7-13

Losing Vietnam

Battles and Campaigns

The Battles and Campaigns series examines the military and strategic results of particular combat techniques, strategies, and methods used by soldiers, sailors, and airmen throughout history. Focusing on different nations and branches of the armed services, this series aims to educate readers by detailed analysis of military engagements.

Series editor: Roger Cirillo

An AUSA Book

LOSING VIETNAM

How America Abandoned Southeast Asia

Major General Ira A. Hunt Jr.
USA (Ret.)

UNIVERSITY PRESS OF KENTUCKY

Copyright © 2013 by The University Press of Kentucky

Scholarly publisher for the Commonwealth,
serving Bellarmine University, Berea College, Centre College of Kentucky, Eastern
Kentucky University, The Filson Historical Society, Georgetown College, Kentucky
Historical Society, Kentucky State University, Morehead State University, Murray
State University, Northern Kentucky University, Transylvania University, University of
Kentucky, University of Louisville, and Western Kentucky University.
All rights reserved.

Editorial and Sales Offices: The University Press of Kentucky
663 South Limestone Street, Lexington, Kentucky 40508-4008
www.kentuckypress.com

17 16 15 14 13   5 4 3 2 1

Library of Congress Cataloging-in-Publication Data

Hunt, Ira Augustus, 1924-
  Losing Vietnam : how America abandoned Southeast Asia / Major General Ira A.
Hunt Jr., USA (Ret.).
      p. cm. — (Battles and campaigns)
  Includes bibliographical references and index.
  ISBN 978-0-8131-4208-1 (hardcover : alk. paper) — ISBN 978-0-8131-4206-7 (epub) —
ISBN 978-0-8131-4207-4 (pdf)
  1. Vietnam War, 1961-1975–Economic aspects. 2. Cambodia—History—Civil
War, 1970-1975—Economic aspects. 3. Military assistance, American—Economic
aspects. 4. Military assistance, American—Vietnam (Republic) 5. Military assistance,
American—Cambodia. I. Title.
  DS559.42.H86 2013
  959.704'3—dc23   2013008898

This book is printed on acid-free paper meeting the requirements of the American
National Standard for Permanence in Paper for Printed Library Materials.

Manufactured in the United States of America.

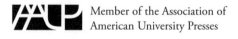 Member of the Association of
American University Presses

This book is dedicated to those
Americans, Vietnamese,
and Cambodians
who so valiantly fought
against communist aggressions.

Contents

Illustrations

Figures

Maps

Photographs

Tables

Preface

As a prelude to the signing of the Vietnamese cease-fire agreement the United States agreed to build up the Republic of Vietnam Armed Forces (RVNAF) and to continue to supply them with essential military supplies and equipment. To supervise that effort and to maintain liaison with the South Vietnamese Joint General Staff (JGS), the U.S. Support Activities Group (USSAG), a major headquarters, was established in northeast Thailand. Most people thought that the cease-fire would herald a stable and lasting peace, but the war continued unabated, much to the consternation of Washington as to which side was violating the agreement.

At a meeting with the JGS in Saigon in October 1973, after inquiring about the initiation of hostilities, I was pleased to learn that RVNAF field reports could provide information as to the origin of combat activities as well as a myriad of other useful data concerning hostilities. Earlier in Vietnam my unit had great success utilizing operational analysis to sharpen our combat edge. I felt that an analytical study of this data could be helpful to the RVNAF to improve its military operations. USSAG offered to analyze the data on a continuing basis. Our initial analysis indicated that 90 percent of the cease-fire violations were initiated by the North Vietnamese in land-grabbing operations. More importantly, it showed that on the few occasions when the RVNAF attacked they were much more efficient than when they were fending off the enemy. It was essential for the South Vietnamese to go on the offensive to prevent the enemy from taking over their country. So, on 3 December 1973 a JGS order went out to the RVNAF to seize the initiative, and during the next ten months or so the RVNAF was very successful in defeating the communists and blunting their attacks. However in July 1974 the U.S. Congress drastically reduced the funding for South Vietnam. The RVNAF was forced to seriously ration ammunition and to appreciably cut back air force flying hours, greatly diminishing its firepower and tactical mobility.

The conflict in South Vietnam greatly affected many of the Southeast Asian nations. In fact, the wars in South Vietnam and Cambodia were always intermingled. Both countries were fighting a common enemy. The deputy commanders of the two armed forces met face to face on a monthly basis to exchange information and intelligence and to ensure cooperation when necessary. In 1970, when the North Vietnamese Army and the Viet Cong (NVA/VC) attacked the Cambodian armed forces, it was obvious that the United States would have to initiate actions to prevent the communists from taking over Cambodia, which would have been very detrimental to the ongoing Vietnamization efforts in South Vietnam. Consequently, the United States organized and equipped the Cambodian armed forces. Concurrently the NVA initiated efforts to organize and field Khmer communist units. For several years the fledgling Cambodian army fought the communists to a standstill—until, as in South Vietnam, Congress drastically reduced its funding for Cambodia.

These severe congressional reductions portended the ultimate defeats of both South Vietnam and Cambodia, and although the warning signs of potential collapses were definitely evident and reported by USSAG, they were generally ignored by superior headquarters. Both countries were doomed—abandoned by the United States' lack of financial support and resolve.

The purpose of this book is to relate the major circumstances leading to the defeats of South Vietnam and Cambodia and to discuss the U.S. military's withdrawals from Laos and Thailand as well as to indicate the value of analytical studies to quantify elusive facets of combat, providing responsible commanders with a basis for decision making to improve military operations. The material contained herein was taken from information and data on hand at Headquarters USSAG, during the period 1973–1975 and is considered to be of historical significance.

As USSAG deputy commander, I was the recipient of the early flow of all Southeast Asia operational reports, reconnaissance activities, and electronic intercepts. I also conducted frequent visits with the senior military echelons of South Vietnam and Cambodia. Consequently, it is believed that as much as anyone, I was in a position to assess the conflicts in Southeast Asia.

Nakhon Phanom

It was with great anticipation that the people of the United States heralded the "Agreement in Ending the War and Restoring Peace in Vietnam"—the so-called cease-fire agreement. Most Americans, myself included, thought that this agreement was the prelude to a stable and lasting peace. I, for one, tried to put the Vietnam War out of mind. The newspapers and television journalists would occasionally cover stories concerning the continuing conflict between the South and North Vietnamese; however, the extent of the ongoing cease-fire violations did not fully register with me. So, in the late summer of 1973 when I was made USSAG deputy commander, to be stationed at the Royal Thai Nakhon Phanom Airbase in northeast Thailand, the successor to the Military Assistance Command Vietnam (MACV), which had the responsibility for supervising U.S. contributions to the wars, I had to get up to speed on the situation in Southeast Asia.

I received a thorough joint staff briefing at the Pentagon; this included the situations in Cambodia, South Vietnam, Laos, and Thailand as well as North Vietnamese logistics. There were also operations and air force briefings and a joint conference at the state department with the assistant secretary of state for East Asian and Pacific Affairs and others.

At my Pentagon briefings I learned of two subjects that required looking into. One, Cambodians were apparently utilizing too much artillery with respect to the funding authorizations, an indication that the Pentagon was already concerned about the adequacy of Southeast Asia funding. Two, the North Vietnamese were stating that the South Vietnamese were habitually violating the cease-fire agreement. A recent Senate Foreign Relations Committee staff study noted: "Lack of respect for the Agreement is so widespread that it is impossible to apportion responsibility for the continued fighting." Which side was initiating the armed conflicts? For propaganda purposes, in their regular weekly news conferences the Viet Cong (VC) always brought up the subject of South Vietnam's cease-fire violations. For example, as late as 20 August 1974, Col. Vo Dong Giang, deputy chief of the VC military delegation to the Two-Party Joint Military Commission, said, "It was obvious that the U.S. Government continues to help Thieu to prolong the war of aggression against South Vietnam." He claimed that from 16–20 August 1974, the Saigon government had committed four thousand cease-fire violations—including 664 land-grabbing operations, 2,593 police and pacification operations, 219 shellings, and 216 bombings, and reconnaissance—bringing the total number of violations since January 1973 up to 428,165.[1] By any type of reckoning, this was an amazing number of cease-fire violations, and it clearly showed that the war had never ended. The cease-fire agreement prohibited all acts of force and hostile acts; both sides were to avoid armed conflict and refrain from using the territory of Cambodia and Laos to encroach upon the security of one another. North Vietnam blatantly violated almost all aspects of the cease-fire agreement.

When the cease-fire agreement was signed on 28 January 1973, and U.S. combat forces were evacuated from South Vietnam, many of the responsibilities of MACV were assigned to the USSAG, which was joined with the U.S. Seventh Air Force (USSAG/7AF). It was a multiservice integrated staff established under a U.S. Air Force commander with a U.S. Army deputy. Our headquarters was under the operational control of the commander in chief of the Pacific (CINCPAC), and its mission[3] was five-fold: to plan for the resumption of an effective air campaign in Southeast Asia; to establish and maintain liaison with South Vietnamese armed forces (RVNAF) joint general staff (JGS); to exercise command over the Chief, Defense Resource Support, and Termination Office, Saigon, usually known as the Defense Attaché Office (DAO); to exercise operational control of all U.S. forces and military agencies that might be assigned for the accomplishment of its mission (this occurred for the evacuations of Phnom Penh and Saigon and the recovery of the *Mayaguez*); and to supervise the Joint Casualty and Resolution Center activities, resolving the status of those dedicated servicemen who were missing in action.[4]

The Little Pentagon

Headquarters USSAG/7AF was established in northeast Thailand at the Royal Thai Air Force Base, a few miles west of the Mekong River town of Nakhon Phanom, slightly north of the parallel delineating the Vietnam demilitarized zone. During its participation in South Vietnam, the United States had constructed a modern facility with the most advanced computer and electronic capabilities for the purpose of monitoring the millions of electronic intrusion devices placed below the demilitarized zone to detect North Vietnamese infiltration. This large, windowless building was dubbed the "Little Pentagon." With its communications, it was tailor-made to control air force units stationed in Thailand—which in January 1973 were supporting the Cambodian armed forces (FANK) with close air support—and, in fact, was the primary reason FANK could withstand the communist attack on Phnom Penh that summer. However, on 15 August 1973 Congress passed a law terminating all combat air operations in Southeast Asia.[5] There remained, however, the important aerial reconnaissance missions and search and rescue operations in Southeast Asia and adjacent waters, the former being conducted to provide indicators of communist intentions and capabilities. In compliance with the peace agreement, unarmed aircraft carried out these aerial reconnaissance activities, which were essential for providing intelligence.

Nakhon Phanom

The Royal Thai Air Force Base at Nakhon Phanom (NKP) was a busy airfield. The U.S. Air Force had several squadrons stationed there, and, of course, there was also Headquarters USSAG/7AF. Nakhon Phanom was a hotbed of activity—50 percent of the population favored North Vietnam. The only landmark, located in the town center, was the Ho Chi Minh Tower, a clock tower donated by North Vietnam. Nakhon Phanom was located across the Mekong River from the Laotian town of Thakhek. Located in Thailand in juxtaposition to Laos with responsibilities in Cambodia and South Vietnam, Headquarters USSAG was totally involved in Southeast Asia (see map 1). I looked forward to this assignment, having served in South Vietnam before. When I was division chief of staff, the Thai component in the Vietnam War, the Queen's Cobra infantry regiment, was attached to the unit, and its liaison officer, Major Narong, whom I had seen almost daily, was now a member of the ruling triumvirate in Thailand. I was also very familiar with the Vietnamese JGS. Brig. Gen. Tran Dinh Tho, the J-3, was a very good friend. So I wasted no time in getting to NKP. The USSAG commander, U.S. Air Force (USAF) General Timothy O'Keefe, was one of the finest officers I ever met. At the time there were ten general or flag officers assigned, and we had over 425 personnel—more than 350 assigned to USSAG and about seventy-five assigned to the Seventh Air Force. The airbase was a restricted area, requiring clearance to visit, so there were few interruptions—our headquarters was focused.

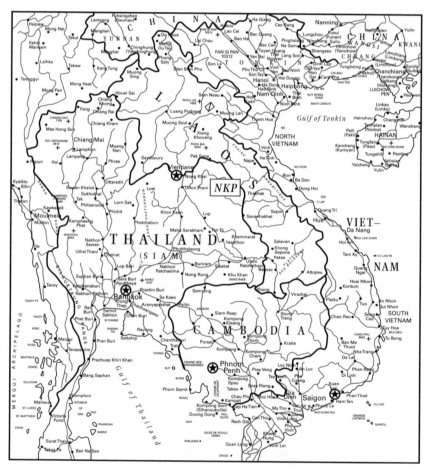

Map 1. Southeast Asia. (Source: Headquarters USSAG, Nakhon Phanom, Thailand.)

2

South Vietnam

The Defense Attaché Office

The U.S. military assistance objectives in the Republic of Vietnam, to be carried out by the DAO, were to "help to achieve and maintain the stable balanced conditions necessary to ensure peace in Indochina and Southeast Asia; assist in the development of an increasingly effective government responsive to the South Vietnamese people's needs and wishes; support a balanced Republic of Vietnam armed force of sufficient size, strength, and professionalism to counter the principal threat facing South Vietnam; and contribute to the healing of the wounds of war and the postwar reconstruction and rehabilitation of South Vietnam."[6]

Unquestionably, these objectives were related to circumstances well beyond U.S. control. Obviously, when they were made public, the Pentagon envisioned that the Vietnamese parties would undertake to maintain the cease-fire and ensure a lasting and stable peace, not a de facto state of war. In reality, the military assistance objectives boiled down to just one: to support balanced Republic of Vietnam armed forces. That support depended directly upon the receipt of sufficient congressionally approved funding to ensure the maintenance and replacement of essential military equipment and to procure necessary supplies, particularly ammunition and petroleum, to enable the country to counter the North Vietnamese threat.

To provide that support was a huge undertaking; consequently the DAO was a major operation. Not only did it support the 1.1 million-man RVNAF, but it had to provide housekeeping activities for the approximately sixty-five hundred U.S. personnel associated with the mission. There were about four thousand direct-hire and contract employees and twenty-five hundred U.S. citizen dependents. Additionally, the total local national workforce exceeded twenty thousand personnel. The DAO had personnel scattered throughout South Vietnam, but its main effort was in a compound at Tan Son Nhut Air Force Base in Saigon.[7]

The DAO's internal budget was about $40 million, and it had an authorized strength of about 940 personnel. It was a huge, busy organization. Maj. Gen. John Murray was the first defense attaché and was succeeded by Maj. Gen. Homer Smith in September 1974. Both were extremely competent managers and outstanding logisticians. The DAO people were dedicated, hard-working personnel and they provided superior support to the RVNAF.

Vietnam Update

I knew that to properly assess the situation in South Vietnam in 1973 I needed to analyze the capabilities of both the South and North Vietnamese armed forces. It was also essential that I learn how the military situation had changed since I had left South Vietnam in 1969—particularly with respect to the Vietnamization program and the major 1972 all-out North Vietnamese Army (NVA) Easter campaign. What follows, then, is an update on friendly and communist capabilities: their relative manpower; the North Vietnamese infiltration of supplies and equipment; a review of the South Vietnamese Air Force, Navy, and Army armor and artillery capabilities; and the key U.S. funding situation, to include the effects of the worldwide oil-induced inflation on South Vietnam. Only after understanding these elements could I answer the important question "How does the RVNAF stack up against the NVA/VC?"

The NVA/VC

Historical Perspective

In late 1973, the intelligence section of the South Vietnamese joint general staff (J-2) produced a study entitled "Communists' Assessment of the RVNAF."[8] In wartime, it is always important to know the enemy, and this enemy's perceptions of the RVNAF were crucial for our understanding of enemy tactics. Although intelligence-gathering necessarily includes considering all sources of inputs, the J-2 study relied primarily on official enemy reports and assessment records on the spirit and combat capabilities of the RVNAF published by communist technical agencies, which were very difficult to acquire because they were classified as VN ABSOLUTE SECRET. However, since there were continuous leaks of important classified information from both sides throughout the conflict, this material was often available.

This study summarized a historical perspective of the Vietnam conflict as well as the enemy's view of our allies. The North Vietnamese analysis divided the war into eight different periods, commencing with the 1954 post–Geneva Accord political struggle and continuing through the 1973 post-cease-fire episode. The NVA called its 1972 episode "The Period of Ending the War," and it opted to launch a spring-summer campaign, hoping to shatter the Vietnamization plan and pave the way to ending the war. In the post-cease-fire episode, it regarded the political struggle as its primary stratagem and armed attacks as its supporting means. It estimated the Vietnamese armed forces would be "utterly confused" at the initiation of the cease-fire and it intended to exploit the situation to grab more land and gain a larger population.

After its historical review, the J-2 study continued to compare the communists' assessments of their opponents in specific areas such as organization, equipment, and combat capabilities.[8] With respect to combat capabilities, the communists viewed the South Vietnamese strengths the same as did the DAO's enemy capabilities versus RVNAF potential review—that is, their strengths were in air and artillery firepower, greater mobility, ability to reinforce the battlefield, and effective logistical support. Thus, the North Vietnamese were well aware of the South's strengths, and with respect to their own shortcomings they had drawn valuable lessons from their mostly failed 1972 campaign.

The North Vietnamese thought the RVNAF overemphasized tactics based on using modern equipment, resulting in reliance on strong firepower instead of infantry to conduct assaults. They stated that the army often deployed in circle formations rather than defense-in-depth, and consequently their formations could be easily broken. They saw a lack of coordination between mobile units and main attacking units.

The North Vietnamese Army was oriented offensively, both tactically and strategically. To the NVA, the defense was a transitory phase to be used to rebuild, reorganize, and refit resources. These assessments originated in the North Vietnamese's offensive operational viewpoint: they saw the RVNAF as a basically vulnerable, defensive, reaction-oriented force. In sum, the communists thought the allied forces relied too much on modern weapons and overlooked the individual fighting spirit.

Notwithstanding this high-level assessment, debriefs of prisoners of war and ralliers (those enemy who surrendered to the GVN) in November 1973 revealed several positives concerning the capabilities of the individual South Vietnamese Army (ARVN) soldiers. One prisoner of war "considers the average ARVN soldier to be daring and dedicated." Another who had fought in two engagements with ARVN stated he found "enemy troops to be spirited fighters." An enemy lieutenant from the political staff of Military Region 3 (MR-3) "considers ARVN . . . now superior to the communists in both spirit and equipment." A source from MR-4 thought "ARVN's use of firepower strong and logistics to be superior to the Communists."[9]

One sunny day I visited one of the RVNAF hospitals. It was hot, and there was no air-conditioning. The patients were dressed only in boxer shorts, bare from the waist up. I stopped to chat with a wounded army noncommissioned officer. I could see several ugly scars on his torso from previous wounds. He told me he had been fighting for seven years and had been wounded five times, yet he was anxious to return to his unit and the war. Considering the length and brutality of the war, the spirit and courage of South Vietnamese soldiers was compelling. Many of the North Vietnamese combatants had been far from home for as long as four or five years. For all involved it was a long war.

The North Vietnamese Army initiated its all-out 1972 Easter Offensive on 30 March 1972, and it culminated by the end of the dry season in late June and early July. The communists launched major attacks on three fronts. At the demilitarized zone, they initially committed three divisions supported by tanks and heavy artillery to seize Quang Tri Province and Hue. Ultimately, eight divisions and fifteen separate armor, artillery, infantry, and sapper regiments were employed. In the central highlands, two divisions with tanks and artillery attacked Kontum. In the area north of Saigon, three enemy divisions from Cambodian sanctuaries struck south along the Saigon River to threaten the city. The communists attacked over a large area in the populated delta, attempting to gain population and territory, but the efforts of their two divisions were easily blunted and the enemy strength in the delta was significantly diminished.[10]

Although initially successful in its efforts, the enemy was forced to commit almost all its forces, and the South Vietnam air forces, tanks, and artillery—superbly supported by U.S. air power, particularly the B-52s—took a terrible toll on the communists' manpower, supplies, and equipment. The RVNAF's counteroffensive late in the year gained back most of the territory it had lost. As a result of the fighting about 750,000 people were displaced, requiring the already stretched South Vietnamese government to provide housing and food. Nevertheless, of the 20 million people in South Vietnam, 92 percent were under government control. Efforts by the communists to control territory and population, thereby thwarting the South Vietnamese pacification program, were to increase greatly at year's end.

The 1972 campaign taught the North Vietnamese several very valuable lessons. First, to fight a conventional war they had to match the South's tremendous firepower. To do this, they would have to infiltrate a great amount of armor and artillery. Second, they would have to nullify the awesome power of the U.S. Air Force, which made the finalization of the peace talks a necessity. Third, they would have to offset the close air support provided by the Vietnamese Air Force (VNAF) by greatly expanding their air defense capabilities. Fourth, they needed a sustained combat capability, which necessitated protected lines of communication all the way from the demilitarized zone to the delta area of South Vietnam, as well as fully stocked and protected base areas close to their combat objectives. And finally, given the manpower, equipment, and supplies necessary to launch a conventional campaign successfully, they would have to master the art of coordinated combined arms tactics.

Political Assessment

So much for the military side of the equation. What was the communist political thinking in early 1973? The North Vietnam chief of general staff outlined the nation's political-military strategy in a series of briefings to key Central Office South Vietnam (COSVN) cadres, which were subsequently reported by friendly agents. The guest lecturers were the North Vietnam chief of general staff, Col. Gen. Van Tien Dung, the Provisional Revolutionary Government's chairman, Huynh Tan Phat, and its lieutenant general, Tran Van Tra. These lecturers emphasized that the Paris Agreement had not changed the original communist objectives in South Vietnam and pointed out that the agreement had achieved the important party goals of getting U.S. forces out of South Vietnam and stopping U.S. bombing raids over North Vietnam and communist bases in South Vietnam. They described the joint talks under way between the communists and South Vietnam as propaganda and stalling tactics while the NVA built up communist forces and strongholds in South Vietnam sufficiently to launch a final offensive to take over South Vietnam. Under the umbrella of the cease-fire, the communists were concentrating on creating serious economic problems for the government of South Vietnam and working with "all opposition groups" to create political unrest, while the NVA were strengthening the communist military forces in the south to strike a final blow "to topple the Thieu Regime."[12]

The party strived until May 1974 "with the assistance of friendly socialist countries to raise the standard of living in VC 'liberated' areas to a level higher than in government-controlled areas, to counterbalance American efforts to strengthen the local economy. It was important to the communists' effort to have the general population of South Vietnam in a neutral mood when the 'final offensive [was] launched.'"[13] Subsequent to these key briefings, COSVN issued its Resolution for 1975,[14] emphasizing the importance of a fundamental defeat of South Vietnam's pacification program. It stated the "VC has the capability of accomplishing [its] 1974 goals as well as winning greater victories in 1975 in preparation for total victory in 1976."

The first phase in the military plan to strengthen communist forces in the South so as to enable them to protect the "liberated" areas had been completed. The current phase was to organize all communist forces in South Vietnam into a modern army capable of launching a sustained offensive.

The COSVN intelligence estimate concerning U.S. post-cease-fire intentions projected that the United States would concentrate on strengthening and modernizing the RVNAF—especially in the fields of armor, artillery, and air support—and that it would continue economic aid at a level sufficient to keep South Vietnam's economy strong. Its troop withdrawal would be permanent; the troops would not be returned even in the face of a heavy communist military buildup in the South. The United States probably would resume bombing raids over VC "liberated" areas in South Vietnam if it was convinced that communist forces in the South were strong enough to challenge the ARVN and were preparing to launch an offensive. U.S. air support would include tactical support of ARVN ground forces if they were unable to contain the communist offensive. Under such circumstances, the United States would not resume bombing of the North or reinsert ground troops. The COSVN estimate concluded that communist forces in South Vietnam could cope with U.S. intervention and still defeat South Vietnam.[15]

The major criteria most people consider when assessing the comparative strengths of the RVNAF versus the NVA/VC is the sizes of the combat forces. Table 1 indicates the NVA/VC order of battle strengths for 1 January 1967 to 1 January 1975. Our intelligence analysts took information from all sources to determine the effective strength of all known enemy units in South Vietnam.[16] They then posited fairly well-known factors, such as integral unit moves into and out of South Vietnam and infiltration of individuals. Then, by analysis they attempted to balance infiltration with reported casualties. The order of battle strengths are reasonably valid numbers, which the gains/losses formula validated. The number of North Vietnamese casualties could well be understated, however, since it was difficult to determine the numbers who died later of battle wounds, from malaria, dysentery, or other medical causes, or in nonbattle accidents. Enemy battlefield medical capabilities were rudimentary. Of course, some believed that the reported enemy casualties were highly inflated. The gains and losses for the NVA/VC order of battle between 1 January 1967 and 1 January 1975 are shown in table 2.

The order of battle data are estimates only. The methodology used to

Table 1. NVA/VC Order of Battle Gains/Losses, 1967–1974 (in thousands)

	1967	1968	1969	1970	1971	1972	1973	1974
1 Jan OB strength	288	301	318	228	205	197	270	298
Infiltration	+100	+220	+90	+89	+85	+183	+95	+100
Integral unit moves to SVN	+11	+17	+12	+10	+15	+30	+20	+25
Local recruiting (mil only)	+35	+20	+30	+30	+30	+25	+15	+15
NVA/VC casualties (KIA, PW, ralliers)	–123	–210	–212	–142	–123	–150	–52	–55
Exfiltration	–10	–20	–10	–10	–15	–15	–35	–42
Integral unit moves out of SVN	0	–10	0	0	0	0	–15	–1
31 Dec OB strength	301	318	228	205	197	270	298	340

Source: Working papers, Headquarters USSAG, Nakhon Phanom, Thailland.

Table 2. NVA/VC Order of Battle Net Gains/Losses, 1967–1974 (in thousands)

	O/H 1 January 1967	Local recruit	Exfiltration	Net unit moves	Infiltration	Losses	O/H 1 January 1975
VC	230	+200	–17			–343	70
NVA	58		–140	+114	+964	–726	270
Total	**288**	**+200**	**–157**	**+114**	**+964**	**–1,069**	**340**

Source: Working papers, Headquarters USSAG, Nakhon Phanom, Thailland.

produce these estimates was far from exact; the USSAG order of battle was based not on a loss/gain methodology but on all source reporting, historical data, and analysis. For example, the range for the 31 December 1974 strength of the NVA/VC was from 295,000 to 350,000, with 340,000 as the best estimate. We continuously monitored all aspects of the conflict to maintain an up-to-date order of battle.

One can readily visualize the episodic nature of the war by noting the annual infiltration as well as casualties. The years 1968 and 1972 were obviously high points. The enemy losses from their abortive Tet

1968 campaign were huge, and the U.S./RVNAF forces conducting a vigorous follow-up seriously weakened the Viet Cong in 1969. The Viet Cong were never able to recover from those two disastrous years. Starting in 1970 the war was almost entirely a North Vietnamese affair, from the enemy's point of view. The all-out 1972 campaign again saw large infiltrations and high enemy casualties. At the time of the cease-fire, the NVA/VC strength in South Vietnam was 270,000 men; this grew to 340,000 by 31 December 1974 and ultimately to about 425,000 troops by 30 August 1975.[17] The 1967–1974 NVA/VC losses exceeded 1 million combatants, a number that boggles the western mind and is in accord with North Vietnamese data.

Integral unit moves out of South Vietnam did not include moves by enemy units into Laos and Cambodia to escape allied security operations, since these were considered temporary. The average annual North Vietnamese Army infiltration rate, about 120,000 men, was in accordance with that nation's demographic capabilities. North Vietnam, with a population of about 23.5 million, had about 4.3 million males between the ages of fifteen and forty-nine years. The number of males reaching draft age yearly was about 200,000 to 250,000, and of those it was estimated that 130,000 to 140,000 were physically fit. Table 3 indicates the probable order of battle strengths for the NVA

Table 3. NVA/VC Order of Battle Strengths, Units in South Vietnam (in thousands)				
	1 January 67	1 January 73	1 January 75	30 April 75 (EST)
Ground Combat Troops	117	148	206	270
NVA	(54)	(123)	(186)	(250)
VC	(63)	(25)	(20)	(20)
Combat Support Troops	50	71	104	125
NVA	(4)	(34)	(84)	(105)
VC	(46)	(37)	(20)	(20)
VC guerrillas	121	51	30	30
Total	**288**	**270**	**340**	**425**
NVA	(58)	(157)	(270)	(355)
VC	(230)	(113)	(70)	(70)
Source: Working papers, Headquarters USSAG, Nakhon Phanom, Thailand.				

and VC components at the beginning of 1967, 1973, and 1975. In 1967 the order of battle was made up primarily of Viet Cong forces; however, after the 1972 campaign the preponderance of enemy was North Vietnamese, and by 1975 it was their war. Even in 1967, the enemy ground combat units were almost evenly distributed between the NVA and VC. None of this data includes the Viet Cong political infrastructure, which was always at least 30,000 people.

When assessing comparable strengths, one must also consider those enemy units along major supply routes and storage areas in Laos and Cambodia, as well as the combat and training divisions stationed in North Vietnam. The North Vietnamese strategic reserve was to play a vital role in 1975. Consequently, an estimate of enemy strengths in late 1974 and early 1975 was 340,000 for South Vietnam, 50,000 for Laos, 30,000 for Cambodia, and 70,000 for North Vietnam, for a total of 490,000 troops.[16]

Infiltration

The enemy used infiltration, the primary operational key to any military estimate, to modernize and rebuild units, replace people, stock supplies, and position units for the end-of-the-war offensive. They learned major lessons from their 1972 Easter Offensive: first, secure logistical bases were necessary to resupply forces until they seized their objectives; and second, to be successful, attacking troops had to employ large-scale combined arms tactics. Also, the enemy learned that the awesome firepower of the U.S. Air Force could disrupt logistical bases, lines of communication, and attacking troops.

The signing of the peace accords eliminated the potential of U.S. air strikes. Afterward the North placed its highest priority on improving and expanding lines of communication, road networks, airfields, and pipelines, to better enable them to push supplies and equipment to the South. In the past, the North Vietnamese had had no problems receiving war matériel from supporting countries, but with the severe air interdiction they had difficulty transporting supplies to the front. The RVNAF, however, had difficulty ultimately in receiving its required war matériel from the United States, but with interior lines it generally had little difficulty in getting what it had into the hands of the troops.

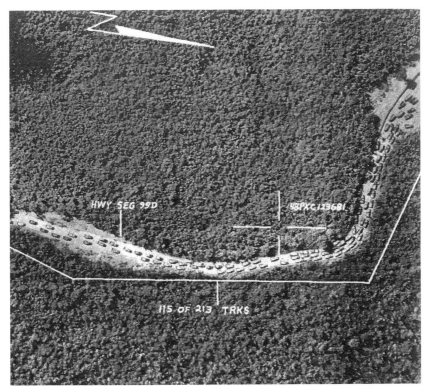

Photo 1. Traffic on the Ho Chi Minh Trail, 21 December 1973. (Source: Headquarters USSAG, Nakhon Phanom, Thailand, produced by the 432nd Reconnaissance Technical Squadron, U.S. Air Force.)

By mid-1974 significant new numbers emerged.[19] The 770-mile stretch of the Ho Chi Minh Trail running through Laos was broadened and improved, much of it even paved. Transport by A-frames was a thing of the past. USSAG's air reconnaissance often showed three trucks abreast traveling south with matériel. The enemy built innumerable roads leading from the jungle areas of the Ho Chi Minh Trail to the coastal plains. They also developed a second major infiltration corridor within South Vietnam; this ran parallel to the Ho Chi Minh Trail, extending from the demilitarized zone to the border area a hundred miles north of Saigon. This second trail, of about 600 miles, terminated in base areas in the northwestern sector of Tay Ninh Province.

The modern equipment being infiltrated required a steady supply of petroleum. The enemy extended its 30-centimeter pipeline through Laos and built a second internal pipeline; in October 1974, the combined length of both was 470 kilometers. During the twenty months since the cease-fire, the enemy had set up an important network of petroleum storage areas that consisted mainly of twenty-thousand-liter containers hidden underground in groups of four to six, linked to the pipeline system. These depots contained 13.5 million liters of petroleum; prior to the cease-fire this number was 1 million liters.

In an effort to modernize the North Vietnamese Army units, the enemy made maximum use of its vastly improved lines of communication to infiltrate men and equipment. Although five divisions and six infantry regiments had been withdrawn or deactivated, the North Vietnamese introduced a sapper division and an antiaircraft division as well as twenty antiaircraft, five sapper, three armored, and three artillery regiments. To commit a modern conventional army in open combat, the enemy was balancing its forces to include a combined arms orientation to offset South Vietnam's capabilities.

The troop levels are indicated in figure 1. Combat troops increased by 54,000 to 206,000, and combat support troops almost doubled, increasing to 108,500. This data varies somewhat from the order of battle data kept by the United States. The increases in combat support were necessary to man the improved logistical support complex fed by the improved lines of communication. The large increases in troop levels were disquieting, but the dramatic reduction of the reinforcing time for infiltration was almost as important. Prior to 1973, troop replacements headed for the delta had taken about four months, whereas in late 1974 the trip took less than two weeks. This ability to quickly relocate reserve divisions in North Vietnam to the battlefield would greatly influence events in March–April 1975. After the cease-fire, the North Vietnamese Army infiltrated more than 200,000 troops.

To modernize the combat capabilities of these troops, the enemy infiltrated numerous tanks, artillery, and antiaircraft equipment. Since most of the armored vehicles were destroyed in battle in 1972, it introduced 655 tanks and tracked vehicles. This included several new types of equipment, such as the T-34 bridge-laying tank.

A substantial number of guns upgraded the artillery capability,

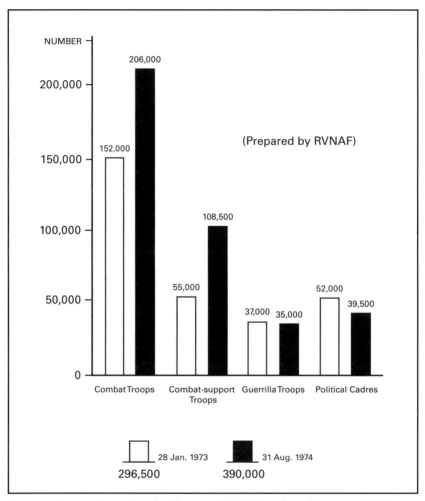

Figure 1. Enemy Troop Levels. (Source: RVNAF briefing, "Logistics," JGS, J-4, September 1974, Saigon, South Vietnam.)

bringing the total to 430 Russian-made 122 mm and 130 mm field guns. The Soviet 122 mm howitzers and the 122 mm and 130 mm guns outranged the U.S.-supplied 105 mm and 155 mm howitzers, which the ARVN primarily relied on. The ARVN did have five 175 mm artillery battalions with twelve guns each that had an effective range greater than the Soviet pieces.

However, the most disturbing aspect of the infiltration was the introduction of twenty air defense regiments and their equipment. No longer required to protect their homeland against an air attack, the North Vietnamese moved ultra-modern and effective radar systems to South Vietnam. This was the unintended consequence of the unilateral U.S. bombing halt of North Vietnam, which in fact negated much of the VNAF's firepower.

These newly infiltrated antiaircraft and radar systems, which provided enemy air surveillance over almost all of South Vietnam, required the South Vietnamese Air Force to fly at altitudes of ten thousand feet, thereby greatly reducing its effectiveness in close air support. These sophisticated systems guarding the lines of communication and military base areas preempted the possibility of the VNAF effectively disrupting the enemy's logistical system, which the U.S. Air Force had done so effectively in earlier years, since the Vietnamese Air Force did not have the sophisticated electronic countermeasures equipment required.

The massive infiltration of equipment into South Vietnam required the North Vietnamese to reorganize their force structure. They reduced infantry divisions and regiments and increased artillery and sapper divisions and separate regiments and substantially increased air defense regiments. Six armored regiments infiltrated to exercise command over the 655 tanks known to be in South Vietnam. The enemy now had the organization and equipment to conduct combined arms offensives. It had fallen short in the past in command and control, which resulted in uncoordinated piecemeal attacks. To remedy that situation, it was reportedly forming four new corps headquarters that would enable control of multidivisional combined arms forces on a conventional warfare battlefield. The communists were also creating additional divisional structures from units already in South Vietnam. Sufficient heavy weapons and artillery were available to provide firepower support for these new divisions.[20]

At the end of 1974, North Vietnam had more troops, more equipment, and more supplies available in South Vietnam than ever before. The stage was set to launch a major dry-weather offensive when they decided to do so. In December, when the NVA was creating new units and infiltrating soldiers at an increased rate, Gen. Cao Van Vien noted that his joint staff was conducting a study to convert all possible rear service personnel into infantry units in a desperate effort to obtain additional combat strength.

The lifeblood of the North's aggression against South Vietnam was the infiltration routes that brought equipment, supplies, and troops from North Vietnam to the South.[11] The enemy could not successfully mount a major offensive without logistical staying power; consequently, it relied on the buildup of base areas located in relatively close proximity to its military objectives. The main infiltration routes ran through Laos and Cambodia and continued to do so, in violation of Article 20, after the signing of the January 1973 cease-fire agreement.

Notwithstanding the importance of the infiltration routes and base areas in Laos and Cambodia, the RVNAF conducted only two major cross-border operations. When Cambodian president Lon Nol closed the port of Sihanoukville (Kompong Som) in 1970, he effectively cut the NVA's supply route to South Vietnam's MR-4. This required the NVA to resupply base areas supporting MR-3 and -4 to infiltrate overland from North Vietnam. The RVNAF's May 1970 joint operation with U.S. forces against the enemy base areas located in Cambodian sanctuaries destroyed great quantities of war materials. Then in February 1971, in another joint endeavor, Lam Son 719, the RVNAF launched a major operation into southern Laos, this one designed to interdict the Ho Chi Minh Trail, now the major resupply route, and to occupy and destroy major enemy logistics bases. Both of these cross-border operations were strategically successful in buying time for the key Vietnamization program so essential since the United States was withdrawing its troops. However, from a tactical point of view Lam Son 719 left very much to be desired, since it did not destroy the enemy base areas and it exposed ARVN inadequacies. While the ARVN may have been seen to have failed, the enemy also showed major weaknesses. Since the cease-fire, ralliers indicated NVA troop morale declined, as it became increasingly clear that the war was not over or even almost over. There continued to be a very definite amount of debilitating friction between the southern and northern communists. In many ways, the loss of morale was not due to any new concrete problems—hardships, friction between northerners and southerners, and the stresses of life under communist control had been present all along—but once the hope of the war's ending was dashed, existing problems suddenly were less bearable than before. Huynh Van Tan, commander of the 200C Sapper Battalion, said he rallied against the fear of being killed, discrimination against southerners, lack of discipline, and the fact that the dissension between northerners and southerners sometimes resulted in fighting and killing.[21]

These communist analyses set the stage for the rest of the war. The communists' strategy was to capture more land and gain a larger population. Their primary targets appeared to be the RVNAF static defense forces and elements assigned to support the pacification program. For starters, they intended to overrun a number of South Vietnamese outposts in remote rural and mountainous areas. Currently, they were organizing all their forces in South Vietnam into a modern army capable of launching a sustained offensive supported by armor, heavy artillery, and antiaircraft.[11] Their goal was to strike a final blow to topple South Vietnam. They thought that as they grew more successful the United States might reenter the war with tactical air support, but they were certain that the Americans would commit no ground forces. In 1973, all sides agreed that the RVNAF had superior firepower, mobility, and logistics support. The communists would do everything to reverse that balance of power. It was up to the United States to see that the RVNAF remained better equipped and supplied. If that occurred, the final outcome would depend on the fighting capabilities of the respective armed forces.

The RVNAF

South Vietnamese Strategy

The South Vietnamese strategy, like all military strategies, was rooted in politics. One of the key articles in the cease-fire agreement was the establishment of an administrative unit, the National Council of Reconciliation and Concord. In the eyes of the South Vietnamese, this would establish a de facto coalition government, which was anathema to the South Vietnamese, who thought that if the North Vietnamese gained a credible amount of territory and controlled a sufficient number of people, they would have a rationale for demanding participation in government. President Nguyen Van Thieu wanted to prevent this possibility, and he adamantly insisted on a policy of no loss of territory or population. The United States supported him in this policy and had crafted the hamlet evaluation survey to measure the number of hamlets and the population under government control on a monthly basis. These concerns were certainly not far-fetched; the communists in Cambodia were demanding that the United Nations recognize the Sihanouk government because it did in fact control about 70 percent of the territory (but only 32 percent of the population).[22] Notwithstanding the perceived political realities, the South Vietnamese policy of attempting to maintain control over all territory and population was, on final analysis, one of the major reasons for the South's downfall.

The strategy of South Vietnam, as General Vien, the chairman of the joint general staff, and others explained to me, was to maintain control over all territory and population, improve and modernize the armed forces, and reinforce the Pacification and Rural Development Program.

This was certainly a coherent strategy, with its centerpieces being the strength, capabilities, and combat effectiveness of the RVNAF. The pacification program had been immensely successful, providing security to more than 5 million additional rural inhabitants, and the RVNAF's ability to provide substantial protection was the key to this success. Without security, there was no pacification. Having deprived the communists of much of their rural base, the RVNAF then had to repel all enemy attempts to retake those hamlets and villages under South Vietnamese control; again, this could only be accomplished by military action.

Although this strategy was coherent, it was seriously flawed. It was primarily a defensive tactic to contain communist expansion. The ARVN was spread thin trying to protect some twelve thousand hamlets; it had very few resources with which to counter enemy aggressions, and many of its troops lost the spirit of the offense, having been positioned so long in a static defensive posture. The strategy gave the initiative to the communists, who could concentrate their forces to attack the smaller outposts and bases, thereby assuring the enemy of local combat superiority.

During the 1972 Easter Offensive, the enemy overran many outposts and besieged several others. The surrounded South Vietnamese outposts required continuing aerial reinforcements and logistical resupply, which was a major drain of friendly assets. So, in late 1972 the JGS recommended that the ARVN withdraw from many of its relatively isolated positions. To the JGS's consternation, President Thieu firmly rejected the request, reiterating with respect to the enemy what came to be called the "Four No's"—no land, no population, no coalition, and no belief (in communist pronouncements).

The cease-fire agreement required the withdrawal of all foreign troops from South Vietnam; at its height, the number included ten divisions and their combat and logistical support units plus the U.S. Air Force and Navy's formidable close air support and strategic bombing capabilities, as well as the naval gunfire of the U.S. fleet, exceeding over 500,000 personnel. Yet the agreement allowed approximately 270,000 armed NVA/VC troops to remain. Thus, the balance of forces dramatically shifted. For South Vietnam, this was the predominant factor influencing the future conduct of hostilities. President Thieu compared the situation to one in which a burglar inside the house breaks out through the front door while the police officer is outside waiting to take action.[23]

Having discussed the South Vietnamese strategy, it is important to review the RVNAF personnel strengths as well as the main firepower and mobility components: air force, navy, and army armor and artillery. In 1967 the RVNAF had 643,000 personnel under arms, and in 1973, as the allied contingents were drawn down, to offset the loss of the allied forces this number increased to 1.2 million authorized troops. After the peace accord was signed, the Ministry of National Defense intended to reduce the size of the RVNAF. However, the continuation of hostilities after the cease-fire precluded this, and there was only a small downsizing of 100,000 men to an approved force size of 1.1 million. Yet, this was less a reduction than an increase in the quality of the armed forces.[24]

The ARVN, the regular ground combat organization, was composed of eleven infantry divisions, an airborne division, and the marine corps division. Additionally, there were seven ranger groups. Artillery and armor supported these thirteen divisions. The approximate number of ARVN personnel in these combat units totaled 210,000: eleven infantry divisions, 105,000; an airborne division, 12,000; a marine division, 14,000; rangers, 28,000; artillery, 36,000 (including 23,000 troops assigned to divisions); and armor, 15,000.[18]

The territorial forces included the regional forces (RF) and the popular forces (PF). After Tet, the JGS placed the territorial forces under ARVN control, and the United States agreed to upgrade their equipment. The regional forces' basic operating unit was the hundred-man company. Many of these were organized into battalions, consisting of four companies each; later in the war these were provided mobile assets. The regional forces generally operated within their own provinces. The popular force operated in platoons of twenty-nine men each, generally within their own districts, villages, or hamlets. The regional force units had more equipment, better training, and more competent leadership than the popular force units. Although it was normal to group the two organizations together, the regional forces were much better qualified in terms of combat capability. Their ranks were filled mostly from local recruiting, and what these troops lacked in combat capability they made up for with their knowledge of local areas. These added another 500,000 troops of varying quality and capabilities: 145,000 in regional force battalions, 155,000 among other regional forces, and 200,000 in popular force units.[18]

Although the ground combat troops (ARVN, RF, PF) numbered about 710,000 soldiers in January 1973, only the army and, to a much lesser extent, the regional force battalions could be considered for deployment to meet enemy combat initiatives anywhere. Thus, more than 50 percent of the ground combat units were primarily disposed in a static defensive posture and were then primarily reactive forces, since it was almost a requirement that the twelve thousand South Vietnamese hamlets had to be protected and the civilian population kept under government control to coincide with President Thieu's policy of losing no population.

The combat support slice, or the necessary personnel to keep combat units in line, amounted to about 328,000 troops. Although these essential units were located throughout the country, the major logistical installations were primarily in the vicinity of Saigon. At any one time the personnel absent from units was about 150,000 soldiers, of which 70,000 were in training.

The approximate overall strength of the South Vietnamese forces at the time of the cease-fire included 210,000 in ARVN/Marine combat units, 145,000 in regional force battalions, 355,000 in other RF/PFs, 328,000 in ARVN support troops, 64,000 in the Vietnamese Air Force, and 41,000 in the Vietnamese Navy, for a total of 1,143,000 soldiers.[18] Subsequent to the cease-fire, the ARVN was chronically understrength. Although the government had passed a general mobilization law, after about a decade of intense conflict the manpower resources were drying up. Considering the demographics of South Vietnam's population of 20 million, the number of physically fit males reaching draft age yearly was probably between 120,000 and 130,000. This should have been enough to maintain a force structure of 1.1 million soldiers. In fact, most observers thought that manpower was not a problem. Yet, it was always a matter of grave concern. South Vietnam had serious difficulties in controlling its manpower. Considering the constant enemy attacks against isolated hamlets and villages, the constant flow of displaced persons, the large urban buildup, and the efforts of draftable youths to evade military service, manpower control difficulties were understandable. The ARVN had continuous attrition because of combat losses and other casualties, discharges, elimination of the unfit, and desertions. By far the most serious drain on manpower was desertions. Efforts to round up draft dodgers and to recover deserters were ineffective. Deserters blended into the overcrowded cities undetected. Some joined the People's Self Defense Force (PSDF) to avoid ARVN combat duty. In 1973 there were 215,023 desertions, 20 percent of the assigned strength. The total losses per month averaged 2.5 percent, of which two-thirds were desertions.[25] There were other personnel problems—such as ghost soldiers, nonexistent names that were nonetheless carried on the rolls; flower soldiers, who were carried on the rolls but were off elsewhere; and those who were absent without leave for prolonged periods—but the desertion rate was by far the most important.

These personnel problems manifested themselves in a chronic shortfall of troops present for duty in combat units. Demographics made it difficult to make up for the loss of manpower resulting from combat losses, desertions, and discharges. Therefore, on the average, combat units had assigned about 85 percent of their authorized strength, and those present for duty were often about 85 percent of the assigned strength. Combat is a team effort; when there are too many soldiers not present for duty, unit effectiveness suffers. Combat units with fewer than 70 percent present for duty are not considered combat effective. Each army infantry battalion generally had an authorized strength of 639 soldiers. Therefore, unit commanders continuously made major efforts to ensure a foxhole strength of at least 450 combatants.

While personnel strengths were a problem, at the senior levels the leadership of the ARVN was good. Most major commanders had been trained at U.S. Army branch schools in the United States, and many were command and staff college graduates. Yet, President Thieu assigned some of the key command billets to officers whose loyalty he could count on, and several of these were considered incompetent. Some of the senior officers lacked the ability to make hurried and decisive decisions in stressful situations. The junior officers lacked the experience of those in higher echelons, but almost all had been battle tested. The intense combat in 1972 had resulted in many company-grade leader casualties. The inadequate pay and long separations from families hurt the morale of the junior officers and noncommissioned officers. Those who had their families close by could not make ends meet. However, in 1973 the overall morale was satisfactory, considering that the war had been going for longer than eight years and showed no signs of ending.

At the national level the South Vietnamese JGS was organized on normal general staff principles. However, the commander of the air force and the chief of naval operations appeared only at the operational level, as did the commanding generals of the four corps. By and large there were few air force and naval personnel at the staff level, which reflected the actual state of the armed forces. Thus it was mostly an army organization instead of a true joint staff.

I had worked with the JGS in 1968–1969 and was very pleased to resume my friendships—particularly with Gen. Cao Van Vien and Brigadier General Tho. Vien was a quiet, intelligent officer, the former airborne division commander, with decades of military experience. A combat-proven officer, he appeared perfect for the job, since he had the respect and loyalty of the officer corps and he could work with President Thieu. Working with the president was not easy. Vien's complete lack of political ambition was undoubtedly an important factor in their continuing relationship.

The chief of staff was Lt. Gen. Dong Van Khuyen, who doubled as the chief of the Central Logistics Command (CLC). He had a phenomenal grasp of logistical matters and was an innovator. His Joint Staff was competent across the board, but two officers stood out. Brigadier General Tho, the J-3, was a superior officer who grasped situations quickly and also had Vien's complete confidence. Col. Hoang Ngoc Lung, the J-2, was also extremely competent. These two officers made a great team.

The military was well supplied with ammunition, petroleum, and rations. The RVNAF's Vietnamization was causing problems with supply procedures, particularly spare parts and maintenance. Thus, there were considerable equipment deadlines. However, the DAO had many U.S. contractors on hand attempting to take up the slack.

The procurement, storage, maintenance, distribution, and transportation of supplies and equipment for a force of over 1 million troops was a formidable undertaking. Particularly when under the Vietnamization program and the pre-cease-fire PROJECT ENHANCE, much equipment was introduced and turned over to the RVNAF in a short period of time. Yet, they managed adequately. The CLC directed and supervised all logistical aspects.[27] Lieutenant General Khuyen headed the Central Logistics Command. The DAO was established primarily to assist the Vietnamese in the critical logistics support area, and it effectively monitored the situation, working closely with the Central Logistics Command. Besides its in-house experts, the DAO provided contract assistance in many critical areas—particularly with respect to aircraft maintenance. In late 1973 there were more than 215 Department of Defense contracts, valued at about $144 million, utilizing about 12,200 contract personnel (Americans, locals, and third-country nationals).[26]

The responsibility for supervising training activities and operating the school and training center system was with the chief of the Central Training Command, Lt. Gen. Nguyen Bao Tri, a member of the JGS. The training system was advanced and almost a mirror image of the one in the United States. It had eight national training centers and nineteen service schools as well as air force and naval training centers. The centers taught basic combat training and advanced individual training. The schools had officer and noncommissioned officer training courses, and there was a national military academy. Many of the personnel in positions of responsibility had been trained in the United States. Compared to the one in Cambodia, the South Vietnamese system was very advanced. In all, the Central Training Command supervised some sixty training centers and schools.

Firepower and Mobility

Toward the end of 1972 it became readily apparent to all that a Paris treaty was in the making, and this set both sides into motion to increase their combat power as they jockeyed for position prior to the signing. The allies, too, learned from the Easter Offensive, in which the awesome firepower of the U.S. Air Force saved the situation. The offensive's most important lesson was that if the Vietnamization program was to be successful, a tremendous effort was required to enhance the firepower and mobility of the military, in order to replace that of the departing U.S. forces.[28] Therefore, the Pentagon undertook projects to accelerate the delivery of equipment to improve combat capabilities. The U.S. Army Matériel Command initiated PROJECT ENHANCE after the 1972 Easter Offensive to replace the heavy losses in equipment and the munitions expended in countering the North Vietnamese and prior to the cease-fire to bring the force structure up to authorized levels. Major equipment delivered to the army included three 175 mm artillery battalions, two M-48 tank battalions, two air defense battalions, and one hundred wire-guided antitank weapons as well as numerous aircraft and ships. The U.S. Air Force established a similar program to modernize the Vietnamese Air Force. The South's main advantages over the communists were in their firepower and tactical and strategic mobility. All three services contributed to these advantages: the VNAF, the Vietnamese Navy, and the ARVN armor and artillery.

The massive North Vietnam Easter Offensive in 1972 included major attacks in MR-1, -2, and -3, which were eventually turned back by allied troops and the U.S. and Vietnamese air forces. Air power played a pivotal role, providing much of the tactical firepower interdicting the enemy supply lines, and ultimately carrying the war into North Vietnam proper. The destruction wrought by B-52 strikes against attacking North Vietnamese forces and their logistical base areas was awesome. However, in situations like the siege of An Loc—where enemy SA-7 shoulder-fired antiaircraft missiles were used—the slow-flying helicopters and C-123s were not capable of sustained operations. At the conclusion of the offensive all sides had learned valuable lessons, but foremost among them was that the ARVN required and relied on close air support to be effective against large-unit attacks. With the dispersed disposition of forces, with outposts generally out of artillery range and ground mobility limited by terrain and distance, the air force's quick response capabilities would also be a very critical element, since aircraft provided firepower and tactical as well as strategic mobility.

One of the purposes of President Richard Nixon's December 1972 resumption of bombing was to force North Vietnam to the peace table. And it did. Among the provisions in the negotiations was that military equipment could be replaced only on an item-for-item basis. This led to an all-out effort to provide the VNAF with the assets necessary to protect South Vietnam. This program to augment and modernize the air force was called ENHANCE PLUS. The improvement of the VNAF had begun in earnest in 1970. Actually, the rate of expansion since 1970 was more than the VNAF could absorb. Also, in the few months prior to the cease-fire, ENHANCE PLUS increased the size of the air force by 45 percent, providing an additional 685 aircraft. When the United States departed Vietnam in early 1973, the air force was left with twenty-five different types of aircraft, including 1,099 fixed-wing aircraft and 1,098 helicopters. This inventory far exceeded the force's capabilities to maintain them.[29] Consequently, U.S. contractors had to fill the gap in maintenance and depot support. Rationalizing the situation, in 1973 the air force retired several types of older and less effective aircraft, thereby reducing the inventory to 1,857 aircraft, organized into sixty-six squadrons. In 1973 and early 1974 the VNAF met its basic requirements of providing close air support, ensuring the critical redeployment of ground troops, providing intelligence, and securing the established lines of communications.

In 1972, the U.S. Air Force flew 58,395 tactical sorties, an order of magnitude greater than the number flown by VNAF. However, the

Vietnamese pilots attempted to pick up the slack caused by the withdrawal of U.S. Air Force combat support. This improved the number of bomber, observation, and helicopter sorties appreciably over the 1972 levels.

In August 1973, the U.S. Congress passed a joint resolution that required the complete disengagement of U.S. combat forces in Southeast Asia.[5] The immediate effect was to stop the U.S. Air Force support of combat in Cambodia; all U.S. air combat activities were terminated. Since the cease-fire, the North Vietnamese had had free reign to improve their lines of communication and move troops, equipment, and supplies into South Vietnam. The relief from potential bombing allowed the sophisticated antiaircraft defenses in North Vietnam to move south. Soon there were at least twenty antiaircraft regiments in South Vietnam, which protected the communist supply and storage areas and supported their combat initiatives. The VNAF's slow-moving helicopters and fixed-wing assets could not cope with the SA-7s and the radar-controlled guns, since they had no electronic countermeasure equipment. Therefore, the air force had to fly A-37 and F-5 aircraft at altitudes of ten thousand feet, and the forward air controllers were completely forced out of the areas of contact.

Our air experts at Headquarters USSAG cited two major VNAF deficiencies, one equipment-wise and the other organizational as the RVNAF faced the forthcoming dry-season campaign in late 1974 and early 1975. First, the South Vietnamese aircraft assets were configured for low-level intensity combat and could not cope well with the mid-intensity conflict now being waged by the enemy. The initial force-planning structure of the Vietnamese Air Force has been severely criticized for not having provided an electronic countermeasure capability or more advanced aircraft like the F-4. One could presume that the planners were counting on a reduction in combat intensity rather than an acceleration and that they did not want to provide the South with the capability to interdict North Vietnam, thereby violating the cease-fire agreement. Unfortunately, they did not consider the possibility after the cease-fire of North Vietnam's highly effective antiaircraft units moving south, which turned out to be a game changer.

The second deficiency was that the air force did not have centralized control over its assets. With the exception of reconnaissance assets, all South Vietnamese squadrons were assigned to the corps. Each corps commander had full control over the tactical air and transport assets assigned to his MR, and he looked upon those assets as *his* air force. The JGS issued directives to the VNAF, which generally followed these only with the acquiescence of the respective corps commander, who, if he desired, would go around the JGS directly to President Thieu. This assignment policy was always a bone of contention with the air force; it violated the basic principle of the flexible use of airpower.[30] With the existing organization, it was difficult for aircraft in one corps to assist in major engagements of another. However, such instances were few. Whenever there was a serious threat, the president could and did step in. More of a problem was that the air force representatives to the corps were generally more junior than their army counterparts and as a consequence often had little impact on the planning of operations. VNAF complained that it was generally utilized solely for protecting ground troops, often bombing (in their opinion) low-priority targets for the psychological effect in lieu of striking enemy troop buildups and storage for petroleum and other supplies. This may have been the case in 1973, but with the enemy antiaircraft buildup to protect such areas, VNAF attacks would have had marginal effect. By and large, army and air force officers functioned very well at the working and intermediate levels of command.

The Vietnamese Navy played an important but relatively unpublicized role in the war. The main missions the joint staff assigned to the navy— all of which were vital—were logistics mobility, coastal surveillance, and riverine operations. Conscious that it had no strategic reserves, the JGS looked to the navy for its sealift capabilities. The JGS was always careful to retain the ability to move the airborne division and marine brigades in MR-1 and MR-2 to Saigon, should the situation demand the protection of the heartland, Saigon, and the delta. The Vietnamese Navy had two major components: the blue-water navy (the large ships that patrolled the China Sea) and the brown-water navy (the riverine forces that patrolled the Mekong Delta and the inland waterways of MR-3 and MR-4). The blue-water fleet had line ships capable of providing supporting fire to land forces as well as combating enemy ships. These ships provided coastal surveillance of the twelve hundred nautical miles of coastline to prevent the North from supplying its forces by water and harbor defense to protect the harbors so essential for logistics support. The navy's tank landing ship fleet, composed of six tank landing ships and two converted cargo carriers modified as troop carriers, was a key element of the navy. This fleet and the air force's C-130s comprised South Vietnam's strategic mobility. The late-1973 navy ship inventory included ninety blue-water vessels, 1,450 brown-water vessels, and 265 army watercraft—1,805 total.

In the 1972 campaign, for the first time, the North Vietnamese Army used armor on a large scale. About four hundred enemy tanks were initially deployed to South Vietnam for the 1972 offensive. There were some further NVA commitments of armor as replacements for combat losses. The enemy's use of tanks was usually ineffective because they were not part of a combined arms operation utilizing infantry and artillery; rather, the enemy generally used them in small numbers to provide supporting fire for its infantry. Notwithstanding that allied ground, air, and naval actions destroyed almost all of the enemy armor, the NVA recognized the advantages of armor and the necessity for coordinated combined arms tactics. To that effect, in 1973 USSAG aerial reconnaissance detected new shipments of tanks on the Ho Chi Minh Trail and the stationing of armor in the demilitarized zone area. All intelligence reports indicated major increases in enemy armor capabilities in South Vietnam since the cease-fire. The enemy armor threats in MR-1 and MR-3 were of the greatest concern to senior Vietnamese officers, who realized that antiarmor capabilities would be essential against a major attack.

On 22 September 1973, North Vietnam's 26th Army Regiment attacked the 80th Ranger Border Defense Battalion in MR-2. The enemy initiated the assault with a heavy artillery bombardment—including 122 mm and 130 mm guns, mortars, and rockets—providing supporting fire for at least six T-54 tanks. Of the 293 men in the ranger battalion, some two hundred were killed or captured. Shortly thereafter, in October, an enemy battalion supported by five T-54 tanks engaged the 2nd Battalion, 40th ARVN Regiment, near Pleiku. It withdrew when confronted by the tanks and fired only one light antiaircraft weapon in defense. From an operational point of view, the situation in late 1973 appeared different than it had been during the 1972 offensive. Reports indicated that the enemy was improving its armor techniques. It was conducting combined arms tactics and had learned how to use armor in the exploitation phase of an attack. But most disturbing was that the ARVN was not standing up to the armor threat.

To assess the RVNAF antiarmor capabilities, I asked the USSAG J-3 to review source documents to determine the allied efforts against tanks during the 1972 offensive. His assessment included U.S. Air Force, Navy, and Marine Corps tactical air attacks, B-52 ARC LIGHT strikes, and engagements by the VNAF, U.S. Army helicopters, U.S. naval gunfire, and ARVN ground weapons.[31] Of the tanks reported as destroyed in South Vietnam, 56 percent were destroyed by tactical aircraft, 31 percent by ARVN ground forces, and 13 percent by naval gunfire and other means. However, when VNAF and ARVN kills were added together, clearly, 63 percent of the armor kills could be attributed to the South Vietnamese, that is, 37 percent were attributed to U.S. activities, which would not be a factor in future battles. It is worthy of note that the ratio between air force tactical air and army ground troops was even, indicating the RVNAF's proven tank-killing capabilities.

The enemy was not only expediting the infiltration of armor, it was greatly fortifying its antiaircraft capabilities. Thus, not only did the RVNAF lose the U.S. tactical air support, its effectiveness was being considerably reduced, as its planes had to fly at higher altitudes to escape lethal antiaircraft fire. Consequently, the main burden of anti-armor defense against a much improved enemy armor capability was primarily with the ARVN. If enemy armor attacks were to be stopped, infantry and armor units would have to do it.

Obviously, the South Vietnamese had the experience and capability to kill tanks. In the future, more reliance would have to be placed on the infantry for antitank kills, thus it was most important that ARVN training techniques be reviewed and assessed. With this in mind, on 24 October 1973 I visited the Quang-Trung Training Center, accompanied by the commanding general of the Central Training Command and DAO representatives. The training center ably demonstrated techniques and tactics, with an emphasis on antiarmor training. Its techniques and tactics were developed to coincide with the reality of the battlefield. Having spent the previous two years with staff responsibility for training in U.S. training centers and schools, I was in a good position to judge the adequacy of the Vietnam training doctrine and performance. The training was excellent, and if conducted elsewhere in country at the same level of performance, from a technical point of view the situation would be satisfactory. The ARVN's problems, highlighted by the two events in MR-2, appeared operational; the infantrymen must stand fast and use their antitank weapons at close range. That required strong leadership.

Because the enemy armor threat was so serious and the antiarmor capabilities of the RVNAF so important, in late October 1973 I asked Maj. Gen. John Murray to see if an expert team from the United States could provide technical assistance to DAO Saigon on the subject of ARVN antitank capabilities. U.S. Army Pacific responded immediately, and on 12 November a team headed by Col. W. F. Ulmer Jr., the commanding officer of the 194th Armored Brigade at Fort Knox, arrived in country with three expert members, including Col. R. S. McGowan, the president of the Combat Arms Training Board at Fort Benning, Georgia, to assess the training and readiness of army units in antitank warfare. The team visited twenty-seven schools, headquarters, training centers, and combat units in MR-1, -2, and -3 and made twenty short-term and sixteen secondary or long-term recommendations.

The team provided excellent insights into antiarmor capabilities.[33] There were sizable enemy armor threats in all three regions, and the corps commanders generally had no viable armor reserves to deploy against unexpected enemy actions. The M-48A3 tanks observed and inspected were in a high state of readiness and, if properly manned, could defeat enemy armor. Thorough antiarmor training was ongoing. The individual soldier was healthy and alert, with well-maintained equipment.

In a late November 1973 letter to me, Colonel McGowan provided a summary of the team's assessment: "The tanks we saw were well maintained and the soldiers appeared confident and competent. The big question—Will they stand and fight?—remains as unanswerable as it always has."

In a conventional war, the most formidable tank-killer is the tank itself. In an aggressive combined arms assault, the tank also provides firepower, shock action, and great mobility. Although still semiconventional, the war in Vietnam was becoming more conventional, as the North Vietnamese, who had the initiative, began to attack with division-size units, using combined arms tactics. Therefore, it was important that we review the ARVN armored capabilities.[34] ARVN had an armored command whose organization had an administrative chain of command that ran from the armored squadrons to the armored brigades to the armored command and the JGS. In this chain, the armored command had no direct control of operations and the JGS had only limited control, since the military region commander exercised almost all of the authority. This dual chain of command, of course, also applied to air force units. As of 26 November 1973, the combat vehicle status of the four armored brigades had 96 percent of their authorized combat vehicles assigned, and 89 percent of them were serviceable, an excellent situation.[35] The units had a high assignment of authorized equipment, and the deadline rate was well within tolerance, considering the need for maintenance downtimes.

On 7 December 1973, the JGS issued a memorandum signed by General Vien, "Improvement of Capability for Countering Enemy Tanks."[32] It included many of the USARPAC team recommendations and highlighted ARVN's battle-tested experience. A JGS briefing on the subject outlined several key points, advising that the South should have confidence in its own armor and in its antitank weapons, should include practical experience in employing and laying minefields, and should develop artillery, air force, and engineer capabilities in anti-armor operations. It also counseled that only teamwork with the air force and all branches and services within the army would ensure a successful antiarmor outcome.

Thus, at the end of 1973 antiarmor capabilities had been emphasized at the highest level and training was ongoing at all levels. Commanders were cognizant of potential enemy mechanized avenues of approach and all corps had positioned their forces accordingly. However, the ARVN defensive positions generally had no great depth (a factor the North Vietnamese had commented upon), and reserve forces so essential to conduct counterattacks were limited. The ARVN and

RF/PF were greatly dispersed, to protect hamlets, villages, and towns. Notwithstanding, the situation on the eve of 1974 was satisfactory for local defense and limited enemy offensives.

The army had an artillery command that, like its armor command, was primarily administrative, since the majority of artillery battalions were assigned to the four corps. In June 1973 it had sixty-three artillery battalions: forty-four 105 mm territorial artillery, fifteen 155 mm howitzer, and four 175 mm gun. In a hurried attempt to beef up South Vietnamese firepower, the United States had delivered the self-propelled 175 mm guns under PROJECT ENHANCE toward the end of 1972. The 175 mm gun was the only artillery weapon that could outrange the communists' 122 mm and 130 mm guns. Besides the army battalions, there were 176 105 mm howitzer sections of two weapons each that supported the regional and popular forces. In all, there were 1,698 artillery tubes in South Vietnam. The RVNAF was proficient in artillery-firing techniques, and when combined with close air support the artillery weapons gave it a decided firepower advantage in 1973. However, this advantage was seriously degraded over time.

Funding

One of the most important factors in the conduct of the war in Vietnam was the support the respective allied countries provided to both sides. The United States, of course, gave South Vietnam funding.[36] Between 1966 and 1974 the United States authorized $4 billion in military assistance. The FY 73 (1 July 1972 to 30 June 1973) program was $1.53 billion. However, in FY 74 support was greatly reduced, to $1.069 billion, which caused the South to initiate a conservation program, particularly in the utilization of ammunition and petroleum products. The military aid was further eroded by the greatly increased inflationary effects of the Middle East oil embargo. Consequently, the FY 74 funding was barely adequate to support the successful conduct of the war.

The large FY 74 congressional reduction in military aid and the inflationary effects of the Arab oil embargo in the post-cease-fire period were highly destructive. The Saigon consumer price index in December 1973 indicated an annual inflation of 65 percent.[37] By mid-1974 inflation had risen an additional 28.5 percent. The spectacular increase in the costs of petroleum products caused by the worldwide energy crisis was responsible for a substantial part of this price spiral. South Vietnam's determination to stem consumption by greatly increasing taxes affected the prices of imports, such as rice, cooking oil, and sugar. Fortunately, the cost of rice increased only 30 percent, the result of a bumper crop due to the great success of the pacification program.

In September 1973 and again in June 1974, noting the serious impact of the economic situation on soldiers, the government gave an across-the-board salary increase. However, it did not come close to ameliorating the inflationary gap. In 1973, military income actually fell between 25 and 40 percent in real terms, and it continued to deteriorate in 1974. Military personnel with dependents (65 percent of the total number), were the hardest hit.

The withdrawal of American forces from Vietnam had a major impact on the economic situation. Foreign exchange receipts evaporated, and the employment opportunities for military dependents as well as the soldiers' ability to moonlight at other jobs disappeared. The declining level of real U.S. economic aid did not help either. So, military families faced with reduced real income had no choice but to consume less.[38] It is disturbing to note that the pay only met about 75 percent of a minimal existence level for married soldiers. Military commanders unanimously stated that no soldier or officer could adequately support his family on his pay and allowances; further, they claimed that of all the factors affecting morale in the military, the soldiers' and their families' dismal economic situation was by far the most important. Connections between the adequacy of pay and combat effectiveness are tenuous at best because of many associated variables, such as the level of hostilities, leadership, and unit pride. Nevertheless, it is clear that the less adequate the real pay, the greater the distraction of the soldier.

South Vietnam's inflation, which had increased about 100 percent since the cease-fire, greatly affected the well-being of the soldier. However, worldwide inflation also seriously reduced the amount of food, ammunition, and petroleum available to the soldier in the field, thereby compounding the morale problem. Between FY 74 and FY 75, the cost of ammunition increased 60 percent, gasoline 150 percent, and clothing 110 percent. The overall across-the-board increase rate was 47 percent.[37]

The effects of inflation on the well-being of soldiers and their families with the unfortunate spillover into desertions and corruption were serious but not critical. The manpower deficiencies at year-end 1973 were manageable.

RVNAF Advantages

Having reviewed the communist and South Vietnamese capabilities, the question then is, "How did the RVNAF stack up against the NVA/VC?" To help answer this, in December 1973 the DAO prepared and forwarded to USSAG a study that listed those factors that favored the RVNAF. The South Vietnamese had greater firepower and tactical mobility. They had a large combat force, more weaponry, more guns and howitzers, more and better communications. They had greater tactical and strategic mobility: helicopters, trucks, armored personnel carriers, air transport (C-130s and C-7s), and naval transport (which included blue- and brown-water fleets). Additionally, they had a modern infrastructure and interior lines of communication, which provided greater staying power. Their logistical support was far more reliable and extensive than that of the communists.

Although ARVN had more combat personnel than the enemy, most of the army battalions were committed to security missions that greatly reduced force flexibility. In 1973, in addition to their troops in South Vietnam, the North Vietnamese also had several divisions in Laos and several more in North Vietnam available for deployment. Therefore, the enemy could move its forces at a time and place of its choosing to obtain battlefield superiority.

The South Vietnamese Air Force had become quite expert in airlift and airdrop operations and could move regiments and division-sized units throughout the country faster than the enemy, whose mobility was limited to trucks and sampans. The country's extensive and modern infrastructure provided great depth and flexibility, and elements of the infrastructure could be mobilized and employed for military purposes on short notice. The enemy, on the other hand, had to make do with what it had moved to the South.

Tactical air power had been decisive in the 1972 campaign. The VNAF had more than eighteen hundred aircraft of all sorts and had experienced combat pilots capable of providing close air support to embattled units. The navy also added to mobility and improvement of security. The blue-water navy could move supplies along the coast to support all four military regions. This sealift capability for shifting major forces and equipment served as a backup to the ground lines of communication and the airlift capability. The brown-water navy had successfully impeded the waterways, the enemy's main lines of communication in the delta.

Looking to the individual combatants, the ARVN had better training. Its soldiers had higher morale, which accompanied good training, greater firepower, and faith in continued U.S. economic and military aid. At this time, the North Vietnamese soldiers had low morale. They had been told that the 1972 offensive would result in the culmination of hostilities. After almost a year of protracted conflict, resulting in major casualties, the individual soldier found himself bogged down far from home with little hope of repatriation in the foreseeable future. The constant monsoonal rains considerably dampened the enemy's spirits. In an April 1974 USSAG briefing, Lt. Gen. Ngo Quang Truong, the MR-1 commander, said an "important point concerning present enemy armed forces in MR-1 is their low morale . . . the majority of enemy do not wish to continue fighting. There has been a significant number of desertions, self-inflicted wounds, etc."[39]

The United States had pulled out all the stops in supporting the Vietnamization program. We had delivered large numbers of aircraft, ships, artillery, and tanks and provided the expertise to maintain the equipment. We also agreed to replace equipment combat losses on a one-for-one basis and built up a large inventory of ammunition, which we would maintain at the cease-fire level. The DAO study concluded that the RVNAF was superior in each area, but noted that it faced security missions that tied its forces to widely scattered defensive positions, enabling the enemy to aggregate his forces to obtain local superiority.

In late 1973, both the DAO and the communists believed the South Vietnamese had major advantages, particularly in the key factors of firepower and tactical and strategic mobility. One then may ask, "What subsequently went wrong?" The answer to that question is the purpose of this book.

Combat Analysis

In early October 1973, I visited the DAO and JGS in Saigon, where I received briefings on the conduct of the war. The four military region commanders controlled the RVNAF field operations, and because of the disparities in terrain, weather, populations, and the makeup of the friendly and enemy armed forces, the situations in each region varied greatly. In fact, there were four very different wars ongoing. Thus, it was not easy for me—or anyone else—to obtain a clear understanding of the overall combat situation. It was apparent that there were many current clashes in each military region as the South Vietnamese attempted to defend against the communists' land-grabbing operations and at the same time the RVNAF undertook what it described as "security operations." I inquired about the initiation of hostile activities, a subject that was vexing personnel at the Pentagon, and with good reason. Expectations, obviously, were that the cease-fire would be effective, producing the opportunity for a reasonable political settlement. The North Vietnamese propaganda machine incessantly referred to South Vietnam's violations of the truce agreement. Which side was initiating the incidents? I was very pleased to find out that the ARVN field reports provided information as to the origination of combat activities as well as a myriad of other data. I thought that the data available—which included the type of incident (for example: attack by fire, including the number of incoming rounds, ground attack, and sabotage), the time of the incident, and the casualties resulting from the incident, including friendly killed and wounded by hostile action and the enemy killed in action—could be displayed meaningfully.

In 1968–1969, my division in Vietnam had had considerable success using operations research to improve its combat effectiveness.[40] Quite simply, operations analysis is an approach to problem solving that makes it possible to use systematic logic and often mathematical techniques to arrive at a decision that will optimize a situation. The essence of decision making is the selection of controllable inputs or factors. In using analytical techniques to suboptimize elements of operations for the 9th Infantry Division, we concentrated on matters that improved operations, tactics, and intelligence. I wanted to know whether such techniques would be helpful on a macro scale for the totality of conflict in Vietnam, where the situation was so complex, varied, and changeable. I thought that by combining military judgment, data collation, and operational research methods we could arrive at useful combat analyses.

Using their combat data inputs, I explained to the JGS that meaningful outputs that would measure combat effectiveness on a macro scale could be obtained, leading to improved efficiencies, saved lives, and a clearer understanding of the overall combat situation. I offered to them that USSAG, with their cooperation, would be pleased to undertake such analyses. The JGS was familiar with our previous analytical approach and, recognizing the requirement, readily agreed.

Fortunately, at NKP we had a plethora of computers and a stable of exceedingly competent young officers well versed in system analysis. With the cessation of the air war over Cambodia on 15 August 1973, these men were available and would be anxious to use their talents for combat analysis.

Right off the bat, some will state that you could not trust the ARVN data inputs that would have to be utilized in making combat analyses. The majority of all inputs were straightforward reporting, such as type of incident, location, timing, unit participating, and incoming rounds. However, naysayers will point out the count of enemy killed would be exaggerated, and often that would be true. In that respect, reports from the field always underreported the friendly killed by at least 20 percent. This too was well known; there was no way the unit commander could count those wounded who subsequently died of wounds after being transported from the battlefield. The same, of course, applied to the North Vietnamese wounded, only more so, since they had no helicopter evacuation or hospitals close to the combat areas and generally had insufficient medical supplies. Thus, the exact casualties resulting from any ground contact could never be known. Nevertheless, it was the trends that counted. We do know that many elements of analysis showed remarkable consistency, such as the ratio of friendly killed to friendly wounded and friendly troops killed per enemy-initiated contact. Experience would show that the data was satisfactory to portray trends and that operational analysis on a macro scale could and did provide commanders and staff agencies with a basis to improve military operations. So, we at Headquarters USSAG initiated the analytical studies with the full support of the Vietnamese joint staff. From the start, I decided to broaden the currently reported field data to include weapons captured and lost, grid coordinates, and the component of the army involved in the incident. Through experience, I learned that personal weapons lost was a good indicator of poor unit morale.

The first order of business was to establish data collection procedures, processing ground rules, and general definitions. We established a matrix of data, with twenty-four elements of information pertaining to the type of unit involved. The memorandum prepared by Capt. Richard Hutchins (USAF) on 2 December 1973 was our initial cut at this massive program (see Appendix A: General Definitions and Processing Ground Rules for Combat Analyses).[41] Hutchins and his fellow officer associates collected, edited, validated, processed, tabulated, updated, and analyzed combat data in an outstanding, expedited manner. To enable responsible military personnel to focus on the more important conflicts taking place, we also established criteria that defined each cease-fire violation as either a major or minor one. (See appendix A, section 3.) Major violations included multiple company ground attacks or any ground attack resulting in twenty friendly and enemy total casualties and enemy attacks by fire (artillery, rocket, and mortar attacks) of more than twenty rounds or that caused five or more casualties. The JGS had inputs into the development of criteria, which, as always, was subjective.

Eight types of enemy-initiated incidents were defined: ground contacts, ambushes, penetrations, attacks by fire, harassment, terrorism, sabotage, and political incidents. The percentages of enemy-initiated incidents by type countrywide as well as the total numbers for January 1973 to January 1974 are shown in table 4. In this post-cease-fire period the enemy aggressively initiated 26,913 incidents.[42]

A review of table 4 indicates that attacks by fire (ABFs) and con-

Table 4. Enemy-Initiated Incidents, Percent by Type, Countrywide, January 1973–January 1974

	MR-1	MR-2	MR-3	MR-4	RVN	Total Number
ABF	9.53	6.12	6.89	23.23	45.77	12,320
CTX	4.06	6.39	7.94	9.49	27.88	7,502
HAR	1.75	6.52	1.52	6.93	16.72	4,503
TER	1.49	.51	1.53	2.69	6.22	1,675
PEN	.53	.45	.27	.58	1.83	489
POL	.19	.10	.36	.06	.71	191
SAB	.10	.10	.22	.19	.61	165
AMB	.03	.03	.04	.06	.26	68
Total	**17.68**	**20.22**	**18.77**	**43.33**	**100.00**	**26,913**

Source: Analysis, "Summary of Ceasefire Statistics," June 1975, Headquarters USSAG, Nakhon Phanom, Thailand.

tacts were the most often occurring incidents. A ground contact was any open engagement between the opposing forces and could be initiated by either side. Ground contacts resulted in 96 percent of all the communists killed in action (KIA) and in 62 percent of all friendly casualties. Other forms of contacts were harassments, ambushes, and penetrations. There were many harassments, and these hit-and-run attacks accounted for about 10 percent of all friendly casualties (see table 16).

Ambushes served the same psychological purposes as terrorism, and they resulted in the highest rate of friendly casualties per incident. Although there were not as many ambushes in the later days of the war, they were particularly effective. The South Vietnamese had thousands of small outposts and hamlets to protect, and a favorite trick of the communists was to initiate an attack on one of them, particularly at night, and then lie in wait to ambush the called-upon reinforcements. This tactic made the ARVN extremely cautious when moving on the ground. Attacks by fire and terrorism were very potent tools of the communists.

To be meaningful to military and civilian authorities, analysis of combat operations must correspond to certain geographical areas and friendly and enemy military boundaries. South Vietnam was divided into four military regions. All army, air force, and territorial forces located within the regional boundaries were under the command and/ or operational control of the respective military regional commanders. The military regions and the major ARVN units assigned are indicated on map 2.

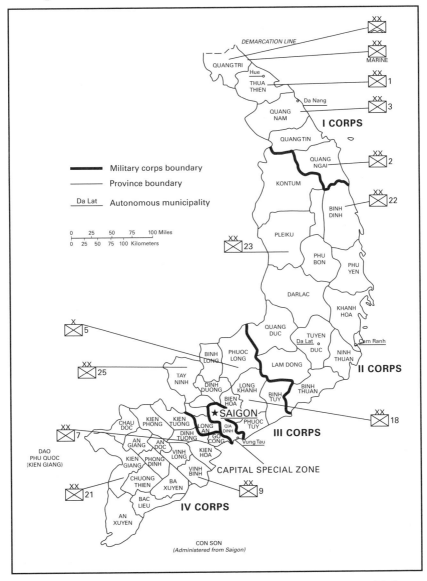

Map 2. South Vietnam Administrative Divisions. (Source: RVNAF, JGS, J-3, Saigon, South Vietnam.)

South Vietnam had forty-four provinces, each completely within a military region—that is, the regional boundaries were drawn to contain a province. Regional forces consisted of units generally assigned to protect areas within provincial boundaries, and popular forces were assigned to protect areas falling within district boundaries. Therefore, when analyzing the performance of the regional forces and popular forces it was essential to tabulate data for incidents occurring within provincial and district regions.

The North Vietnamese Army had several major commands, or fronts. Its B-5 front, in North Vietnam, was responsible for the demilitarized area. The three principal fronts in South Vietnam were the MRTT in the north, which included Quang Tri and Thua Thien Provinces; the B-3 front, which included the highland provinces of Kontum, Pleiku, Daclac, Phu Bon, and Quang Duc; and the COSVN, which had six military regions in the southern and eastern provinces (see map 3). Sometimes Viet Cong MR-5, which included the coastal provinces from Quang Nam in the north to Khanh Hoa in the south, was considered a separate front. Each of the North Vietnamese fronts acted independently but under the communist central command. Each front had its own obvious objectives. To understand the enemy's conduct of the war, it was necessary to analyze it within these geographical areas.

Therefore, our analysis considered parameters for each district, province, and military region as well as for the country as a whole and for the enemy regions. We further subdivided results by ARVN, RF, PF, and PSDF categories. Consequently, the outputs were available for many levels of command.

The first statistical output defined was the initiation ratio, that is, the friendly-initiated contacts divided by the enemy-initiated contacts, which was a measure of aggressiveness. A ratio of 1 would mean that the RVNAF initiated as many ground contacts as the enemy did. Subsequently, we got into the habit of measuring friendly-initiated ground attacks as a percentage of total ground contacts, in which case a ratio of 0.50 would indicate equal aggressiveness.

$$\text{Initiation Ratio} = \frac{\text{Fr Int Cntc}}{\text{En Int Cntc}} \text{ or aggressiveness}$$

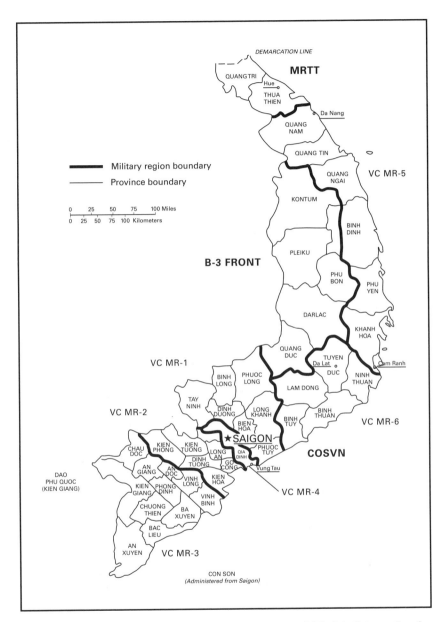

DEMARCATION LINE

MRTT

QUANG TRI

Hue

THUA
THIEN

Da Nang

QUANG
NAM

QUANG TIN

QUANG
NGAI

VC MR-5

KONTUM

BINH
DINH

B-3 FRONT

PLEIKU

PHU
BON

PHU
YEN

DARLAC

KHANH
HOA

QUANG
DUC

TUYEN
DUC

Da Lat

Cam Ranh

VC MR-1

BINH
LONG

PHUOC
LONG

LAM DONG

NINH
THUAN

TAY
NINH

VC MR-2

DINH
DUONG

LONG
KHANH

BINH
THUAN

VC MR-6

BIEN
HOA

BINH
TUY

CHAU
DOC

KIEN
PHONG

KIEN
TUONG

LONG
AN

SAIGON

GIA
DINH

PHUOC
TUY

COSVN

AN
GIANG

DINH
TUONG

GO
CONG

Vung Tau

DAO
PHU QUOC
(KIEN GIANG)

AN
DOC

VINH
LONG

KIEN
HOA

VC MR-4

KIEN
GIANG

PHONG
DINH

VINH
BINH

CHUONG
THIEN

BA
XUYEN

BAC
LIEU

AN
XUYEN

VC MR-3

CON SON
(Administered from Saigon)

Military region boundary
Province boundary

0   25   50   75   100 Miles
0   25   50   75   100 Kilometers

Map 3. NVA/VC Military Regions. (Source: RVNAF, JGS, J-3, Saigon, South Vietnam.)

Other major statistical outputs were those I previously found the most valuable in measuring combat effectiveness.

$$\text{Exchange ratio} = \frac{\text{En KIA}}{\text{Fr KHA}} \text{ or friendly efficiency}$$

$$\text{Enemy casualty ratio} = \frac{\text{En KIA}}{\text{Cntc}} \text{ or friendly effectiveness}$$

$$\text{Friendly casualty ratio} = \frac{\text{Fr KHA}}{\text{Cntc}} \text{ or enemy effectiveness}$$

$$\text{Fatality ratio} = \frac{\text{Fr KHA}}{\text{Fr KHA} + \text{Fr WHA}}$$

The enemy casualty ratio, or friendly effectiveness, was measured both for friendly- and enemy-initiated attacks. The same applied for the friendly casualty ratio, or enemy effectiveness.

One should always approach the interpretation and use of data derived from initial field spot reports with caution. Unfortunately, errors can and do develop in reporting as a result of the confusion inherent in combat. Some reporting—such as date, time, location, type of incident, and the initiator of the incident—should be reliable. All data was initially manually reviewed and then machine checked for consistency and reasonableness. Other data—such as friendly and enemy casualties and weapons gained and lost—would not be as reliable. Should we, therefore, use the data and their ratios as if there was no uncertainty associated with them? Comparing spot report data of friendly killed over a monthly period with the actual data, we sought a relationship through linear regression analysis and obtained a very good linear fit. For the purposes of our analyses, this allowed us to assume that all the data such as weapons gained or lost by incident type had an ordinal relationship between actual data and reported data and consequently comparison of ratios by various time periods should also be valid.

I briefed both the JGS and the DAO concerning our requirements for data inputs to support our operational analysis, and both were extremely helpful in the collection and dissemination of data. With the data the JGS had collected since the cease-fire, we made an initial operational analysis and presented it to them in early December 1973. We divided the data into two periods: 28 January 1973–14 June 1973 and 15 June 1973–1 December 1973. These coincided roughly with the semiannual dry and wet seasons. Since the data prior to 2 December 1973 did not identify the generic type of friendly unit involved in an action—ARVN, RF, PF, or PSDF—all data was aggregated and treated only as RVNAF.

Our initial emphasis was to determine the initiation ratio, a measure of friendly aggressiveness, which the Pentagon sought particularly. For 28 January to 14 June 1973, 90 percent of incidents, which included friendly and enemy ground attacks, enemy attacks by fire, sabotage, harassments, terrorism, et cetera, were enemy-initiated. From 15 June to 1 December 1973, 94 percent were enemy-initiated. Enemy-initiated ground attacks were more than four times greater than the friendly-initiated ground attacks. Obviously, the communists had the initiative and had no intentions of abiding by the cease-fire. After North Vietnam's immediate attempts to grab land before and after the cease-fire, South Vietnam counterattacked to reclaim lost territory. Having effectively accomplished that task, they generally settled into a mode of static defense. Considering that the incessant bombardment of North Vietnamese propaganda about South Vietnam's cease-fire violations was affecting American outlooks, the South Vietnamese limited their combat initiatives and couched them as "security operations." The reality of the situation was that the North was aggressively reinforcing its troops in South Vietnam with supplies, weapons, and personnel and doing its best to control both land and population.

Analysis also indicated that the exchange ratio (En KIA/Fr KHA), or friendly efficiency, was much greater when the ARVN initiated ground attacks than when the enemy initiated attacks. The same was true for the enemy casualty ratio (En KIA/Cntc), or friendly effectiveness. The data indicated that three times as many enemy soldiers were killed when the ARVN initiated the contact. When we completed our initial analysis, I met with General Vien, the JGS chairman, and Brigadier General Tho, the JGS J-3, to speak to them about the data. They were very pleased and relieved to learn we had definitely concluded that the communists were initiating the great majority of combat incidents because they were being pressured by Hanoi and somewhat by Washington concerning the initiation of combat operations. I also informed them that the army's effectiveness was high when they had initiated contacts. I suggested it was imperative for the RVNAF to seize the initiative to keep the enemy off balance and to prevent it from systematically massing forces to attack the thousands of outposts and hamlets throughout South Vietnam. The JGS recognized the situation, and as a result orders went out for the RVNAF to take the initiative.

In early 1974, South Vietnam still had the advantage of firepower and maneuver. Its army was better trained and had higher morale than that of North Vietnam, whose personnel had been led to believe that the 1972 Easter Offensive was to be the final blow to South Vietnam and that they would be returning home to their families.

USSAG monitored the combat in South Vietnam through the daily situation reports and by frequent visits to the DAO and JGS. We also had the important advantage of the Seventh Air Force's aerial reconnaissance of the active fronts in South Vietnam. We continued to collate the enhanced combat data that was available by field reporting commencing on 2 December 1973. In early April, after four months of data, we presented the operational analysis to the DAO and JGS. For the first time, this included data on the relative performance of the component forces (ARVN, RF, PF, PSDF) as well as on weapons captured and lost. By this point, we also were able to analyze the results of attacks by fire and booby traps. Many important factors, of immediate concern to the JGS, emerged from the April presentation. We kept the two periods of our initial assessment and added a third, which included data from 2 December 1973 through 31 March 1974. Subsequently, we organized our analytical outputs into twenty-six-week periods, extending from mid-June to mid-December and mid-December to mid-June, to provide equal intervals for comparative purposes, which roughly corresponded to the wet and dry seasons and thereby aligned analysis with seasonal variations in South Vietnam. The five periods for analysis were 28 January 1973–15 June 1973, 16 June 1973–15 December 1973, 16 December 1973–14 June 1974, 15 June 1974–14 December 1974, and 15 December 1974–19 April 1975. Several of the combat analyses obtained by utilizing the broadened data inputs are discussed subsequently.

Aggressiveness. The spirit of the offensive is measured by this factor, and the aggressiveness of the friendly ground attacks greatly improved from an anemic 15 percent in the second period to 43 percent in the third period. After the JGS directed the ARVN to take the initiative, in the third period there were more friendly-initiated contacts than enemy-initiated ones in MR-1 and MR-3. However, MR-2 was still badly lagging, initiating only one contact in five.

Exchange Ratio. This factor is a measure of friendly efficiency. On a countrywide basis, the ratio of enemy killed to friendly killed was a respectable 4.3 for 28 January 1973 to 31 March 1974. The exchange ratio for friendly-initiated attacks was 6.7, compared to 3.5 for enemy-initiated attacks, again indicating that aggressiveness paid off. This was true for the country as a whole but did not apply to MR-3, which had an unfavorable ratio (see table 5).

Enemy Casualty Ratio. This factor is a measure of friendly effectiveness, the ratio of enemy killed per friendly-initiated contact to those killed by enemy-initiated contact. It remained high from 28 January 1973 through 31 March 1974, 5.0/1.6, or three times as many. However, the average number of enemy killed per contact countrywide was 2.1 to 1, since the enemy initiated more attacks. The RVNAF in MR-4 was particularly effective when it initiated attacks, but this was due solely to the ARVN divisions.

Major/Minor Violations. Unquestionably, most of the incidents were of a small-unit nature. Minor violations outnumbered major violations during the total period by more than ten to one. The communists, recognizing the South's superior firepower, were reluctant to mass their forces for major attacks; instead they kept hammering away with minor assaults upon South Vietnam's far-flung outposts.

Table 5. Exchange Ratio, Friendly Efficiency, Enemy KIA/Friendly KHA, 28 January 1973–31 March 1974

Contacts	MR-1	MR-2	MR-3	MR-4	RVN
Friendly-initiated	8.0	14.6	3.4	6.8	6.7
Enemy-initiated	3.2	5.9	3.7	1.2	3.5
Combined	**4.8**	**6.2**	**3.6**	**3.1**	**4.3**

Source: Analysis, "Summary of Ceasefire Statistics," June 1975, Headquarters, USSAG, Nakhon Phanom, Thailand.

Fatality Ratios. The ratio for the total period was surprisingly constant for each military region, providing good verification of the data. However, the ratio increased noticeably in each succeeding period both for friendly- and enemy-initiated contacts and for attacks by fire. The tempo of combat was definitely increasing, and that could be the causative factor; however, there could also be a problem with medevacs or medical treatment.

Attack by Fire. The number of attacks by fire more than doubled in MR-4 between the first and third periods, accounting for 64 percent of the total, whereas the numbers in the other military regions remained almost constant. For the total period, the casualties per casualty-producing incident—which was 41 percent of all attacks by fire—amounted to 3.1. Almost 27 percent of all RVNAF casualties during the period since the cease-fire were caused by attacks by fire. This alarming statistic conveyed a lack of troop discipline; it suggested, for example, troops congregating in the mess line without taking adequate protective measures. Multiple casualties also resulted from booby trap incidents; the 4.0 booby trap casualties per casualty-producing incident indicated bunching (walking too close together) on operations.

RF/PF Comparisons. Reporting data by components allowed them to be compared. Obviously, the better-trained and -equipped ARVN outperformed the territorials—that was to be expected. However, our analysis indicated the territorials in MR-4 were definitely not performing well; not only were they not aggressive, but they performed poorly when in contact. The popular force had more troops killed than the enemy, and both the regional and popular force lost two weapons for every soldier killed in battle—a sorry state of affairs. The territorials were very important to MR-4's defense, since there were five times as many of them (206,000) as ARVN troops (40,000). To undertake actions to remedy the situation, when provided this data the JGS directed a study to determine why the territorials' performance in this region was lacking.

This second presentation of combat analysis highlighted several new situations resulting from the broadened data-collection requirements. It also verified that the RVNAF was becoming more aggressive, taking the battle to the enemy, and that when it took the initiative it was more efficient and effective. That attacks by fire caused 27 percent of all casualties was disturbing. Also upsetting were the multiple casualties resulting from booby trap incidents. Obviously, both of these areas required command attention. But most important was that the combat performance of each of the army components was available. In this case, it highlighted the poor performance of the territorials in MR-4. Since these units provided the preponderance of forces in the rich delta region, the disparity required immediate remedial action.

The analysis of the 2 December 1973–15 June 1974 period further highlighted the serious situation with the territorial forces in MR-4. Table 6 breaks out the friendly weapons lost per friendly killed by hostile action; note that the RF/PF in MR-4 lost more than two weapons per friendly killed, bringing the total average to greater than one weapon per friendly killed. The disparity between the ARVN and the territorials is obvious—except in MR-1, where the ARVN was having a difficult time. This alerted us to potential problems in MR-1, which manifested themselves later in the year. The same is true for operational initiatives or aggressiveness, particularly in MR-4, where the popular forces initiated only one contact out of thirty. This does not include attacks by fire. The overall efficiency of the ARVN in this period was 6.91, compared with 3.30 for the regional forces and 1.38 for the popular forces. Again, the popular forces in MR-4 had more friendly than enemy killed (.93), while the ARVN had an order of magnitude greater success (9.84).

Now that our attention was focused on the poor performance of the territorials in MR-4, we noticed in late 1974 that there was a large increase in the number of those killed compared to the number

Table 6. Friendly Weapons Ratio, Weapons Lost, Friendly Killed/Total Contacts (period 3, 16 December 1973–14 June 1974)

MR	ARVN	RF	PF	Total
RVN	.63	1.41	1.52	1.18
I	1.08	.72	.40	.83
II	.49	.72	.64	.57
III	.53	1.05	.86	.81
IV	.55	2.06	2.12	1.83

Source: Analysis, "Summary of Ceasefire Statistics," June 1975, Headquarters USSAG, Nakhon Phanon, Thailand.

wounded; the ratio of killed to total casualties increased from 24 percent in period 3 to 32 percent in period 4. This could be an indication that medical evacuation had been curtailed or that medical treatment was lacking, either of which could seriously affect morale. I asked the JGS to look into the matter. Its findings were fascinating. According to reports from the field, medical procedures and treatment had not changed during the period. However, the territorials in MR-4 had lost so many M-16s to the enemy that the enemy was using these weapons against them. According to the ARVN, the lethality of the M-16 was so much greater than that of the AK-47 that the wounded were succumbing in greater numbers.

The topography and the climate varied appreciably for each military region, greatly affecting military operations. Two major seasons characterized the climate: the southwest monsoon (wet season), which occurs generally from May through October, and the northeast monsoon (dry season), which usually runs from November through April. A major exception is the weather in the North Vietnamese panhandle south through MR-1 and -2 during November, December, and January, which are wet because of heavy coastal precipitation associated with the active tropical storm season. Figure 2 highlights the dry season for Southeast Asia. All values are the mean monthly precipitation for the larger areas, and the precipitation values for specific locations can vary considerably from the mean. This provides insight to the tempo of combat operations; for example, it suggests why communist attacks in MR-3 were often initiated in December, whereas in MR-1 and MR-2 they usually did not commence until February or March.

As additional data became available, particularly with respect to the times of day when attacks were initiated, the JGS could obtain a much better understanding of communist tactics and the RVNAF responses. Since the enemy regional commanders had relative autonomy concerning day-to-day operations, the spectrum of the times enemy ground attacks were initiated against separate South Vietnamese military regions varied greatly. They peaked in MR-1 and -2 at 0600 hours, in MR-3 at 0100 and 0200 hours, and in MR-4 at 1900 hours. Although there were definite peaks in each MR, overall the enemy initiated contacts equally over a twenty-four-hour period; thus, almost half of the attacks came at night.

Sea Precipitation (inches)

	J	A	S	O	N	D	J	F	M	A	M	J
N. LAOS	15	20	15	4	1	.5	T	.5	1	2	6	10
ST	20	22	15	6	2	1	T	.5	1	1.5	4	12
KORAT	10	12	12	4	1	T	T	.5	1	2	2	6
NVN	12	12	8	4	1.5	1	1	1	1.5	3	4	10
NVN PNHDL	6	8	20	20	10	6	2	2	2	2	3	4
MR I RVN	8	6	14	22	20	12	10	3	3	3	6	6
MR II RVN	8	8	16	20	20	12	10	5	2	2	6	8
MR III, IV RVN	10	8	10	6	3	1.5	1	.5	.5	2	10	10
KHMER	10	10	12	8	3	1.5	T	.5	1	2	8	10
S.W. KHMER	20	24	30	10	4	1	1	1	2	4	12	20

Note 1. All values are monthly, areal averages derived from 1st Weather Wing Special Studies 105-11/X. Precipitation values for specific stations can vary considerably from the mean for the area. If such specifics are desired please contact a USSAG Staff Weather Officer (2851 ext. 107, or 2234).

Note 2. NVN is dry from November through April, however they do experience extensive cloudiness in the form of low stratus.

Note 3. The wet November and December from the NVN Panhandle south through MR II in RVN is due to heavy coastal precipitation associated with the active tropical storm season.

Prepared for MGen Hunt on 9 March 1974

Leon I. Zimmerman

Leon I. Zimmerman, Capt, USAF
USSAG Staff Weather Officer

Figure 2. Dry-Season Analysis. (Source: Headquarters USSAG, Nakhon Phanom, Thailand.)

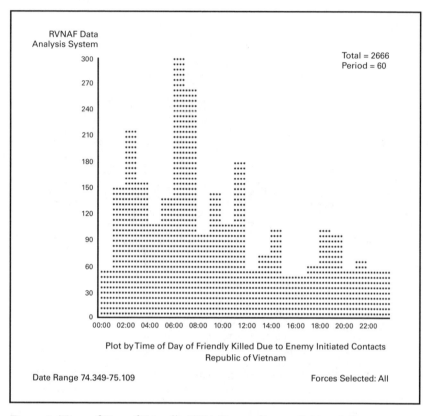

Figure 3. Time of Day of Friendly KHA Due to Enemy-Initiated Contacts. (Source: "Republic of Vietnam Ammunition Conservation Study," June 1975, Headquarters USSAG, Nakhon Phanom, Thailand.)

Considering the friendly casualties resulting from the enemy-initiated contacts, one might expect the time spectrum of casualties to mirror the enemy attacks. However, while there were spikes at 0200 hours and between 0600 and 0800, this did not hold true for the early evening hours, even though that was the period of maximum enemy contacts. The RVNAF was most vulnerable to both enemy ground attacks and attacks by fire between 0600 and 0800 hours; it just had a difficult time getting started in the morning (see figure 3). The enemy attacks by fire were mostly in the daytime, the opposite of my 1968–1969 experiences.

RVNAF-Initiated Operations

The South Vietnamese initiated operations predominantly in the daytime. When informed, the JGS, recognizing the importance of night initiatives, brought this matter to the military region commanders' attention. Between 16 December 1973 and 14 June 1974, the ARVN initiated about 1,620 contacts between 2200 hours and 0600 hours. However, between 15 June and 14 December 1974, it conducted about 5,280 friendly-initiated night contacts, over three times as many operations. A big improvement. The results of the friendly night initiatives, however, were poorer than those of daytime forays. Unfortunately, the ARVN did not have the night vision devices that enabled the U.S. forces in South Vietnam to be so successful with nighttime operations.

The JGS's prodding of commanders had some immediate effects with respect to aggressiveness. The RVNAF continued to expand its operational initiatives throughout the war. In 1975 it initiated more contacts than the enemy. This had been true for MR-1, -2, and -3 since the summer of 1974. No longer was it sitting in its bases; it was effectively taking the battle to the enemy.

When considering communist casualties, it is important to note that the number of enemy killed by air when ground forces were not in contact are not included in these statistics. Air force attacks on enemy troop movements, bivouac areas, supply points, and lines of communications were carried out throughout the post-cease-fire period. Enemy casualties resulting from the massive amounts of unobserved harassment and interdiction artillery fires also were not included. The numbers of enemy killed by these two actions, particularly by air, were substantial.

Attacks by Fire

The JGS, concerned in April 1974 that enemy attacks by fire caused 27 percent of casualties, alerted the field commanders in April and again in October 1974. Subsequently, USSAG carefully monitored the problem. One measure of the enemy's ABF effectiveness was the number of friendly soldiers killed per attack by fire: 0.12 fatalities, an average of one killed in every eight attacks. This takes into account multiple fatalities. However, there were more than six wounded per those killed.

Period	Weeks	ABF	WHA	KHA	WHA+KHA ABF
Table 7. Casualties from Attacks by Fire					
18 January 1973–16 June 1973	20	4,051	5,764	809	1.62
17 June 1973–15 December 1973	26	6,311	5,438	841	.99
16 December 1973–15 June 1974	26	7,317	5,657	901	.84
16 June 1974–14 December 1974	26	10,141	8,085	1,248	.92
15 December 1974–19 April 1975	18	7,709	4,880	734	.73
TOTAL	**116**	**35,529**	**29,824**	**4,533**	**Avg .97**

Source: Analysis, "Summary of Ceasefire Statistics," June 1975, Headquarters USSAG, Nakhon Phanom, Thailand.

Without our operations analysis, there was no way the field commanders could have realized the overall effects of enemy attacks by fire on the troops. By directing unit commanders to focus on this problem, the JGS was able to cut the enemy's effectiveness between 28 January 1973 and 20 April 1975 from 1.62 casualties per ABF to 0.73 casualties per attack by fire, even though the intensity of the attacks (rounds per attack) continued to increase throughout the periods. Countrywide summary statistics concerning friendly casualties from enemy attacks by fire are given in table 7.

There were 6.6 wounded by hostile action (WHA) per 1 killed by hostile action (KHA) resulting from attacks by fire, twice the 3.2 ratio resulting from all ground attacks. Thus, the importance of taking defensive measures against attacks by fire to protect the troops is evident. If the ratio of casualties to attacks by fire in the first period (1.62) had continued throughout the subsequent four periods, there would have been 23,211 more friendly casualties. ARVN protective measures created a huge savings in manpower and costs, to say nothing of morale.

There were several major attacks in early August 1974, particularly at Plei Me in MR-2, where the 320th NVA Division expended more than ten thousand artillery and mortar rounds attempting to defeat the 82nd ARVN Ranger Battalion.[42] Even though the intensity (rounds/ABF) increased somewhat in later periods, the friendly losses per attack were reduced by half from the earlier periods. Nevertheless, the casualties were much too high and reflected poorly on small unit leadership across the board. As an example, in period 3 there were 11,725 ARVN casualties resulting from enemy-initiated contacts and 6,558 casualties from attacks by fire.

Of all friendly casualties caused by enemy-initiated actions in period 3, 36 percent were the result of attacks by fire. When the 1,818 KHAs and 5,637 WHAs resulting from the 2,387 friendly-initiated attacks are added to the totals above, 25.5 percent of all casualties resulted from attacks by fire. We sliced the combat data in many, many ways, and generally the lessons learned were very valuable and often when implemented saved lives. The aforementioned examples are but a few.

Terrorism

The fourth major type of enemy-initiated incidents after attacks by fire, contacts, and harassments was terrorism, an important weapon of the communist insurgency, one continually practiced by the Viet Cong Infrastructure (VCI). Terror tactics constituted an integral part of communist strategy, and the assassination of civilians by terrorists was therefore deliberate and systematic. Terrorism could also be nonlethal, as manifested by taxation, abduction, and political agitation. An October 1973 review indicated enemy terrorism had declined somewhat in intensity since the January cease-fire agreement.

It was impossible to draw an exact comparison between the 1973 incident rate and those of 1969, 1970, and 1971, as tabulating procedures had changed. In gross terms, however, there appears to have been a steady four-year decline in the number of civilian casualties. Through October 1973, the number of victims killed, wounded, or abducted/ missing was running about one-half of what it had been in 1969 and 1970. The number of civilians wounded in 1973 (6,841) nearly equaled that in 1971 and was higher than in 1972, which indicated that communist harassment and shellings continued to affect populated areas. Basic government controls in urban and other normally secure areas were not affected by increased military activities in 1972 or 1973.

A U.S.-funded public survey, the Pacification Statistical Analysis System, from which the foregoing data is taken, confirmed the trends in the statistical reporting and the recent shift toward nonlethal terrorism.[43] This system was an important guide to terrorist activity, which is "successful" only if it actually persuades or coerces the target—in other words, affects the population's attitudes. Its findings indicated a lack of success nearly everywhere in South Vietnam.

In 1973, assassinations (attacks on select single individuals in which only they were killed) accounted for 393 of the 2,487 civilian deaths. Moreover, the assassination rate since the cease-fire declaration had remained close to thirty cases per month despite an upturn in civilian casualties (killed) in September. The communists evidently did not have sufficient access to target those who most threatened them politically. The more important government officials remained beyond their control.

As in the past, however, the communists continued to rely on shellings, road mining, and other techniques that did not require precision targeting to eliminate low-level government officials and PSDF troops in communist-accessible areas. Hamlet and village officials were being killed, abducted, and wounded in much larger numbers since the cease-fire. More fell victim during September 1973 than in any other month.

Urban terrorism had become almost nonexistent in 1973. According to the Pacification Statistical Analysis System, the number of urban respondents nationwide who had observed no terrorism in their own subwards or precincts rose from 27 percent in January to almost 100 percent in September.

One explanation for the decline in terrorism was implicit in the analysis system responses about the VCI. Of the September 1973 urban respondents, 98 percent rated the VCI ineffective or nonexistent. In rural areas, nearly 50 percent of the respondents offered the same assessment (compared with only 23 percent in January 1973). In September, only 4 percent of the total respondents believed that the VCI had become more effective during the previous year, whereas 16 percent had given this response in January.

The falloff of terrorism reflects on the performance of three elements of the VCI in particular: the armed reconnaissance teams, which conducted assassinations for the security sections of province and district party committees; the armed propaganda units of the propaganda sections; and the sapper (sabotage) units under the control of the military affairs committee or military headquarters of each party echelon. These specialized agencies were largely responsible for the enemy's terrorist campaigns.

The number of civilian casualties reported by the military increased each year after the cease-fire, and the number of incidents primarily against civilians also remained high in 1975. In fact, the 1975 casualty rate exceeded those of all other years. In all, since the cease-fire there were 44,296 reported civilian casualties—and the actual number was undoubtedly much higher.

When incidents occurred in the field, the friendly element involved in the incident filed a report, often hourly, with its operation center, which forwarded the report to the JGS (see appendix A, section 2). The JGS formatted the information contained in these field reports in a "Daily Results of Ceasefire Violations" form and transmitted it daily to USSAG, where our staff analyzed the data received and presented it weekly in a myriad of useful statistics. USSAG reported weekly summaries of twelve parameters relating to combat activities in South Vietnam: friendly-initiated contacts; enemy-initiated contacts; the ratio of friendly-initiated contacts to total contacts; total incidents; friendly killed; enemy killed; the ratio of enemy killed to friendly killed; friendly killed per enemy-initiated contact; number of attacks by fire; enemy rounds; rounds per attack by fire; and occurrences of terrorism, sabotage, and political events. USSAG utilized the combat data to compute the weekly intensity of combat for all regions. (See table 15.)

In addition to the detailed daily reports, the JGS compiled a "Summary of RVN Activity,"[44] which was immediately transmitted to the DAO, where Col. William LeGro, its operations and plans division chief, transmitted it to me at Headquarters USSAG. Additionally, a JGS compilation of major and minor incidents was also forwarded daily to Headquarters USSAG.[45] These two summary reports enabled USSAG to focus on the major conflicts on a daily basis. Consequently, we were privy in near real time to all the combat activities in South Vietnam.

RVNAF Improvement Efforts

MR-4 RF/PF Upgrade

In May 1974, after the JGS attempted to determine the causes that made the territorial units in sixteen sectors of MR-4 downgrade in operational effectiveness, the JGS instructed IV Corps to initiate a plan to improve and upgrade the territorial forces. The plan was to enhance the combat effectiveness of territorial units, make the outpost system effective, and develop leadership, the spirit of anticommunism, and the capabilities of the cadre and troops.

A most remarkable aspect of the IV Corps implementation had to do with the redeployment of forces. To withstand the incessant enemy attacks, the army had to consolidate its positions. Between June and September, MR-4 abandoned 752 static positions out of 3,335 organic positions. Those abandoned included two fire bases, seven bases of operations, forty company-level outposts, 527 platoon-level outposts, and 176 watchtowers. This suggests the dispersion of troops necessary to ensure territorial integrity. The RVNAF's hanging on to so many minor positions had allowed the enemy to mass troops, ensuring its local troop and fire superiority in attacks.

An important aspect of JGS planning was upgrading regional force units into mobile units. The regional force battalions and the territorial artillery battalions were to be consolidated into group commands, providing a mobile combat capability. The JGS placed these group commands under the direct control of the corps commanders and they were no longer restricted to deployment within provincial boundaries. By 30 September 1974, MR-4 had seventy-eight mobile regional force battalions and fifty-two separate companies, compared with seventy-two battalions and twenty-nine companies previously.

One may ask why the joint staff was so concerned with the performance of the territorials in MR-4. Most observers focused on MR-1, where the communists continually maintained pressure, which they could do easily because of their internal lines and huge logistical bases in North Vietnam, and on MR-3, where, from their sanctuaries in Cambodia and large border base camps, the North Vietnamese also kept moderate pressure on the approaches to Saigon. For those reasons the JGS positioned five divisions of 87,000 ARVN/Marines in MR-1 and 55,000 regulars in MR-3—over two-thirds of the regular forces. But the war for South Vietnam was being fought daily in the delta, with its population of 7 million and preponderance of arable land. The communists kept maximum pressure on the delta with the goal of affecting the pacification program by controlling the rice-producing areas and thereby disrupting the South Vietnamese economy, which was so dependent upon rice. As a consequence, the largest RVNAF contingent, three divisions with 246,000 troops, was located in MR-4, although only 40,000 were regulars. The remaining 206,000 were territorials. The distribution of the troops in the other regions was as follows: in MR-1 there were five divisions, with 87,000 ARVN/Marines and 70,000 territorials, 157,000 personnel total; in MR-2, two divisions, 28,000 ARVN/Marines and 116,000 territorials, 144,000 total; in MR-3, three divisions, 55,000 ARVN/Marines and 108,000 territorials, 163,000 total. In all four regions, the forces included thirteen divisions of 210,000 ARVN/Marines and 500,000 territorials, 710,000 total.[18]

Obviously there were major differences in the effectiveness of the components (ARVN/Marines, RF, PF, and PSDF). The ARVN, which was better trained and equipped than the others, had comported itself very well in the war. However, the performance of the RF/PF, particularly in MR-4, was poor. Improvements had to be effected! And they were.

Upon review of the daily combat reports and the weekly compilation of combat data, it became obvious that there were many more enemy initiatives in MR-4 than anywhere else in the country. This was not surprising, since the communists' objective was to conquer people and territory and the delta had the most arable land and the largest population. In MR-4 there were more incidents, more friendly killed and wounded, and more enemy killed. Additionally, more large battles (arbitrarily defined as those having fifty or more casualties) were fought in MR-4 than in any other military region. No doubt about it, the war was lost in the northern military regions—but major battles were waged in the delta, off the radar screens of most observers.

In the last analysis, the JGS's Territorial Force Improvement and Upgrade Plan[46] did greatly increase the combat effectiveness of the regional force mobile units in MR-4; during the final weeks of the war I observed that they performed very well under heavy enemy pressure.

On 11 October 1974, General Vien published a memorandum about assessment on friendly and enemy activities after the cease-fire, which was distributed to all corps and divisions. This memorandum, included in appendix B, recognizes that the North was launching large-scale, division-level campaigns with "tremendous intensity" and notes the increasing tempo of attacks by fire and the continued casualty toll. The data enables gross comparisons between military regions. The memorandum concentrates on regular force (ARVN) activities. The strategies included in its summary emphasized ARVN weaknesses: study enemy habits so as to preempt attacks, be vigilant, take effective measures to counter enemy attacks by fire, conserve weapons and equipment, and increase and improve unit activities at night.

Because of the disparities in terrain, weather, population, and the makeup of the friendly and enemy armed forces, there were still four different conflicts ongoing in the military regions. However, the joint staff now had a much greater understanding of each corps' efficiencies and effectiveness, as well as those of the enemy. It was obvious from General Vien's memo and other joint staff actions that our operational analyses provided important information, useful in making decisions to improve military operations.

The Pacification Program

Hamlet Evaluation Survey

One of the foundations of U.S. policy in Vietnam was the pacification program, the purpose of which was to extend the control of the government to the maximum throughout South Vietnam. The Hamlet Evaluation System (HES)[47] was designed specifically as a means of evaluating the effects of insurgency upon the people of Vietnam. Essentially, the system permitted a set of questions to be asked about the people and their environment and evaluations to be derived from the responses. The system provided information in three fundamental areas encompassing pacification—military, political, and community development—from a set of 165 multiple-choice questions. HES data originated at the hamlet and village level with information gathered monthly from various sources. It was designed to meet several objectives: monitor the progress of the pacification effort in hamlets and villages throughout South Vietnam; provide the capability of analyzing trends in various aspects of projects within the pacification program; make available analytical reports that reflected the military, political, and community development aspects of the pacification program; and supply a geopolitical profile of South Vietnam.

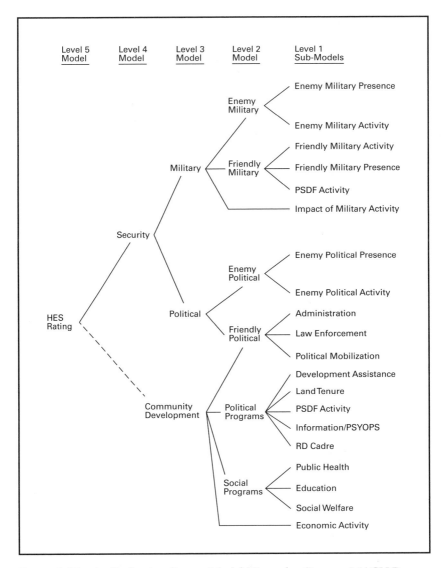

Figure 4. Hamlet Evaluation System Model Hierarchy. (Source: MACV Document, DAR R70-79, Hamlet Evaluation System [HES], 1 September 1971, Saigon, South Vietnam.)

The general types of inputs to the system are shown in figure 4. The output of the system was a rating for each hamlet/village in the country. There were five basic alphabetic ratings forming a progressive scale, from best to worst. An "A" rating represented the best situation; an "E" rating represented the worst. An "N" rating was assigned if there was insufficient information to evaluate a hamlet, and a "V" rating was assigned when the hamlet was considered under Viet Cong control.

The 9th Infantry Division, the only major U.S. unit in the populated delta when I was chief of staff in 1968–1969, utilized the HES extensively to integrate our combat operations with our pacification efforts to ensure the optimum support for the pacification program. When the Accelerated Pacification Program was initiated in late 1968, it had clear-cut objectives, the most fundamental of which was to choose key hamlets and villages in a contested status with the Viet Cong and, through security and civic efforts, raise these hamlets to a more secure status. We initially had little faith in the HES, since it appeared that it could be a pencil exercise with little validity. Therefore, we undertook a detailed hamlet evaluation survey for all the hamlets in one district of Dinh Tuong Province. We told our G-2 to be hard-nosed in his evaluations. At its conclusion, we compared our survey with the MACV advisory-team survey and were amazed to find a difference of less than 10 percent between the evaluations. This gave us new and substantial confidence in the hamlet evaluation survey. With the peace accord, the responsibility for the HES was transferred from MACV to the Saigon embassy, and the tasks of supervising the recording of data were transferred from U.S. district advisers to South Vietnamese district local personnel. Between 1973 and 1975, the survey became less reliable, primarily because the local personnel were not as capable or as well trained. The special assistant to the ambassador for field operations, Col. G. D. Jacobson, was responsible for publishing the HES, and he did so through a U.S. contractor. Sorting through the surveys for more than ten thousand hamlets each month and portraying meaningful outputs depicting the effects of insurgency on the people of Vietnam was extremely complicated and difficult. Because of the complexity, the contractor considered himself irreplaceable. In 1974, when the contractor pulled out over a disagreement, Jacobson asked me if Headquarters USSAG could produce the hamlet evaluation survey. We had the computer capability and many hard-working young officers, so we took on the job. Maj. Leonard F. Vernamonti (USAF) and his associates not only had the survey up and running but greatly improved the output and its timeliness. We had already become the collator and analytic focus for military combat data for Cambodia and South Vietnam. Consequently, USSAG was the periodic recipient of almost all of the vital Southeast Asia data inputs.

To be an "A" or "B" hamlet with respect to friendly military presence, the reaction time for the nearest friendly ground reaction force during the hours of darkness when called upon for support by local security forces had to be shorter than two hours 65 percent of the time. Obviously, for this capability a military unit would have to be stationed in close proximity to the hamlet. In January 1973 there were 12,091 hamlets in South Vietnam, of which only 750 were under VC control— these numbers give a sense of how extremely difficult it was to provide reasonable security. That January 2,248 hamlets (18.6 percent) were in D, E, V, or N categories, whereas of the 19,390,753 people, only 8.1 percent were in hamlets/villages given these categories.[48] A review of the population under Government of Vietnam (GVN) control (HES ratings A and B) from January 1973 (14,764,410) to February 1975 (14,554,723) indicates a peak of control in March 1974 (16,666,540).

The State Department always highlighted the necessity for the control of population and territory; thus, this was where the South Vietnamese government and the military placed their emphasis. The peace treaty did not provide an answer to the all-important question of who would ultimately control South Vietnam. Therefore, to obtain legitimacy and bargaining power the North Vietnamese, both before and after the signing of the Paris accord, sought to seize and control population. In counterattacks, the RVNAF fought to deny the enemy this control.

The RVNAF was under tremendous strain to defend more than twelve thousand widely dispersed hamlets, many in difficult terrain. These static defenses greatly sapped its combat capabilities, while the enemy was free to choose its objectives and in almost all cases to amass a local preponderance of troops and firepower. As long as the enemy retained even a modest military capability in an area, pacification was impossible. Strong military and civic action efforts integrated with the South Vietnamese pacification program achieved notable results. As an aside, all U.S. military units in South Vietnam participated in civic action programs to some degree. The 9th Division pacification program,[40] for example, had at its foundation five major civic action themes: psychological operations to win the hearts and minds of the people, assistance to victims of the war, assistance in health matters, educational support, and repair and construction of facilities. The individual American soldier has always helped to alleviate the suffering and anguish caused by wars, and Vietnam was no exception.

Pacification and Rural Development Program

The Pacification and Rural Development Program (PRD) was the centerpiece of the GVN and U.S. policies in South Vietnam. It required the total integration of military and civic action efforts. As such, it was a great success, and by mid-1974 almost all of the major populated areas of South Vietnam were pacified. This included the absorption of almost 750,000 refugees driven from their homes by the 1972 general offensive. The areas under government control had been expanded, and the security provided brought about confidence in the South Vietnamese government. The relative stability of the rural areas plus economic aid substantially improved the living conditions of the rural populace.

The PRD program took the combined efforts of the United States and South Vietnamese utilizing all available resources and capabilities. It required the total integration of civilian and military means, for without security there could be no development. By 1973 the government had trained more than 2 million local personnel in the PSDF, and, coordinating with the territorial forces, they provided the security for the hamlets, which enabled many social and economic programs to take hold.[49] A measure of the success of the Pacification and Rural Development Program is the index of agricultural production. In 1967, agricultural production was at 91 percent of 1961–1965 levels, and it gradually improved, until 1973, when it was 115 percent.

It was obvious that the Pacification and Rural Development Program was a success, particularly since the 1975 COSVN Resolution emphasized the importance of a fundamental defeat of South Vietnam's pacification program and indicated that the communists would give top priority to counterpacification.[50] The North's stated requirements for fundamentally defeating pacification were to kill one-third of South Vietnam's main, regional, and popular forces in 1975 and to neutralize one-third to one-half of the PSDF.

The enemy understood that there could be no pacification without security, and the territorial forces, some five hundred thousand troops, had security as their major objective. To protect all the hamlets and villages from the enemy, they had to remain colocated with the people. To accomplish this, they established outposts (5,453 of them) to interdict the enemy; operational and fire support bases to protect larger concentrations of people and support the outposts; and ARVN main force units to intervene, support, and attack major enemy incursions. It took time, months, to eliminate enemy local forces; thus, the majority of all troop strengths were stuck in static situations. The ennui of prolonged periods of static duty severely denigrated the aggressive spirit of many friendly main force units. The areas to be secured were vast, so a linear defense protected the perimeter of South Vietnam. Almost all military units were committed, and none of the four corps had a satisfactory reserve.

The COSVN current affairs committee assessed the situation in the third quarter of 1974:

> Militarily, the enemy mobile forces are compelled to contend (with attacks by us) from many directions, their mobility declines and the rescue forces "to quell the fire" are weaker day by day. As a result of this, they cannot hold on to territory even in some important areas, and the consolidation of their rear areas is also limited. The personnel strength has decreased, particularly in the regional forces to the point that it has affected greatly their tactics, the soldiers' morale and their fighting force and limited their capability to come to the aid of outposts.[50]

Naturally, COSVN always exaggerated the situation, but there was fact to this assessment.

Although the strategy of protecting all of the national territory and maintaining control over all the population was a flawed concept, it did work very well until the enemy had the strength and the resources necessary to initiate major unit combined arms attacks, shifting from a guerrilla war to a conventional one, which they were able to do because of their increased artillery and armor and the serious diminution of friendly airpower. Thus, in late 1974 the RVNAF was spread woefully thin with little defense in depth and no strategic reserves. The success of the Pacification and Rural Development Program, which required the military to provide local security for pacification areas, became a major drawback to an effective combat capability.

Ammunition

By early 1974 it had become obvious to USSAG that in addition to assisting with tactical matters, we had to do everything possible to help both Cambodia and South Vietnam, with their U.S. advisers' support, to reduce current expenditure levels so that they would have the funding with which to procure essential supplies and equipment. This was war by budget! That in itself is not bad, if the budget fits the combat situation. In FY 74, the budget was tight but workable. We had to ensure that our allies maximized their combat power within the budget restrictions. Currently, the rates of ammunition expenditures in both South Vietnam ($544 million) and Cambodia ($301 million) were far greater than the approved congressional funding would support, thereby necessitating the undesirable drawdown of ammunition stocks as well as precluding the requisitioning of other necessary items. The major expenditures creating across-the-board funding shortfalls were in ammunition, so this was where we concentrated.

The estimated quantity of conventional ammunition required per day to sustain operations in an active theater is called a day of supply (DOS). A DOS is calculated by multiplying the weapons density by the supply rate. The force structure that determines the weapons density and the rate of supply are the key factors. Some ammunition definitions are in order. First, required supply rate (RSR) is the amount of ammunition expressed in rounds per weapon per day for ammunition to support tactical operations. Authorized supply rate (ASR), now called the controlled supply rate, is the amount of ammunition estimated to be available to sustain operations of a designated force for a specified time if expenditures are controlled at that rate. Daily expenditure rate is the average rate of expenditures per day, over a given period of time. And, finally, intensive combat rate is the amount of ammunition expressed in rounds per weapon per day required to sustain heavy-intensity combat.

All of the supply rates in Southeast Asia varied with combat intensity, which could be seasonal and/or dependent upon friendly and enemy actions. The DOS varied with the weapons densities. The optimum situation was to have sufficient ammo so that the controlled supply rate (ASR) equaled the tactical commander's requirements (RSR) and to have daily expenditure rates equal to or below the ASR. However, in Southeast Asia the unavailability of funding, transportation, or stockage levels required the authorized supply rate to be below tactical requirements (RSR), and, generally, the daily expenditure rate was in excess of the authorized supply rate.

Comparative RSRs

Our first step was to compare the RSRs of the ARVN and the Cambodian armed forces (FANK) to those of the United States. Table 8 compares the Cambodian and South Vietnamese rates at the time with those of the United States under inactive combat. Both Southeast Asia RSRs were significantly below the lowest level of American RSRs. Measured against U.S. standards, ammo expenditures in South Vietnam and Cambodia were low. However, measured against the restrictive congressional funding levels, they were excessive.

Table 8. Comparative Required Supply Rates, Rounds per Weapon per Day, October 1973			
	Cambodia	South Vietnam	U.S. inactive situation
M-16 rifle ammo	6.6	3.6	30
7.62 machine gun ammo	30.0	31.0	131
.50 cal machine gun ammo	20.0	20.0	53
M79 grenade launcher ammo	1.8	0.8	6
81 mm mortar ammo	3.1	2.5	29
105 mm howitzer ammo	22.7	10.0	40
155 mm howitzer ammo	43.1	13.0	47
106 mm recoilless rifle ammo	1.0	0.8	8
Source: Authorized country RSRs as of October 1973.			

Ammunition Conservation

In mid-December 1973, General Vien, the RVNAF chief of staff, asked Major General Murray if the DAO could make an analysis of army artillery expenditures. Murray passed this request to USSAG, knowing that we were already attempting to get a handle on the Cambodian ammunition situation. It was obvious to all concerned that with the reduced FY 74 funding levels some solution concerning ammunition expenditures had to be found. Since artillery ammo made up 75 percent of ARVN ammo tonnage and more than 50 percent of the costs, artillery was the critical line item in South Vietnam.

In South Vietnam, shortly after the cease-fire and before the full departure of American forces, the JGS arrived at the understanding that there had to be a cutback in ammunition expenditures. On 12 March 1973 a JGS memorandum from General Vien with the subject of "Restricted Employment of Artillery and Tactical Air" was distributed to all corps, divisions, and major units as well as the air force. It stated that if responsible officials did not restrict the usage of ammunition, a shortage would certainly come and that artillery and air should be employed only when the unit's organic crew-served weapons (machine guns, mortars, and recoilless rifles) had been fully employed. It also restricted the use of harassment and interdiction fires. Units were authorized to fire only within their prescribed ammo loads. The memorandum concluded: "The abundant and nearly unlimited artillery and air support in the recent past does not exist at present, so it is necessary to get the troops morally prepared to accept it and to get familiarized with our restricted means in this phase of self-sufficiency and self-development."[295]

Relating Ammunition Usage to Combat Levels

The RVNAF was indeed predisposed to the conservation of ammunition—they just required assistance in getting a handle on the problem. The question, then, was whether current artillery expenditures were reasonable and whether steps could be taken to ensure adequate firepower at reduced rates. There are many factors in the ammunition equation: rates of supply, density of weapons, organization of forces, types of ammunition, cost of line items, conservation measures, and levels of combat. Of these, only the level of combat was in part dictated by the enemy—all other factors were under friendly control. Therefore, it was important to relate artillery responses to known combat activities. The ARVN had kept excellent data on enemy attacks by fire and ground contacts. USSAG then considered four types of activities that resulted in artillery expenditures: counterbattery in response to enemy attacks by fire, artillery support of minor contacts, artillery support of major contacts, and harassment and interdiction fires. Close air and artillery support of troops in contact is a function of the intensity of conflict and is less for minor contacts and more for prolonged intensive fighting. In late 1973, this was still a war of attrition; 50 percent of all ground contacts reported resulted in one or fewer casualties—that is, friendly killed or wounded or enemy killed. Not much artillery should be employed in support of minor contacts. However, in major contacts, where fierce fighting often occurred over prolonged periods, a large amount of artillery support was absolutely essential to meaningful fire and maneuver tactics. There was obviously a requirement for counterbattery fires in response to enemy attacks by fire and also a requirement for limited interdictive fires.

USSAG responded quickly to the DAO and JGS request for an analysis of artillery expenditures. We initially calculated artillery allocations for 29 June through 6 December 1973. We took the number of tubes in each military region into consideration and computed the total rounds per tube fired. The results were eye-opening; some military regions, particularly MR-2, used far more artillery ammo than others, even considering the level of combat. As a result of this initial analysis, the joint staff set about drafting an ammunition conservation memorandum, issued to corps commanders on 24 January 1974. The staff also asked USSAG to develop an ammunition conservation program. It required a formula for what could be considered a reasonable response to enemy activities, using as its base the four aforementioned types of combat. It was important to keep in mind the interrelationship of ammunition and tactics. The Army Field Manual 101-10-1 states: "Ammunition directly influences tactical operations. Therefore, tactical commanders must plan their operations and commit their forces with full awareness of the support capabilities of the ammunition service support structure . . . an imbalance of either tactics or ammunition service may decisively influence operations. . . . Ammunition demands vary in direct ratio to the intensity of combat."[296] The joint staff recognized the interrelation of tactics and ammunition when it succinctly stated in its memo that ammo consumption must be related to enemy actions. No conservation plan is sound unless correlated with combat activities, and, conversely, there can be no understanding of ammunition expenditures without concomitant knowledge of the tactical situation.

Considering the tactical situations as they related to artillery ammo, I arrived at a formula that primarily provided a measure for the level of combat intensity.

Combat Intensity Factor =
[18 ABFs + 36 Minor Cntc + 360 × Major Cntc × $\frac{\text{Casualties}}{20}$] 1.15

It must be pointed out in the strongest terms that no formula will provide an exact measurement. A major advantage for calculating periodic combat intensity factors (CIFs) was that they provided meaningful measurements of combat intensities over time. It was obvious from the streams of combat data that the North Vietnamese were increasing their combat levels. They conducted many more attacks by fire, and at the time the scope of their ground attacks was escalating from regimental to divisional units. Therefore, we believed that measuring and reporting on the intensities of combat would allow the parties in Washington to judge whether or not additional funding was required to enable the South Vietnamese to combat the increasingly blatant communist aggression. The CIF was developed as a macroscopic measurement of the combat level and was considered an average over many units within a military region. We emphasized that the recommended rates were gross estimates only and should be used as such.

This measurement of the combat intensity level related artillery responses to combat activities. It provided limited artillery allocations for counterbattery, close ground support, and 15 percent for interdictions. It was event oriented in that it considered the number of attacks by fire and ground contacts, and intensity oriented in that it provided additional artillery for major contacts depending upon casualty rates. Battle casualties are the most realistic measures of combat intensity, and 25 percent of all RVNAF losses were from ABFs (table 16). When the ABF portion of the CIF was computed for four six-month periods it varied from 22 to 25 percent, closely correlated to actual battle casualties.

To provide the ARVN with a conservation plan aimed at determining a reasonable level of artillery capabilities, it was necessary to relate expenditures to the level of combat, choose a baseline for computation purposes, take measurements weekly for each MR and the country as a whole, and take measurements that provided absolute as well as relative criteria. The chief of the joint general staff had issued his ammo conservation memorandum to the corps commanders on 24 January 1974. Consequently, the baseline was taken from 29 June 1973 to 24 January 1974, a period without any conservation. Five weeks were allowed for the units to adjust to the new conservation program, and the conservation period was then measured from 1 March 1974 through the final data input on 27 March 1975. We computed the levels of combat, and thus the artillery allowances, every week for each military region and the country as a whole. This enabled absolute as well as relative comparisons to be made. In that way, the JGS could compare conservation results among the military regions.[52]

The army made great progress conserving ammunition in the first twenty-four weeks of the conservation period, 1 March 1974 to 15 August 1974. It reduced artillery expenditures by 40 percent, although troops were still firing in excess of the computed allowances. Regardless of their progress in conservation, however, by August 1974 ground ammunition was a very pressing problem. The ARVN's FY 75 ammo budget was only $262 million; in July expenditures amounted to $28 million and in August $50 million, an annual rate of expenditures of about $470 million. Thus, in two months it had spent 30 percent of its budget, creating a potentially serious drawdown of stocks. But the level of combat had increased greatly because of a substantial increase in both friendly and enemy initiatives.

So again, in September 1974, the JGS felt compelled to issue still another memorandum, subject: "Ammo Conservation."[53] It considered "ammo . . . a decisive factor on the battlefield besides morale, *so it cannot be deprived or short of in combat.*" Noting the enormous annual expenditure, it stated, "Conservation is the most urgent action of all possible courses of action." Addressing what ammo conservation meant, the JGS wrote, "Ammo conservation does not mean privation or shortage of ammo *to destroy the enemy when we see him, find him or when he comes to attack us.* We have to use ammo *in the right place at the right time and accurately.*"

In December 1974, I prepared a "SEA Ammunition Perspective" for CINCPAC and the JCS in Washington to provide a background for all concerned in coming to grips with Southeast Asia's most pressing problem—greatly reduced funds which, due to high inflation, reduced the amount of ammo available to use in escalating combat in Southeast Asia.[54] We had previously requested, as had the DAO and Military Equipment Delivery Team Cambodia (MEDTC), additional funds generated through a reduction of Department of the Army–directed funding offsets (set-asides) or an increase in the current appropriation level.

We noted that both countries had implemented stringent conservation programs and that the FY 75 ammo expenditure rates were approximately the same as for FY 74, even though the levels and intensity of combat had increased appreciably. As requested, we provided a forecast of annual expenditures for ground and air ammunition for FY 75 computed at the current levels of combat, not for general offensives. Ammunition expenditures would amount to approximately $845 million, several hundred million dollars in excess of available funding, which would mean a serious drawdown of stocks.

Tripartite Deputies Meetings

As the USSAG deputy commander, I traveled monthly to Phnom Penh to attend the tripartite deputies meetings. Phnom Penh was a bustling city of about 3 million people located on the Mekong River, with vestiges of its French colonial past everywhere. A big benefit of these meetings was that I could coordinate with MEDTC, which was providing logistical and training support to the Cambodian armed forces. USSAG was actively assisting this small, overworked organization with both operational planning and logistical management.

The tripartite concept was that South Vietnamese and Cambodians could improve their resistance to the communists by coordinating their military activities. To this end, the deputy commanders of the South Vietnamese, Cambodian, and U.S. forces met monthly, always at Phnom Penh, for face-to-face discussions. These were formal meetings with papers prepared and presented in three languages. The first order of business was to review and discuss the past month's military operations. We also attempted to resolve any actual or perceived interoperability problems between the two countries.

These were two different wars. In Cambodia, President Lon Nol had withdrawn his forces into the major population centers and rarely conducted offensive operations, leaving the countryside largely under communist control. In South Vietnam, President Thieu insisted on protecting all of his far-flung hamlets and villages and pacifying the countryside, so the ARVN was consistently on the offensive to keep the enemy off balance, thus securing the population. Until now, the superior ground and air firepower of both countries had inflicted heavy losses on the enemy whenever it massed to attack.

The major advantage the Vietnamese and Cambodian armed forces had over the communist enemy was in firepower. Since the January 1973 cease-fire in Vietnam and the 15 August 1973 bombing halt in Cambodia, this comparative advantage had been reduced more than 50 percent, if one considers tons of steel on target. Even though firepower had been reduced, the results obtained by our allies had been much greater than is generally recognized. In the previous twelve months (December 1973 through November 1974), the Vietnamese and Cambodian armed forces had killed approximately 23 percent of the combat forces of the enemy. More precisely, in Vietnam, of between 190,000 and 215,000 enemy combat personnel, 49,500 (24 percent) were KIA, and in Cambodia, of 59,850 enemy combat personnel, 13,800 (23 percent) were KIA.[52, 55] Until December 1974, whenever the enemy moved to initiate a major attack, the allied artillery and airpower had generally chewed it up and the enemy losses in those situations were great. For that reason, combat had become a war of attrition, with a large number of small, enemy-initiated, limited-objective ground attacks and a large number of standoff attacks by fire. It is a fact that the major single inhibitor to enemy-initiated all-out major assaults on strategic targets had been allied firepower.

To date, allied firepower had been very effective. But the balance was changing rapidly as the enemy accumulated more and more equipment and supplies, particularly antiaircraft guns, which negated the air force's potent punch, and long-range artillery, which could outgun the ARVN's pieces. Besides, the RVNAF had to reduce greatly its firepower and mobility because of severe funding restrictions.

The daily expenditure rate continued to exceed the authorized supply rate in both countries; this was the root of the ammo problem. Both countries faced considerable drawdowns in stocks, perhaps to dangerous levels. Funds dictated the authorized supply rate, and the authorized supply rate mix should approximate the daily expenditure rate. Either excessive line-item expenditures had to be reduced or the authorized supply rate had to be adjusted to reflect the combat situations—that is, each country needed to obtain an increase in funding. The required supply rates, the amount of ammunition the tactical commanders would like to have to conduct their respective wars, were far greater than the authorized supply rates, but in reality they were much less than the previous U.S.-Vietnam expenditures.

The daily amount of ammunition expended on targets in Vietnam from all sources in 1969 was 6,410 short tons. This compares to the RVNAF's stand-alone 1974 expenditures of 808 short tons, which, incidentally, was less than the 983 short tons the RVNAF itself expended in 1969. Both the ARVN and the VNAF, whose weapon densities the Vietnamization program had appreciably increased, were expending less munitions in 1974 than they had in 1969 while now fighting a much better equipped enemy whose battle strength was 50 percent greater (see table 1), and they no longer had the support of the free world forces. The allies spent eight times the ammunition in 1969 that the RVNAF alone spent in 1974.

In February 1975, the South Vietnamese were expecting a major North Vietnamese dry-weather offensive to commence in late February or early March. We knew that there would be a great increase in combat intensity in South Vietnam (already for 6–12 December 1974 the factor had reached an all-time high of 98,821), which could result in substantial ammo expenditures. Therefore, in an attempt to prevent a complete drawdown of stocks, we calculated an intensive combat rate to enable us to properly forecast ammunition requirements. The calculated ground ammo intensive combat rate of 1,809 short tons, or 54,270 short tons per month, was well below ARVN's expenditures of 75,700 short tons per month between April 1972 and February 1973 (when the formidable U.S. firepower had been available).

As we at NKP anticipated the NVA dry-weather offensive, it became clear that by the end of FY 75 the ammunition situation in South Vietnam would be desperate. Notwithstanding all the discussions and message exchanges Headquarters USSAG had with CINPAC and Washington, we never really got their attention on the criticality of ammunition in Vietnam. There was a large amount of ammo stored on the ground in South Vietnam, and it was difficult to visualize the severe drawdown an all-out enemy offensive would cause.

Although according to the peace agreement ammo stockage could be maintained at 177,800 short tons, the funding situation created an endemic shortfall from period to period, so that on 1 July 1974 the ammunition stocks on hand had been seriously drawn down, to 114,000 short tons. I do not fault those who thought the ARVN stockage of ammo on 1 July 1974 was a substantial quantity; it was. Nevertheless, it was insufficient to support the ARVN in combating a North Vietnamese general offensive. We had seen the huge consumption in the 1972 Easter Offensive, and the same increases were bound to occur if the enemy again initiated a major offensive, which all intelligence reports unequivocally said it intended to do in February or March 1975. Thus, we repeatedly alerted higher headquarters that ARVN ground ammunition was inadequate.[56] Three months of intense combat would require more than 160,000 short tons of ammo, much more than was available.

Table 9 shows the ARVN ground ammunition issues for 1968 through 1975. In 1972, the year of the NVA Easter Offensive, ammo issues averaged 66,355 short tons per month, or 2,200 short tons per day, greater than the 1975 intensive combat rate of 1,809 short tons.

Table 9. Army Ground Ammunition Issues (short tons)		
Year	Total	Monthly average
1968	222,200	18,517
1969	292,606	24,384
1970	376,299	31,358
1971	444,228	37,019
1972	796,264	66,355
1973	333,067	27,756
1974	205,450	17,121
Source: "ARVN Ammo Issues," ARVN Records via DAO, March 1975, Saigon, South Vietnam.		

The air munitions expenditures for April, May, and June 1972 far exceeded ground expenditures.[57]

The 1972 ammunition supplies were issued during a period of massive U.S. tactical air support. There had not been a major communist offensive in 1973 or 1974, so observers could have forgotten the extensive ammo requirements for intensive combat. ARVN ammo consumption in 1974 was lower than it had been in any year since 1968 and was only 26 percent of the 1972 rate.

On 11 March 1975, the beginning of the enemy's dry-season campaign, we sent CINCPAC a message: "Considering current enemy initiatives and future enemy capabilities, the ammo supply in South Vietnam is critical."[59] The ARVN would be almost out of ammo by the end of FY 75 if it consumed only 55 percent of the ammo expended in 1972, when the army had far fewer artillery pieces, tanks, and antitank weapons, all of which were introduced as the result of the huge pre-cease-fire equipment buildup, when the U.S. Air Force was providing close air support and strategic bombing. We fully realized that the congressional funding limitations circumscribed CINCPAC and the Pentagon in providing ammunition. However, we hoped that if we brought the critical ammunition situation to their attention, both could influence Congress to increase the funding.

On 5 April, after the withdrawals from MR-1 and MR-2, where the unusual loss of ammo storage was about 16,000 short tons, only 43,471 short tons of ground ammunition remained in MR-3 and -4. At the rate of expenditures over the previous two weeks—1,351 short tons per day—there was less than a month's supply, considering that critical line-item shortages would occur. There was a due-in quantity of 32,630 short tons, but it was very doubtful whether any could be effectively delivered to the besieged troops around the Saigon perimeter. Even if it could be delivered, there would be no stocks on hand on 31 May 1975, leaving the troops with only their basic loads. The same type analysis applied to the air force, which had approximately 20,000 short tons at Bien Hoa, Tan Son Nhut, and Bien Thuy. They were expending 270 short tons per day, so they would be out of munitions about 7 June 1975. Therefore, on 8 April we sent another message to Washington: "The ammunition situation in South Vietnam is critical."[60] This assumed that the due-in quantities of ammo could effectively be delivered, which was very doubtful. Within two weeks Tan Son Nhut was being interdicted. Also, after a sustained enemy attack on Saigon, the large ammo supplies in Bien Hoa would not have been available.

So, to carry on, in early April the South Vietnamese desperately needed the close air support of the U.S. Air Force and a herculean effort to resupply critical air and ground munitions. Given the political situation in the United States, the Vietnamese would wait in vain for the United States to reintroduce its air support and adequate logistics. Had the RVNAF stood and fought it would have been effectively out of ammo within days.

Ammunition Costs

The cost of ammunition directly affected supply availability. As the limiting factor with respect to ammunition was funding, costs were vital. In the past there had been a tendency to analyze ammunition situations (expenditures and stocks) by aggregating tons of ammunition. The assumption that costs per ton are constant had underlain such analyses. Nothing could be further from the truth: these costs vary appreciably over time because of inflation and weapon densities, and they also vary among types of ammunition.

In 1974, the cost of ammunition rose well out of proportion to the inflationary increases in the U.S. economy as a whole, although U.S. depots provided various reasons for the dramatic rise in costs. The ammunition costs both in Cambodia and Vietnam increased 60 percent in one year. The costs per ton varied between the countries, and price increases fluctuated widely, depending on the line item of ammo. Yet, the net increases in both countries for a day of supply was about the same. Using the November 1974 day of supply rate with the cost of ammo variable, between November 1973 and November 1974 the cost of daily supplies in South Vietnam rose from $1,251 to $1,997 per ton, a 60 percent increase; in the same period in Cambodia the cost rose from $1,553 to $2,553 per ton, a 64 percent increase.[54]

Force structure has a great impact on the cost of ammunition. The accelerated delivery of equipment in 1972 to replace combat losses and to enhance firepower had substantially increased weapons densities and consequently the cost of a day of supply. In November 1974 the costs per ton of each type of ammunition varied considerably, with individual weapons ($3,991) and mortars ($3,575) being much more expensive than artillery ($1,463). Yet, artillery expenditures in South Vietnam drove their costs, accounting for 54 percent of total ammunition expenditures. Mortars and individual weapons (which included rifles, machine guns, light antiaircraft weapons, and M-79 grenade launchers) each accounted for 19 percent of total expenditures, with miscellaneous items accounting for 8 percent.

The main point concerning costs is that although the cost per ton of ammunition varied with weapon densities and the type of ammunition, the major factor affecting Cambodia and Vietnam was the 60 percent inflationary increase in the cost of a day of supply. Funds that could purchase a full year's supply in FY 73 could purchase only 222 days' worth in FY 74. The question remained: Could troops cut back enough to meet the stringent authorized supply rates and still be effective? To answer this, it is necessary to compare the ASR (which was established to limit ammo expenditures to a given dollar level as dictated by funding) to the daily expenditure rate.

The RVNAF was over its authorized target by 52 percent. By any measure, the intensity of combat in South Vietnam had been steadily increasing. In Vietnam, the 1974 dry season saw at least a 60 percent increase in combat activities over the previous year. The number of attacks by fire and minor contacts had increased appreciably, and major contacts had either increased or remained steady. To date, the war in South Vietnam was one of attrition. The majority of incidents were either standoff attacks by fire, with no contact involved, or minor contacts in which the number of casualties on both sides averaged about three personnel. This "retailing concept," with a large number of small actions, adds up, and more than half of all ground casualties resulted from minor contacts. The enemy, however, had the capability to go "wholesale"—with large-scale conventional attacks. When one looks at the average weekly combat statistics for South Vietnam in late 1974, two factors stand out: the level of conflict was increasing, and the majority of incidents were minor contacts and attacks by fire, which required limited responses only. Major contacts occurred only about 3 percent of the time.

Even though Vietnam initiated a strict conservation program, utilizing combat data as its basis, by mid-December 1974 it was obvious that the daily expenditure rates consistently exceeded the authorized supply rates. Its already low ammunition stocks were being perilously drawn down, and without conservation by the end of the year it would have either run out of ammunition or required supplemental funding. However, the ARVN did appreciably conserve ammunition. If the rates of artillery consumption in effect during the six-month base period were continued thereafter, the army would have expended more than 2 million more artillery rounds, the equivalent of $110 million.

It must be emphasized that the current levels of ammo expenditures in Vietnam were low, particularly when compared to the U.S. levels. If the United States had provided ample military aid, it would have been desirable to maintain these current levels of expenditures and perhaps to increase them. However, the current expenditures were running several hundred million dollars over the FY 75 appropriation, and belt-tightening was essential. The necessity to buy ammunition was leaving no funds available for other purposes. In effect, the conservation program computed allowances based on measurements of combat intensity and represented a pragmatic approach to saving ammunition in a balanced fashion so that military capabilities were not excessively reduced in the efforts to shoehorn expenditures into a much smaller military assistance program. In December 1974 combat levels were increasing, and the budget should have been geared to the level of conflict. The rising combat intensities coupled with inflationary costs had greatly affected the situation.

Was Ammo Conservation Hurting Morale?

In his memorandum to corps commanders on 2 April 1974, General Vien stated: "We have to adopt the slogan *Win over the enemy by morale and not by material means.*" At the end of 1974, the question was whether the required conservation of ammunition, petroleum, and other supplies was affecting the morale of the soldiers. There is no doubt that tactics and the supply of ammunition are closely interrelated. A reduction in the amount of ammunition available would have a decided impact on the tactics employed, would affect a unit's efficiency and morale, and could impinge severely on a unit's combat personnel losses. In Vietnam, the U.S. Army left a legacy of ample ammunition expenditures. It was our philosophy to maximize the utilization of firepower to minimize the loss of American lives.

Ammunition rationing can have a dramatic impact on an infantry soldier's morale. A man who has been used to having three bandoliers of M-16 ammo, a frag grenade hanging from each shoulder strap, and a light antitank weapon in his left hand feels naked going into battle with less. Consequently, without any one of these, he is less prone to take chances and eventually loses the offensive spirit. It is important, therefore, to ensure that the infantryman is provided with sufficient ammunition—his basic load is part of his way of life.

The conflict in Vietnam to date was indeed a war of attrition: over 96 percent of all contacts were minor, and there was about one enemy attack by fire for every ground contact. The number of times an infantryman needed massed artillery or close air support was lower than 5 percent; therefore, in a war of attrition individual weapons were the key. Conservation, then, should focus on supporting fires and not on individual weapons. However, an infantryman's failure to receive supporting fires or close air support when absolutely required could also have a shattering impact. In the past, there had been a tendency for the artillery to fritter away supplies on harassment and interdiction fires, trying to hit an enemy that would not mass.

In November 1974, a South Vietnamese infantryman received 19 percent of the ammo dollar. This may have been too little. It must be accepted that ammo conservation measures adversely influenced morale; the question was whether ammunition conservation practices affected the efficiency of the forces materially. One might measure troop efficiency by the ratio of enemy killed to friendly killed, which is perhaps the most easily quantifiable measure. Other possible measures are territory or population controlled and battles won or lost, comparing previous data to the period since ammo rationing. We cannot substantiate the statement that there had been an exchange of lives for ammo. Perhaps reduced morale would in time dictate a decided reduction in efficiency; or if more stringent ammo conservation measures were taken, there could be a major deterioration. The JGS believed that to ensure that such a situation did not occur, the ARVN should continue to provide maximum individual support for the infantryman in his day-to-day combat and maximum supporting fires during the relatively infrequent major attacks. However, the North recently had initiated large-scale combined arms attacks and had outgunned the South in tanks, artillery, and antiaircraft weapons. Even though to date the South Vietnamese had been making their bullets count, the deteriorating logistics situation had materially affected the balance of power. There was no doubt morale had already been adversely affected.

Two of USSAG's primary missions were to establish and maintain liaison with the South Vietnamese military and to exercise command over the DAO. Consequently, I visited Saigon at least monthly to coordinate with both the JGS and the DAO. I always stopped by the DAO, which was established to ensure that the South Vietnamese armed forces were logistically well supported, for a briefing. During the war everything was in constant flux, and a logistics area that had no problems today could very well be the source of tomorrow's flap.

My visits to the joint staff were always pleasant and useful. It was most helpful that I had close relationships with staff members. They were generally very candid in reviewing their operations, and we would discuss our latest statistical analyses of operational activities. Normally I met with Gen. Vien, Lt. Gen. Le Nguyen Khang, the assistant chief of staff for operations, and Brigadier General Tho, the J-3, on operational matters and with Lt. Gen. Khuyen to discuss logistics.

On 5 August 1974, Maj. Gen. John Murray, who had accepted a transfer to the United States, made departing visits to the corps commanders. Several of their comments were very cogent, and he relayed them to us. At II Corps when he asked Lt. Gen. Nguyen Van Toan if he had observed anything new in the enemy's tactics, Toan reeled off four items: First, the enemy had much more firepower. Second, to take advantage of his increased artillery strength, the enemy employed more daylight attacks deploying artillery observers. Third, with its added antiaircraft, the enemy worried less over the air force. Fourth, the enemy now tended to attack all over the place rather than make a single strong effort so as to prevent ARVN's use of superior mobility.[61]

When Major General Murray visited Lieutenant General Nguyen Vinh Nghi, the IV Corps commander, and 7th Division commander Major General Nguyen Khoa Nam the next day, Nghi was really worked up.[62] He said that before the cease-fire he had been getting 248,500 rounds of 105 mm a month to offset thirty to forty enemy attacks a day. Now he was getting just 45,000 rounds to offset seventy attacks a day—an 82 percent cut. Prior to the cease-fire, the enemy had been using 82 mm mortars and a few 107 mm rockets. Now the enemy was freely bombarding IV Corps with 82s, 107s, 122s, and 12.7 antiaircraft in a direct fire role. (Hoping to obtain more supplies for their troops, almost all commanders exaggerated their situations, and Nghi was no exception. In FY 74, the year prior to his meeting with John Murray, with respect to artillery ammunition the IV Corps fired 1,147,894 rounds, or 95,657 rounds per month, not 248,500 rounds. In FY 75, the nine-month period following, IV Corps fired 763,397 rounds, or 84,821 rounds per month, not 45,000 rounds.[63] This was an 11.3 percent decline. Without letting facts get in the way, in reality it is often the perception that counts.)

Major General Nam said his biggest problem was that he needed more ammunition—grenades and M-79 ammo. When General Murray asked why he wanted the grenades, Nam replied, "For safety and aggressiveness. Now I give each soldier two grenades, then they use only one and keep one. One is always for their own protection. My soldiers continually ask for more."

There you have it in a nutshell in early August 1974 from the top army leaders! The enemy had increasing firepower to support more combat initiatives, while at the same time the ARVN was faced with a reduced ammunition allocation, resulting in a loss of aggressiveness.

On 9 August, General Vien was reported to have said that because of increased casualties caused by the limitation of artillery ammunition and helicopter and air support, there would be a lowering of morale and, consequently, combat effectiveness. Those were strong words, but Vien did not go so far as John Murray, who had commented earlier in a message to General O'Keefe at USSAG: "But when I look at the ammo usage going down, I also note that the casualties are going up, and it's rather sad that while we used to trade ammo for lives, they are compelled to trade lives for ammo. I wish we could get this message to the Congress."[64]

Murray would be greatly missed. He was an outstanding logistician, having directed the DAO from its inception and helped build it into an excellent organization. However, Homer Smith stepped in without missing a beat and was equally effective. Most important, both had the confidence of the embassy and the Vietnamese.

Murray had suggested rather vividly that while the United States "used to trade ammo for lives, they [the RVNAF] are compelled to trade lives for ammo." General Vien and other senior officers stated this as a fact; at that time I tended to agree with those assessments. But in subsequent months it began to gnaw at me. "Is the conservation of ammo costing lives? Are we trading blood for ammo? In specific local instances this might be true. But is it true on a countrywide basis?" I had my doubts.

I also recalled the balanced JGS memoranda Vien had published, in which he stated: "Ammo conservation does not mean privation or shortage of ammo to destroy the enemy when we see him, find him or when he comes to attack us. We have to use ammo in the right place at the right time and accurately." None of the officers wanted to deny the soldiers the means to fight. The question was how much was required. Psychologically, without a doubt, the ammo conservation program was bad for morale. It could reduce aggressiveness. But did it appreciably increase casualties, as most instinctively thought?

This was a very unsettling thought—so I tried to measure all enemy-inflicted casualties (KHA and WHA) against the intensity of combat (CIF), which includes both enemy and friendly casualties, and the expenditures of ammunition over four major periods. The first period had no conservation measures, the second was an interim conservation period, the third was with full conservation, and the fourth was the first two months of 1975 for which data was available (see table 10).

Table 10. Ratio of Casualties and Ammo Expenditures to Combat Intensity

Period	Average monthly combat intensity factor	Average monthly ammo exp. S/T	Average monthly casualties KHA & WHA	Casualties per CIF	Ammo/CIF
1) July 1973– December 1973	23,701	16,177	11,717	.49	.68
2) January 1974– June 1974	34,652	15,320	14,389	.42	.44
3) July 1974– December 1974	46,409	16,146	16,765	.36	.35
4) January 1975– February 1975	60,545	22,558	14,280	.24	.37

Sources: Analysis, "Summary of Ceasefire Statistics," June 1975, Headquarters USSAG, Nakhon Phanom, Thailand; "Republic of Vietnam Ammunition Conservation Study," June 1975, Headquarters USSAG, Nakhon Phanom, Thailand.

The combat intensity doubled between the first and third periods, yet the ammunition expenditures remained the same. Obviously, ammunition was being conserved. Although the average monthly casualties did increase between these two periods, when one considers the increased intensity of combat, the ratio of casualties to combat intensity decreased. Between the third and fourth periods, the ammunition expended per combat intensity factor remained about the same, yet there was a major reduction in casualties per combat intensity. On a countrywide basis, then, it is difficult to rationalize that casualties increased due to the conservation of ammunition.

The ratio of friendly casualties to combat intensity decreased in each period and was ultimately cut in half because of ARVN's improved effectiveness and its appreciable reductions in casualties from attacks by fire. Additionally, the joint staff's efforts to improve and upgrade the territorials that commenced in July 1974 had definitely improved their effectiveness. Contrary to others' intuitions, there was not a trading of blood for ammo.

The 1 October 1974 National Intelligence Bulletin supported this outcome, stating that the recent cutbacks in the use of artillery by South Vietnamese forces—partly as the result of less combat and partly as the result of orders to conserve supplies—had not yet led to higher casualties or the loss of significant new territory to the communists.[65] The reduction of firepower, however, made the South Vietnamese more willing to abandon remote outposts and contributed in making them less aggressive in their operations to take lost ground.

Ammunition Conservation

The artillery ammo expenditures and conservation data were carefully monitored. In the thirty-week base period (29 July 1973–24 January 1974) the ARVN computed allowance was 754,680 artillery rounds, but it fired 1,926,891 rounds, which was 1.553 times in excess. The ARVN managed to cut back slightly in the five-week adjustment period. However, in the fifty-six-week conservation period (1 March 1974–27 March 1975) it reduced artillery expenditures appreciably. The computed allowance was 2,610,434 artillery rounds and the ARVN fired 4,578,744 rounds (168,584 short tons), or 0.754 times in excess—a conservation of 51 percent.

If the ARVN had continued the rate of ammunition consumption throughout the conservation period as it had during the base period it would have expended 6,664,438 rounds (2,610,434 times 2.553), more than 2 million more than it actually fired with conservation. This resulted in a savings of $110 million, or 42 percent of the total FY 75 ammunition budget; had the ARVN not conserved, it probably *would have run out of ammunition before January 1975.*

During the battle for the Iron Triangle, MR-3 had huge ammunition expenditures, for several weeks exceeding allowances four-fold. Over 16–22 August 1974, it fired 58,383 rounds, which was 3.5 times the computed allowance of 12,916 rounds, a rate that was never exceeded in any military region except in MR-1 in the last three weeks of March 1975. This exceptional use of firepower in MR-3 in June–September 1974 paid off, since it repulsed the enemy's corps-directed multidivisional combined arms attack on the Iron Triangle. If the RVNAF had had unlimited ammo, the final result in South Vietnam might have been different.

There is no doubt that in its policy the United States has always attempted to use firepower to save lives. The statistics clearly indicate that the South Vietnamese soldiers held their own and in later periods took the war to the enemy. They rose to the occasion—conservation or no. Had they had more artillery and close air support, they would have done better. There is no question but that the RVNAF's effectiveness and efficiency were reduced from mid-1974 onward.

General Vien and the JGS recognized early on that there had to be a cutback in ammunition consumption. Little did they anticipate that the U.S. Congress would reduce the initial available funding from $1,530 million to $1,069 million in FY 74 and then to $583 million in FY 75. Neither could they have envisioned that inflation would increase the costs of petroleum by more than 100 percent and ammunition by more than 60 percent, thereby greatly reducing the amounts that could be purchased with the fewer dollars available. The storage levels of the ammunition on hand at the time of the cease-fire had been continuously drawn down from 177,000 short tons to 114,000 short tons on 1 July 1974, which was only a two months' supply at the intensive combat rate. Consequently, the JGS was forced to initiate an ammunition conservation program even though it realized this would result in reductions in offensive spirit and morale. Consider that the RSR was already a small fraction of the comparable U.S. rate. Nevertheless, the JGS had to reduce consumption further—and reduce it did.

Unfortunately, by conserving ammunition South Vietnam prolonged the war and the killing, a war it had no chance of winning because the U.S. Congress refused to authorize adequate funding for ammunition and other combat supplies.

At the end of 1973 my notes[66] concerning enemy intentions, which were distilled from NVA/VC documents and intercepts, were as follows: they intend to draw South Vietnamese main forces into combat and inflict casualties that will reduce their military initiatives and facilitate communist local force strikes against the government pacification program and increase operations in contested and government-controlled areas in conjunction with their main force operations. Actions would be focused on PSDF elements, terrorism, and with impressment of local inhabitants into military and other services. As usual, the communists intended to attack the South's weakest elements. These were not grandiose plans and were in keeping with the North's current doctrine advocating military activities to support the political struggle.

1974

This was a crucial year. The RVNAF, cognizant of the effects of the communists' attriting attacks, took the offensive and aggressively and successfully confronted the enemy. Pacification was working well, and the number of South Vietnamese living in secure areas peaked in March. The JGS reorganized mobile regional force units and was systematically improving force capabilities. In May, North Vietnam launched its first multidivisional combined arms attack against the Iron Triangle and South Vietnam successfully beat it back. However, mid-summer was a high point of South Vietnam's defenses. In August, the United States dramatically reduced its supporting funds, which forced the RVNAF to make major cutbacks in firepower and mobility. Concomitantly, the enemy initiated a major logistical campaign, infiltrating large numbers of men, matériel, and supplies. Instead of adjusting its strategy to the situation, South Vietnam waffled, putting its hopes into supplemental funding. In December, the enemy in COSVN launched a major attack in Phuoc Long Province, managing to capture their first provincial capital. By year's end the balance of power had shifted greatly, yet the RVNAF was still capable of carrying the war to the enemy and defending its country. For those of us monitoring the war, the long-term situation looked bleak as all focused on the 1975 communist dry-weather campaign that was sure to come. Following are several highlights of 1974.

President Thieu's War Policy

On 2 April 1974, the joint staff published an exclusive memorandum to the four corps commanders and the heads of the navy and air force, subject: "The President of RVN's Instructions on the Present War Policy." On the occasion of Tet, the year of the tiger, President Thieu traveled by helicopter to visit many of the military posts. His usual instructions to the troops were:

> During the past when the U.S. forces were still here, we fought with unrestricted abundant means, that is fighting on a large scale . . . employing many means and ammo, bombs lavishly.
>
> Now foreign aid has been restricted and tends to diminish due to difficulties happening right in our allied countries which have assisted us, so it cannot continue indefinitely, as well as the energy crisis in the world which has significantly affected the economy of RVN.
>
> Therefore, we have to resort to the purely Vietnamese tactics to be in conformance with our self-sufficient and restricted means.
>
> In the field of tactics, large scale attacks with combined arms which require ample costly support are no longer appropriate, partly because our supporting capabilities are limited. . . . Therefore, we have to return to the purely Vietnamese tactics, putting emphasis on small unit activities. . . . Units will not depend and entirely rely on air and artillery support.[67]

This was a far-reaching and very important change in military tactical philosophy, definitely an unpopular message. In a way, it showed that President Thieu, far more than others, was reading the minds of the U.S. Congress and instinctively knew that military aid was to be further cut. He was trying to position the armed forces for the future. This policy was dubbed "the necessity to fight a poor man's war."

Tong Le Chan, a ranger camp on the Saigon River along the border of Tay Ninh and Binh Long Provinces, had been under siege by the enemy since the cease-fire. Its location, in the heart of enemy-held territory, created problems for the enemy lines of communication—thus the enemy was determined to overrun the camp. For months, the outpost, manned by the 92nd Ranger Battalion, could only be resupplied by airdrop because heavy antiaircraft fire precluded helicopter resupply. Communist artillery for an extended period pounded the base like rain. The enemy had attempted multiple infantry and sapper assaults but had always been repulsed; air strikes helped keep the communists off balance. However, for the 260-plus survivors, the situation inside the camp was becoming desperate. On 11 April 1974, Lt. Col. Le Van Ngon requested permission for his men to break out, but the corps commander denied this and ordered the battalion to defend at all costs. Everyone recognized the bravery of the 92nd Rangers, and their stubborn resistance against such odds was a source of pride for the nation. Ignoring his orders, that night Ngon ordered his men to break out of the encircled position and withdraw to An Loc, about ten miles to the northeast. The 92nd Battalion brought all its wounded (about thirty) along. The ranger defense had been admirable, but the battalion's breakout was spectacular, and the populace took great pride in its accomplishments.

As always, there were those (many of them newspaper reporters) who sought to put an odd spin on the situation. They claimed that the communists had collaborated and permitted the evacuation. However, Vu Hoa, the deputy commander of an enemy reconnaissance unit that participated in the communist attack, had a different story:

> When our [NVA/VC] infantry troops and tanks began to approach the Ranger base, the Rangers knew they could not resist us and evacuated the base. Before evacuating they managed to plant an unbelievably large number of mines. It took our infantry much time and effort to break into the base. When we entered, we found that the base had been deserted, all the equipment destroyed, and nothing left intact. There were more than 50 wounded troops at that base and all of them had been carried out. We found only two dead troops when we followed the Rangers' trail.

It has been widely rumored that we captured about 100 prisoners, but in fact we captured one. I was there when we overran Tong Le Chan, and the Rangers had evacuated the base a day and one half before we entered. The day we overran the base, I saw all the equipment was destroyed and there were no bodies in the base. About 250 men carrying at least 50 wounded had managed to leave the base safely under our fire. Their discipline was very high indeed. If it had been our men, they would have left the wounded behind. Headquarters gave the order to have the Rangers intercepted but a lower echelon disobeyed it. The element that saw them leaving was afraid to attack them for fear of aircraft and artillery fire and let them escape.[294]

On 16 May 1974, the North Vietnamese Army initiated a coordinated attack with two divisions in the Iron Triangle area, more than twenty miles north of Saigon. The 7th NVA Division attacked in the east, toward Phu Giao, and the 9th NVA Division attacked from the west, toward An Dien and Ben Cat. Tanks and artillery supported them. The enemy attacked to inflict casualties, catalog ARVN weaknesses, and test combined arms tactics. This was the first major multidivisional attack with combined arms since the cease-fire, and we monitored the results most carefully. Although the NVA forces initially were overwhelmingly successful against the South Vietnamese defenders, the ARVN counterattacked on 18 May and by 6 June had regained several key areas. The conflict continued well into November, by which time the RVNAF had regained all territory.

I watched this attack with great interest. My analysis of the enemy's conduct here indicated a lack of effective command and control. Once the attack was launched, the enemy showed no flexibility. The divisional objectives were such great distances apart that there was no mutual support, allowing the RVNAF to deal with each division separately. The enemy also applied its forces in a piecemeal fashion; it did not effectively use its armor and artillery as combined arms teams. There was just enough enemy armor and antiaircraft for ARVN to see its capabilities. When required, the communists did not utilize their reserves. These glaring deficiencies in the use of large-unit tactics made the South Vietnamese more comfortable. However, both sides had steep learning curves. This battle ushered in a new period of corps-type tactics.

Reduced Congressional FY 75 Funding

The reduced FY 74 military aid authorization had caused great consternation, but the real shocker came in August 1974, when Senator Ted Kennedy and others, emboldened by President Nixon's difficulties, pushed through Congress a bill that limited the FY 75 defense assistance to Vietnam to $700 million. The in-country reaction to such reduced funding was total dismay. Maj. Gen. John Murray summed up the situation succinctly in a message to USSAG on 14 August 1974: "The $700 million level will place the RVNAF in a position of being unable to maintain a viable defense of the country."

On the same date, shortly after we had been alerted to the potential of major congressional reductions in funding, General O'Keefe met with General Vien; Lt. Gen. Nguyen Khuyen, special assistant to chief, JGS (Operations); Lt. Gen. Dong Van Khuyen, chief of staff; Maj. Gen. Vo Xuan Lanh, deputy commander VNAF; and Brigadier General Tho, J-3. Maj. Gen. John Murray, DAO, Saigon, and I accompanied him. The Vietnamese were obviously preoccupied with the current military situation and the ramifications a $700 million aid program would have upon their military capabilities. Vien mentioned that the current stringent ammo conservation program had caused serious concern among the corps commanders and was having an adverse effect on troop morale. He also foresaw more desertions and ineffectiveness resulting from the lack of fire support. General O'Keefe made the JGS aware that offset charges might reduce the $700 million to between $450 and $500 million and that their planning should proceed within those bounds.

O'Keefe then suggested that the broader question was what effect the new funding ceiling would have on the strategy and associated tactics employed in the defense of the country. He further said that it would be impossible to maintain the level of activity in all areas and on all fronts at the current rates—and that spreading the reduced resources among all the activities currently consuming them would only cause an early drawdown with no tangible objective, resulting in a war of attrition of resources.

He also said that the South Vietnamese thinking might have to change to a strategy of prioritized defense of critical areas and that their manpower and resources should be applied more selectively. General Vien agreed with this from a purely military viewpoint. However, he stated strongly that a change in strategy in that direction would have overriding political implications to his country and to his people. The loss of territory and people currently under government control would be unacceptable.

The conversations intentionally avoided the subject of hardware and unit reductions except in general terms, since everyone thought these considerations should follow the development of strategic and tactical planning, which the logistical support provided by any forthcoming program would drive. We then discussed the FY 75 ammunition and petroleum buys under consideration and related them to the current levels of combat activity.

In sum, the proposed level of military aid concerned and dismayed the Vietnamese, and they had to develop military plans for the defense of the country constrained by the support that would be available, even at the expense of loss of territory and people. They probably would be compelled to reduce forces, but until they developed supportable strategies and tactics, they would be hard-pressed to identify which and how much they would reduce. This was all in the face of the current increased level of enemy operations as well as its ongoing logistics offensive, which we were witnessing every day.

In a memorandum for the record, General O'Keefe afterward said it appeared "that if the intent of Congress, as stated in the press, was to force President Thieu to negotiate—that will happen. But he will not negotiate from strength nor even from parity, but as a loser, or worse, he will hang on until the last dog is dead. A sad return for the level of effort the U.S. had expended over the last ten years."[68]

As it turned out, O'Keefe was prescient. Vien made available to us the memorandum he sent to President Thieu reporting on the aforementioned meeting, in which Vien suggested, "There will be additional losses of land and population." However, Thieu and the JGS never seriously undertook consideration of a change in strategy necessitated by the reduced funding level or initiated negotiations with the communists.

Initially the JGS believed that the full $700 million was to be available; however, the appropriation did not provide this full amount of assets to the military, because under the new rules being established for the FY 75 Defense Assistance to Vietnam Program, the program's funds were to bear all support costs, including administrative expenditures and the packaging, crating, handling, and transportation of supplies. These were not previously programmed. In all, directed set-asides amounted initially to $230 million, so $470 million was available, only 30 percent of the FY 73 funding (much less, actually, considering the high inflation).

Not only had Congress greatly reduced the funding, but it had established new rules that reduced the funding even more. These set-asides were indeed dire. The DAO would have to fund $55 million for the ammunition pipeline—that is, the cost of ammo shipped from the States but not yet received in Vietnam. Not only were the pipeline costs set aside, but costs of packaging, crating, handling, and transporting supplies were added—and these were escalating tremendously. Inland U.S. transportation increased 14 percent. The sealift command rates for deliveries from the West Coast to Vietnam increased from $78.70 to $141.60 per ton of ammo and from $39.90 to $71.80 per ton of general cargo. These costs were estimated to be $47.0 million.[69] The inflation of costs hit hard in all aspects of the budget. Another major set-aside was for DAO operations, excluding personnel costs, estimated to be between $34 and $40 million. In an effort to upgrade the Vietnamese Air Force, the JGS had requested that the DAO allot $77.4 million for the purchase of seventy-one F-5E fighter aircraft. This purchase had to be cancelled to provide RVNAF the ability to procure basic warfighting essentials.

Notwithstanding the seriousness of the initial shock of the congressional action, the funding situation only became more confusing as the Departments of the Army and Defense found additional mandated charges while they tried at the same time to effect relief from these set-asides. Earlier in the funding cycle, a senior official visiting Saigon stated: "The situation is really fouled up. DAO is completely confused as to what they are authorized and where their bank balance stands. The Ambassador refuses to accept any reduction in the level of effort or tell the GVN that there will be a decrease in funding."[70]

However, after the congressional action, so that adequate planning could go forward, the South Vietnamese had to be told of the funding situation. Near the end of August, Maj. Gen. John Murray left for his stateside transfer. During the three weeks between his departure and the arrival of his replacement, Maj. Gen. Homer Smith, I was in Saigon as the acting head of DAO. This was an extremely critical and busy time. The South Vietnamese had just been told of the major cuts in the military funding, and the JGS was shocked at the magnitude of the reductions. However, they set about to make the best of a terrible situation by tightening their belts. At the time, there was no discussion of a possible change in strategy to apply their manpower and reduced resources to a prioritized defense of critical areas. General Vien and others in the joint staff understood the reality of the situation—but in their guts they knew that additional funding would be forthcoming, because the United States would never abandon them. The hopes of the South Vietnamese political side for a supplement prevented the military from considering strategic alternatives.

The DAO and JGS worked closely together to prepare a revised FY 75 budget. Fortunately, the Defense Assistance to Vietnam Program[71] allowed the JGS to move funds from one service to another, which facilitated the tailoring of a balanced force, although a much less powerful one because of the severe cutbacks. Understandably, the RVNAF was consternated, trying to allocate funds within a budget of about $500 million when it required $1.219 billion. DAO personnel worked long and difficult hours with the Vietnamese joint staff to develop a balanced military budget within the restricted funding. The JGS performed truly exemplarily in this critical funding exercise. Across-the-board service cuts were required, and a strong conservation program was necessary. The RVNAF's 28 August 1974 response to the budget is included here as appendix C. Vien stated: "The combat efficiency and the morale of the RVNAF troops will be severely hurt. . . . Even with a tremendous effort, the RVNAF feels it is impossible to operate with *such a small military aid fund* mostly during the period of communist readiness for a *possible* general offensive in Winter or Spring."

He noted that the communists had replenished their supplies and with new resupply routes could quickly reinforce the front in South Vietnam with reserve divisions stationed in the North. He then listed five possible recommendations for additional funding: put off the purchase of F-5Es, reduce ammo pipeline costs by resupplying from U.S. depots in Southeast Asia, reduce other set-aside items, cut off support of the Mekong convoys resupplying Cambodia, and increase military aid funds to $1 billion.

The JGS recommendation to reduce the ammo pipeline was, in fact, a DAO input that USSAG favored as having the best opportunity for immediate implementation to improve the funding situation in Southeast Asia. Most of the ammunition consumed by our allies came directly from continental U.S. production lines; that is, our allies were firing new ammunition, even as the U.S. stocks of ammo stored in Korea and Okinawa were getting older. The DAO suggested that the U.S. ammo stocks in the Pacific should be rotated to reduce maintenance costs and to ensure that newer serviceable ammo would be available for American forces, should they ever need it.[72] The delivery time from Korea and Okinawa would be at most half of that from the States, thus greatly reducing the ammo pipeline and its associated $55 million cost. In October 1974 the Department of the Army responded positively and authorized ammunition to be delivered by the most expeditious response at the least overall cost, thereby authorizing replenishment from Pacific storage sites.

The last recommendation, a supplemental funding of $300 million—which incidentally had the support of both the State Department and the Defense Department—held out a strong ray of hope for the South Vietnamese. They believed this funding would be approved and thus provide them the wherewithal to carry out the war. The State Department reported that President Gerald Ford and Secretary of State Henry Kissinger were pushing congressional leaders to remove the restrictive funding limitations. Although stated FY 75 requirements were for $1.219 billion, the RVNAF could, with strict financial management and some relief from set-asides, get by with $1 billion.

The new single appropriation strengthened the JGS's hand: it placed the staff in the position of determining service-funding allocations and establishing priorities. The joint staff was obliged to keep President Thieu fully informed, and he participated in funding allocations and was well aware of their impact on the services. Obviously, with the overall budget drastically reduced there could be no thought of any major new investments, and the purchase of the F-5Es was put off. The Pentagon, CINCPAC, and the DAO worked assiduously to reduce the amount of set-asides where possible. The JGS had a very healthy attitude; it was aware of the effect of the reduced level of funding and was tightening its belt rather severely. In the backs of their minds, staff members were hoping for a supplemental appropriation in the long term and reductions in the large current set-asides in the short term. Its position was to shepherd its resources unless these were needed to respond to enemy combat initiatives, in which case it would use the forces and resources it considered essential. Although the staff had taken steps to reduce expenditures, it had done nothing as yet to rethink strategy and associated tactics required as the result of the drastic reduction in funding.

Once the new requirements for set-asides were finally resolved, they amounted to $117 million. Therefore, the net available military assistance funding for FY 75 was $583 million. In FY 74 dollars, however, FY 75 funding was only about $396 million.[73] The military assistance funding in constant dollars in FY 75 was only 37 percent of that available in FY 74. Congress, Department of Defense procurement regulations, and inflation had created an untenable situation, which was obvious to all. In the *Los Angeles Times,* George McArthur wrote that the South Vietnamese had been put on a "starvation diet."[74] The ARVN combat capabilities would become weaker, while the North was becoming stronger. Without additional funding to procure the sinews of war, South Vietnam was doomed.

Adm. Noel Gayler visited Saigon to assess the impact of the recently greatly reduced funding. He received a thorough briefing at the DAO, after which I accompanied him on a visit to President Thieu, who was obviously disappointed with the current level of U.S. support yet most cordial. The president focused on two major subjects. First, when the more than five hundred thousand U.S. troops pulled out of South Vietnam, they left a tremendous void in the military's capabilities to protect its country, particularly since all the enemy forces had been allowed to stay in place. Second, the recent major reduction in funding was creating a very serious situation, which must be offset with supplemental funding. The absolute necessity for a supplemental continued to be a subject uppermost in the minds of senior Vietnamese.

These two subjects were the seminal events affecting South Vietnam's military capabilities. It was now well past the time for President Thieu to reconsider his "four no's."

Loss of Mobility and Firepower

The RVNAF's main advantages were indeed firepower and mobility. The reduced funding seriously degraded the capabilities of the nation's air force and navy, which together provided substantial firepower and strategic mobility to the ground forces. The air force had to seriously cut back its force structure and flying hours. The original 1973 program called for 2,073 aircraft in sixty-six squadrons operating 708,000 flying hours. In September 1974, the program called for 1,494 aircraft in fifty-six squadrons operating 332,290 flying hours, and that greatly reduced program could not be sustained within the overall $700 million DAO authorization. As of 3 September 1974, the FY 75 air force programming level was $165.0 million, of which $63.5 million was for direct flying.[75]

The North Vietnamese complained about peace agreement violations when the air force attempted to upgrade its F-5s to the newer F-5E models. However, with the FY 75 budget crunch, the $77.4 million for the F-5Es was redirected and the VNAF was left with its older models. So, in mid-1974 a low-intensity-configured Vietnamese Air Force faced a mid-intensity-capable enemy—much to its detriment.

The JGS took immediate actions in late August 1974 to cut back air force expenditures so as to maximize their operating capabilities within the restrictive budget.[76] They grounded eleven squadrons consisting of eight types of aircraft; reduced flying hours drastically, by 67 percent; withdrew those students who had not reached the final stage of pilot training in the United States; and considered eating into their ammo stocks so as to generate more flying hours.[75]

The severity of the reduced funding caught everybody by surprise. The impact was even greater because the air force had operated full-bore for the first two months of FY 75 and then had to cut back and shoehorn expenditures into a ten-month period. In July and August, they flew 108,148 hours, a monthly average of more than 54,000 hours, and expended $19.9 million. The average monthly flying hours for the remaining ten months had to be reduced to 24,000 hours (for a total of $43.6 million), less than half the earlier number.[77]

The FY 75 funding deficiencies also required the DAO to eliminate U.S. contractor maintenance support. The air force was struggling to keep up its maintenance and supply. Because of the reduction in the types and numbers of aircraft and the availability of aircraft to cannibalize, this did not create an immediate problem; however, in the long term it would have been extremely serious. CINCPAC's message stated: "Equipment is certainly going to fall apart and disintegrate."[78]

The cutback in available flying hours necessitated by the funding reduction was so serious that General Vien as chief of the joint general staff sent this message to all corps commanders: "The Corps and Military Regions will give their subordinate units a thorough understanding of the current limitations of the VNAF and explain that Air Force assets should be used only when absolutely necessary to meet their needs." The air force was hit with a double whammy—fewer sorties and a more hostile air environment as the result of the enemy's increased antiaircraft defenses.

The funding cutback also seriously affected the navy. When the joint staff allocated only $11 million to the navy in August, we reviewed the situation carefully. There was to be no problem with navy peculiar ammo, since the navy was estimated to end the fiscal year with forty-one hundred tons, as compared with its annual requirement of eighteen hundred tons. However, the budget would severely reduce the availability of spare parts, which were essential for keeping the older fleet operating. The allocation was $8.1 million for the blue-water fleet and $0.7 million for the brown-water fleet.

Clearly, the blue-water fleet was given considerable importance. Unfortunately, the budget did not provide the funds for the activation costs and material support for the additional six tank landing ships that were to be transferred to the navy. This shortfall was critical. The ships were to provide an urgently needed capability to move division-size forces and cargo between various ports. In the 1975 withdrawals from MR-1 and -2, the lack of additional tank landing ships deprived the ARVN of the ability to retrograde several major troop elements, which were lost to the enemy.[79]

In summary, the army's necessity to conserve ammunition and

petroleum; the air force's reduced force structure, available sorties, and maintenance capabilities; and the navy's gutted ship inventory added up to a serious loss of firepower and tactical and strategic mobility—this at a time when the enemy was increasing its combat intensity. Not only was the enemy increasing its attacks by fire, but its ground assaults were division-level combined arms attacks accompanied by tanks, artillery, and more sophisticated air defense weapons. The situation would not look too promising when the 1975 dry season rolled around.

It is important to note that, according to a joint Central Intelligence Agency/Defense Intelligence Agency study, during this period of reduced military and economic aid to South Vietnam, communist military and economic aid to North Vietnam was higher (in 1975 dollars) than in any other previous year. In 1974, the delivery of ammunition to Hanoi markedly increased over 1973 and reached a level as high as that of 1971. According to this study, published on 5 March 1975, "North Vietnamese forces in South Vietnam, supported by record stockpiles of military supplies are stronger today than they have ever been." But the Central Intelligence Agency and the Defense Intelligence Agency, like other stateside agencies and CINCPAC, could not properly assess the importance of this disparity between forces and concluded, erroneously, "The GVN's force will not be decisively defeated during the current dry season."[80]

North Vietnam's communist supporters also increased their economic assistance in the same period. In 1974, their food and petroleum commodity shipments, for instance, were over four times the average of the previous four years. While it is always difficult to compare the exact levels of military and economic assistance, the conclusion that communist aid to North Vietnam was appreciably increasing while U.S. aid to South Vietnam was drastically decreasing was clear and as such had to be factored into the balance of military power equations.

USSAG Study

In August 1974, the Headquarters USSAG staff prepared a study in response to a draft CINCPAC study addressing "RVNAF Future Force Structure Alternatives 31 July 1974." Rather than comment on the level and use of individual hardware items, we considered strategy and tactics in the light of the current situation and the available funding level to determine what was necessary for the RVNAF to best accomplish its mission—in other words, to determine the impact of U.S. funding levels on the strategy, tactics, and organization of RVNAF. We did exactly what General O'Keefe strongly recommended to General Vien that the joint staff should do.

The USSAG study concluded that U.S. funding of $1.4 billion (a FY 74 equivalent of $1.1 billion) was required to sustain RVNAF forces at a level that allowed the continued defense of territory and population currently under government control and that funding of less than $1 billion ensured the early demise of South Vietnam.[81] The study assumed that *no* U.S. forces (ground or air) would be deployed in South Vietnam under any conceivable circumstances. However, to maintain the status quo, our staff held out hope for a major supplemental, that is, a total funding of at least $1.1 billion. At that time, all concerned—from President Ford on down: our ambassadors to Vietnam and Cambodia, our military establishment, and particularly our Southeast Asian allies—were hoping for a supplemental. The belief that Congress would authorize additional funding warped the decision-making capabilities of both South Vietnam and Cambodia until mid-March 1975, when it was too late to change the outcome even if emergency funding had been made available.

The USSAG study was particularly insightful in its discussion of four potential force structure alternatives. It considered as one alternative that the severe constraints imposed by the reduced U.S. funding, particularly in ammunition and air support, could in the long run only be offset by reducing the areas to be defended. While the South Vietnamese government might not willingly yield territory or population, it might do so as the result of communist actions. In which case, the most probable strategy would be to fall back along successive defensive lines to ultimately protect Saigon and the highly populated and rich delta region.

Any strategy that sacrificed population would have several immediate results: refugees in large numbers would take to the roads, attempting to escape communist control, which would exacerbate the military situation; the morale of the people and the military would plummet; and military personnel whose families were in abandoned areas would desert in large numbers to protect their kin.

However, adopting such a strategy to give up major portions of the country, most probably MR-1 and MR-2, would have several advantages. As the area to be defended would be greatly reduced, there could be defense in depth and interior lines, which would enable rapid reinforcements to points of enemy attack. The disadvantages, as stated, would be a significant reduction in morale, a large-scale refugee problem, and greatly increased desertions.

The adoption of a strategy to give up major portions of the country was very dangerous and required careful planning and coordination. A conscious yielding of territory, say, MR-1, should be effected only when it could be done most advantageously—that is, when the South Vietnamese were not under enemy pressure. Any strategy to hold enclaves in ceded regions should be considered only as interim measures.

Realistically, without additional funding, each of the four force structure alternatives foresaw a South Vietnamese defeat. In every case, the RVNAF would run out of resources. Even though a truncated territory to defend would provide a more concentrated defensive capability, a major North Vietnamese breakthrough would eventually result in the collapse of the defense of Saigon, and the South Vietnamese government would fall.

The 1974 summary of the assessment of the threat to the Republic of Vietnam concluded, "With reinforcements of one to five NVA divisions, the enemy would be capable of making significant military gains in MRs -1, -2, and -3, securing control of rice growing regions in MR-4, forcing major political concessions, and possibly bringing about the downfall of GVN." This study was forwarded through U.S. channels only.

In early September I attended a Saigon embassy briefing on the military situation. This was professionally done, but its content disturbed me greatly. The embassy staff's interpretation of military events had a decidedly optimistic spin. At the time, the hamlet evaluation survey showed that the government controlled 92 percent of the population. However, it downplayed the increasing strength of the North Vietnamese and glossed over the declining RVNAF capabilities. I returned to the DAO compound that day very concerned. Previously, I had thought that the ambassador generally interpreted events over-optimistically. Now I understood why. When Ambassador Martin had testified before Congress with respect to the military situation just a month earlier, he stated: "Even with the North Vietnamese military buildup since the Agreement, I am confident the South Vietnamese can continue to handle the military threat on their own, provided we continue to replace military supplies on the permitted one-for-one basis. . . . It is now crystal clear that the North Vietnamese cannot conquer South Vietnam militarily."[82] He sincerely believed that, but the situation was rapidly changing.

Martin strongly pressed the Congress for increased funding. The embassy's focus on supplemental funding gave the South Vietnamese government what turned out to be false hopes. Rather than adapt its military strategy to the greatly reduced funding levels, it continued to operate in the same manner as it had previously. As late as mid-April 1975, when the situation was dire, President Thieu, oblivious of the military situation, was still hoping for a supplemental.

This was also a period of tension between South Vietnam and its neighbors in Southeast Asia over the discovery of oil among offshore islands claimed by several countries earlier in the year. The South Vietnamese Navy had already sparred with Chinese warships at the Paracel Islands and had its nose bloodied.

And now in late summer there was a possible confrontation between Cambodia and South Vietnam over U.S.-French oil drilling in the Gulf of Thailand.[83] The dispute centered on the ownership of Puolo Wei Island, claimed by South Vietnam, Cambodia, and Thailand. The South Vietnamese demanded the removal of the oil rig owned by Global Marine of Louisiana. Diplomatic sources reported that Lon Nol had ordered three hundred marines to reinforce a small garrison on an island near the drilling site. He recalled his ambassador to South Vietnam back to Phnom Penh for consultation. The military of each country had taken a bellicose stand.

Brig. Gen. William "Jack" Palmer had called me earlier from Cambodia about the matter, stating that Lt. Gen. Sosthene Fernandez and the entire Cambodian military establishment were worked up over a report that the South Vietnamese Navy was circling the island. There was talk of the Khmer Navy being ordered to take the offensive. Jack was very concerned that neither side should take provocative actions; there was no question but that this was a very serious matter. The Saigon embassy was understandably upset to see our two main allies at each other's throats. Wolf Lehman, the deputy chief of mission and acting ambassador while Ambassador Martin was in the States, asked me if I could discuss this matter with the JGS to see whether we could head off this ridiculous state of affairs. I took advantage of a social gathering at the JGS compound to discuss the situation with the senior officers, emphasizing that the communists were our enemy and South Vietnam and Cambodia should concentrate on defeating them and that they should continue to work closely together with the Cambodians to that end. The senior Vietnamese officers understood the situation and were very calm about it. They would discuss it with their president. The situation subsequently cooled off, yet both of the economically stretched countries harbored the hope that oil would be their salvation.

In the fall of 1974 the Pentagon indicated a much increased interest in the RVNAF casualty data because casualties were an indication of combat intensity and the Department of Defense was at the time trying to convince Congress to budget for the expanding Vietnam War effort. Admittedly, reported casualty data could be confusing, since there were four sources of data: First, the Joint Operations Center (JOC) reported on a daily basis the friendly and enemy killed and friendly wounded based on compiled battlefield spot reports. Second, the Adjutant General Casualty Report Branch reported two casualty categories from hostile actions: first, those killed or wounded in action (casualties resulting from ground contacts), and second, those other troops killed or wounded by the enemy (casualties from booby traps, grenades, or indirect fire). Third, the Adjutant General Personnel Computerized Center reported only those killed based upon morning report changes. The J-1 used these figures for unit replacements. Finally, the surgeon general's office reported all wounded and died in the hospital from hostile and nonhostile causes.[84]

In December 1974, U.S. Army Pacific Command requested that we clarify the casualty data. In our reply, we expressed surprise, since it had stated that Washington had been using the spot report data. It was known in military channels that this data was greatly underestimated. It was only natural that initial casualty reports were understated, since no commander wanted to exaggerate losses in the field and unit commanders had no way of knowing what happened to seriously wounded soldiers after they left the battlefield area. It is worthy of note that the numbers of KHA listed in morning reports were higher than in the ultimate resolution by the adjutant general; this would tend to indicate the commanders were reporting casualties accurately, once there was time for a proper determination.

In addition to those soldiers killed by hostile causes, a substantial number were casualties from nonhostile actions—for example, those injured or killed in vehicle accidents or from training mishaps. In 1973, 9,617 were killed from nonhostile action, whereas 27,901 were killed by hostile actions. In the same year, 2,668 of the 27,901 KHAs (9.6 percent) died in the hospital.[85]

We ascertained also that the wounded in action data had been understated. Prior to August 1974, the surgeon general reported only those wounded who were absent from duty for one or more days. Effective in August, the surgeon general included those treated and returned to duty immediately. Thus, minor shrapnel and bullet wounds would be properly recorded as wounded by hostile action.

To clarify the situation the DAO requested that the official JGS casualty data be provided for each year from 1965 through 1972 and for each month beginning in 1973. After serious study, the JGS decided that the official sources for casualty data would be the Adjutant General Personnel Computerized Center (known as J-1 data) for all casualties killed outright by hostile and nonhostile sources and the surgeon general's office for all who were wounded or injured and died in the hospital from both hostile and nonhostile causes. The killed by hostile action data is shown in table 11.

Table 11. RVNAF Soldiers Killed by Hostile Action (official data)	
Year	KHA
1965	14,092
1966	11,592
1967	13,572
1968	26,872
1969	22,783
1970	24,052
1971	26,956
1972	39,195
1973	27,901
1974	31,219
Source: Message, "Casualty Reporting," 211045Z February 1975, DAO, Saigon, South Vietnam.	

A fax from the office of the secretary of Defense principal deputy assistant secretary (comptroller)[86] stated that during hearings before Congress on the Vietnam budget an understatement of casualties had provided an effective argument for the reduction of assistance to the $700 million level. It is true that casualty figures are an important measurement of the level of intensity of combat and that the Senate Armed Services Committee gave a 75 percent decline in RVNAF casualties in 1973 as one reason for cutting the Department of Defense's FY 75 military assistance request.[87] It appears this was wishful thinking and that Congress supposed the cease-fire agreement was curtailing the conflict. It amazed me that the official figures used reflected 38,697 South Vietnamese combat deaths in 1972 and only 11,093 in 1973. They were comparing the morning report data in 1972 with the understated spot reporting data in 1973. The 1972 data was essentially correct, but the J-1 data for 1973 should have been 27,901 KHA.[88] The Department of Defense was well aware that the spot report data was understated, and the mistake in not presenting accurate casualty data led in great measure to major reductions in funding. The insatiable appetite in Washington for immediate data on all matters at every level—in this case, the need to know battle casualties as they occurred—led to this most serious misunderstanding. The Defense Department could have utilized USSAG's reports on the levels of combat intensity, which took into consideration the number of casualties and definitely indicated a continuous escalation of levels of combat in South Vietnam. The fact was that the RVNAF casualties during the cease-fire period exceeded the casualties of every other year of conflict except the 1972 high point (39,195).

One day about noon I was returning from a meeting in downtown Saigon to the DAO compound at Tan Son Nhut airfield in my chauffeur-driven official car with U.S. flags posted on the front fenders. As we were driving we were startled by incessant police sirens coming from the rear. Looking back, I saw by the flags flying from an escorted limousine that it was the North Vietnamese delegation, probably headed to Tan Son Nhut for a flight back to North Vietnam. I told my driver not to pull off the road and to continue normally. When the limousine carrying the North Vietnamese delegation passed us, it purposely swerved to the right to cut us off, and our front left bumper caught the right rear fender of the North Vietnamese limousine, ripping the fender completely off. They continued on, and when we got to the airfield I returned to my office as if nothing had happened. Later I looked out the window into the yard below, and there were about twenty South Vietnamese employees huddled around my sedan listening to my proud Vietnamese driver tell his story. He was hailed as a hero! Such was the dislike the southerners had for the communists.

In the fall of 1974, Deputy Secretary of Defense William P. Clements visited Saigon. He was the highest-ranking U.S. government official to visit Vietnam since the cease-fire. In a speech prior to his trip he claimed that cuts in military aid had put our allies "on the military equivalent of starvation rations," this after the United States had told the Vietnamese that America would provide the tools and expect them to do the job. So, General Vien and the Vietnamese government officials looked forward to Secretary Clements's visit, which would allow them a personal briefing on the deteriorating situation. In preparing for a private luncheon for Clements with Vien and his staff, the general asked me what special measures he should take. I told Vien to just do it normally but suggested the centerpiece might be yellow roses, since Clements was from Texas. Sure enough, the secretary picked up on this cue and told the group the story of the mulatto girl, the Yellow Rose of Texas, responsible in large part for the defeat of the Mexican general Santa Anna at San Jacinto. Clements was polite and charming and listened well to the RVNAF situation, unlike many arrogant congressional types before and after him. He discussed that the administration would attempt to get a supplemental bill for more military aid, although this would be extremely unpopular in Congress. In a press conference later, Clements stated that the return of U.S. air and naval forces "would have to be considered" in the event of a major North Vietnamese offensive. He further stated that the inability to replace lost equipment or to train enough soldiers adequately was weakening South Vietnam's long-term capability. His strong personal support for additional funding gave the senior Vietnamese officers continued hope for a supplemental.

At the same time, on an extended trip to the United States, Ambassador Martin was relaying to the South Vietnamese government assurances that the administration would keep trying for more military aid. There was no doubt Martin was taking part in a strong lobbying effort to increase the military aid so desperately needed, while at the same time those in Saigon were totally preoccupied in reducing the level of expenditures required by the cuts in U.S. military aid to South Vietnam.

These events and others like them left the South Vietnamese with high hopes that a supplemental bill would be forthcoming after the November elections, enabling them to conduct the war aggressively. They fully understood that their previous success in blunting the 1972 all-out North Vietnamese Easter Offensive was accomplished with tremendous U.S. air power support. They strongly believed that the United States would intervene in the case of a major communist .offensive in the future.

In January 1973, during the final stages of the negotiations leading up to the cease-fire agreement, senior South Vietnamese officials stated that President Nixon personally wrote to President Thieu pledging to actively assist South Vietnam, should North Vietnam seriously violate the cease-fire. Since Nixon had reinstated bombing of military targets in North Vietnam and had mined Haiphong Harbor in the closing months of 1972, the South Vietnamese had confidence that the United States would react vigorously. Additional credibility was assured when the United States continued to maintain the Seventh Air Force bases and equipment in Thailand. When MACV phased out and its remaining functions were transferred to USSAG at NKP, the JGS insisted upon a twenty-four-hour hotline to Headquarters USSAG so it could call upon U.S. air support when it was reintroduced.

It was an article of faith with the South Vietnamese that the United States would intervene to save the military situation if it were required. President Thieu always held out that hope up to the very last. So did many others. In December 1974, Vien, when discussing communist intentions and capabilities for 1975, opined that there would be no enemy countrywide general offensive in 1975 as there was in 1972, because, according to JGS reasoning, the communists feared U.S. Air Force intervention and therefore would not escalate the war beyond the limits the communists believed would result in a U.S. reaction. Later that month the JGS J-2, Colonel Lung, briefed that he thought an all-out North Vietnamese offensive, although well within communist capabilities, would cause a U.S. intervention, which they wished to avoid.

Not only the South Vietnamese believed that U.S. intervention was probable; so did the communists. As mentioned, the North Vietnamese estimate in September 1973 stated that the U.S. troop withdrawal would be permanent and U.S. troops would not be returned even in the face of a heavy communist buildup in the South. However, the United States probably would resume bombing raids over communist "liberated" areas in South Vietnam if it were convinced that communist forces in the South were strong enough to challenge the ARVN and were preparing to launch an offensive. U.S. air support probably would include tactical support of Vietnamese ground forces if they were unable to contain the communist offensive.

President Thieu's hope that the U.S. Air Force would intervene unfortunately colored South Vietnam's decision-making. Not until early January 1975, when Phuoc Long Province fell, did a more realistic mind-set begin to emerge. Yet, even in April 1975 the hope of U.S. intervention still existed at the highest levels of government, particularly with President Thieu.

Rumors concerning military corruption surfaced periodically, and in late August 1974 *Time* magazine reported, "President Thieu has not taken any strong action, perhaps because he fears that by eliminating the military's traditional involvement in corruption, he would cause unrest among his most powerful supporters."[89] However, in late 1974 an anticorruption campaign was organized to attempt to force President Thieu to clean up the upper echelons of his regime. Several antigovernment demonstrations were staged in Saigon and other major cities. To defuse the situation, the president replaced several senior officers, among them the II Corps commander, Lieutenant General Toan, who was charged with corruption; he was replaced by Maj. Gen. Pham Van Phu. As events later unfolded, this personnel change was one of the major causes of the complete debacle in MR-2 in March 1975.

In early November 1974 we reviewed our operational analysis as well as all other intelligence to determine major trends in the prosecution of the war. In compliance with President Thieu's instructions on war policy, the RVNAF had emphasized small unit activities and had dramatically cut back on air and artillery support. At the same time, the North Vietnamese had stepped up their tempo of attacks. They greatly increased the number of attacks by fire, and although the number of ground attacks remained constant, they were emphasizing large-unit tactics.

As a consequence, the ARVN efficiency (Enemy KIA/Friendly KHA) when faced periodically with the large-unit enemy offensives was continually being degraded, having been reduced from 3.98 in period 1 to 1.81 in period 4. This was due to a major swing in relative firepower of the two forces. Ammunition conservation and the greatly reduced air sorties rapidly diminished South Vietnam's initially superior firepower, just as the enemy's firepower was increasing.

In like manner, enemy effectiveness for its initiated contacts increased 42 percent between the third and fourth periods, particularly in MR-1 and MR-2. At the same time, there was a great increase in weapons lost per soldier killed by hostile action in MR-1 and -2. The 3.06 weapons lost per KHA in MR-1 was previously unheard of. Countrywide, the number of weapons lost increased 48 percent (see table 12). It was these rather large reductions in the ARVN's efficiencies that led to my pessimistic assessment provided at year's end.

Not only was the enemy becoming more effective in its tactical attacks, but for the first time the RVNAF's effectiveness when it took the initiative dropped appreciably. Although the foregoing indicates that the situation was deteriorating, it was also true that the RVNAF, particularly the army, was acquitting itself well. The friendly efficiency

Table 12. Friendly Weapons Ratio (weapons lost/friendly killed)			
MR	**Period 3**	**Period 4**	**Total**
1	.87	3.06	**1.82**
2	.60	1.26	**.89**
3	.77	.86	**.81**
4	2.11	1.75	**1.95**
Total	1.28	1.89	**1.55**
Source: Analysis, "Summary of Ceasefire Statistics," June 1975, Headquarters USSAG, Nakhon Phanom, Thailand.			

of 3.52 in period 4 was lower than the earlier periods, but it was still respectable. ARVN's efficiency, at 5.40, was good, and the regional forces were improving, but the popular forces in MR-3 and -4 were still struggling.

Notwithstanding that the efficiency of units in MR-1 increased in the June–November 1974 period from the previous six months, they did not fare as well against enemy initiatives, and they lost more than three weapons per soldier killed. But disquieting to me was that in the DAO's "Major Engagement Won-Lost Ledger" between July and September 1974, units in MR-1 had six major engagements and lost them all. Because of the high respect they had for Lieutenant General Truong, most U.S. observers thought MR-1 was the most effective military region. But in late 1974 and in 1975, MR-1 had major problems. Our analyses foretold the serious morale problems in MR-1 that would lead to the debacle during the communists' 1975 major offensive.

In November 1974, having followed the war on a daily basis, we believed the South Vietnamese had reached their high point that summer and that the situation was getting worse as the year progressed. Particularly distressing was the lack of logistics support to enable them to pursue an aggressive military posture. In the realm of firepower, not only was South Vietnam's air force circumscribed in the number of sorties available, but the North's twenty-two antiaircraft regiments were so dominant that the close air support sorties were not effective because they were flown at high altitudes. Although the RVNAF continued to perform well, its combat superiority declined as the enemy grew stronger and stronger. From here on out it was going to be all downhill.

As a military man, President Thieu should have been able to foresee the severe consequences of the drastically reduced funding upon which the success of war depended. Since the country was at the time in a position of strength, it was an opportune time to initiate negotiations with the communists or, at a minimum, to reassess the government's political and military strategies. However, he was blinded by the hope of supplemental funding and the belief that U.S. forces would intervene if the military situation deteriorated—so he took no action.

The snowballing effect of inflation on South Vietnam led to sub-subsistence standards of living for soldiers and their families, caused increased desertions and corruption, and was exacerbated by the greatly reduced military aid funding. This state of affairs was not lost on the communists. The COSVN Resolution for 1975, issued in mid-November 1974, stated:

> Their desertion rate is twice as great as their casualty rate. Their main force divisions are experiencing troop shortages. Their local forces cannot become mobile and take the place of their main forces as they expected. On the contrary, their local forces are having troop shortages, too. The enemy has had to abandon many outposts in the Mekong Delta. The enemy's troop morale is sinking further below its low level in 1973. The enemy's air and artillery capabilities are now limited as a result of the reduction in U.S. Aid. Air sorties and artillery firings are unquestionably fewer than before; the abundance and mobility of the old days are gone. In short, the enemy is declining militarily and has no chance of regaining the position they held in 1973.[90]

USSAG *Threat Assessment*

Recognizing the deteriorating situation, Lt. Gen. John J. Burns, a well-known fighter pilot who had effectively replaced General O'Keefe as commander in late August, decided to pull together a briefing, the South Vietnam Threat Assessment,[91] which Headquarters USSAG thought would present the realities of the conflict by analyzing key indicators, reviewing enemy capabilities, and focusing on possible enemy courses of action.

Our operations and intelligence staffs, which put together the assessment, noted several indicators that might reveal the North's estimate of the situation and the probable courses of action to be adopted by them in the first half of 1975: the enemy's reorganization, its training emphasis, its logistical and infiltration activities, and its directives and resolutions.

The enemy redesignated its military regions to return to the pre-1962 military region organizational structure, emphasizing the current North Vietnamese propaganda, "One Vietnam." More important, however, was the formation of possibly four new corps whose purposes obviously were to control large combined arms forces on a conventional warfare battlefield. The corps would assume responsibility for major tactical unit operations, and the military regions would primarily be responsible for logistical and administrative tasks. Also, new divisions and regiments were being formed primarily by upgrading local forces and through infiltration.

The most significant training emphasis was on combined arms operations. Major artillery and antiaircraft units were assigned to the direct support of their divisions. This was noted in the May 1974 multidivisional attack on the Iron Triangle.

In the first ten months of 1974, the communists demonstrated their improved lines of communication and logistical system by transporting more than three hundred thousand tons of matériel to South Vietnam. At the time of the USSAG assessment, this huge transportation offensive was under way, moving large amounts of ammo and weapons.

Infiltration of personnel was always a hallmark of increased enemy activity, and during 1974 the North infiltrated at least a hundred thousand soldiers. There were more enemy soldiers in South Vietnam now than at any other time.

Finally, intelligence obtained by personnel (HUMINT) indicated that heavy fighting would take place in 1975. COSVN Resolution No. 12 and the recent COSVN Resolution for 1975 corroborated this. The new resolution indicated a new widespread dry-season campaign. It implied that the fighting would be heaviest in northern South Vietnam. The overall purpose was to defeat pacification and destroy the South Vietnamese armed forces, thereby accelerating the communists' territorial and population expansion.

In summary, these indicators led us to conclude that North Vietnam believed the South was weaker, the NVA was stronger, and communist forces could launch major offensive activities that would defeat the government of South Vietnam's pacification, increase communist territorial and population control, and attain victories that would lead to the removal of the present South Vietnamese government and eventually to a communist government. The indicators pointed toward a significant intensification of military activity in late December 1974 and the first half of 1975. Knowing this, what were the enemy capabilities?

The South Vietnamese were still acquitting themselves well in the field. They maintained initiatives, but their efficiency and effectiveness were decreasing. They were, because of a lack of support, forced to fight a much improved adversary with one hand tied behind their back. They had much less ammunition to expend, for example, than U.S. troops and the RVNAF had expended earlier in the war to fight an enemy that had been generally utilizing small-unit tactics without modern weapons and had an inadequate support base. In 1972 and earlier, the formidable U.S. tactical air and B-52 bombers had supported the allies, whereas in November 1974 South Vietnam was rationed not only on ammunition but also petroleum and short on repair parts. Its forces were highly dispersed, required to support a policy of giving up no territory or population, and facing a vastly improved enemy force utilizing large-scale combined arms tactics, supported by modern tanks, artillery, and antiaircraft weapons, and backed up by an adequate logistics system. Compounding the situation, the armed forces had no strategic reserves and the U.S. Air Force was not available. In other words, the communists could choose the time and place to attack, always with an initially superior force.

Headquarters USSAG believed that a general coordinated offensive probably would not occur but that major regional offensives would take place. The enemy definitely would attempt to annex Quang Tri Province and isolate the cities of Hue and Da Nang in MR-1, isolate Kontum and Pleiku Provinces for the purpose of annexing Kontum Province in MR-2, isolate Tay Ninh Province and eliminate friendly enclaves in Binh Long and Phuoc Long Provinces in MR-3, and increase territorial and population control in the delta and interdict highway QL-4 in MR-4. But the North Vietnamese had the capability to launch a general offensive, and the reinforcement of their current force structure was the key variable.

In MR-1, with a commitment of two to four strategic reserve divisions, the enemy would be capable of seizing all territory north of the Hai Van Pass and would eventually capture Da Nang. In MR-2, with two additional division-size forces, the enemy could capture both Kontum and Pleiku, and the coastal areas of northeast Binh Dinh Province would eventually fall, thus severing MR-1 from the rest of South Vietnam. Finally, in MR-3, reinforced by two divisions and coupled with heavy fighting in the other military regions, it could possibly isolate Saigon, inflict heavy damage on the Bien Hoa complex, and cause the

downfall of the South Vietnamese government. Thus, with the reinforcement of two to five infantry division equivalents, either through
infiltration or commitment of its strategic reserve divisions, the enemy
could achieve significant gains, which might lead to the eventual removal of the present South Vietnam government.

When Charles Whitehouse, the U.S. ambassador to Laos, visited
NKP in late November 1974, we decided to have him review our assessment briefing, which had not yet been shown to anyone outside
the command. He was a highly competent and respected Vietnam
hand, for several years having been the senior State Department official in MR-3, where I had had close contact with him, and we were
anxious for his comments. I can still vividly recall his reaction. He said,
"That was an outstanding briefing and very distressing. You should
take this briefing to Washington." We thought very seriously about his
advice, and Lieutenant General Burns decided to send the briefing to
CINCPAC, our next higher headquarters, to see if they would pass it
on to the Pentagon.

About 10 December, our two briefing officers, a major and a captain, flew to Hawaii and presented the briefing to CINCPAC. This was
a very thorough briefing consisting of thirty-six charts. Subsequently
Brigadier General Doyle E. Larson, the CINPAC J-2, called me to
very politely inform me that our "Threat Assessment" briefing was not
well received; it was too pessimistic, and CINCPAC was sending our
briefers back to NKP. I thanked Larson for his comments. They just
did not get it; like the embassy in Saigon, CINCPAC was not as yet facing the rapidly deteriorating situation. That the U.S. military chain of
command could not grasp the implications of South Vietnam's serious
loss of firepower and mobility precluded a realistic comprehension by
our politicos. I always thought that if the briefing had been forwarded
to the Pentagon, its substance would have galvanized a more intensive
JCS approach to obtaining the critical supplemental funding.

Although USSAG did not forecast a general coordinated offensive,
the most likely scenario for the upcoming enemy dry-season campaign
was not too difficult to hypothesize, should the NVA commit its reserves. A major B-3 front effort against MR-2 with the objective of
driving to the coast and dividing the upper provinces from the South
was almost certain. At the same time, the new MRTT Corps could be

expected to attack MR-1, hoping to seize Hue and Da Nang. If success-ful, these forces would link up and drive south along the coastal plain and attack MR-3 defenders. In the meantime, the COSVN forces from bases in MR-3 would attack toward Saigon down the Saigon River cor-ridor while the enemy's troops in the delta would use limited ground attacks and attacks by fire to tie down South Vietnam forces in MR-4. The enemy would then converge on Saigon from all directions for the last great battle. We believed that if the enemy committed its reserves in an all-out general offensive, this scenario could possibly occur in late spring or early summer. This was how we briefed the potential situation in November 1974. However, no one could have predicted the debacle in MR-2 that led to the rapidly deteriorating situation and the North's responsive commitment of all its reserves. This threat assessment brief-ing and the August USSAG study were kept in U.S. channels and were not disseminated to the government of South Vietnam.

As mentioned, Headquarters USSAG also processed the data for the hamlet evaluation surveys. When we looked at the population con-trol macroscopically, it appeared that South Vietnam still had excellent control. However, in November 1974 the South began losing control of the people in the densely populated areas, particularly MR-4. In one month, those living in contested areas or under communist control in MR-3 and MR-4 increased 24 percent, and by the end of December 1974, following the Phuoc Long offensive, the number had increased greatly in these two MRs.

Commencing with the cease-fire in 1973, the DAO kept a ledger of major engagements. The choices of the incidents considered major were subjective: the DAO applied no firm criteria, as USSAG had in its combat analyses. However, Colonel LeGro and his staff were highly experienced officers and their judgments were sound. They also determined which side had the upper hand in the major engagement—and so the Won-Lost Ledger was created. It contained histories of the major engagements dur-ing the 1973–1975 period, which are summarized in table 13.

Clearly, the last half of FY 74 was the high point for the RVNAF. The situation started downhill in FY 75, particularly in December 1974. By reviewing the ledger, one could note that the situation in MR-1 definitely was not good, the South having lost six out of seven major engagements.

Table 13. The Won-Lost Ledger			
	Won	**Lost**	**Tied**
January–June 1973	6	6	2
July–December 1973	6	11	1
January–June 1974	12	6	—
July–December 1974	7	16	—
Source: DAO, Operations and Plans Division, "Major Engagements Won-Lost Ledger."			

One of the incidents considered a major engagement was the attack on the petroleum storage depot at Nha Be. On the evening of 3
December 1973, the DAO reported that an enemy rocket attack had
destroyed or damaged thirty fuel tanks, causing the loss of approximately six hundred thousand barrels at the Nha Be Petroleum Storage
Facility, the largest in South Vietnam. However, neither of the adjacent
Shell or Exxon storage facilities was hit. Fortunately, the civilian in
charge of the DAO petroleum section was on hand, and he reportedly
braved numerous incoming rounds to attempt to put out the fires and
limit the damage. The DAO cited him for his bravery and quick reaction. This was a major catastrophe, and it was listed as one of the major
battles the South had lost to the enemy.

I was familiar with Nha Be, as I had landed there many times to
have my helicopter refueled while on operational missions in 1968–
1969. Nha Be was within the 9th Infantry Division's tactical area of
interest but not in our tactical area of responsibility. I recall that in
the fall of 1968 the Viet Cong had fired twelve to eighteen rockets at
the storage facility, destroying one storage tank. About a week later,
Gen. Creighton Abrams, the commander of the U.S. Military Assistance Command Vietnam, invited our division commander, Maj.
Gen. Julian J. Ewell, and me to his quarters in Saigon for dinner. We
were having pleasant, business-type conversations before dinner when
Abrams turned to his aide and said, "Bring in the gift I have for General
Ewell." The aide left the room and returned with the tail fin of a rocket
mounted on a wooden base with a brass plaque, inscribed somewhat
as follows: "To MG Julian Ewell, Commander 9th Infantry Division,
The last rocket to hit Nha Be." We all had a good laugh, and Julian
said, "Abe, I've got the message." After dinner we headed back to Dong

Tam, concerned about how we were going to stop future rocket attacks. We concluded that the Viet Cong had to have some ground control and were probably using old French maps. With some difficulty we found one of these maps, and by noting the benchmarks in the dense growth of weeds that surrounded Nha Be we found their firing point, which, to ensure no further rocket attacks, we checked out periodically with ambushes and helicopter flyovers.

The loss of one storage tank in 1968 was of such importance that Abrams took a personal interest. The Viet Cong had fired over a dozen rockets and hit only one tank. Yet, in the 3 December 1973 attack thirty tanks were damaged or destroyed. Something stank—particularly since none of the storage tanks in the adjacent civilian storage compounds were damaged. Rather than take my doubts to the DAO, we asked USARPAC to send two demolition experts to assess the situation. They inspected the storage area on 15 December 1973, with the purpose of determining the probable cause of extensive damage to the area. The experts, W. R. Dobbing and J. J. Koebl, concluded, "All tanks appeared to have been damaged or destroyed either by placed charges containing approximately 1–3 lbs of explosives or by the resulting fire which spread from adjacent tanks. No evidence that rockets or mortars were used was found."[92]

All detonation points except on one tank were close to the ground, in locations where charges could easily be placed and concealed—that is, on concrete pads, behind stairs, on or under fuel lines and valves. And the damage to the other tank was obviously caused by placed charges rather than projectiles. The experts stated that with such an extensive sapper-type operation conducted, it seems unlikely that a rocket or mortar attack would have been deemed necessary.

In late November 1973, at the height of the oil crisis, to assure sufficient petroleum supplies the U.S. government made arrangements to deposit funds monthly in a special Saigon account, from which a designated DAO official could issue checks to oil companies for delivery of stocks. Such commerce was generally negotiated in Singapore. This new procurement initiative could have been the impetus for an insider to destroy the petroleum reserves; the storage was destroyed by a sapper attack and definitely not an attack by fire, as reported. Could it have been an inside job, or was it an enemy sapper attack?

Phuoc Long

On 8 December 1974, a COSVN-wide general offensive kicked off in MR-3 and MR-4. The number of enemy-initiated incidents was the greatest since the cease-fire. The combat intensity factor approached a hundred thousand, the highest of the war. It was strictly a COSVN offensive, since the tempo of battle did not pick up in MR-1 and -2. The beginning of the expected North Vietnamese winter-spring offensive would come later. Nevertheless, the tempo of these attacks was an indication of what could occur. A look at the percentiles of activities clearly demonstrated the COSVN high point. By December 1974 we had collected data on all friendly- and enemy-initiated incidents for the ninety-nine weeks since the cease-fire. Therefore, a percentile of 99 would indicate the level of combat activities that week was the highest since the cease-fire. A reading of 2, for example, would indicate that the level of activities were low and had been exceeded in ninety-seven other weeks. We could easily discern trends by presenting the data in four-week increments. Percentiles were a useful tool, enabling us to quickly review the levels of combat activities in the many various geographical areas.

A review of the combat intensity factors for the period of the main attack on Phuoc Long and the four previous weeks graphically illustrates that it was business as usual in MR-1 and -2, with a great upsurge in MR-3 and -4.

Subsequently, it became obvious that the COSVN-wide offensive was to fix South Vietnamese forces in MR-3 and MR-4 in place so that the 301st NVA Corps could successfully attack Phuoc Long Province. The total incidents and combat intensity factors in MR-3 and -4 were

Table 14. Weekly Percentile of Activities, 6–12 December 1974				
	Enemy-initiated ground contacts	ABF	Sabotage/ Political	**Total incidents**
MR-1	36	78	68	**76**
MR-2	21	50	84	**59**
MR-3	98	96	97	**99**
MR-4	99	99	93	**99**

Source: "Republic of Vietnam Ammunition Conservation Study," June 1975, Headquarters USSAG, Nakhon Phanom, Thailand.

Table 15. Combat Intensity Factors, 8 November–12 December 1974					
Dates	**MR-1**	**MR-2**	**MR-3**	**MR-4**	**Total**
8 November– 14 November	14,903	6,913	4,636	19,784	**46,236**
15 November– 21 November	7,286	4,885	6,561	18,402	**37,134**
22 November– 28 December	7,255	3,539	3,560	13,868	**28,222**
29 November– 5 December	12,292	7,865	4,864	17,429	**42,450**
6 December– 12 December	14,220	5,154	22,832	56,614	**98,820**

Source: "Republic of Vietnam Ammunition Conservation Study," June 1975, Headquarters USSAG, Nakhon Phanom, Thailand.

never exceeded, not even in the 1975 general offensive. The RVNAF had been expecting an enemy attack on Phuoc Long Province since November as the result of information it had obtained from intelligence sources, including agents and enemy prisoners of war as well as usually reliable intelligence (intercepts). All sources indicated ongoing enemy preparations.

Even with all the intelligence information, unfortunately, few if any preparations were made to defensively prepare for the expected attack. In the overall scheme of MR-3 defense, Phuoc Long Province, with its population of only 44,000 inhabitants out of the total MR-3 population of 5,838,000 and its relatively minuscule economic impact, was not high on the MR-3 priority list. Consequently, only five regional force battalions, with 2,598 troops, and some forty popular force platoons, with 1,837 men, defended the province. These units were highly dispersed, to protect the provinces' sixty-six hamlets and four district towns.

Phuoc Long was also a relatively secure province, with 86.4 percent of its population in HES categories A and B and only nine of its hamlets contested. Phuoc Binh, the provincial capital, was about seventy-five miles northeast of Saigon, and an airfield several kilometers from the city at Song Be served it. During the NVA land-grabbing offensive in early 1973, Phuoc Binh and its district towns had their main supply routes cut by the enemy and became dependent upon the airlift of men and supplies to Song Be and thence to the district towns by helicopter. That airlift had proved successful then, and perhaps the corps commander thought it could be successful again, if necessary.

At any rate, the secondary enemy assaults against outposts along Highway 13 northeast of Tay Ninh and then against Nui Ba Den in the eastern sector of MR-3 and against friendly units in Long Khanh and Binh Tuy Provinces in the western sector were successful in fixing the III Corps units in place. Thus, when the main attack against Phuoc Long came five days later, the corps commander was indecisive; he had to protect the more strategic and populated provinces.

The communists launched a coordinated attack on 13–14 December 1974 with elements of two divisions. One of these was the 7th NVA Division, which had participated in and learned lessons from the May attack on the Iron Triangle. First, the enemy cut all routes of communication. Then they introduced an antiaircraft regiment to prevent aerial attack on their forces and prevent aerial resupply to the surrounded territorials. Heavy artillery with 130 mm guns, which outgunned the ARVNs few 105 mm and 155 mm howitzers, supported the enemy troops. The enemy used tanks and infantry in combined arms tactics, and its massive observed artillery fires were accurate and highly effective. Even though the ARVN's light antitank weapons were relatively ineffective against the enemy tanks, which had standoff protection, the greatly outnumbered South Vietnamese fought doggedly and, with concentrated close air support, managed to destroy many enemy tanks. (This battle was an example of the JGS's ability to employ tactical aircraft from other military regions, specifically MR-2 and MR-4.)

Yet neither III Corps nor the JGS had a general reserve that could be utilized for counterattacks—a glaring general weakness for which the South would pay dearly. On 28 December, one regular infantry battalion, three reconnaissance companies pulled from the three MR-3 divisions, and ten tubes of artillery reinforced the territorial forces. Later, when the situation at Phuoc Binh was desperate, the corps commander inserted elements of two airborne ranger companies on 3 January 1975. Total reinforcements amounted to 933 men—obviously grossly inadequate for any chance of success. Phuoc Binh was lost on 6 January.

The battle for Phuoc Long portended things to come. The enemy was now conducting multidivisional corps-type operations supplemented with armor, artillery, and antiaircraft units. The formerly effective U.S. and South Vietnamese tactical air support was no more—the U.S. had withdrawn and the Vietnamese were forced by the enemy's antiaircraft units to fly at altitudes that generally rendered their support ineffective. The enemy carefully chose his objectives, ensuring that he always had greater numerical superiority. MR-3 and the JGS had no general reserves and imprudently sent minor reinforcements to be chewed up by the numerically superior enemy.

The communist tactics were simple and effective. Surprise was to them a major ingredient, but in this case that strategy failed, although the RVNAF was not prepared. They cut all ground lines of communication to prevent resupply and reinforcements. They then utilized coordinated multidivisional combined arms tactics against the highly dispersed South Vietnamese forces. The combat results of the enemy tactics at Phuoc Long were bad. Two weeks after the battle had terminated, out of 5,368 soldiers only 776 beaten remnants had made it to Quang Duc. Fewer than 10 percent of the popular force troops, who were mostly Montagnards, escaped. Although the loss of Phuoc Long hurt militarily, its psychological and political effects were even worse. This was the first provincial capital to be lost, and it was now obvious that the North had no intentions of abiding by the Paris peace treaty. That the United States did not react to this loss demoralized the South Vietnamese. With President Nixon gone and the U.S. antiwar sentiment, it was evident that no active military support could be expected.

During my previous tour in Vietnam I had noticed that enemy ground attacks were greatly reduced for an extended period prior to a major enemy attack. I assumed this occurred for two reasons: First, the communists were careful planners, going into every detail, and they did not want an allied counterattack against one of their ground forays to disturb these carefully laid plans. Second, it was a long supply tail to North Vietnam and they had to carefully husband their ammunition and supplies to have enough for a successful operation. I also noticed that to keep pressure on their intended objectives, they continued to conduct attacks by fire, but with much less frequency and with fewer rounds than previously. The communists had used the subterfuge of a cease-fire to prepare for the 1968 Tet attack, and they did it again in our area for Tet 1969. In the latter case, without any intelligence reports, we put Dong Tam Base on full alert in anticipation of an attack, which on 22 February 1969 turned out to be the largest ever on the base. So, when the enemy attacked Phuoc Long on 13–14 December 1974 I had my staff break out the statistics for Phuoc Long Province. Sure enough, there was an appreciable reduction in enemy-initiated ground attacks for a prolonged period prior to the main attack. There had been only one ground attack in the previous five months, compared to about twelve per week earlier. Such an analysis could be a useful indicator of communist intentions in the future.

The government dictum to protect all territory and pacify all population created a major military problem. The army was highly dispersed and spread too thinly along the perimeter, with little defense in depth and a sparse strategic reserve. No one understood this critical problem better than General Vien, who in July 1974, to provide depth, directed the regional forces' reorganization into mobile battalions. At every opportunity, he attempted to provide a strategic reserve near Saigon. As part of this, he formed two ranger divisions from existing ranger battalions, to provide command and control elements. The lack of a strategic reserve was a matter of great concern to me, and I had several conversations with Vien about this subject. I recall vividly one from mid-January 1975 at his joint staff compound office, with General Khang, who was also the marine corps commander. I asked Vien how he intended to protect Saigon without a strategic reserve. He said he would recall the airborne and the marines from MR-1 to protect Saigon. Having previously been an airborne division commander, he had the highest regard for the fighting capabilities of the airborne soldiers; obviously, Khang had the same for his marines. The home base of the airborne and marine divisions was in the Saigon area, so their dependents were not generally in MR-1; thus, these troops would fight more effectively knowing that their families were safe.

More than anything else, it should have been a wake-up call to President Thieu and the joint staff. They were now facing a determined modern North Vietnamese force, one that had superior equipment and abundant logistics support capable of fighting a conventional war. The South Vietnamese could no longer expect to protect every one of their twelve thousand hamlets. They could no longer effectively react without adequate reserve forces. It was time—really, past time—to consolidate and defend critical territory only.

In 1973, greatly concerned about U.S. reactions to the incessant North Vietnamese propaganda concerning alleged RVNAF cease-fire violations (more than four hundred thousand blatantly claimed by North Vietnam), the South Vietnamese maintained an almost completely defensive posture against the continued enemy aggressions. This was reflected in their reports of their minimal (10 percent) offensive actions as security operations. The cease-fire agreement required all foreign troops (at one time well over five hundred thousand) to evacuate. This included the U.S. Air Force's and Navy's formidable close air and strategic bombing power—while at the same time allowing the communist forces, at an all-time high, to remain in place throughout South Vietnam. In other words, anticipating reduced U.S. assistance, President Thieu issued instructions to fight a poor man's war. When the anticipated reductions in funding became a reality in 1974, the JGS issued several directions requiring the conservation of ammunition and other resources. RVNAF ammunition expenditures were the lowest since 1968. Meanwhile, the North Vietnamese were free from the previous U.S. air interdiction, but with our aerial reconnaissance we were able to observe that they were improving their road and petroleum lines of communication and initiating a major logistical offensive, transporting tanks, artillery, air defense weapons, and supporting supplies in great numbers to South Vietnam. The North Vietnamese also continued to infiltrate tens of thousands of troops and to organize the forces into divisions and corps capable of conducting coordinated combined arms operations. By the end of 1974, the balance of power had shifted greatly, although the South Vietnamese were still capable of carrying the war to the enemy and of defending their country.

Recognizing the aforementioned in late December 1974, I prepared for Headquarters USSAG a "South Vietnam Assessment,"[297] which I include here in its entirety:

South Vietnam Assessment

Since the ceasefire on 28 January 1973, the communists have continued to improve their military posture in South Vietnam. Today, the NVA have more troops, more artillery, more tanks, more antiaircraft, and more logistical supplies on the ground than at any other time since the beginning of the war. The enemy has also continued to escalate his military activities against the South Vietnamese. His strategy has been to maintain a constant pressure across the board to attrit the RVNAF, while, lately, he has initiated large scale combined arms attacks (infantry, tanks, artillery, sappers) against selected strategic targets.

On the other hand, RVNAF has been circumscribed by a static force ceiling and declining weapons inventory because it has not been able to replace military equipment losses on a one-for-one basis. Additionally, operational funds have been reduced to the point that stockpiles are dwindling seriously. In April 1975, the communists will have more ammunition on the ground in South Vietnam than the RVNAF. Right now, the RVNAF has the manpower and the will to fight. Combat analysis indicates that the RVNAF, because of its superior firepower and mobility, gives much more than it takes, utilizing our military assistance with great skill. However, recent severe reductions in funds have caused a diminution in tactical mobility (particularly helicopters) and firepower (ammunition has been severely limited by conservation measures). The efficiency of RVNAF, as measured by the ratio of enemy killed to friendly killed, has fallen off and the number of RVNAF weapons lost per RVNAF soldier killed has increased appreciably until it is now at the pre-1965 level—indicating a deteriorating morale situation. The current situation can be summarized by the following two tables, which show the greatly reduced military funding with a concomitant increase in combat intensity. We have reduced military aid over 63 percent while the level of combat activities has increased by more than 75 percent.

Military Assistance Funding (in millions)			
	FY 75 in CURRENT DOLLARS	FY 75 in FY 74 DOLLARS	**FY 74**
TOTAL	$700		$1,069
Less Set Asides	117		
Net Available	$583		
Ammo	$268	$168	
POL	87	38	
Other	228	190	
	$583	$396	$1,069

Combat Data, Average Weekly Incidents				
	ATTACKS BY FIRE	MINOR GROUND CONTACTS	MAJOR GROUND CONTACTS	ADJUSTED WEIGHT FACTOR
BASE PERIOD 29 JUNE 73– 24 JAN 74	287	301	9	25156
CURRENT YEAR 28 JUNE 74– 26 DEC 74	487	503	16	44183

In summary, the enemy has more troops, more weapons, more equipment than before and is using them with increased intensity while the South Vietnamese have a static force ceiling, a depleting weapons inventory, and a decreasing supply level, which, in time, will reduce their current superiority in firepower and mobility, ultimately requiring the GVN to trade territory and population to maintain strategically essential areas. If the level of military assistance is not materially increased soon, the balance of military power in South Vietnam will swing dramatically in favor of the communists.

In mid-January 1975 General Vien summarized his viewpoints, concluding, ". . . if RVNAF's superiority in firepower and mobility is maintained . . . ." It was an assumption that depended upon increased aid—that is, FY 75 supplemental funding. Make no mistake, in January 1975 the RVNAF was comporting itself very well, holding its own against a superior enemy force. However, the lack of effective air power, the reduction in supplies, the ravages of inflation, and the requirement to defend all the territory were taking their toll—time was running out.

Following are pertinent excerpts from his assessment:[93]

It became obvious in 1974 that if the GVN did not increase their tactical activities that the enemy could deal their Armed Forces severe blows. Therefore, beginning in Dec 1973 the ARVN began to take the tactical offensive and for the past two months we have maintained parity with respect to tactical initiatives. However, we do not have the equipment or supplies to undertake strategic objectives . . . our forces are utilizing the equipment and supplies provided by the United States while employing our own tactics in order to conserve these precious supplies to inflict appreciably more casualties on the enemy than we are receiving. Yet, despite his losses the enemy remains totally committed to their aggressions and they get stronger in equipment and supplies while we struggle to maintain the status quo. . . .

In summary, if RVNAF's superiority in firepower and mobility is maintained we will be able to protect our vital areas through tactical initiatives and responses to enemy strategic aggressions.

On 28 December 1974, to provide an insight into the latest upsurge in fighting and to look into the future, we sent CINCPAC an "Executive Summary" of South Vietnamese combat activities.[94] It analyzed each of the twelve indicators of combat activities. It was noted that during the four weeks enemy activities in MR-2 had been very low, which presaged a round of increased activities in the future. Also, it was not generally realized that the level of terrorism, sabotage, and political incidents had been the highest since the cease-fire. We concluded for the 1974 year-end executive summary: "Country-wide the incident levels of the past several weeks have been the highest since the ceasefire. Enemy activity levels in MRs -3 and -4 have been high. ARVN efficiency in MR-4 has been good but performance in MR-3 has been low. Enemy activities in MR-2 have been very low level while in MR-1 the NVA has maintained average pressure. We look for another week of continuing pressure in MRs -3 and -4 and an increase in activities in MR-2 in the near future."

It is worth noting what the communists had in mind for 1975.[95] South Vietnam's National Level Intelligence Agency, utilizing all source intelligence-gathering techniques, provided us with insights into the communist plans: the early 1975 campaign—which might end in June 1975—would be aimed at "occupying a number of provences and districts." During this time, the communists would weaken the South Vietnamese economy, forcing the government to support 1 million refugees. To avoid U.S. intervention, they would occupy only some provinces. In the event the United States did intercede, the communists were convinced that no ground forces would be used, only air force and navy elements, and they had confidence in their antiaircraft networks. South Vietnam had to defend its territory and its lines of communication. It would be constantly on the defensive, unable to eliminate the contradiction between concentrating its troops and dispersing them. U.S. aid would decrease gradually. The South Vietnamese troops would see their firepower decrease, their morale would be lowered, desertions would develop, and the political and social structure in the country would not be able to improve.

In December the communist headquarters sent a long motivational letter to all combat units on the eve of their departure for the 1974–1975 dry-season offensive that read in part: "Attack strongly . . . destroying as many enemy outposts and units as possible and liberating people. Defeat the enemy's pacification and landgrab plans and move forward heroically."[96] In reality, for the 1975 dry season, these were only limited objective plans to attrite the RVNAF and gain as much land and population as possible.

1975

Combat activities remained at a relatively high level from the end of December to the first week in March, but with the exception of the wind-down of the North Vietnamese Army attack on Phuoc Long the enemy undertook no major initiatives. There were some increases in major contacts during February, but these were predominantly due to the aggressive friendly tactics. From 27 December 1974 to 6 March 1975 there were 5,172 ground contacts; the South initiated 3,095, or 60 percent of these. The average combat intensity factor for January through 6 March was 44,162, equal to the 44,183 average of the previous six months. The January and February hamlet evaluation survey indicated a population gain of 69,500 people in secure areas. The RVNAF was performing well and definitely more than holding its own. Everyone anticipated a North Vietnamese Army dry-season offensive, and the RVNAF's aggressiveness was calculated to keep the enemy off-balance.

In early 1975, some officials wondered about the number of South Vietnamese aircraft lost or destroyed. Thus General Vien directed that the Tactical Operations Control Center make an accounting.[97] So on

27 January, this section, subordinate to the Air Operations Center of the JGS, prepared a summary of all aircraft and air crew losses for the cease-fire period, 28 January 1973–27 January 1975. According to the report, 424 aircraft were destroyed or damaged by enemy action and 99 air crew members were killed, 165 wounded, and 18 missing in action. Of the 424 aircraft destroyed or damaged, 104 were lost or completely destroyed and the remaining 320 were damaged. On 3 February 1975, 85 percent of the damaged aircraft were inoperative because of a lack of spare parts or of inability to perform repairs. Almost three-fourths of these aircraft were Huey helicopters. Obviously, this does not include the tremendous March and April 1975 losses. None of these aircraft losses were ever replaced by the United States, notwithstanding the U.S. government's agreement to do so.

To illustrate the aircraft operating environment from 1 January through 31 March 1975, there were twenty-five SA-7 firing incidents against VNAF aircraft. Of these firings, eighteen successfully hit aircraft. As a result of those hits, fourteen aircraft were destroyed. The enemy improved its hit ratio to 72 percent and its kill ratio to 50 percent, compared to 33 percent and 23 percent during the previous quarter. The increased hit ratio may be attributed to a combination of improved missiles, better-trained crews, and an increased aggressiveness on the part of the South Vietnamese. The VNAF was under tremendous pressure.

Attack against the Central Highlands

The COSVN Resolution for 1975 indicated a new widespread campaign would be initiated by the communists in late December or early January and would last until June. North Vietnamese party editorials also indicated a 1975 general offensive. When one collated intelligence data, there was no doubt in the minds of the joint staff that there would be a major offensive, and it estimated that the major initial attacks would be against the central highlands at the end of the rainy season, in late February or early March.

There was no doubt in our minds, either, that the North Vietnamese dry-weather attack would be against MR-2. We sent the JGS the "Executive Summary SVN Combat Activities, 104th Week"[98] for the four-week period ending 25 January, which clearly indicated that the enemy-initiated ground attacks in MR-2 had all but dried up. Data also indicated that RVNAF forces in MR-2 were keeping a moderately high pressure on the enemy, which was helpful in disrupting enemy plans and obtaining intelligence.

The central highlands in MR-2 straddled the enemy's approaches to the lush coastal plain and, should a communist attack be successful, provided the enemy the opportunity to cut South Vietnam in two, isolating the forces in MR-1. To allow the army to provide successive defensive positions and the ability to concentrate massive artillery and air force fire superiority, successful defense of the highlands greatly depended on an early warning.

As it was to turn out, the enemy's attack against the central highlands was almost an exact replay of the December–January attack against Phuoc Long, but on a larger scale. Intelligence sources indicated an attack against MR-2; this was verified by USSAG's operational analysis of enemy ground initiatives against the region, which came to a halt six weeks before the initiation of the attack.

The enemy conducted the battle for the central highlands in three phases. Again, its strategy called for surprise, and in this it was successful. First, the enemy cut the ground lines of communication. Then it conducted a corps-directed multidivisional combined arms offensive against dispersed South Vietnamese forces. Next, it concentrated a massive artillery and tank attack on the main objective, Ban Me Thuot. Finally, to sever MR-2 the enemy drove down the east-west highways toward the coast, relentlessly pursuing the withdrawing RVNAF.[99]

The major difference between the Phuoc Long attack and the highlands operation was that in February–March 1975 the enemy successfully confused II Corps regarding its main objective. The II Corps intelligence chief pieced together aerial reconnaissance and ground sightings of major North Vietnamese troop movements, captured documents, and other bits of information and correctly predicted Ban Me Thuot as the enemy's objective. The JGS intelligence section supported him in this assessment. However, the corps commander, Major General Phu, believed the conventional assessment that the main attack would be against the Pleiku-Kontum area, as had occurred in the past. However, in early March—when II Corps was alerted to movements of the 320th NVA Division to the south—he did send a small divisional headquarters detachment and the 53rd Infantry Regiment to reinforce Ban Me Thuot. Only 20 percent of the friendly forces in MR-2 were regulars, and the bulk of them were in the Pleiku-Kontum area, where II Corps Headquarters, the 23rd Division with two regiments, and several ranger groups were located. The 22nd Division was in Binh Dinh Province protecting the coastal region. While the small divisional headquarters detachment and the 53rd Infantry Regiment were in Ban Me Thuot, a ranger group was located at Buon Ho, about twenty miles north of the city. Like Phuoc Binh before it, Ban Me Thuot was defended primarily by territorials, mostly Montagnards.

The North Vietnamese Army campaign opened on 4 March, when the 95B NVA Regiment and the 3rd NVA Division cut the main supply route from Pleiku to the coast, QL-19, in several places. At the same time, the F-10 NVA Division cut the second major highway to the highlands, Route QL-21, which connected Ban Me Thuot to the coast. Thus, on the first day major enemy units closed the two major roads to the central highlands. Then, on 8 March, units of the 320th NVA Division attacked ARVN units on QL-14, the principal north-south route connecting Pleiku and Ban Me Thuot, effectively closing this main artery. As a result, the forces at Ban Me Thuot had no road communications to II Corps at Pleiku or to Nha Trang on the coast. The battlefield was now isolated (see map 4).

On 10 March, six days after the initial attacks, the communists launched a massive artillery barrage against Ban Me Thuot. This was followed by a tank-infantry combined arms attack by the F-10 NVA Division and supported by the 316th NVA Division, which had clandestinely moved from Laos, and the 320th NVA Division. The RVNAF fought doggedly and inflicted severe casualties on the enemy. Tactical air support, along with the infantry, knocked out many enemy tanks. Notwithstanding the determined defense, the attacking forces overran Ban Me Thuot by the evening of 11 March. By achieving tactical surprise and committing three of its divisions supported by massive artillery and armor against an ill-prepared, numerically inferior force, the outcome was all but certain in favor of the North Vietnamese.

The North Vietnamese Army held off on its attacks by fire against the RVNAF in MR-2 before the 10 March all-out attack, just as it had done with ground contacts. In the previous five weeks it had fired an average of four hundred rounds per week in MR-2, but between 10 and 13 March it fired over eleven thousand rounds—mostly at Ban Me Thuot, overwhelming the defenders. The intensity of enemy attacks by fire also greatly increased in the other military regions between 7 and 20 March.

Although it initially concentrated on MR-2, the 1975 general offensive was a countrywide North Vietnamese coordinated effort. From 8 to 10 March, enemy activities, contacts, ABFs, and terrorism in every military region were at or near their all-time highs since the cease-fire.[100]

The combat intensity countrywide of 104,307 for 7–20 March was more than 2.7 times greater than the average of the five preceding weeks. It was obvious that the enemy's major dry-weather offensive had been initiated. The loss of Ban Me Thuot, a major provincial capital, coming on the heels of the loss of Phuoc Long, stunned the South Vietnamese and precipitated several hasty, unplanned, disastrous decisions by President Thieu.

President Thieu's Momentous Decisions

Thieu had for some time realized that his military was overextended everywhere, with no defenses in depth and, in reality, no strategic reserve. The reduced military assistance had greatly affected combat capabilities. With the loss of Phuoc Long Province and the inevitable loss of Darlac Province, he now resolved to redeploy his forces so as to defend only the most populated and economically viable regions, that is, MR-3 and MR-4.

On 11 March, unbeknownst to the U.S. embassy and military personnel, President Thieu held a meeting to discuss this major change from his previously implacable "defense of all territory" to a "truncated defense." His idea was reasonable, but his timing was atrocious. A redeployment of forces during a slack period would have been extremely difficult—but to do so under pressure was all but impossible. Such a major endeavor would take careful and detailed planning. We were told subsequently that President Thieu informed Lieutenant General

Truong on 13 March about his plan to evacuate the highlands, at which time Thieu also told him to prepare a plan for the evacuation of MR-1. Then on the next day Thieu flew to Cam Ranh—accompanied by General Vien, Prime Minister Tran Thien Khiem, and Lieutenant General Dang Van Quang—to meet with Major General Phu, the II Corps commander. Phu briefed the group on the current situation—that is, he told them that QLs 14, 19, and 21 had been effectively cut, isolating Ban Me Thuot, which had been overrun, as well as Kontum and Pleiku. Given the current status of forces and the necessity to clear the routes, it was doubtful that the South could retake Ban Me Thuot.

President Thieu then ordered Phu to redeploy the troops at his disposal at Kontum and Pleiku and the 22nd Division in Binh Dinh

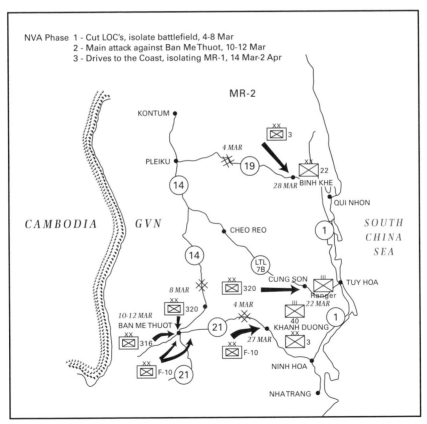

Map 4. The Battles for MR-2. (Source: Maj. Gen. Ira A. Hunt Collection.)

Province to retake Ban Me Thuot. Phu, when asked how he would accomplish this, said that to retrograde his troops from the highlands he would use LTL-7B, a small secondary route that branched off of QL-14 twenty miles south of Pleiku and ran some 150 miles to Tuy Hoa on the coast. He would then reassemble his forces at Nha Trang and drive up QL-21 to recapture the city. This planned withdrawal was to be considered secret and the VNAF was not fully integrated into the withdrawal planning. Phu hoped that surprise would allow his forces to reach Tuy Hoa before the enemy caught on and reacted.[101]

Such was the stuff dreams are made of! Phu returned to Pleiku and, we were told, drafted an outline plan. The order to evacuate was issued on 16 March, without any in-depth planning. Phu turned the operational responsibility for the corps' withdrawal over to a newly promoted subordinate, and he and elements of the II Corps forward command post immediately flew to Nha Trang.

The Americans first learned of this momentous decision when the RVNAF began its retrograde movement from Pleiku. Only then did the joint staff discuss the situation. Our aerial reconnaissance documented the withdrawal. Route LTL-7B was a narrow road, overgrown in many places with brush, and it had several bridges out. When the civilian population sensed what was occurring, it panicked and joined the exodus en masse. The convoys backed up at the town of Cheo Reo, waiting for army engineers to build a pontoon bridge over the Ea Pa River. A 19 March aerial photo of LTL-7B showed a huge backup of vehicles there: 26 armored personnel carriers, 45 tanks, a pair of 175 mm guns, 14 engineer vehicles, 669 military trucks, 279 civilian vehicles, and 53 unknown ones.

As the retrograde progressed, more and more vehicles became mired at the fords (see photo 2). In fact, MR-2 lost all of its newly issued M-48 tanks in the mud. Ultimately, the enemy caught up and attacked, creating heavy military and civilian casualties. Pursued relentlessly by the 320th NVA Division, on 27 March the tattered troops and fleeing families and refugees finally made it to Tuy Hoa.[102] Out of twenty-six thousand soldiers, fewer than six thousand made it to the coast from Pleiku and Kontum.

During this period, the North Vietnamese were also driving to the coast along the two major east-west highways, QL-19 in the north,

Photo 2. Tank Mired in the Mud. (Source: Headquarters USSAG, Nakhon Phanom, Thailand, photo file.)

which connected Pleiku to Qui Nhon, and QL-21 in the south, which connected Ban Me Thuot to Ninh Hoa and Nha Trang. (See map 4.)

In the north, the 22nd ARVN Division met the 3rd NVA Division at Binh Khe, and a vicious battle ensued. The 22nd was well supported by the air force, and together they inflicted heavy casualties on the enemy. The division fought a stubborn defense, but when the 95B NVA Regiment reinforced the 3rd NVA Division it had to fall back, and the Vietnamese Navy evacuated it from Qui Nhon. The division commander had turned himself into the hospital sick, so his assistant, Colonel Leu Tho Cuong, provided the essential leadership for the 22nd's stiff resistance. This well-disciplined division was to fight again later at Saigon.

In the south, two North Vietnamese divisions pursued the 23rd ARVN Division down QL-21. To stem the tide, the JGS offloaded the 3rd Airborne Brigade—on its way by ships from MR-1 to Saigon— at Nha Trang, and with two battalions of the 40th Infantry set up a blocking position on QL-21 at Khanh Duong. In the ensuing battle, the 3rd Airborne Brigade was chewed up and, with the remnants of the 23rd Division and 40th Infantry Regiment, fell back to Nha Trang. Obviously, there was no further thought of retaking Ban Me Thuot.

The five ranger groups and the logistical troops retrograding from

Pleiku down Route LTL-7B, which had also fared very badly, also straggled into Nha Trang, where the navy evacuated them and the other troops from MR-2 on 2 April. The evacuations from MR-1 and -2 would have been much more effective if the navy had had the six FY 75 tank landing ships deleted for lack of funding.

According to the joint staff, upon entering the port of Nha Trang the commander of an artillery unit seeking to evacuate his men found it free of both enemy and friendly troops. However, the city was under siege by a large number of military and civilian convicts who had been released from local jails amid the confusion of earlier troop withdrawals. With several on-the-spot executions of criminals engaged in various forms of terrorism, looting, and rape, the colonel reestablished control and discipline within the city. Subsequently, he reestablished communications with the JGS, whose members were dumfounded because Nha Trang was supposed to be under enemy control.[103] Granted, there was great confusion during the ill-planned hasty withdrawal, but it appeared the majority had little stomach for putting up defensive positions and fighting, although several units fought very bravely.

President Thieu's decision to evacuate the highlands under pressure was poorly made. Yet on 14 March, when Phu received his orders, there was little pressure on Pleiku and Kontum. A review of estimated troop dispositions in MR-2 prior to the initiation of the dry-weather offensive indicated there was a minor buildup of communist combat forces from thirteen to sixteen infantry regiments. Considering that MR-2, and specifically Ban Me Thuot, was a prime objective in the initial communist offensive, the increase of one North Vietnamese division (three regiments) was not overwhelming. Phu had time to prepare detailed evacuation plans, to notify the air force so as to gain maximum air support, and, most important, to provide the bridging necessary to utilize Route LTL-7B. Not only did he not do his proper staff work, but he left the area in the command of a subordinate and withdrew II Corps Headquarters to Nha Trang. North Vietnamese General Vo Nguyen Giap, referring to General Phu, said, "He was an ineffective general who enjoyed no confidence within military circles."[293] The results were catastrophic. MR-2 lost more than 75 percent of its soldiers, almost all of its heavy equipment, and all of its supplies and ammunition.[99] From psychological and political points of view, this loss's profound effect on the South Vietnamese was immeasurable. The nation was in shock.

According to the USSAG order of battle, the enemy buildup of combat forces in MR-1 between January and March was only one infantry regiment and one artillery regiment. Previously, the MR-1 troops had successfully held their own. Past successes aside, however, we now know that President Thieu made his fateful decision to redeploy forces from MR-1 and -2 on 11 March. The next day, he ordered the airborne division to redeploy from northern MR-1 to Saigon. He and the JGS intended to also redeploy the marine division so the two elite outfits could concentrate as the strategic reserve to protect Saigon. On 13 March, he met in Saigon with Lieutenant General Truong, the I Corps commander, and informed him of his decision and ordered him to prepare an evacuation plan. This was one day before he briefed Major General Phu. At that time, Truong said he was concerned that the withdrawal of the airborne division would seriously weaken his defensive posture in Quang Tri Province and asked that the scheduled departure be postponed from 18 March to 28 March. However, the 3rd Airborne Brigade was loaded on ships on 18 March only to be offloaded two days later at Nha Trang to help block the enemy attacking down QL-21. As events unfolded, this plan to constitute a strategic reserve went awry, greatly weakening the army's capability to resist the enemy in MR-3 later.

The recall of the airborne and marine divisions had always been foremost in the minds of the joint staff members. Some pundits said the order was given to embarrass Truong, whom many favored as a replacement for President Thieu. Such speculation was ridiculous; the withdrawals of those two units were, of course, a military necessity.

Thieu intended to hold Da Nang at all costs. The military situation in MR-1 was stable for a week, providing plenty of opportunity for careful and detailed planning, which did not occur. As was the case in MR-2, there was not a major increase in the estimated enemy forces in MR-1 prior to the initiation of the dry-season offensive. MR-1 probably could have withstood the enemy attacks, had President Thieu not been spooked by the loss of Ban Me Thuot and ordered the withdrawal of the airborne division. However, once the civilian population in Quang Tri saw the withdrawal, it began to leave, in a trickle, toward Hue and

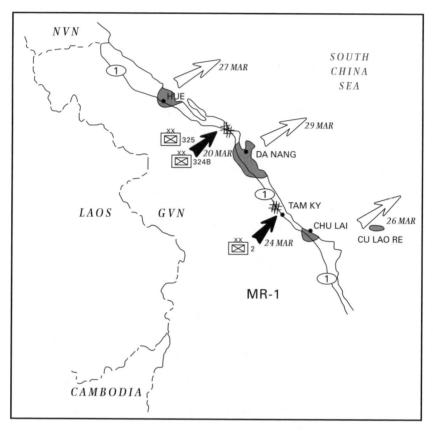

Map 5. Withdrawal from MR-1. (Source: Maj. Gen. Ira A. Hunt Collection.)

Da Nang. In time, this exodus became a torrent of panicked refugees, which seriously interrupted military activities. Many soldiers with families in the area deserted to ensure their families' safety.

The initial plan was for I Corps units to withdraw to an enclave at Da Nang, where they would put up a spirited defense. About 20 March, the North Vietnamese began to attack in earnest. Enemy long-range artillery firing from the hills above Cua Tu Hien just north of the Hai Van Pass massively interdicted troops withdrawing from Hue along QL-1, and the 1st Division and the marines took severe casualties. The communists also managed to cut QL-1 between Chu Lai and Da Nang. Consequently, the I Corps plan was revised to establish enclaves at Hue in the north, Da Nang in the center, and Chu Lai in southern MR-1 (see map 5). In the south, the 2nd Infantry Division had to fight its way toward Chu Lai, and the dispirited troops did not establish defensive positions there; rather, they moved offshore to Cu Lao Island to be evacuated by ship. Subsequently, the navy evacuated the units at both Chu Lai and Hue, intending the forces to reconstitute at Da Nang to take up defensive positions.

All of this time refugees had been fleeing to Da Nang, and the city was teeming with well over a million frightened people. The government undertook emergency efforts to evacuate, both by air and by sea. The refugees were desperate: When a chartered commercial aircraft landed at Da Nang to assist in the evacuation of the city, frantic refugees (and some military) overran the airport and the maddened crowd attempted to force its way onto the aircraft. Some of the people grasped struts in the wheel wells and went aloft with the plane. A few eventually lost their holds and plummeted to the earth.[104]

Little effort was made by the military in Da Nang on 27 March to reconstitute forces, restore order, and attempt to organize defenses. At NKP, I received a telephone call from Al Francis, the senior adviser to I Corps, who was in Da Nang. He said that the senior military officers in MR-1 had abandoned Da Nang and taken cover aboard a navy vessel in the harbor. No one was organizing the defense of the city. I relayed this message to Brigadier General Tho, the JGS J-3, and asked if he could verify the situation. He contacted the navy, and the admiral provided the names of the general officers on board. All the MR-1 general officers were there except one, who had been killed. Such was the leadership in those trying times. The loss of Da Nang occurred during the night of 28–29 March, when the communists launched a massive attack by fire with artillery and rockets against the city's air and navy bases. On 29 March the city was evacuated.

General Truong, the I Corps commander, was considered by many to be an outstanding leader, yet like his II Corps counterpart he made no in-depth withdrawal plans even though there was plenty of time to do so. What plans were made did not include the VNAF, whose assets could have been very effective in the fluid situation. Although President Thieu's orders were to defend Da Nang, no organized defenses were effected and General Truong and his generals retired to the safety of an offshore naval vessel.

The government's inability to evacuate the hundreds of thousands of refugees in an orderly manner was a major factor in creating the chaos and panic that led to a severe breakdown of law and order in Da Nang. On 30 March 1975, within three hours of North Vietnamese Army troops' occupation of the city, in a draconian effort to restore order the North Vietnamese divided Da Nang into ten sections and took about one hundred people from each at random and shot them in an open mass execution. Those chosen were primarily uniformed military men, police, long-haired "hippies," and looters. There were no women or children identified in the mass execution. This measure quickly put an end to the rioting and looting that had been going on for several days.

On 1 April, convoys of trucks began hauling refugees who had fled to Da Nang back to their original places of habitation. In a few days this reduced the population of the city from about 1 million to an estimated three hundred thousand.

While Da Nang was being evacuated, Secretary Henry Kissinger held a news conference that included questions on Vietnam.[105] He said that Congress's failure to send more military aid to South Vietnam and Cambodia raised questions of whether the United States wanted to "deliberately destroy an ally" at the time of crisis and that the "consequences we now see" in the two nations were a result of the United States' not giving enough aid. Further, he stated that the United States "projected" South Vietnam into the conflict.

The secretary's last-minute attempt to shame Congress into providing the required military reinforcement was laudable. However, it was much too late; the lack of support had taken its military and psychological toll. The country felt abandoned. The die had been cast.

As was the case in MR-2, more than 75 percent of the troops in MR-1 had been lost. The 1st Division, once the cream of the army, was almost totally destroyed and later disbanded. However, five thousand men of the marine division were relatively successfully evacuated. As the South had lost both MR-1 and MR-2, the stage was now set for the enemy's final drive on Saigon.

A hasty count of lost equipment indicated that 294 armored personnel carriers, 225 tanks, 676 artillery pieces, and 278 aircraft were gone. However, the major South Vietnamese loss resulting from the withdrawal was the one of morale. That U.S. support was not forthcoming engendered a profound feeling of abandonment and defeat.

The withdrawal from the highlands and MR-1 was intended to reduce the territory to be defended by the RVNAF forces, thus facilitating the defense of South Vietnam's heartland. The seven divisions in MR-1 and MR-2 were essential to such a defense; however, instead of a combat-effective force, they made up a disillusioned, disarranged, and defeated remnant as they found their way to the ports of MR-3. Only two brigades of the airborne division were intact. To be combat effective, the other units needed to be reequipped and reconstituted. Of the 399,000 troops in MR-1 and -2, only about 45,000 were recovered.

The DAO prodded the joint staff into planning the reorganization and refitting of the evacuated military units. Once it was under way, the RVNAF made great progress, but the equipment losses were so great and unit integrity so disrupted that the task could not be completed on time. There was enough equipment available to quickly refit a marine brigade, and since the 22nd Division was in fair shape, its ranks were filled with regional force soldiers and it was transferred to Long An Province. The territorial units were so beaten up that their soldiers could only be used as fillers. The 1st and 3rd Divisions were never properly regrouped, but the 2nd Division had one regiment reconstituted and assigned to Phan Rang. Fortunately, there was a weeklong lull in the combat following the 2 April evacuation from Nha Trang. Obviously, the enemy, too, had to regroup and assess the startling turn of events.

Between 18 March and 2 April, the navy was constantly moving troops from the northern military regions to southern ports, starting with the 7th Airborne Regiment from Da Nang to Nha Trang and culminating with the evacuation of the remnants of MR-2 from Nha Trang. It also had to support by fire the enclaves in MR-1. Short on repair parts to keep its blue-water fleet of older ships operating, the navy performed this daunting task very professionally.

Neither the I or II Corps commanders integrated the air force into their evacuation plans. Even so, in support of the army in MR-2, the 6th Air Division doubled its sortie rate under extremely difficult situations, from an average of 237 sorties a week from 31 January to 6 March to 593 a week from 7 to 20 March. However, for some reason the air force support in MR-1 was not accelerated—at a time when it was so essential to impede the advance of the enemy by either interdiction or close air support. The air force performance later in the final battles in Vietnam left much to be desired. Unlike the Cambodian Air Force—which stayed and fought, inflicting heavy casualties on the Khmer communists even after the United States had evacuated Phnom Penh—instead of heading toward the enemy, the South Vietnamese headed toward the safety of Thailand.

During the evacuation from the north, the enemy had actively attacked selected areas of MR-3. Northwest of Saigon, it attacked Tri Tam, finally overrunning it. It also attacked in the Tay Ninh sector. East of Saigon it besieged Xuan Loc, and to the south the marines and regional forces repulsed the enemy in Long An Province. These were tough fights, with severe casualties on both sides. However, by 1 April the situation was stable.

Enemy activities in MR-4 continued heavily. There was a great increase of attacks by fire, and there were several major ground probes. However, in the upper delta the 7th and 9th Divisions were containing the enemy, and in the Can Tho region the 21st Division was effective. Success in the delta depended on the territorials, and the recent upgrading appeared to have paid off: they performed well. The key focus was now on Saigon.

The JGS gave General Toan, formerly the II Corps commander, command of III Corps. A superb soldier and tactician, he infused a fighting spirit into III Corps. However, Lieutenant General Toan had only the 5th, 18th, 22nd, and 25th Divisions, the 1st Airborne Brigade, the 3rd Armored Brigade, and three ranger groups to hold off a vastly superior array of North Vietnamese forces.

Lieutenant General Toan placed the 25th Division and the three ranger groups to protect the northwest corridor between the Saigon River and the Vam Co Dong River; the 5th Division to the north, at Ben Cat astride QL-13; the 22nd Division at Tan An in the southwest; and the 18th Division, the 1st Airborne Brigade, and the 3rd Armored Brigade to the east at Xuan Loc (see map 6).

Subsequent to the withdrawal of II Corps soldiers from Nha Trang, Lieutenant General Nghi, the former IV Corps commanding general, volunteered to lead the territorials in the three southern

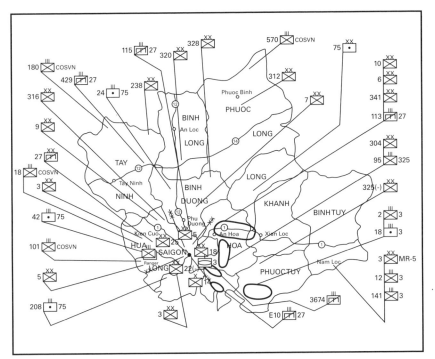

Map 6. Troop Dispositions, Saigon, 28 April 1975. (Source: RVNAF, JGS, J-3, Saigon, South Vietnam.)

coastal provinces of MR-2 in what resulted in an aggressive defensive action. He had available a ranger group, a regiment of the 2nd Division (reorganized), and the 2nd Airborne Brigade. Brig. Gen. Phan Ngoc Sang's 6th Air Division provided effective close air support from the air base at Phan Rang.[106] Colonel Tran Van Tu, the province chief of Ninh Thuan Province, commanded the RF/PF units protecting its critical airfield. President Thieu personally assigned him to head his "home province"; he was known to be a tough, dedicated leader. He and many of his men had "KILL COMMUNISTS" tattooed on their arms—obviously, these stalwart soldiers would be in peril should they ever be captured by the North Vietnamese Army. Lieutenant General Nghi's provisional group, composed predominantly of territorials, put up a valiantly stubborn defense, managing to blunt the North Vietnamese surge southward along the coastal corridor—killing many of the enemy's troops and destroying many of its tanks. On about 15

April they were ultimately overwhelmed. I have often wondered what happened to Colonel Tu.

On 9 April, the communists resumed their assault on Xuan Loc, which strategically controlled the main highways of QL-1 and QL-20 and was the gateway to the Bien Hoa–Long Binh military complex. The enemy attacked initially with its 341st and 7th NVA Divisions. A fierce battle ensued, with hand-to-hand combat in Xuan Loc itself. The 45th ARVN Infantry Regiment repulsed the enemy. By the third day of battle the enemy had committed another division; however, the brave South Vietnamese forces not only held on but inflicted huge losses. The communists kept throwing troops at the friendly defenses in a desperate attempt to dislodge them. In the first three days of fighting, at least thirteen hundred enemy were killed and thirty tanks destroyed. The regular troops stood tall, and regional forces and the air force provided outstanding support. The close air support very effectively broke up the massed enemy attack.[107] The VNAF modified a C-130 and dropped a fifteen-thousand-pound bomb, the so-called Daisy Cutter used to clear jungle terrain. I was told that the explosion was so loud that the morale of the ground troops was improved because they thought that B-52s were supporting them again. Field reports from Brigadier General Tho indicated that the bomb fortunately had exploded over a enemy corps headquarters, killing the corps commander and an estimated eight hundred troops.[108]

When the ARVN counterattacked with tanks, local Vietnamese civilian observers reported that the 341st NVA Division, when confronted with the unexpected reaction, suffered heavy losses, lost its "spirit," broke formation, and fled in all directions.

Finally, the 325th NVA Division joined the battle, and the 18th Division had to fall back toward Long Binh. The 1st Airborne Brigade retrograded to the south to protect QL-15 and the key port of Vung Tau. This was well planned, well led, and well executed, resulting in only minor losses of men and equipment—unlike the debacles in MR-1 and MR-2. Xuan Loc was the last great battle of the war. The South Vietnamese stood and fought, and inflicted heavy casualties on the enemy. In this case they were well led by Lieutenant General Toan, Brigadier General Le Minh Dao, the 18th Division commander, and the regimental commanders and were well supported by the 4th Air

Division.[109] Dao, the hero of the Battle of Xuan Loc, was one of eight South Vietnamese general officers who after the war were required to spend eighteen years in the dreaded communist indoctrination camps.

As an aside, years before, the 10th ARVN Division had been an inept organization. In some countries in Asia the number "10" has a negative connotation, so the joint staff changed the name of the division to the 18th ARVN Division. The formerly incapable outfit covered itself with glory in those final days.

On 20 April, during the battle for Xuan Loc, Lieutenant General Toan expressed great confidence in his corps' ability to repel the expected enemy attack, even with four new North Vietnamese divisions. He stated he had summarily executed more than one individual for cowardice. He attributed the failures in I and II Corps to leadership's not remaining with the troops during difficult times. He said that too many officers went to take care of their families rather than their troops. He left little doubt; he believed he could have held the highlands. He did not intend to give up Tay Ninh without a fight and planned to defend Bien Hoa along the Song Be River. This called for an attack out of Ham Tan north, then west along QL-1 to link up with forces attacking on an axis from Xuan Loc. He stated that III Corps would give a good account of itself in coming major attacks.[110]

Unprecedented NVA Major Unit Reinforcements

Regardless of Lieutenant General Toan's confidence, the military situation appeared hopeless. III Corps faced sixteen enemy infantry divisions with supporting armor, artillery, and sapper units—in all about 115,000 combatants (see map 6). The majority of the reserve divisions in North Vietnam had been hastily deployed to the south. In early February 1975, there were seven divisions in North Vietnam, two of which were deployed to South Vietnam in preparation for the dry-season campaign. The 316th NVA Division moved to the B-3 front and was a key participant in the attacks on Ban Me Thuot, and the 341st NVA Division relocated to COSVN in Long Khanh Province in MR-3. In March, reacting to the RVNAF collapse in MR-2, the North Vietnamese quickly deployed the 312th NVA Division to MR-2 and the 320B NVA Division to MR-3. Then in April the 338th NVA Division, which had been in Thanh Hoa Province in North Vietnam, deployed to Tay Ninh Province in MR-3 to participate in the attacks on Saigon. The enemy's much-improved lines of communication enabled these five major units to redeploy to South Vietnam in a period of weeks. (Recall that in August 1974 the USSAG study referring to a general offensive had stated that with reinforcements of up to five divisions the enemy would be capable of making significant military gains, possibly bringing about the downfall of the South. The December 1974 "USSAG Threat Assessment," which was briefed to CINCPAC, had reiterated this conclusion.)

The unprecedented reinforcement by five reserve infantry divisions overwhelmed the valiant residual South Vietnamese forces, whose ranks the losses in MR-1 and -2 had severely depleted. Between November 1974 and April 1975, the communists had infiltrated more than a hundred thousand personnel, half of whom were destined for COSVN, so by 30 April there were 425,000 communist troops in South Vietnam.

After the fall of Ban Me Thuot, the political pot in Saigon started to boil. President Thieu had never been a popular leader. On 6 March 1975, prior to the withdrawal, former vice president Maj. Gen. Nguyen Cao Ky reportedly said that Thieu had lost the support of the armed forces and of the population. He claimed that the generals would not fight for the president and that General Vien was depressed and suffered from low morale. He also claimed Thieu was a lonely, friendless man who, although effective in the past, had served too long.[111] Of course, there was a lot of politics involved in those statements; Ky was very ambitious.

However, it was true that the president's orders to evacuate the highlands had severely damaged the morale of senior officers. The officers of the badly battered 22nd ARVN Division were rumored to be openly calling President Thieu a traitor and warning that he had better leave the country before they returned to Saigon—threatening to kill him when they got there. A field-grade officer at the joint staff said that those people with whom he had daily contact were overjoyed by the 8 April bombing of the presidential palace, but they were sad because the pilot missed the president.[111] Clearly, the inevitable major loss of military and civilian morale and support resulted from the withdrawal and defeats.

There were many rumors and counterrumors being aired. Many

blamed President Thieu for the rapidly deteriorating situation. Prime Minister Tran Thien Khiem put the blame elsewhere. On 22 March, in a discussion with several close associates, he attributed the public loss of morale to the U.S. failure to provide military assistance.[113] He believed the American Congress's attitude had created a terrible crisis in South Vietnam. But beyond what happened to Saigon, he thought that the "American sell-out" would have continuing effects in other parts of the world. Now the United States could no longer hide its lack of bravery in foreign policy with an elaborate facade. Khiem, the Vietnamese people, and a large segment of the military believed the United States had betrayed and deserted them.[112]

Yet, the postmortems on the demise of South Vietnam almost always heaped the blame on President Thieu for his untimely order to evacuate and on Major General Phu for his lack of planning and the poor execution of the II Corps retrograde. Actually, Truong's performance in MR-1 was just as bad. There, too, was a lack of planning and a failure to exercise initiative, as well as a breakdown in leadership. On 21 April, in his farewell speech upon resigning, President Thieu would insist that the generals had failed him. This was certainly the case in MR-1 and -2.

President Thieu's decision to evacuate the northernmost provinces was ill conceived and at the time unnecessary. The friendly losses at Phuoc Long and Ban Me Thuot were not that great. There was little pressure on Pleiku and Kontum. The enemy attack on MR-1 was containable. The RVNAF probably could have held off the offensive as it had done in the past. To attempt to withdraw under pressure with no advanced planning was just ridiculous. The joint general staff, which had consulted with the Americans on all previous military matters, kept this momentous decision totally secret. Many Americans thought General Vien should have spoken up against this ridiculous presidential decision. And he should have. And so should have Lieutenant General Truong. But within the Vietnamese culture, that would have been difficult for them to do. Indeed, some of President Thieu's generals had failed him—the withdrawals from MR-1 and -2 were poorly planned and executed. But his own decision caused the debacle. The effects of such a withdrawal were well known—the refugee problem, the massive troop desertions to assist families, which would greatly reduce unit effectiveness, and the tremendous loss of morale. No, the faulty implementation can be laid on a few generals, but the ill-fated, poorly considered decision was President Thieu's alone.

On 2 April, the Vietnamese senate adopted a resolution holding President Thieu responsible and asking him to form a more inclusive cabinet. Some thought that a broader group might have the influence to initiate negotiations with the communists. According to rumor, the senior generals had lost faith in President Thieu after the disasters in MR-1 and MR-2 and wanted him to resign. This I seriously doubt. Vien had told me that in a conversation he had with General Le Quang Luong, the airborne division commander, speaking to Luong as a father to a son, he said "as an old man" he did not hate anyone and believed it was morally wrong "to mess around in domestic politics" and that those who want to use one element of the army against another to "play those kind of games" open the gates to defeat. Vien went on, "While we were fighting among ourselves, the communists would come in and destroy both sides."

Near the end of March, President Ford directed Gen. Frederick C. Weyand to the Republic of Vietnam to conduct a fact-finding mission. The president could not have picked a more knowledgeable person for the job. Weyand concluded that the current military situation was critical and the probability of the survival of South Vietnam was marginal at best. He believed the country was on the brink of total military defeat and noted that the United States went to Vietnam to assist the South Vietnamese people and he believed we owed them that support. Besides immediately increasing military aid, he suggested that the best option for saving the country would be the reintroduction of U.S. military power to supplement the Vietnamese capabilities—particularly air power and naval gun support. However, he recognized the legal and political limitations of such a course of action.[114]

Late on 21 April, in a nationally televised ceremony, President Thieu resigned and Vice President Tran Van Huong assumed the presidency. Immediately after Thieu's resignation, the sixteen North Vietnamese divisions surrounding Saigon generally stood in place and there was a definite lull in the fighting. Some say the enemy was making plans, re-supplying its forces after their long movement southward and gathering information about the friendly defensive positions. Others believe that there were high-level intergovernmental discussions going on to reach a political settlement. That evening the American embassy contacted USSAG, requesting a plane to take President Thieu and his wife to Taiwan, and the president left the country.

In April the intrigues within Saigon were at a feverish pitch. Gen. Duong Van Minh, for one, aggressively attempted to convince the leaders and members of the general assembly that if he were installed as president he would be able to broker an accommodation with the communists—after all, he said, his brother was a Viet Cong general with access to the highest levels of communist leadership. Vien informed me that around 20 April Minh called him and requested a meeting, which was held in Vien's office at the JGS compound. Minh was effusive and friendly as he attempted to convince Vien to join his crusade. However, Vien flatly denied support. In relating this meeting to me, Vien said he did not trust Minh, and rightfully so. At the time of President Ngo Dinh Diem's overthrow in 1963, Vien had been the commander of the airborne division stationed in Saigon. The coup planners, led by Minh, thought that Vien would remain loyal to President Diem and consequently put out instructions to have him assassinated. Then and now, in 1975, Vien had always been a loyal military man with no political ambitions. He recently had been asked several times to join in the overthrow of President Thieu, and he always refused to be a part of such efforts. Nonetheless, it soon became known in Saigon that President Huong would resign and that the general assembly was prepared to appoint Minh president, hoping he could broker a truce with the communists. Faced with this situation, Vien believed he could not be loyal to Minh. Therefore, true to his principles, he prepared his resignation and took it to Huong, who signed his retirement papers. That done, Vien turned over his JGS command to his deputy, Lt. Gen. Dong Van Khuyen, and departed Vietnam on 27 April. Few people outside of the joint staff were ever aware of this event.[115]

On 26 April the communist attacks began again, and there could be no doubt that they had elected to gain a total military victory and not a diplomatic solution. The next day, the general assembly voted to grant the presidency to General Minh. Rumors were rampant that the communists would be willing to negotiate with Minh—but like all the other rumors, these had no substance.[116] The enemy attack on Saigon continued. Obviously, the situation was hopeless, and it was time for the United States to evacuate. The end had come.

Time to Evacuate

Evacuation Planning

In early 1974 the responsibility for preparing a noncombatant emergency and evacuation plan for South Vietnam was initially assigned to the American embassy in Saigon. Headquarters USSAG had the responsibility of preparing the same plan for Phnom Penh. Both plans obviously required air assets, and therefore Headquarters USSAG had to be intimately involved in the planning process. Our staff completed the detailed planning necessary for Phnom Penh, with the close coordination of the American embassy in Phnom Penh. However, we could not obtain the desired cooperation—nor, really, any interest in the matter—from the embassy in Saigon because it was reluctant to undertake any activity which, if leaked, could upset the Vietnamese.[117] Consequently, we asked CINCPAC to attempt to transfer the authority and responsibility for evacuation planning for Vietnam to Headquarters USSAG. On 10 April 1974, CINCPAC asked us to develop a contingency plan (CONPLAN) in support of CINCPAC CONPLAN 5060 for the evacuation of South Vietnam.

Shortly afterward, I called in our operations personnel who had successfully completed the Cambodia evacuation plan—Col. Ed Bronars and Lt. Col. Joseph Lutz. Bronars was a marine who eventually was promoted to lieutenant general and became the deputy chief of operations for the Marine Corps, and Lutz was a savvy army armored type. Lutz was due to rotate in August, and I told him that the evacuation plan had to be completed before he rotated or, because of his expertise, we would have to hold him over. They asked what was so urgent, and I responded that I believed Vietnam could fall before Cambodia. Consequently, we established a planning schedule that provided for the submission of a draft CONPLAN to CINCPAC by 15 July 1974.

Most people did not know that the future of Cambodia depended almost entirely on the viability of South Vietnam because the Mekong convoys, so essential to the lifeblood of Cambodia, originated in Vietnam and were escorted initially up the Mekong by the Vietnamese Navy.

However, the entire planning process was slowed because the American embassy in Saigon was revising its emergency and evacuation plan. Coordination meetings were held at NKP on 26–27 June and again in Saigon on 1–3 July. On 30 July 1974, a draft USSAG/7AF CON-PLAN 5060V, called TALON VISE, was forwarded to CINCPAC for approval. It planned for approximately ten thousand evacuees. In late September 1974, we were informed that coordination difficulties (navy originated) had arisen over certain command relationships and thus early approval no longer seemed likely. Then, on 12 December 1974, CINCPAC directed that CINCPAC Fleet assume responsibility for the preparation and implementation of the evacuation plan for Cambodia, Laos, and Vietnam not later than 1 June 1975, when Headquarters USSAG was to be inactivated. CINCPAC obviously did not view the military situation in Vietnam as being as critical as we did. (It was sometime early that month that they had returned our Vietnam assessment briefing as being much too pessimistic.)

Since USSAG/7AF was to retain the responsibility for evacuation planning until 1 June 1975, Lieutenant General Burns requested CONPLAN approval so that the tasked units could prepare supporting plans. The plan was accepted, subject to directed changes that included the redefined command relationships, and on 26 March 1975 the revised plan was sent to all concerned.

The situation in Vietnam was deteriorating rapidly with the withdrawal of the South Vietnamese from the central highlands, and the pace of planning activities increased greatly. The evacuation plan consisted of four options: first, ambassadorial control, using either civilian or military transportation assets, or both; second, military control, using fixed-wing aircraft; third, military control, using sealift assets; and fourth, military control, using a combination of fixed-wing, sealift, and helicopter assets. On 14 April, CINCPAC directed development of detailed plans for the evacuation of fifteen hundred, three thousand, six thousand, and two hundred thousand personnel. The plan for the evacuation of two hundred thousand was called option five.

Lieutenant General Burns was the coordinating authority for any emergency evacuations conducted in Southeast Asia. Under his command, the air force, navy, and marines had just completed the flawless evacuation of Phnom Penh on 12 April. So, at the 15 April major planning conference held at Headquarters USSAG there was a strong feeling of confidence that the planning for the evacuation of Saigon would also go well. The detailed planning based on the Saigon enclave did not begin in earnest until 2 April 1975, and then, because of the uncertainty as to the potential number of evacuees, an open-ended plan was required. In this case, the presence of representatives from both the fleet and the marine ground security force working in conjunction with our planners was absolutely essential to the time-compressed development of a workable plan. We maintained this joint planning group throughout the actual evacuation. On 15 April, the name for the South Vietnam evacuation was changed from TALON VISE to FREQUENT WIND.[118]

The lack of even reasonably accurate estimates of the number of evacuees, coupled with the requirement to submit proposed plans to handle different estimates on both the numbers to be evacuated and the method of evacuation, swamped the small planning staff at NKP. Changes in the details of aircraft flow and integration as well as the time to complete the evacuation were continuous. The undetermined length of the operation required the integration of supporting air forces (air force, navy, marine) to protect the helicopters, ground support forces, and evacuees. It was assumed that the evacuation would be accomplished in a daylight period of twelve hours.

To provide an idea of the number of potential evacuees, Ambassador Martin sent a cable to Secretary of State Kissinger in Washington, D.C., on 14 April (one day before the planning conference) that gave the total number of evacuees as 175,533—that is, 4,765 American citizens and 170,768 aliens.[119] All four military options were completed and approved by CINCPAC: Option IV (helicopter) on 11 April, Option II (fixed wing) on 20 April, Option III (sealift) on 21 April, and Option V (200,000 evacuees) on 25 April. The operational plan now in place possessed the flexibility necessary to accommodate the changing tactical situation and the fluctuating number of potential evacuees. No one could envision how vital this flexibility would become.

Evacuation

At the end of March 1975, there were appreciably fewer American citizens in South Vietnam than there had been the previous summer.

The termination of DAO support contracts in September 1974 as a consequence of reduced funding had resulted in hundreds of U.S. contract personnel returning to the States. On 31 March, the American embassy estimated there were about eight thousand American citizens in country. It started the evacuation of American citizens at that time, and by 23 April the number was just 1,681, of which only 179 were dependents.

In early April a relief group in Saigon sheltering orphans of mixed parentage received permission to fly the children on military aircraft to the States. Only hours before the plane was scheduled to depart, the relief group recognized that the infants and very young children needed adults to hold them while in flight. I was at the DAO when it received a frantic call asking for female employees to volunteer to accompany the flight. There had been artillery fire just over twenty miles north of Saigon for weeks, and the office workers needed little persuasion to leave. Maj. Gen. Homer Smith authorized them at the DAO to volunteer to assist the orphans. These wonderful women rushed off to pack and ready themselves for their return trips home. Air control informed us that the rear door of the C-5 blew out shortly after takeoff and the crippled plane was making a valiant attempt to return to Tan Son Nhut airfield. We rushed to the window to watch the approach, only to see it crash about a mile short of the runway, killing half the passengers on board, including thirty-six of the thirty-seven escort volunteers. This terrible tragedy cast a pall over the DAO. Fortunately, it was to be the only major accident in the continuing evacuation from South Vietnam.

On 19 April, Admiral Gayler flew to Saigon to assess the situation. During the meeting with Gayler and the DAO staff, I received a note stating that General Vien wished to see me on an urgent basis. I requested that Major General Smith accompany me for any discussion with Vien. Gayler agreed and excused us, and we met with Vien at 1630 hours on 19 April.

Vien had just returned from the palace, where he had had discussions with President Thieu. The president was extremely pleased with the information that he had received from Minister Hung, in Washington trying to obtain military and economic assistance. Hung had related that events in the Senate Armed Services Committee meeting indicated that South Vietnam would receive about $375 million in assistance. We mentioned that this, of course, was good news but that in all probability the military situation had deteriorated to the point that primary consideration should be given to the current tactical situation. Vien agreed that the assistance was probably too late. He was personally perplexed that the president did not seem to grasp the seriousness of the deteriorating military situation but explained that he had briefed the new minister of defense in great depth concerning the situation on Friday, 18 April. That morning Minister Dong had told him that he had explained the seriousness of the Vietnam situation to President Thieu. Yet, Vien said, the president did not refer at all to the military situation and seemed to be ignoring it. This was not a good sign; Thieu always had his hand heavily in all military matters.

The conversation then turned to evacuation. Vien understood that the Americans had a plan whereby helicopters would pick up personnel at the race track and at Newport, the port facility. Major General Smith confirmed that we were preparing to evacuate Americans and their dependents. Vien stated that as a soldier it was his duty to stay with the troops, but he was hopeful that Vietnamese military dependents could be evacuated as well, and said that as long as the United States provided a large number of Vietnamese with the means of evacuation, we could expect cooperation. He requested that after a governmental breaking point the United States remain offshore from Vung Tau for at least two weeks with platforms to pick up Vietnamese people, who would reach them either by swimming or by boat.

Vien reiterated that these discussions were extremely sensitive and should not be shared with others. We asked him if he had talked about evacuation plans with anyone else. He said he had not done so yet but that he could trust Lieutenant General Khuyen and Brigadier General Tho. He said, though, that he could not rely on the marines. We asked if we could strongly rely on the airborne forces for assistance. He replied that this was very important and he would have to think about it for the next few days. We agreed to meet again on Tuesday, 22 April, to pursue the matter further.[120]

Afterward, Smith and I relayed the substance of the meeting to Admiral Gayler. I was distressed to learn that the president was still mentally relying on a supplemental and that he did not grasp the seriousness of the situation. Gayler allowed that the navy could and would stand by offshore of Vung Tau. We also thought that if the families of key military personnel could be evacuated, then the RVNAF could stay and fight. As a consequence, these families were integrated into the American embassy/DAO plan to use safe houses to marshal personnel the evening before and then guide them to the aircraft at Tan Son Nhut. So, on 21 April 1975, in coordination with the ambassador through the DAO, USSAG/7AF scheduled an around-the-clock evacuation from the airfield using C-130 and C-141 aircraft. Between 21 and 28 April, 170 C-130 and 134 C-141 sorties evacuated 42,810 personnel. The last C-141 flights were on 27 April, CINCPAC having terminated them because of increasing small arms fire around the airfield.

On 24 April, the JCS authorized CINCPAC to direct the execution of Options II, III, and/or IV when the ambassador requested. The operational units completed FREQUENT WIND force deployments on 27 April, and Headquarters USSAG directed the forces to assume a one-hour readiness posture in anticipation of execution on 28 April. However, CINCPAC made no decision to execute, and the forces reverted to a six-hour posture.

This was a huge undertaking and many forces were available for the operation:

- A U.S. Navy task force of approximately forty-five ships, including two aircraft carriers for tactical air and helicopters and one LPH
- Ten Air Force and thirty-four Marine Corps H-53 helicopters, of which forty-two were used in actual evacuation operations
- Twenty-seven Marine Corps H-46 helicopters, of which fourteen were used
- Three Marine Corps battalion landing teams
- Navy tactical air
- Air Force tactical air
- Thirty-six Air Force KC-135 tanker aircraft
- Four Air Force KC-135 radio relay aircraft
- Five Air Force HC-130 rescue aircraft
- Four Air Force EC-130 airborne battlefield command and control centers[118]

The situation at Tan Son Nhut began to deteriorate rapidly. On 28 April, at 1800 hours, a flight of three A-37s equipped with MK-82 500-pound bombs attacked the flight line area. Six bombs hit the VNAF parking area, destroying numerous aircraft, at least three AC-119s and several C-47s. The enemy used dive-bomb tactics, with an estimated roll-in altitude of five thousand feet. The VNAF believed that the A-37s were piloted by captured South Vietnamese pilots.

Two C-130s from Clark AFB in the Philippines landed at about 2030 hours and loaded about 360 passengers and departed without incident. At the same time, the flow of C-130s from Clark AFB was reinstated under the previously scheduled Option I evacuation airlift. Between 0100 and 0330 hours on 29 April, the first three C-130s arrived from Clark. Two of the three were loaded with passengers, and the third was getting ready to pick up passengers, when at about 0400 hours the enemy began an intense rocket attack. The taxiing USAF C-130 was hit and set on fire while on the ramp near the Air America operations. The crew of the destroyed aircraft boarded adjacent aircraft, and the two remaining craft departed without injuries to crew or passengers.

At 0625 hours, COMUSSAG/7AF directed the launch of all U.S. Air Force support aircraft (tankers, radio relay, airborne command and control) to provide communications and control for the C-130 operation, even though Option II had not yet been directed. All indications were that Option II was imminent, and the Seventh Air Force launched C-130s from Clark in anticipation of execution. However, due to the chaotic conditions at Tan Son Nhut, the C-130s never landed and COMUSSAG/7AF ordered them to withdraw and return to base at about 0730 hours.

During the earlier attack by fire, two enemy rockets hit the gate guarding the DAO compound, killing two embassy marine guards.[121] The attack by fire continued for several hours, with about forty rounds per hour of 122 mm rockets and 130 mm artillery hitting throughout the airport complex. Then, to make matters worse, senior Vietnamese Air Force officers panicked and closed up shop, and several F-5 pilots jettisoned their fuel tanks and armaments on the Tan San Nhut runway as they hastily departed for safe havens in Thailand instead of attacking the surrounding enemy forces, thus precipitating the closing of runways and effectively precluding additional C-130 evacuations. In addition, one F-5 with engines running was blocking the entrance taxi-way to the Air America operations ramp and passenger-loading area. About forty vehicles and several hundred local nationals occupied the runway area, trying to board two VNAF C-130s attempting to take off. To top it off, a South Vietnamese gunship was hit and destroyed near the northern perimeter of Tan Son Nhut.

The USSAG personnel on the ground at Tan Son Nhut believed the resumption of fixed-wing evacuation was not possible. Thus, the runway was closed and the airport was deemed unusable. Ambassador Martin visited the DAO compound to assess the damage and receive a briefing from Major General Smith, after which he belatedly decided against continuing the fixed-wing evacuation and turned control of the evacuation over to the military.

Martin's concern about the effect of the evacuation of U.S. and se-lected Vietnamese personnel on the rest of the population had resulted in an overly cautious use of available aircraft in the previous days and had caused an unreasonable delay in the decision to request military airlift. As a result, the movement of evacuees to planned primary land-ing zones was disrupted, forcing more people to the embassy, which had the least capable landing zone in the operations plan. The plan called for evacuating one hundred personnel from the embassy, not the eventual twenty-one hundred.

At 0951 on 29 April, CINCPAC directed execution of Option IV (helicopters), and for tactical air reference timing purposes L-hour (launch hour) was set at 1100 hours. Tactical aircraft were launched and with support aircraft were all on station by 0945 hours. Unfortu-nately, the marine ground support and helicopter forces, which were on separate navy vessels, did not commence the cross-decking operations required for their integration until L-hour was established. Thus, sev-eral hours of valuable daylight passed, necessitating a night operation. As a consequence, the first evacuation helicopter did not land at the DAO compound until 1406 hours, when the evacuation by helicopters commenced.[118]

The DAO compound, although in the same general location as the airport, was separate from where the fixed-wing evacuation was taking place. The situation at the airfield was becoming very tense,

Photo 3. Tan Son Nhut Airfield, 28 April 1975. (Source: Headquarters USSAG, Nakhon Phanom, Thailand, produced by 432nd Reconnaissance Technical Squadron, U.S. Air Force.)

with Vietnamese Air Force officers and civilians demanding evacuation and attempting to commandeer aircraft. Therefore, all Seventh Air Force, Air America, DAO, and marine guard personnel were taken from the flight-line area, many by Air America helicopters, to the DAO compound (see photos 3 and 4).

About 0815, VNAF commander General Tran Van Minh and other top air force officers had entered the compound and requested evacuation by American aircraft. This event signaled the complete loss of the Vietnamese Air Force command and control and magnified the continued deterioration of an already volatile situation. Major General Smith ordered them disarmed and segregated until their evacuation could be accomplished.[122]

In the early morning, two A-1s and an AC-119 had provided air cover for Tan Son Nhut. At 0605 hours SA-7 fire shot down the AC-119, and only one A-1 was left airborne. Almost all of the F-5s had left South Vietnam, and by 0920 at least twenty had landed at the U-Tapao Airbase in Thailand, with more in the air. There was little doubt that at the urging of Pentagon personnel the VNAF aircraft were flown to

Photo 4. Tan Son Nhut Airfield, 30 April 1975. The Aftermath. (Source: Headquarters USSAG, Nakhon Phanom, Thailand, produced by 432nd Reconnaissance Technical Squadron, U.S. Air Force.)

Thailand to save them. The almost complete collapse of the air force was devastating. By the end of the day there were six C-130s, three C-119s, thirteen C-47s, twenty-seven F-5s, ten A-1s, six U-17s, three DC-3s, and more than two thousand refugees received at U-Tapao, as reported by the American embassy in Bangkok. The South Vietnamese Air Force has been severely criticized for its performance in those last days. Prior to that, its performance at Da Nang had left much to be desired. The air force of course had many moments of glory—but they weren't in the last days.

A navy tank landing ship and a U.S. military sealift tug with a barge waited at the commercial wharf (Newport); by 1130 hours these were loaded and preparing to depart downriver. They were attempting to establish communications, should air cover be required during the voyage. An estimated six thousand evacuees were on board, including about one hundred American citizens. I was happy to see that the joint staff took to heart the idea of evacuating from Saigon by ship. True to Admiral Gayler's word, the U.S. Navy stood off Vung Tau for days, enabling forty thousand additional refugees to escape.

Lieutenant General Burns, acting as the designated subordinate commander and coordinating authority for CINCPAC in the conduct of FREQUENT WIND, exercised operational control of the air force units and of the ground support force and overland helicopters. CINCPAC Fleet retained operational control of supporting forces at all times for navy tactical air and when over water for the ground support force helicopters. COMUSSAG/7AF exercised command and control from the Seventh Air Force Tactical Air Command Center at NKP through the airborne mission commander in the airborne command and control aircraft, initially Col. J. S. Roosma Jr., and the marine ground support force commander on the scene, Brig. Gen. Richard E. Carey.

Upon landing at the DAO compound, Carey and his battalion of marines (865 men) took immediate charge of the security situation. The compound had seven designated landing zones, three of which were easily used during daylight hours. With darkness, helicopters could land on only the two with existing lighting, augmented by auto headlights and portable lighting equipment. The steady flow of choppers to the compound was thus maintained.

There were some difficult moments transporting evacuees. At about 1500 hours, the national police blocked nine busloads, escorted by Captain Wood, U.S. Marine Corps, from entering the compound. Wood negotiated with the police and secured safe passage for the buses when he allowed several of the senior police to join the convoy. Elsewhere in the city, Air America choppers picked up U.S. citizens from rooftops and deposited them at both the embassy and the DAO compound. The helicopter airlift assured a steady flow to the compound, and the evacuation went smoothly. The total number evacuated from the DAO was 395 Americans and more than 4,475 Vietnamese and third-country nationals.[123] About 0030 hours, the last of the marine ground support forces was evacuated from the compound. The DAO personnel all deserve tremendous credit for the smooth evacuation.

The situation at the embassy was a horse of another color. The plan called for a minimal helicopter lift from the American embassy roof to evacuate those working in the main building. The majority of the personnel who rendezvoused at the American embassy were to be moved by bus to the DAO compound. The in-town pick-up locations were no longer usable, and bus movement had become tenuous, so a large number of evacuees made their ways to the embassy grounds. To the consternation of those directing the airlift, the estimate of the number to be evacuated kept growing with time. It was obvious the rooftop landing zone, which could only accommodate a CH-46, was not sufficient. The marine security personnel took the initiative to clear the parking lot next to the main embassy building. The lot had a beautiful old tree that earlier even in this critical situation some at the embassy wanted to save. Notwithstanding, the parking lot was cleared so that CH-53s could land. About 1430, the first helicopters were inserted with two platoons of marines.

As the evacuation proceeded from the main embassy grounds, the very large number of personnel in the recreation areas adjacent to but separated from the main embassy by a high wall and gate became panicky and highly agitated. Additionally, the number seemed to keep growing, although a realistic head count had not been made. The lack of numbers for planning in the helicopter flow was a problem; however, once the people in the embassy grounds had been evacuated, those in the recreation area entered the grounds and the situation became more manageable.

At about 2400 hours there was a major lull in the helicopter flow. This caused all hell to break loose on the command net. CINCPAC asked, "Why no '53s in the Embassy at this time?"[124] It appeared that out of concern for flight safety Admiral Whitmore (CTF 76) had made an independent decision to halt flight operations. All CH-53 helicopters were directed to return to base for aircraft servicing and crew rest. Needless to say, the flow was turned back on and by 0200 hours a CH-46 and a CH-53 were landing at the embassy about every ten minutes.

At 0121 hours, Blue Chip (USSAG/7AF command and control) received a message from CINCPAC, which I roughly copied: "Pass message to Ambassador Martin from Admiral Gayler. I have been directed to send following message to you by the president: On basis of a reported total of 726 evacuees CINCPAC is authorized to send 19 helicopters and no more. The president expects Ambassador Martin to be on the last helicopter. For your info: the Sec Def wishes that the last lift to depart NLT 0345 hours (2045Z) and we will do our best to meet that request. Warm regards. End Message. FYI request that Martin acknowledge this presidential message."

At 0400 the airbase command center reported that a code 2 (Ambassador Martin) was on board Lady Ace-09. With that, only the 130-man ground support forces and a few Americans had to be lifted off to conclude the evacuation. The final extraction was the most dangerous. At 0433, a Lady Ace (CH-46) was forced into an immediate takeoff. Apparently the enemy was using riot-control gas (CS) on the embassy. At 0439 the Specter C-130 gunship saw much fire (mostly small arms) around the embassy. It was cleared to provide suppressive fire. At 0451 there was an antiaircraft threat at the presidential palace only six blocks southwest of the embassy. Earlier, there was a SA-7 warning published three miles west of the embassy in a cemetery. At 0517 the airbase command center reported that Swift-33 had become disoriented and had withdrawn because of riot gas but was coming in again.

With daylight, A-7s replaced the AC-130 gunship and provided overhead cover. At 0646 hours Swift-22 lifted the last of the ground support forces out of the embassy.[125] One of the A-7s covering the helicopters had its engine quit and was lost at sea. Fortunately, the pilot ejected and was recovered. Thus ended FREQUENT WIND.[126]

The head count showed that 2,098 personnel (978 U.S. and 1,120 Vietnamese) were evacuated from the embassy.[127] In all, 8,048 personnel (including 995 ground support forces) made their way to safety on the naval ships offshore, in the largest helicopter evacuation in history. Under Lieutenant General Burns's outstanding leadership, all of the Americans and thousands of foreign nationals both at Phnom Penh and Saigon were successfully evacuated, with the loss of only the two Saigon embassy guards.

Obviously all concerned with the evacuation deserve plaudits—the DAO and embassy staffs; the air force, navy, and marine pilots; the ground support forces; the navy ships and crews; and the battle staff at USSAG. The helicopter pilots flying into small landing zones at night and braving the antiaircraft fire, however, deserve special recognition. The incoming artillery and rockets at Tan Son Nhut created the only casualties, but there was constant small-arms and automatic weapons fire aimed at the evacuation aircraft. At the tactical control center, we plotted all firing incidents other than small-arms and automatic weapons fire, of which there were many. The envelope of enemy firing kept getting smaller and smaller as they moved in on the evacuation routes.

If a halt to helicopter flights had not been called when it was, we could have lost some helicopters soon. At least seventy-six FREQUENT WIND antiaircraft incidents were reported, of which thirty-six were SA-7 firings.[128] During the previous three months the enemy had effectively shot down fourteen South Vietnamese aircraft with twenty-five SA-7 firings; with this as an example, the danger to U.S. evacuation aircraft is clear.

We learned several important lessons from the evacuation. First, in a rapidly deteriorating military situation a flexible operational plan with decentralized command and control arrangements is necessary. The midday initiation, unexpected increase in evacuees at the embassy, restriction of the embassy's landing zones, breakdown in smooth helicopter flow, difficulties of night operations, and continuing enemy harassment by fire extended the operation well beyond the time anticipated. Yet, the participants quickly and effectively adapted to these situations. Second, there was occasional confusion between controlling agencies, as some used local time and some used Zulu time (Greenwich Mean Time). The planning and execution of an operation should always be in accordance with Department of Defense/International standards—that is, Zulu time. Third, the late requirement to provide detailed information to higher headquarters on a real-time basis complicated the command, control, and communications task. This was a high-interest operation, and many agencies required current information. A review of the communications log shows how higher headquarters from the National Military Command Center, CINCPAC, and others took over the radio net—mostly on minor matters—contributing to occasional saturation of communications.[129] During the planning phase, agencies should agree as to the frequency and content of reports required. Finally, directives to execute the operation came through CINCPAC to both COMUSSAG/7AF and to the Commander-in-Chief of the Pacific Fleet. This dual channel of command allowed the unilateral interpretation of alert postures, making it difficult to coordinate joint forces. Authority for the overall operational control of a joint operation should be centralized at the lowest possible joint command.

The newspapers blamed Ambassador Martin for the "catastrophe" in Saigon. Photographs of evacuees ascending the ladder at the embassy rooftop were printed everywhere as a sign of failure. There was no failure on Martin's part. Yes, he held out hope to the very end that the situation would improve. In the final days, however, the normally decisive ambassador could not face the fact that South Vietnam was falling. In 1974, he had not supported proper evacuation planning, concerned that it would send a negative message to the Vietnamese. Then he refused to allow a stepped-up airlift, again concerned that it would panic the Vietnamese. On 29 April he wasted valuable daylight hours before he acquiesced to a military evacuation option. Finally, he would not leave the embassy as long as the airlift could continue to evacuate the Vietnamese supporters of the United States. In the end, President Ford had to order him to leave.

In testimony before Congress, Martin did fight hard to obtain the military and economic aid necessary to keep South Vietnam operating. He would not stand by and see American promises to the Vietnamese vitiated. Ambassador Martin was an honorable man, intelligent and strong and quite gutsy. Once the fall of the government was obvious, he did his best to evacuate the maximum number of Vietnamese supporters possible. In Cambodia we evacuated hundreds of supporters; in Vietnam we evacuated over a hundred thousand. Martin deserved much better treatment than he received from the press. If there was any failure, it was Congress's for not properly supporting the war efforts in Southeast Asia, certainly not Martin's for attempting to evacuate the maximum number of U.S. supporters.

Summing Up

Subsequent to the cease-fire, the war in South Vietnam was a North Vietnamese–initiated conflict primarily directed against the South Vietnamese pacification program to gain population and territorial control so as to establish a claim of sovereignty. The ultimate goal, of course, was to overthrow the government of South Vietnam. It was a war of attrition that the communists incrementally ratcheted up in intensity by increasing their number of attacks by fire and by increasing the scope of ground attacks from regimental to divisional size and finally to coordinated corps actions. Studies of wars normally focus on the final cataclysmic battles; however, in this war it would be misleading for a summation to neglect the thousands of minor engagements that were continuously fought in the rural countryside. This war of minor skirmishes took a heavy toll of human lives and caused much suffering for the peasants whose allegiances both sides fought over. Numbers rather than words best describe the conduct of the war: During the 116-week period from the cease-fire on 28 January 1973 until the last few data inputs were received on 19 April 1975, there were 85,210 incidents and more than 155,000 combatants were killed in hostile actions. Of these incidents, 69,011, or 81 percent, were enemy initiated—of which 52.2 percent were attacks by fire, 39.4 percent ground incidents, and 8.4 percent terrorism, sabotage, or political acts. On the flip side, 16,199, or 19 percent, were friendly-initiated ground attacks. The 116 weeks were divided into five periods, during which the enemy-initiated ground attacks remained relatively constant at about 235 per week. However, as its logistics improved, to keep pressure on the RVNAF the enemy kept increasing its attacks by fire both in number and in intensity. The 203 attacks by fire per week in the initial period more than doubled to 428 in the final period. In December 1973, after our initial analysis, to keep the enemy off balance the South Vietnamese increased their friendly-initiated ground contacts from an average of thirty-nine per week in 1973 to 273 per week in period 5, which, incidentally, exceeded North Vietnam's 255 ground contacts per week in the same period.

The types of incidents portrayed can be further categorized as ground contacts, other ground incidents (ambush, penetration, and harassment), attacks by fire, and other enemy-initiated incidents (mines, terrorism, sabotage, and political) (see table 16).

Table 16. Total Incidents, 28 January 1973–19 April 1975

Type	Number	Enemy KIA	Friendly casualties
Ground contacts	30,807	96,067	85,556
Ambush, penetration, harassments	11,097	4,462	12,724
Attacks by fire	36,029	—	34,357
Mines, terrorism, sabotage, political	7,277	16	4,775
Total	**85,210**	**100,545**	**137,412**

Source: "Republic of Vietnam Ammunition Conservation Study," June 1975, Headquarters USSAG, Nakhon Phanom, Thailand.

Ground incidents include contacts, ambushes, penetrations, and harassments. The definition of each is explained in appendix A. There were relatively few ambushes and penetrations but 10,038 harassments, which resulted in 3,122 enemy killed. Although few in number, the 250 ambushes resulted in by far the greatest number of casualties per incident (4.56). The most important ground incidents were the 30,807 ground contacts (attacks), which accounted for 96 percent of the enemy killed and 62 percent of friendly casualties. Sabotage and political acts by the communists resulted in no casualties. However, the enemy acts of terrorism and the ubiquitous mines and booby traps caused 4,775 casualties. The other primary source of friendly casualties was the attacks by fire, which caused 25 percent of all friendly casualties.

In December 1973, USSAG informed the joint staff that the communists had taken the offensive everywhere in South Vietnam and that the RVNAF was both more effective and more efficient when it initiated attacks, and as a result the word went out for it to become more aggressive. From December 1973, when we initiated coverage by type of unit, until April 1975 the ARVN initiated more ground contacts (12,974) than the enemy. The army attacked the enemy more than twice as often (5,799) than it was attacked (2,498). The territorials initiated about as many ground contacts (7,175) as the communists initiated against them (7,391) and more than those initiated by the army. As expected, the enemy attacked the territorials almost three times as often as it did the army. Obviously, the North Vietnamese were selective in choosing their targets. This reflected that territorials—who, incidentally, had very little in the way of firepower compared to the regulars and whose troop strengths were usually depleted—protected the South Vietnamese hamlets, generally the North's objectives to gain territory and population and disrupt the pacification program, and, of course, there were twice as many territorials as regulars. Of all communist-initiated ground attacks, 75 percent were against territorials. Even the communist multidivisional attacks against Phuoc Long and Ban Me Thuot were directed at units composed primarily of territorials.

There is no doubt that the territorials' outposts and units bore the brunt of frequent enemy attacks and consequently paid a high price, with more friendly territorials killed than regular troops. However, the 30,146 enemy killed by the territorials was a surprising number. Yet the better-trained and -led regulars were even more successful, eliminating 42,123 enemy, with an effectiveness ratio of 6.27, almost double that of the territorials.

The army was the glue that held the RVNAF together; it backed up the territorials and repeatedly took the battle to the enemy. Even circumscribed by lack of equipment, ammunition, petroleum, and spare parts, the ARVN was an effective combat organization, although it paled in comparison with U.S. combat forces.

The large number of friendly casualties resulting from enemy attacks by fire was reduced somewhat over time as the matter received more command emphasis, but it was always too high. Again, more than twice as many attacks by fire were launched against the territorials than against the regulars, whose defenses against attacks by fire were not satisfactory. Of all enemy attacks by fire, 61 percent resulted in no casualties, which indicates multiple casualties were often taken.

The communist strategy of conducting thousands of minor attacks against the weakest elements of the military enabled the North Vietnamese to slowly gain territory and some population while forcing the highly dispersed South Vietnamese forces into a defensive posture, "protecting all territory and population." It also allowed the North Vietnamese to expand their command and control, upgrade equipment, and increase their manpower in preparation for massive multidivisional combined arms attacks against outnumbered friendly troops defending selected enemy objectives. Yet, this was a war of minor skirmishes punctuated by a few major battles. The casualties added up—and quickly, because of the total number of incidents. Every day, there were an average of two major incidents and 140 combatants killed.

Why Did South Vietnam Fall?

The United States reneged on almost all of the pre–peace treaty promises made to South Vietnam. It did not replace major combat system losses on a one-for-one basis; it did not maintain the pre-treaty level of the stocks of ammunition; it failed to intervene militarily when North Vietnam overwhelmingly renewed its aggression; and most importantly it did not continue to provide adequate financial support. In August 1974, a USSAG study had concluded, "U.S. funding of less than 1 billion dollars ensures early demise of RVNAF." The congressional funding available to South Vietnam for FY 75 was only $583 million, definitely not sufficient to successfully conduct the war. In April 1975 the South Vietnamese would have been completely out of ammunition within days; they were doomed to defeat. The question then should be "Why did South Vietnam fall when it did?"

A contributing factor to South Vietnam's ultimate defeat was President Thieu's dictate that the military must protect all territory and population, which overrode his joint staff's recommendation to withdraw from many of its relatively isolated positions. This required the military to become thinly spread throughout the country, protecting more than ten thousand hamlets and villages. As a consequence, it had no reserves with which to combat a potential major communist offensive. The great reduction in the FY 75 U.S. funding greatly exacerbated the situation. Rather than changing its current strategy to one of a prioritized defense of critical areas so that the South Vietnamese manpower and greatly reduced resources could be more selectively utilized, the government continued on as before until early March, when the enemy's attacks spooked President Thieu.

However, in early March 1975 South Vietnam was holding its own. The December–January COSVN offensive in MR-3 and MR-4 had netted the enemy Phuoc Long Province and some key outposts and population in the delta. From a military point of view, the localized Phuoc Long defeat was not great, although the first loss of a provincial capital was a psychological blow to the South Vietnamese. There were no major enemy inroads in MR-1 and -2; the RVNAF was on the offensive and was still effective, although not as much as it had been in the summer of 1974. It still had superior mobility, but the enemy antiaircraft capabilities and the infiltration of a great number of tanks and artillery had seriously eroded its firepower advantages. The necessity to dramatically cut back on flying hours and conserve ammunition and the inability to replace combat equipment losses was having a deleterious effect. Additionally, while the RVNAF was scraping the bottom of the manpower barrel to bring units up to strength and to form a strategic reserve, the North Vietnamese were infiltrating a large number of combatants and organizing their regimental units into divisions and corps capable of conducting large-scale combined arms offensive operations. The force pendulum was swinging inexorably in favor of the North Vietnamese. Yet, for all of this, the South Vietnamese soldiers were still seriously attriting the enemy and still had a strong military capability. Man for man, they were probably superior to the enemy. (Many American Vietnam War veterans, who were better equipped and better led, do not have a high regard for the ARVN, usually comparing its capabilities to those of U.S. troops. However when one compares the South Vietnamese military to the Cambodian or Thai military, both of whom I was very familiar with, and the NVA/VC, the ARVN looked good.)

So what happened? The II Corps commander's inability in March 1975 to properly interpret the intelligence information about the communists' intent to attack Ban Me Thuot prevented the precautionary reinforcement of the principally territorial units in the area, enabling the enemy to overwhelm the greatly outnumbered defenders and resulting in the second loss of a provincial capital in two months. This obviously caused President Thieu to abandon his firm policy of giving up no territory or population, and he made his catastrophic unilateral decision to hastily withdraw from MR-1 and -2. His order to withdraw was ill-conceived, poorly executed, and unnecessary at the time.

The North Vietnamese pressures in March were high initially but subsequently not overwhelming. The communist buildup of combat forces in MR-1 and MR-2 was not large. The most difficult of all tactical maneuvers is a withdrawal. It takes careful planning and strong execution—particularly under pressure. After his fateful decision, the JGS staff told President Thieu that probably only 25 percent of the combat forces could be saved. They were entirely correct. The retreat lacked both careful planning and strong execution; the air force, for example, was not fully integrated into the planning. The unfortunate situation could only be saved by a massive introduction of U.S. air power, and this was not forthcoming. The end had come quickly and dramatically, the result of President Thieu's decisions and of poor ground execution by senior military leaders.

The Pacific Command Intelligence Unit summarized the situation:

Reduction in U.S. aid coupled with inflation crippled the GVN economy and demoralized its armed forces. The combination of these and other factors resulted in serious psychological problems for the GVN. A sense of isolation, defeat, and abandonment became widespread, especially after the defeat in Phuoc Long Provence and the Central Highlands. Likewise, the absence of massive air and artillery support, which the RVNAF had come to rely on as a result of U.S. training, added another significant psychological blow to the GVN's will to resist.[102]

Congress's failure to adequately fund the conflict had, in the words of Secretary of State Henry Kissinger, "deliberately destroyed an ally." The United States abandoned South Vietnam, which it had projected into the global fight against communism.

After the Fall

After South Vietnam surrendered on 30 April, the communists moved swiftly to organize the South under a military management committee, whose priorities were establishing order, population control, and resettlement.[130] To effect these goals, it organized the population into people's revolutionary committees at all levels. These steps were not unlike those taken by the Cambodian communists. However, in Vietnam the aftermath was definitely much less violent than in Cambodia. Although there were rumors of specific cases of retaliation against South Vietnamese officials and military, no general purge was noted. Still, the communists established many dreaded indoctrination camps, in which some senior military personnel were to languish for as long as eighteen years. According to information culled primarily from the press and communist news services, life in South Vietnam outwardly changed little. Apparently (after the dismantling of the South Vietnamese system), economic unity between North and South was the immediate goal, to be followed by complete political reunification.

3

Cambodia

Background

From its inception, the war in Cambodia was closely associated with the conflict in Vietnam. The Khmer communist insurgency began as an offshoot of the North Vietnamese Communist Party in the late 1930s. Full-scale insurgency against the French, however, did not break out until 1947. After the French evacuated Southeast Asia in 1954, the communists were permitted to function overtly and did so until the early 1960s, when Prince Sihanouk began to crack down. The French had crowned him prince in 1941, at the age of nineteen, because they believed the fun-loving playboy was more controllable than his relatives. In 1953, Prince Sihanouk took control of Cambodia. Shortly thereafter, he stepped down from the throne, organized the Sangkum political party, and continued to govern the country as "the Father of Independence."[131] He sought political and economic ties with China, and although not a communist himself, he was partial to the North Vietnamese in their war with South Vietnam, collaborating with them to protect his own position and mollify his left wing. As a result, the United States cut off its economic aid to Cambodia. Sihanouk's leftist economic policies, associations with the Chinese and North Vietnamese communists, and repressive police measures caused unrest in Cambodia. In March 1970, peasants from the border area of the country demonstrated in Svey Rieng, demanding the Cambodian government take action to prevent the North Vietnamese from taking their farmland and precipitating border incidents with the allied forces. Additional demonstrations followed in Phnom Penh, in which the Viet Cong and North Vietnamese embassies were sacked. Sihanouk, traveling in Europe, threatened to punish the offenders upon his return. The government leaders were afraid for their lives, and on 18 March 1970 the Khmer National Assembly unanimously voted to depose Sihanouk, who, incidentally, had handpicked them. Lt. Gen. Lon Nol headed the government at the time.[132]

Lon Nol's government pledged to continue a neutral course in Southeast Asia, as long as the Vietnamese communists withdrew from Cambodian territory. He closed the port of Kompong Som to the North Vietnamese, thereby cutting off one of their major supply routes to South Vietnam's MR-3 and MR-4. The border areas of Cambodia and South Vietnam were significant sanctuaries for four communist infantry divisions and more than fifty thousand communist logistical support troops targeted against South Vietnam. Consequently, on 29 March 1970 the NVA/VC forces in the Cambodian sanctuaries initiated attacks against the Khmer military outposts. The thirty-five-thousand-man Cambodian Army, whose main mission until then had been to perform road construction and act as the palace guard, was no match for the NVA/VC, and it was decisively overrun. The North Vietnamese Army made serious advances toward Phnom Penh.

It became obvious that without assistance Lon Nol's pro-Western government would be overturned and Cambodia would become totally communist controlled. This would be a catastrophe for the United States, since in 1970 it was pulling troops out of South Vietnam and had initiated the Vietnamization programs for the South Vietnamese Armed Forces. To alleviate the situation, President Nixon authorized the use of U.S. combat forces in cooperation with the RVNAF to make a strategic raid into Cambodian NVA/VC sanctuaries in the Parrot's Beak area west of Saigon. The Cambodian raid began on 1 May 1970 and was successful in that the North Vietnamese retreated, abandoning huge supplies and base areas. The amount of captured enemy equipment exceeded all expectations and probably set back enemy plans by at least the year or more that it would take them to resupply. It definitely bought time for the Vietnamization program, and it took the communist pressure off of the Cambodian armed forces.

Although some in the United States were upset with the Cambodian raid, many U.S. soldiers in Vietnam were very pleased. The Parrot's Beak was like a dagger pointing into our area. The North Vietnamese often would conduct surprise attacks out of the Parrot's Beak into South Vietnam, and when they were aggressively engaged by our units would retreat back into Cambodian territory, where U.S. forces were forbidden to pursue them further. The raid into Cambodia definitely put such attacks on hold, thereby saving lives of our troops.

One unwelcome side effect of this invasion was the antiwar demonstrations in the United States. In June, the Senate passed the Cooper-Church amendment,[133] which, although rejected by the House, would be presented again later and ultimately would hamstring American military efforts to support Cambodia by not authorizing the introduction of U.S. ground combat troops into Cambodia or providing U.S. advisers to or for military forces there. Further, Section 756, PL 92-226, limited to no more than two hundred the total number of civilian officers and employees of the U.S. government and members of the armed forces present in Cambodia at any one time.[134]

One of the new Cambodian government's first actions was to request a reinstatement of aid, and Congress allocated $8.9 million in Military Assistance Program (MAP-CB) funds to support Cambodia for the remainder of FY 70. Subsequently, Congress authorized $185.0 million in Cambodian MAP funds in FY 71, $172.7 million in FY 72, $180.0 million in FY 73, $375.0 million in FY 1974, and $275 million in FY 1975.[135] These funds were obviously to improve the Cambodian armed forces to ensure the maintenance of a neutral Cambodian government friendly to the United States that would in effect allow the Vietnamization program in South Vietnam to better proceed. The military assistance for Cambodia was to be implemented through the U.S. Military Equipment Delivery Team Cambodia.

Military Equipment Delivery Team Cambodia

The Military Equipment Delivery Team Cambodia (MEDTC) was to determine the needs of the fledgling Cambodian military forces, arrange for the delivery of equipment and materials, and then report on the utilization of the U.S. logistical and training support. Unlike the DAO in Saigon, congressional dictate limited the MEDTC organization in number. It had seventy-four U.S. personnel in Cambodia and fifteen outside Cambodia in the joint liaison office at Samae San and Bangkok, Thailand. Like the DAO, it had army, navy, and air force divisions—plus one ammo and service division. MEDTC's responsibilities were formidable, since the Cambodian armed forces were recently formed and did not have mature logistical or personnel systems. The grateful Cambodians referred to Maj. Gen. John Cleland at times as the "Lafayette of Cambodia," for all the great support MEDTC provided. In February 1974 Cleland rotated and was replaced by the equally effective Brig. Gen. William "Jack" Palmer. USSAG supported MEDTC in operational planning, ammunition inventory and funds management and the Khmer Air Force airlift self-sufficiency program, but MEDTC itself accomplished the difficult on-the-ground implementations.

In addition to MEDTC, there was a U.S. military attaché office, comprising seventeen personnel with attachés from each military service. Col. Pete Burnell, the defense attaché, his successor, Col. L. B. Martin, and the other attachés also did a wonderful job. The reports of the assistant army attachés who made frequent visits to the field were invaluable in assessing the military situations. The naval attaché was vital in the planning for Mekong convoys, and the air attaché deserves great credit in the resurgence of the Khmer Air Force.

The March–May 1970 events initiated major efforts by the North Vietnamese Army to organize and field Khmer communist (KC) forces, whose purpose was to effect the overthrow of the government of the Khmer Republic (GKR), and by the United States to equip and assist the Cambodian armed forces (FANK) so that they could counter the enemy and protect the country. Should the FANK be successful, the final outcome of the Cambodian war would always be determined by the final situation in South Vietnam.

Khmer Communist Organization

In 1970 and 1971, the North Vietnamese Army/Viet Cong gained control of northern Cambodia and most of the territory east of the Mekong. The communist forces received their basic grounding from a Khmer communist cadre trained in North Vietnam who returned to Cambodia in 1970. That year, the KC rapidly moved to consolidate their holdings in areas overrun by the NVA/VC. The North's primary objective was to reoccupy its sanctuary bases and ensure the control of its primary lines of communication, so essential to combat operations

Table 17. Khmer Communist Command and Control Organizations
(total entities identified at end of month)

	May 1973	August 1973	January 1974	April 1974	June 1974	August 1974	January 1975	March 1975
Divisions	0	0	2	3	3	4	9	9
Battlefield commands	4	7	8	11	11	11	8	8
Brigades	—	—	—	—	4	4	7–9	7–9
Regiments	12	13	19	27	27	36	41	43–46
Battalions	109	126	174	193	197	203	230	250
Troop strength	32,400	38,700	61,300	61,900	57,600	63,000	65,000	60,000

Source: "Khmer Communist Order of Battle Document," DAO, Phnom Penh, Cambodia.

in South Vietnam. It was quite content to have the KC pursue the war against the government, since this allowed it to concentrate on the war in South Vietnam. To ensure Khmer communist successes, the North Vietnamese provided cadres, training facilities, advisers, and, most important, military supplies and equipment.

The North Vietnamese controlled sufficient territory and population to allow the communists to conscript a regular army. Initially they formed village militias, which, after training, filled territorial units; and as the territorial units gained combat experience, they were formed into regular well-equipped main-force battalions. They communized the peasantry by ruthlessly imposing discipline and by indoctrinating the population. Those who rebelled were often executed. Offered the opportunity, thousands of Khmer escaped to government strongholds, while those who remained were captive to the iron grip of the communists.[136] So, in three years, the KC evolved into an expanded, well-developed, battle-tested force equipped with modern weapons and was increasingly better supplied. The growth of the enemy is indicated in table 17. Note the doubling of forces between May 1973 and April 1974.

Khmer Armed Forces

In 1970 and 1971, patriotic Cambodian youths flocked to the army to defend their country from the despised North Vietnamese. As the young patriots rallied and local commands recruited, FANK grew to more than three hundred thousand men organized in more than five hundred battalion units. These soldiers had neither training nor equipment and lacked organization. The disparate group undertook several poorly planned and executed operations against the NVA/VC, which ended in a disastrous defeat in late 1971. In 1972 FANK was saved primarily by the U.S. Air Force's close air support.

Recognizing the necessity to reorganize the military into a standardized, better-equipped and -trained force, and working with the Cambodian joint staff, MEDTC designed a balanced MAP-CB–supported army force structure of 220,000 personnel. FANK established a 253,000 strength limit, the additional 33,000 men to be supported by payroll assistance only. The organization called for thirty-two infantry brigades and 202 infantry battalions. Twelve of the brigades were organized into four divisions of three brigades, and each division was supported by a 155 mm battery and an armored cavalry squadron. Each of the brigades also had a 105 mm battery.[135] Lon Nol insisted upon forming a fifth division, the 9th Division "Palace Guard," which diverted both personnel and equipment. Implementation of the planned force structure was not easy. However, with emphasis in early 1973 on the delivery and formation of artillery and armed cavalry troops, the force structure was almost completed.

The Khmer peasants were sturdy, rugged individuals able to withstand privation and difficulty. When well led, they were very heroic. Unhampered by an inexperienced officer corps such as the FANK was saddled with, the communists could promote their officers based on performance. Consequently, through a winnowing process the KC were able to staff their units by and large with intelligent and, in the latter stages, innovative officers with combat experience who demanded ruthless discipline from their soldiers. A major difference between the forces, then, was the quality of combat leadership.

The remnants of Cambodia's colonial peacetime officer corps, which had no combat experience, initially primarily composed the FANK leadership. Consequently, key leadership positions were unavailable to the younger combat-experienced officers, and this created a stifling situation. MEDTC stated that on its inspections it often found large-scale officer absenteeism. The Cambodian officers rarely conducted inspections. They were notorious for padding their ranks with phantom soldiers. Lacking experience and professionalism, the leaders generally failed to seek innovative solutions to combat situations; their offensive tactics were often unimaginative and plodding. Whereas the enemy most often attacked at night, the FANK almost always initiated daytime attacks at mid-morning. Its fire coordination was poor, so that its firepower advantage was not optimized. On top of all this, FANK basic training lasted only six weeks, and much of it involved political indoctrination rather than protracted hands-on experiences, such as marksmanship, preparation of defensive positions, or night exercises. Therefore, the soldiers were inadequately prepared for combat, which led to high casualties and a high desertion rate. The communists, with their aggressive attacks, and the FANK, with their inept defensive posture, both created many casualties. This was a bloody war.

For the Khmer, the South Vietnam peace accords signed in January 1973 had the immediate effect of requiring the relocation of the MEDTC logistical base in South Vietnam to Thailand and the termination of Cambodian training programs being conducted in South Vietnam. With respect to logistics, however, the net effect was positive. Ammo resupply and air force responsiveness were improved, and there was no change in rice and petroleum product procedures. The transshipping of equipment and general cargo, particularly that transiting the Mekong, was made more difficult because Saigon was much closer to the Mekong waterway than Vayama, Thailand, was. Overall, the transfer of logistics went smoothly, and in the long run, particularly when the requirement for airdrop and airland of supplies arose, it was a blessing. The government's in-country training base consisted of five national training centers and fourteen service schools. The quality of in-country training, completely staffed by Khmer, improved as those who completed out-of-country training were assigned to the cadre. However, the constant enemy combat pressure precluded optimum attendance, and the field commanders' indifference to sending good people for training reduced the effectiveness of the program. This cost FANK dearly. Stateside training, which required English-language proficiency, was minimal, with only about 150 students per year. However, those young officers who attended the armor school returned knowledgeable and enthusiastic and led the new cavalry squadrons with élan.

In 1973, FANK did not have the manpower to fortify its defensive positions on Route 4, and the battalions of the newly formed 1st Division had less than 50 percent of their authorized strength during their first operation on this route. There was a serious chronic manpower shortage, particularly with the intervention battalions. Therefore, some amplification of the military personnel situation is necessary for a better understanding of the conduct of the war.

Combat capabilities were measured by the number and strength of battalions. The standard battalion size was 512 soldiers. Most of these were intervention battalions, under the control of the centralized joint staff (EMG), and territorial battalions, generally controlled by the military region commanders. There were also separate marine battalions, controlled by the navy, which protected navy bases and the Mekong at choke points, and separate air force battalions, which defended the airbases.

In July 1974 there were 91 intervention battalions,[138] 187 territorial battalions, and nine marine battalions. The aggregate number was 287, with an effective strength of 105,460 troops out of a total of 244,457. The total strength of the 91 intervention battalions was 27,868. At that time, the separate territorial battalions had 74,187 troops, and the marine battalions had 3,405 soldiers. The residual army strength—which included EMG headquarters, support troops, and the pipeline, but not the 20,488 men in the air force and navy—was 118,509 personnel.

Many units were still not fully filled. As a glaring example, the 7th Division Headquarters had an effective strength of 217.6 percent, versus the full (or authorized) strength, while its battalions had only 38.0 percent, and the headquarters were always overstaffed. This strength disparity was always a severe problem; although many efforts were made to do so, the combat battalions were never brought up to strength.

Those Khmer youth volunteering for military service, who made up about 85 percent of all new recruits, compared with the 15 percent who were draftees, generally opted for territorial units. They elected for service with units close to home because they wanted to stay near their families. Any decision to circumvent this would surely result in major desertions—which were too high as it was. Often, conscripted young men pulled strings to be assigned to FANK headquarters and service support units. There were more than ten thousand troops in EMG headquarters alone. However, the air force and navy, with effective leadership at the top, had no problems recruiting and were generally always up to strength. The same was true for the armored cavalry squadrons.

The practice of reporting soldiers present for duty when they were off moonlighting, deceased, or nonexistent was common. Although the ambassador and MEDTC both repeatedly requested that FANK purge itself of the ubiquitous phantom soldiers, it was reluctant to do so—obviously, since such reporting was so common and the unit commanders lined their pockets with the phantoms' pay. The phantom soldiers and a huge desertion rate kept the actual strength of the intervention and territorial battalions below authorized numbers.

In October 1974, after the Cambodian government made an all-out effort to enforce conscription, the country's forces reached their manpower high point. There were 117,704 soldiers in 289 intervention, marine, and territorial battalions, but only 56.4 percent of the intervention battalions had effective strengths of at least 70 percent of the authorized strength. Units with lower than 70 percent authorized strength are considered marginally combat effective. By April 1975, only 13.8 percent of the 116 intervention battalions were at 70 percent. There was a continuous drawdown of the intervention battalions' effective strengths to 43.6 percent on 12 April 1975. FANK's severe 1975 casualty losses could not be replaced.[139]

As mentioned, the territorial battalions always had a much greater strength per battalion than the intervention battalions did. In early April 1975 their average strength, 358 personnel, was right at 70 percent while the intervention battalions had only 240 troops per battalion, or 47 percent. In other words, the territorial battalions had almost 50 percent more personnel than the intervention battalions, which bore the daily brunt of the enemy attacks.

MEDTC systematically collected manpower data, which USSAG collated to highlight these deficiencies. Brigadier General Palmer and his team repeatedly discussed the situation with the joint staff, as did the ambassador with the political leaders of the government—but to no avail. The chronic manpower shortfall in the intervention battalions, which were conducting most of the combat, was critical; it effectively prevented FANK from seizing the offensive. The lack of adequate military manpower, and the reluctance to remedy the situation, was undoubtedly one of the major causes of Cambodia's defeat. The failure to enforce mobilization, the padding of headquarters, the system that allowed volunteers to serve at home (in the territorial troops), the phantom troops, and the high desertion rates together were a colossal manpower management failure.

MEDTC designed the force structure of the Khmer Air Force primarily for counterinsurgency missions. It had an authorized strength of about ten thousand and had no problems maintaining that level. Only about two thousand personnel were associated with the operational missions—that is, flying and logistic functions—and about eight thousand were in standard battalion units responsible for airbase defense. Squadrons were organized to operate each type of aircraft. There were two main operating bases (Pochentong and Battambang) and three forward operating locations (Kompong Cham, Kompong Chhnang, and Ream). In January 1975 the air force had 131 aircraft, of which 101 were operationally ready. That month it flew a remarkable 7,208 sorties, as compared to 5,134 sorties in January 1974.[140]

By 1975 the air force logistics system was capable of keeping up with the increased operational missions, even after Pochentong came under intense artillery and rocket fire. That in itself was an extraordinary feat. A U.S. Air Force detachment conducted Khmer training in FY 75 at the Udorn Royal Thai Air Force Base in Thailand, for both pilots and maintenance personnel.[141] This realistic training, duplicating as much as possible the actual tactics and maintenance support required in Cambodia, raised the air force effectiveness to new heights. Air crews increased from ninety in January 1974 to 141 in January 1975.

In the summer of 1974 the air force was fully competent to support the immediate transfer of troops from Phnom Penh to outlying surrounded enclaves. In fact, it had been effectively supplying much-needed ammo and other supplies to enclaves on a daily basis by both airland and airdrop. There had been significant improvements by the air force in all areas. The most impressive improvements were in command and control and tactical operations coordination.[142] During January 1975, 62 percent of all strike missions were controlled, and the air force began to use an airborne command and control system for complex joint operations.[141] The operationally ready rate for the T-28 aircraft was 79 percent, compared to the U.S. Air Force standard of 71 percent.[143]

There were still problems in management, logistics supply, and maintenance. However, effectiveness had increased to the point that FANK attempted no major Mekong convoy or ground maneuvers without precoordinated direct air support. The C-123 squadron airdrops were instrumental in the survival of enclaves, and were a prime determinant in the army's ability to deploy sufficient intervention forces into the Phnom Penh perimeter to stop the determined communist offensive against the capital. Although not self-sufficient, the air force was striving toward that end. Its improvement since the end of the American bombing in August of 1973 had been truly dramatic.

The main deterrent to optimizing air force assets was the poor coordination between air force and army units—that is, the army's failure to comprehend and effect joint operations. Although matters improved in 1975, joint operations certainly were not routine. Naturally, the failures of coordinated actions at the upper echelons were exacerbated at the lower unit levels. In the matter of coordinated fire support, the Khmer suffered greatly because U.S. law prevented American advisers from training troops in country. The fluid tactical situations rendered air-ground coordination and cooperation much more difficult in the final months of the conflict.

Nevertheless, the accolades Ambassador John Gunther Dean gave Brig. Gen. Ea Chhong, the dynamic air force commander, and his force were certainly warranted; he paraphrased Winston Churchill's comment on the Royal Air Force, "Never have so many owed so much to so few." After the United States vacated Phnom Penh, the Khmer Air Force was the last effective fighting force in Cambodia. It continued to attack numerous communist units advancing in the open until they had overrun Pochentong and destroyed the stocks of fuel. Then it retrograded its flyable assets to Thailand. The Cambodian Air Force's determined resistance at the end sharply contrasted with the South Vietnamese Air Force's almost total capitulation.[144]

The Khmer Navy (MNK) was authorized 15,461 personnel (including the marine units) and had been issued about 208 vessels of all types.[145] Within this organization, there were twelve battalions of naval infantry (battalions of fusilier marines) whose mission was to defend major naval installations and occupy key choke points along the lower Mekong River. Before January 1975 the navy had lost twenty-eight craft from enemy action.[146] However, in the 1975 dry-weather campaign one of the communists' main thrusts was to interdict both the Upper and Lower Mekong River in an all-out effort to strangle Phnom Penh. The river craft constantly escorted convoys to and from the vital enclave of Neak Luong as well as from South Vietnam in January. Navy craft and crews sustained constant and heavy attacks by fire from the enemy dug in on the riverbanks. Navy and marine casualties were high. The navy lost forty-five craft, and, more important, more than 70 percent of their riverine operators were casualties. The MNK was exhausted, having lost more than 25 percent of its operating assets in less than 3½ months. Therefore, Rear Adm. Vong Sarendy, perhaps the strongest of the Cambodian military leaders, stood his forces down and reorganized them. Although it was actively operating until the end, the MNK had lost all capabilities for offensive operations.

Although similar in many ways, the wars in Cambodia and South Vietnam were entirely different because of cultural and economic matters. The political leaders of both countries attained their positions as the result of coups. Both were senior military officers who used the armed forces for military and political purposes. Both promoted to positions of responsibility officers whom they were certain would be loyal, and sometimes these men were not capable. In important matters, both presidents often bypassed the joint staffs and gave orders directly to the commanders. This compromised the staffs, rendering them less effective. Similarly, whenever the joint staff of either country issued an unpalatable directive, its senior commanders bypassed these and went directly to the president.

The joint staffs in both countries were not truly joint; they were staffed primarily by army personnel to the exclusion of the air force and the navy. Thus coordination was difficult. The military region commanders in both South Vietnam and Cambodia considered the troops under their command to be "theirs" and jealously guarded their utilization outside of the local military regions.

In both countries, the military's pay at all grade levels was insufficient to meet basic needs, particularly for the lower ranking soldiers with families. This necessitated "moonlighting" and, notably, corruption, absences without leave, and desertions. The effect of rampant inflation brought on by the worldwide oil crisis exacerbated the situations in both countries.[147]

The RVNAF, comparatively speaking, was a sophisticated military organization. Nearly all of its senior officers had been trained in the United States. They had worked closely with the allied military for many years and were battle-tested. The RVNAF also had a decent training base, a mature logistics system (although it still required outside contractor support), and an effective personnel management system. Its force structure included tanks, comparatively higher performance aircraft, and a much larger blue-water navy. However, South Vietnam's long years of fighting created a war-weariness that manifested itself in desertions (this problem plagued the Cambodian armed forces as well).

The South Vietnamese Army troops were more skilled in fire support coordination and combined arms tactics than were the Cambodians, whose skills were almost nonexistent in 1973. But most important, the RVNAF took the initiative and mounted hundreds of offensive operations against the much more effective North Vietnamese force. The FANK, in contrast, after its abortive 1971 offensive to open the highway to Kompong Thom—the CHAM LA II Operation—assumed an almost totally defensive posture. There were, of course, local offensive actions that were largely frontal type assaults.

President Lon Nol was willing to cede the territory gained by the communists in their 1970–1971 assaults. President Thieu, however, was unwilling to give up any territory or population, which required the RVNAF to be spread much too thinly and allowed the enemy to pick and choose its offensive targets, always with local force superiority. Lon Nol's primary objective was to retain and solidify the territory and population centers currently under government control while building and training the armed forces. By 1973, this was a defensive effort to hold on to population enclaves while attempting to maintain key lines of communication, primarily, Routes 4 and 5 and the Mekong River. This had the salutary effect of consolidating forces, but it created a difficult logistical problem of aerial supply to isolated enclaves.

The level of U.S. personnel support differed greatly in Cambodia and South Vietnam. A congressional mandate strictly limited the number of U.S. advisers in Cambodia to only two hundred total personnel, including military, embassy, and USAID people. Conversely, there were thousands of U.S. personnel supporting the war effort in South Vietnam, including contract technicians to maintain equipment. Additionally, U.S. MAP-CB funding procedures were extremely burdensome, whereas the Defense Assistance to Vietnam Program funding gave the South Vietnamese much more leeway in their planning and requisitioning of supplies.

The situation in Cambodia revolved around funding or the lack thereof. Almost all funding was utilized to purchase ammunition, and the Cambodians were expending ammunition at rates that far exceeded the available support. Ammunition was shipped by U.S. contractors predominantly by barges on the Mekong River, the critical main supply route. The outcome of the war greatly depended on ammunition and the Mekong.

Ammunition

Military Assistance Funding

In midsummer 1974 a matter of grave concern had surfaced: the inadequacy of MAP-CB funds, a situation exacerbated by the cumbersome rules for requisitioning supplies. The military assistance program was not designed to provide the flexibility necessary to support a war. Requirements had to be planned for and funded during prior year programming, and, to make matters worse, the funding was effected through a continuing resolution authority, which required that the allocated funds be made available in quarterly increments. Thus, at the beginning of each quarter MEDTC had to allocate funds for those items considered the most critical. This played havoc with long lead-time investment items, which were often postponed to satisfy critical requirements. Not only did ammunition requirements, which obviously were a function of combat intensity as well as force structure, have to be predicted a year in advance, but bureaucratic bullet counters in stateside depots were dramatically increasing the costs. Those responsible for maintaining and reconciling the Cambodia ammunition program were frustrated because of conflicting accounting directives.[148]

Necessity to Manage Ammo

In April 1974, ammunition expenditures averaged $1 million a day, and the necessity to fund this critical item was driving out other potential procurements. In FY 74, 83 percent of authorized funding was spent on ammo. To make matters worse, the intensity of combat was greatly increasing. It was critical to manage ammunition. The U.S. joint staff's concern of the previous fall was valid; the problem was not only artillery expenditures, but ammunition expenditures across the board. Like South Vietnam's conflict, Cambodia's was a "war by budget."

On 3 May 1974, recognizing the seriousness of the situation, Ambassador Dean, accompanied by Brigadier General Palmer, called on Marshal Lon Nol to focus his attention on the need for FANK to cut down ammunition consumption. Dean explained that ammo expenditures precluded spending funds on hardware items, such as armored personnel carriers and airplanes. He strongly stated it was imperative that FANK and the American military mission more effectively control the release of ammo and the FANK instill ammo discipline in field commanders. Shortly thereafter, Palmer met with Lt. Gen. Sosthene Fernandez, who subsequently put out the word to all his field commanders.[149]

Analysis of Ammunition Situation

MEDTC, with its limited staff spread thin, asked Headquarters USSAG for assistance in managing the ammo situation. We had already been assisting in the accounting, storage, and call-forward aspects and now developed a method to measure ammo expenditures as a function of several variables and to establish a conservation program. In June 1974, CINCPAC asked Headquarters USSAG to provide comments on the logistical considerations and plans for the Cambodian wet season, reflecting funding constraints and ammo conservation measures. CINCPAC also requested MEDTC comments on the need to limit the Cambodian ammo expenditures to 290 short tons per day to align consumption with fiscal realities. On 2 July 1974, I prepared a message in answer to CINCPAC's inquiries by providing an analysis of the previous year's ammo expenditures in Cambodia that forecasted ammo requirements through December 1974, the end of the wet season.[150]

I began the analysis with discussion of the wet season. The intensity of combat in Southeast Asia ebbed and flowed with the seasons. The southwest monsoon brought tremendous rainfall, ushering in the wet season and its miserable field conditions and decreased trafficability for the combatants. There were three indicators of the wet season in Cambodia: the southwest monsoon, reversal of the flow of the Tonle Sap River, and general flooding. Both the reversal of the Tonle Sap and the monsoons normally occurred in early May. Flooding in the vicinity of Phnom Penh occurred when the river reached the eight-meter level at its waterworks.[151] Therefore, we closely monitored the Mekong River levels. A channel at Phnom Penh links the Tonle Sap Lake, a remnant of an ancient sea gulf, to the Mekong. When it reaches the eight-meter level, waters flow through the channel, flooding the lake, which then expands to an area of 770 square miles, inundating the land at its borders. During the dry season the Tonle Sap shrinks to one hundred square miles, and its depth falls from about forty-five feet to a maximum of five feet. It is no wonder military operations cease in the vicinity when the lake floods (see map 7). The earliest yearly flooding on record occurred in 1971, on 16 July. In 1973 the Tonle Sap flooded on 15 August, and the communists called off their attack on Phnom Penh on about that date. River stages in 1974 closely paralleled those of 1971. For our analysis we assumed general flooding would occur in central Cambodia in early August.

The wet season favors defense. Constant rain and the muck are detrimental to the morale of troops in the field. There is an upsurge of malaria. Transportation and cross-country mobility are difficult. The enemy's major weakness was its logistical support capability, which the wet season exacerbated. The enemy could attack in areas not greatly affected by flooding, such as along Highway 4, Kampot, Kompong Som, Kompong Cham, and other major population centers at the edge of the flood plain around Tonle Sap Lake. However, it would be difficult to move supplies, and I believed that the KC would have to concentrate on one or possibly two enclaves. In any case, the wet season should have seen a diminution in enemy initiatives because of their reduced capabilities and because the situation favors defense.

The combat intensity in June 1974 was the highest of the war to date. Thus, when assessing ammunition expenditures in Cambodia, it was necessary, as it was in South Vietnam, to consider not only the

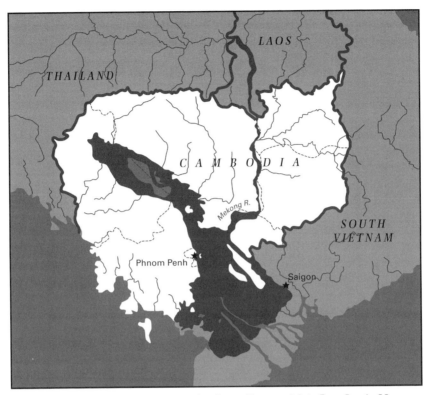

Map 7. Mekong River Wet Season Flooding. (Source: Maj. Gen. Ira A. Hunt Collection.)

authorized supply rates and the changing weapons densities that combined to make up the authorized day of supply—which in this case was a function of the limited funding situation—but also the varying intensities of combat as well as ammo conservation measures. These four variables together provided the insights essential to understanding the ammunition consumption picture.

MEDTC requisitioned the Cambodian munitions through the U.S. Air Force and Army. Air force munitions made up approximately 20 percent of the total tonnage but at the time less than 10 percent of the cost, since a day's supply of air ammunition cost less than half of a day's supply of ground munitions on a per-ton basis. Naval munitions had negligible costs; they made up less than 1 percent of the total on both a cost and tonnage basis.

A review of previous ground and air munitions daily consumption rates, tallied on a weekly basis since the termination of U.S. air support on 15 August 1973, indicated that the air force's utilization had pretty much leveled off at about 65 short tons a day. The munitions requirement was primarily a function of the number of close air support sorties flown. Since there were generally more air missions requested than existing capabilities allowed, the aviation assets were used to capacity. Of course, weather always influenced the sortie rate. Nevertheless, the capacity utilization meant a more even ammo consumption rate, thereby facilitating predictions.

The consumption of ground munitions, however, was highly variable, depending on such major factors as the intensity of combat and the flooding of the area around Phnom Penh. During the 1973 wet season (15 August to 28 December), the average usage of ground munitions was 273 short tons a day. The initiation of the communist offensive against Phnom Penh saw consumption jump to over 765 short tons daily. Thereafter, during the dry season, ground ammo usage varied greatly from week to week, averaging about 430 short tons a day.

The Effect of Weapons Density

Seven line items made up about 85 percent of the tonnage of ground munitions.[152] Table 18 shows the authorized supply rate for 1 November

Table 18. Effect of Weapons Densities on Ground Munitions					
	ASR	**Weapons densities**		**Day of Supply**	
	November 1973	November 1973	June 1974	November 1973	June 1974
105 mm HE	22.7	178	236	119.9	158.9
81 mm HE	3.1	1,052	1,260	30.3	36.3
155 mm HE	43.1	12	24	25.8	51.5
60 mm HE	3.2	2,553	2,594	22.4	22.7
5.56 ball	6.6	129,855	162,500	17.1	21.5
.30 cal machine gun	66.7	5,822	6,396	19.4	21.3
40 mm	1.8	21,900	18,840	14.6	12.6
All others	—	—	—	51.3	65.8
				300.8 S/T	390.6 S/T

Source: Message, Maj. Gen. Ira A. Hunt, "Reply to CINCPAC ASG 190324Z Jun 74," 020819Z July 1974, Headquarters USSAG, Nakhon Phanom, Thailand.

1973 and the weapon densities for 1 November 1973 and 1 June 1974 and computes a DOS, using the 1 November ASR and the weapon densities on 1 November and 1 June. Between November 1973 and June 1974, as shown, the influx of ground weapons to build up FANK's firepower and mobility created a ninety-short-ton increase in a day of supply, a 30 percent increase in requirements. There was no attendant increase in air or naval weapons densities at that time.

Measurement of Cambodian Intensities of Combat

The most important variable in determining ammunition expenditures was the intensity of combat. Obviously, the same variables used to measure combat intensity in South Vietnam obtained for Cambodia. In Vietnam, the problem was initially one of curtailing artillery ammunition expenditures, and the measurement formula was developed to assist with that. The RVNAF had good combat data; in fact, we had a data card on every incident generally within forty-eight hours of its occurrence. However, in Cambodia we had to develop a data collection system to obtain basic casualty and incident data from each Cambodian military region on a weekly basis. Using the same combat inputs as for the RVNAF formula—that is, the number of contacts, the number of attacks by fire, and casualty data—we developed the following formula to give us a rough handle on combat intensity and therefore ammo expenditures:

$$\text{Cambodian CIF} = \frac{\text{Total Casualties}}{\text{Friendly Strength}} \left(\text{Total Contacts} + \frac{\text{enemy ABFs}}{3}\right)$$

This Cambodian CIF was derived for macroscopic use only—that is, for the country as a whole or for a military region, not for individual battles. In Cambodia, because of the enclave strategy, the number of attacks by fire was double the number of minor contacts, and such factors as the duration and intensity of attacks by fire would be accounted for by the number of casualties. This also would apply roughly for minor contacts, more than 96 percent of all contacts. The wars in Southeast Asia were primarily a series of minor incidents punctuated periodically by major battles. The Cambodian CIF was necessarily more simplistic initially than the South Vietnamese CIF. When we obtained more detailed data on Cambodia, we applied the RVNAF formula to both countries.[55] As a matter of interest, when applied to Cambodian data, both formulas had a good degree of correlation, except for very intense combat situations. The CIF formula shown here is only one of many possible measures of combat intensities.

We had the inputs necessary to make a relative analysis of ammo expenditures as a percentage of an adjusted day of supply. For comparative purposes, we used the same November 1973 authorized supply rate and took into consideration the increasing weapons densities to compute the actual day of supply, which we then adjusted to reflect varying combat intensities, using a scale of 1.00–1.50 (with 1.00 being the lowest level [October 1973] and 1.50 being the highest level [June 1974]). This gave an adjusted day of supply. Actual ammo expenditures divided by the adjusted DOS for the same period provided what we then called the conservation ratio.

As the conservation ratios for the 23 May to 24 June 1974 period of high-intensity conflict (thirty-seven daily contacts, forty-four daily attacks by fire, eighty-five daily friendly casualties, and forty-two enemy KIA per day) was 0.63, it appeared reasonable to establish an ammo reduction goal of one-third, an ammo conservation factor of 0.67. Therefore, during periods of high-intensity combat, ammo consumption should equal the authorized supply rate (the adjustment of 1.5 multiplied by the conservation factor of 0.67 equals 1). In other words, FANK should never exceed the ASR—and for slack combat periods expenditures should be only two-thirds of the authorized supply rate, with variations depending on the level of conflict.

CINCPAC had requested that we forecast Cambodian ammunition consumption for the wet season, 1 July through 31 December 1974 (the first half of FY 75).[153] I was very pleased to do so, since it enabled us to use systems analysis in an extremely complicated situation with many real-life variables to determine a quantifiable factor. To forecast reasonable levels of ammunition expenditures, we had to accept the MEDTC-authorized supply rate, a function of the various line items and the equipment densities associated with the line items, and adjust the densities for additional equipment deliveries; adopt a conservation goal; and predict the intensity of conflict, taking into consideration the enemy's intentions and capabilities, the effect of flooding on friendly operations, and the air force's operational readiness, which was its ability to generate sorties. Our forecast of ammunition expenditures, important in assessing the critical funding situation, could be verified in January 1975 from actual utilizations.

In July, MEDTC reviewed the daily expenditure rates for the previous year and adopted line-item ASRs to reflect those expenditures. The results, which used the July 1974 equipment densities, indicated a DOS of 390 short tons. Therefore, accepting the authorized supply rate of 390 short tons and noting that additional artillery tubes were scheduled for delivery, we forecasted a day of supply to vary between 390 and 400 short tons.

We believed the intensity of conflict should remain relatively high in July (1.30), decrease when the Tonle Sap flooded (1.00), then pick up again late in the year (1.30). Considering the high level of U.S. and Cambodian interest in ammo conservation and the weekly MEDTC personnel ammo inspections in the field, I believed that a conservation factor of 0.67 was feasible.

We thought the air force would continue to improve its maintenance and that the wet season should not materially reduce its capability to generate sorties. The wet season also favored riverine operations; navy forces could resupply enclaves like Prey Veng. Consequently, air and naval ammo expenditures should increase slightly throughout the next six months.

We predicted that the daily ground ammo expenditures would average 310 short tons a day, a 21 percent reduction from the authorized supply rate, appreciably less than the just concluded dry-season consumption of 430 short tons a day. We estimated the air force and navy ammo expenditures at seventy short tons a day, a slight increase from the current level, because of the improved air force situation resulting from its self-sufficiency program.

Thus, as shown in table 19, our operational analysis predicted a consumption of 69,983 short tons during the six-month wet season.[150]

Some at CINCPAC doubted the efficacy of using the CIF adjustment factor to forecast variations in ammunition expenditures from the authorized supply rate, but, as always, the proof would be in the results. In early January 1975, when all ammo utilization data was in, the

Table 19. Projected Total Ammo Expenditures (short tons)

Month	Ground	Air and Navy	Total S/T per day	Total Monthly
July	340	65	405	12,555
August	295	65	360	11,160
September	261	70	331	9,930
October	295	70	365	11,315
November	322	75	397	11,910
December	348	75	423	13,113
Average	310	70	380	Total: 69,983

Source: Message, Maj. Gen. Ira A. Hunt, "Reply to CINCPAC ASG 190324Z Jun 74," 020819Z July 1974, Headquarters USSAG, Nakhon Phanom, Thailand.

actual depot issues as well as the weekly MEDTC ammo field reports were compiled for July through December 1974. We had predicted ground and air utilization at 57,108 and 12,875 short tons, or a total of 69,983. The actual amounts issued were 59,315 for ground, 10,950 for air, a total of 70,265 short tons[154]; field reports had this total at 68,958 short tons.[155] The predicted ammo utilization was only 0.4 percent, or 282 short tons, lower than the 70,265 short tons actually issued. Considering all the variables, this result could be chalked up to pure dumb luck. Obviously, there was a lot of that; underutilization in some months compensated for overages in others. Nevertheless, operational analysis provided clear insights into the variables and gave results that were very helpful for planning purposes.

The purpose of the foregoing combat analysis was to predict ammo consumption in order to evaluate the first half FY 75 procurement costs and determine whether the MAP-CB–allocated funds were sufficient to purchase essential munitions. Four factors influenced the funding determinations: ASR, combat intensity, ammo conservation, and costs.

One would think that once given the quantities of ammo consumption, it would be simple to determine total costs—and it should have been. However, the army arsenal system increased the costs of ammunition every few months, so those responsible for munitions management in Vietnam and Cambodia were frustrated at having to constantly juggle orders and were angry at the apparent unfairness of the system's inflationary trends, which greatly exceeded the U.S. producer price index. The cost increases had a great effect on the amount of ammo Cambodian military assistance funds could purchase. A comparison of costs of ground and air munitions in November 1973 and June 1974 indicated that there was no increase in the costs of air munitions but that in this very short period the cost of ground munitions increased by 64 percent. In fact, CINCPAC indicated that the cost of ammo would continue to increase at approximately 2 percent per month. From MEDTC's point of view, the FY 75 ammo procurement costs for Cambodia were about double those for FY 74, when greater funds were available, a result of both the price increases (64 percent, as mentioned) and increased weapons density (30 percent).[150] Headquarters USSAG called CINCPAC's attention to the escalating cost problems on several occasions. In June 1974, a day's supply of ammo cost slightly more than $1 million. The FY 75 approved ammo funding was for only $160.4 million. Obviously, this rate of expenditure could not be supported.

There were several surprises with respect to ammo costs. Fortunately, the latest army pricing actually reduced the costs of a day's supply of ground ammo by about 15 percent.[157] We learned subsequently that higher headquarters had taken action on the pleas for an ammo cost review. However, the air force's increase in the price of the MK-82 bomb, from $190 to $269 and later to $313, partially offset the ground ammo price reduction. Since these bombs made up a large percentage of the cost of an air day of supply, this increased the total cost by about 26 percent. If our prediction of the first half FY 75 ammo consumption of 69,983 short tons was correct, however, the net result of the cost changes represented a $14 million saving, in effect balancing the ammo funding situation, should Congress approve the $140 million continuing resolution authority for the first half of FY 75.

In late December 1974, the office of the secretary of Defense comptroller evaluated the basis used by the U.S. Army Armament Command to compute the cost of ammunition provided Cambodia during FY 74 and discovered its unit prices were inflated. It cited one example, the 60 mm mortar high explosive round. Effective 18 March 1974, the price of one round had been changed from $10.00 to $17.83. However, documentation on file supported a standard price of only $11.96, and on 1 July the price of the round was rolled back to $12.80.[158] It was no stretch to state that the major variable on the cost of ammunition was its pricing.

Congressional Authorization

Finally, on 19 December 1974, Congress passed the Foreign Aid Authorization Act, which imposed a MAP-CB ceiling of $275 million.[159] This was substantially below the FY 74 program but in line with the $70 million quarterly program in effect. However, there was a serious drawback: MAP-CB would have to fund the costs of packing, crating, handling, and transporting supplies, for which the initial estimate was $51 million. Thus, on 19 December only $224 million was available to the program. As of 31 December 1974, MEDTC already had expended $142.5 million out of the then effective ceiling of $224 million. To make matters much worse, in keeping with the congressional mandate, Washington determined more set-asides each successive month, until finally, on 12 April 1975, the effective ceiling was only $196.7 million. There was little funding available for anything other than vital ammunition. Obviously, this was definitely grossly inadequate to properly support Cambodia.

For budget purposes, MEDTC had forecasted the FY 75 munitions funding requirement at $380.8 million. In its review CINCPAC reduced this to $299.8 million.[156] Ultimately, the funding ceiling was

Table 20. MAP-CB Funding (millions of dollars)

	FY 74 program	FY 75 authorized program as of 12 April 75
Ammunition	$310.4	$160.4
ARMY/SVCS	36.4	23.2
NAVY	9.2	2.0
AF	13.2	7.5
Training	5.8	3.6
Subtotal	$375.0	$196.7
Mandatory set-asides	0	77.1
Total	**$375.0**	**$273.8**

Source: Message, "FY75 CB MAP CRA Funding," 191048Z June 1974, CHMEDTC, Phnom Penh, Cambodia.

$160.4 million, where it had been $310.4 million in FY 74. But in FY 75, FANK's equipment density had increased and the cost of ammunition had escalated, so that in real terms the Cambodians had only one-third of the comparable funds to expend on ammunition in FY 75 as they had in FY 74.[157] The funding crunch meant no equipment replacement and serious shortages of spares, clothing, and other supplies. It was obvious that Cambodia could not survive without additional funding.

The funding situation was dire, and all concerned hoped for additional funding. But what if Congress refused to approve a supplemental? Obviously, Cambodia would have to attempt to survive with the funds in hand—in which case, only the basic tools of war could be requisitioned: ammunition, petroleum, and medical supplies. More than 80 percent of available funding was by necessity spent on ammunition. Distressingly, there could be no funds for uniforms, field gear, or the replacement of combat equipment losses. Now that the packaging, crating, handling, and transportation costs came off the top of approved funding, it was mandatory that these expenditures be held to a minimum. That meant reduced airland supply, which was expensive. Stockage levels had to be expertly managed to preclude airland calls forward when supplies were low. The Mekong resupply must be cost effective and have no ammo barge losses. It is clear why in August 1974 the logistical management of ammunition and the Mekong convoys were so important. FANK had its back to the wall, and all concerned were doing their best with the meager funds they had been given. Cambodia's only hope, like South Vietnam's, was for the U.S. Congress to have a change of heart and approve a supplemental.

The 19 December 1974 congressional authorization was absolutely shocking. It required a massive reduction in ammo utilization. Consequently, in its guidelines for ground ammunition, MEDTC recommended draconian cutbacks, effective 1 January 1975—the day the communist dry-season offensive commenced. The total recommended cost allocation was $650,000 per day, and the total daily tonnage was 290 short tons, the limit CINCPAC had recommended in June 1974.

These guidelines meant major reductions in ammo expenditures just at the commencement of the dry season's increased combat intensity. When confronted by the enemy, the soldiers always used every means possible to fight back, and they would, when necessary, expend their basic loads of ammunition, which they fully expected would be replenished. The individual soldier was not rationed. Could there be some method of munitions management to ensure the discipline necessary to reduce consumption this much without completely demoralizing the armed forces or endangering the combat soldier? Obviously, the answer was *No!* Ammunition would continue to be consumed to meet the level of combat intensity. Therefore, without a supplemental congressional authorization Cambodia was doomed—it would run out of ammunition.

Even though the level of combat had increased, the Cambodian soldiers made great strides in conserving ammunition between 30 January 1974 and 15 November 1974. However, this was in no way proportional across the board. The army made appreciable reductions in artillery, but only a small reduction in mortar use. Consequently, the cost of a day of supply of mortars increased by 10 percent, from $2,315 to $2,553 per ton, as mortars became the primary cost category. However, conservation still brought substantial cost savings. More important, conservation measures create different tactical patterns, so it is vital to continually review consumption patterns to ensure that artificial constraints do not affect battlefield performance (see table 21).

Between the end of January and the middle of November 1975, Cambodia's ground forces cut back daily expenditures greatly, particularly in artillery (from 20,493 rounds to 6,149 rounds) even though the intensity of combat had increased. In January 1974, FANK fired

	30 January 1974		15 November 1974	
	Rounds (DOS)	**Percent of cost**	**Rounds (DOS)**	**Percent of cost**
Individual weapons	—	25	—	27
Mortars	14,822	26	12,555	37
Artillery	20,493	42	6,149	28
All others	—	7	—	8
		100		100

Table 21. Analysis of Cambodian Daily Expenditure Rate of Ammunition

Source: Message, "SEA Ammunition Perspective," nine sections to multiple addressees, 131930Z December 1974, Headquarters USSAG, Nakhon Phanom, Thailand.

0.7 mortars for each artillery round, but in November 1974 it fired two mortars for each artillery round—a huge change in tactics. It is important to note that the intensity of combat had reached a new and much higher plateau, and when a soldier's back is to the wall he will use all the ammo available to him to fight. And rightly so.

The conservation factor for the total conservation period of 26 June 1974 to 24 March 1975 was 86 percent. However, from 1 October 1974 to 24 March 1975, during which period the 1975 general offensive was fought, FANK was 18 percent below the computed allowance. Ambassador Dean, MEDTC, and the joint staff had much more command interest in ammunition conservation than their counterparts in Vietnam because the ground ammunition supplies were visibly critical.

During the conservation period, the army consumed 2,164,000 fewer 105 mm rounds than it had during the base period of 2 January to 25 June 1974. However, to offset this large reduction in artillery, FANK fired over 600,000 more mortar rounds than it had during the same base period. Considering the artillery and mortar mix and the various types of rounds (high explosive, illuminating, smoke), the conservation efforts amounted to a huge saving of $76 million, or 47 percent of the FY 75 $160.4 million ammunition budget.

Cambodia's combat intensity peaked at 83,441 in the first week of January and remained high each week thereafter during the Khmer communist dry-weather offensive. Figure 5 compares the FY 75 combat intensity factors for South Vietnam and Cambodia and vividly displays the dry-season high points.

It is of interest to compare Cambodian and South Vietnamese combat intensity factors and their total ground ammunition expenditures. South Vietnamese artillery ammunition expenditures for FY 75 were double that of the Cambodians, yet the ARVN CIF was only 53 percent greater. As a percentage of the cost of a day of supply, you find the artillery expenditures were 54 percent in South Vietnam, and only 28 percent in Cambodia. FANK greatly increased its mortar use while cutting back on artillery expenditures, which largely accounts for the disparity. Therefore, to me it was of great interest to compare the combat intensities in South Vietnam with those in Cambodia and then to compare the total tonnage of all ground ammunition consumed by both armies. I chose the wet season of 1974 because during it there were

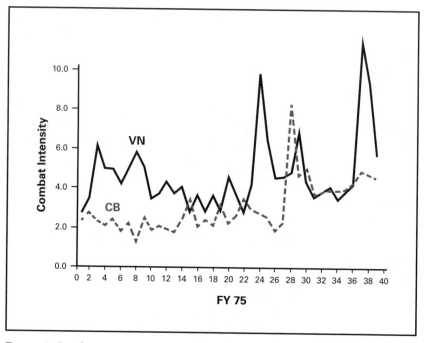

Figure 5. Combat Intensity, in Tens of Thousands, by Week. (Source: "Republic of Vietnam Ammunition Conservation Study," June 1975, Headquarters USSAG, Nakhon Phanom, Thailand; "Khmer Republic Ammunition Conservation Study," June 1975, Headquarters USSAG, Nakhon Phanom, Thailand.)

no major campaigns by the communists and ground ammo consumption data was available for the twenty-six-week period. It should be instructive to see if there were any major differences in relative ammo expenditures.

The combat intensity factors for the twenty-six-week July–December 1974 period in South Vietnam was 46,409 and 24,198 in Cambodia. The ground ammo consumption for the same period for the ARVN was 113,526 short tons, and 59,315 short tons for the FANK. The respective ratios of ammo consumption to combat intensities were then:

$$\text{RVNAF} = \frac{113,526}{46,409} = 2.45 \text{ tons per CIF unit}$$

$$\text{FANK} = \frac{59,315}{24,198} = 2.45 \text{ tons per CIF unit.}$$

With respect to their combat intensities, the two armed forces were expending ammunition at identical rates. Therefore, if one presumes that the responses to a given level of combat intensity should be the same by both armed forces, then the combat intensity factor was indeed an adequate measurement tool.

Utilizing the combat intensity factors as a guide to reasonable firepower responses to enemy initiatives—and accepting that ammo conservation did adversely affect morale and did reduce combat effectiveness—the key question is, "Were the ammunition conservation programs in South Vietnam and Cambodia effective in reducing expenditures from the levels of usage during the base periods?" The answer is unequivocally that the conservation programs in both countries were very effective—much more so than generally realized.

Both countries reduced their ammunition consumption substantially, for which they paid a definite price. If the rates of artillery consumption in effect during the six-month base periods had been continued, then each would have expended over 2 million more artillery rounds than they did with conservation, which gave cost savings of $110 million for South Vietnam and $76 million for Cambodia. As a consequence, when the all-out communist 1975 dry-season attacks began, both countries had more ammo stocks available, which were then rapidly drawn down as the result of the large increases in ammunition consumption rates—that is, the intensive combat rates. Had both forces not conserved ammo, then they both probably would have run out well before January 1975. Thus, by conserving ammunition, they both prolonged the wars and the killing, wars they had no chance of winning because the U.S. Congress refused to authorize adequate funding for ammunition and other combat supplies.

As it was, even with conservation, if the military in both countries had hung on and fought the communists, they both would have completely run out of ammunition within days of their capitulation. The people of South Vietnam and Cambodia could not, and would not, believe that the United States would stand by and abandon them—so they fought on, anticipating forthcoming U.S. air power and supplemental funding. Their faith was misplaced.

The Lifeline of Cambodia

The two main military priorities were always, first, to defend the Phnom Penh enclave, since the capital region, with its seat of government and its population of 3,250,000, was in fact the heart of Cambodia, and second, to maintain the Mekong River line of communications. With all the landlines severed, without the Mekong the crucial logistical support items of food, fuel, and ammunition could not be delivered to the capital enclave in sufficient quantities and Phnom Penh would surely fall to the communists. Logistical airlift support could substitute for the Mekong for short periods, but certainly not for any extended time. A major U.S. effort, then, was to assist the Cambodians in keeping the Mekong open so that Phnom Penh and Cambodia could survive. The efforts to maintain the critical Mekong line of communication, the "lifeline of Cambodia," were little known but vital.

SCOOT

The United States initiated the logistical program to Support Cambodia Out of Thailand (SCOOT) to provide vital ammunition supplies to the Cambodian armed forces via the Mekong River from Vayama, Thailand, to Phnom Penh.[161] The transportation of ammunition was a strictly military function, to be fulfilled by both aviation and waterborne assets. However, two factors became obvious: one, the amount of ammunition required was far greater than the programmed water assets could transport, therefore requiring major airland support, which was, of course, much more expensive; and two, other logistic supplies besides ammo were critically required. Consequently, the SCOOT assets had to be increased to carry the required supplies, thereby reducing airlift requirements, and an administrative and security system for the waterborne Mekong River convoys was required to integrate all supplies and transport them safely. The tripartite deputies assumed the vital administrative and security operations.

The initial SCOOT program went into effect in January 1973 with five tugs and seven barges programmed to carry two thousand short tons of ammo per month. This quantity was woefully inadequate, thus placing primary reliance on airlift delivery. Security was such that there were large losses of cargo. The program remained in effect through December 1973.

The Expedited SCOOT program went into effect in January 1974. Its assets included seventeen tugs and twenty-one barges, and the program was to transport thirteen thousand short tons of ammo per month. Thus, it placed on Mekong convoys primary reliance for the delivery of not only ammo but all supplies to Phnom Penh, where the cargo was redistributed throughout Cambodia. Standoff barges were used to protect the ammo barges and the tugs. Since their inception, the improved protection resulted in no losses. The estimated annual cost was $12 million. Whereas previously only 25 percent of the ammo was shipped via the Mekong, the amount was increased to 75 percent under Expedited SCOOT.

Since all continental U.S. ammunition receipts were transported to Vayama, Thailand, by deep-water vessels, USSAG decided to offload as much of the ammo as possible at Vung Tau, South Vietnam, thereby saving both the deep-water vessel transport to Vayama and the four- to five-day barge trip from Vayama to Vung Tau. There was also much pilferage on the Vayama barge leg by Thai pirates. Thus SCOOT-T (T for transship) was initiated in July 1974.[162]

The SCOOT-T program assets called for thirteen tugs and fifteen barges (plus thirty shield barges) and was designed to transport eleven thousand short tons of ammunition per month,[163] with savings of several millions of dollars that MEDTC then used to purchase ammunition and other essential supplies.[164] By July 1974 the necessary storage level of ammo had been reached at Phnom Penh and the resupply was only necessary to replenish ammo usage. During the SCOOT-T period (July–December 1974) 96 percent of all Cambodian resupply was by the Mekong, 3 percent by airdrop, and less than 1 percent by airland.

All commodities that the Mekong convoys transported to Phnom Penh initiated their voyages in South Vietnam, with the exception of the ammunition barges loaded at Vayama and a few petroleum vessels from Singapore. Rice and general cargo were normally loaded at Saigon, petroleum at Nha Be, and ammunition at Vung Tau. The Mekong River transit distance from Saigon to Phnom Penh was 304 kilometers, of which only ninety-two kilometers were in Cambodian waters. Assembling those disparate cargoes, transported with different types of vessels, operating with different owners, and originating from different ports was a headache, to put it mildly, and it was the responsibility of the tripartite deputies.

The Tripartite Deputies Concept

The basic idea behind the tripartite concept was that the nations of Southeast Asia could improve their resistance to the communist enemy attacks by coordinating their military activities.[165] Soon after the overthrow of Prince Sihanouk in March 1970, the United States began to show its interest in the newly created Khmer Republic by sending officers on fact-finding missions. U.S. and Vietnamese activities in the Khmer soon followed, with the joint Cambodian raids in May 1970. However, no basis for regular contact between the leaders of the respective military forces existed. In December 1970, General Weyand paid a call on Marshal Lon Nol in Phnom Penh, and, although the record is not complete, it appears that they discussed the concept of organizing regular deputy commander–level meetings between the armed forces of the three nations. In any case, such a meeting did take place in January 1971. Weyand was apparently dissatisfied; in his opinion there were far too many attendees. Apparently, however, he could not convince his counterparts that a three-man meeting, of just the deputies themselves, would work best. Since then, almost all tripartite meetings had forty to fifty attendees, including the deputies themselves, their immediate assistants, and the chiefs of the major joint staffs, as well as defense attachés of all three countries, representatives of other interested U.S. agencies, and other minor figures. To conduct the important discussions and agree upon decisions, the principals and their chief advisers normally met before or after the regular session in a group of about a dozen.

The next tripartite deputies' meeting took place in May 1971, at which time the deputies established a monthly schedule. Initially, the meetings were held at MACV headquarters in Saigon, but after the cease-fire agreement in January 1973 the venue was changed to Phnom Penh and the deputy COMUSSAG replaced the deputy commander of the U.S. Military Assistance Command Vietnam as the U.S. representative. The tripartite organization slowly evolved, and the necessary machinery to support the meetings was established. In late 1973 the

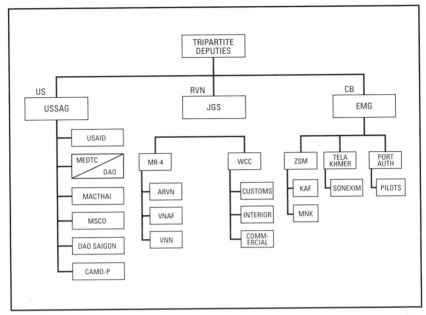

Figure 6. Tripartite Deputies Organization. (Source: Tripartite Deputies Working Group.)

tripartite deputies were Maj. Gen. Thong Van Fanmoung of Cambodia, Lt. Gen. Nguyen Van Manh and Brig. Gen. Tran Dinh Tho for South Vietnam, and myself, representing the United States. The tripartite deputies organization was as depicted in figure 6.

There were four tripartite committee study groups: cross-border operations, coordination of intelligence, communications, and the Mekong air-ground-riverine operations. From the beginning, the U.S. representatives to these groups knew they were to facilitate the solution of their allies' problems and not direct the meetings or promote their own solutions. By late 1973, only the Mekong operation study group had regular U.S. representation. Lt. Cdr. E. M. Graham and Cdr. F. W. Cronin of the U.S. Navy were my senior representatives to these groups, and they did an outstanding job of coordination and assistance.

Working groups would meet during the month to review the situations, discuss problems, and make recommendations. When important matters were not resolved here, they were elevated to the deputies. The monthly meetings had a standardized format. The meetings always commenced with a summary of the military situation in South Vietnam, followed by the one in Cambodia. Then there were discussions of the four working groups, always with the air-ground-riverine Mekong operations (the most important) first. All briefings were published in English, French, and Vietnamese and distributed to the plenary participants in folders. The intelligence and operational situation summaries prepared by the RVNAF and FANK were of inestimable value, as they provided us with insights as to how our allies perceived the military situation. In late 1974, Maj. Jerome Pogorzelski, U.S. Army, and Maj. Barnard Caradec, U.S. Air Force, pulled all this paperwork together for the American side.

FANK's presentation at the 7 February 1975 tripartite meeting illustrates the importance of receiving briefings on the military situations in their respective countries.[166] FANK summarized the military situation around Phnom Penh during the period between 7 January and 3 February 1975:

> During this four-week long period, the enemy exerted his heavy pressure progressively, however no significant action was recorded.
>
> After some limited offensives against our positions around the PP/SMR as well as against our garrisons of Kompong-Cham and Kampot Provinces, there was a new pause.
>
> However, the enemy maintained his firm pressure on our positions locating along the Mekong River and continued his efforts against our boat convoys.

It concluded:

> After one month of offensive around the PP/SMR and along the Mekong River, the enemy fails in his undertaking. In fact, if he can achieve some local success at the beginning, such as the dislodging of our defense line, particularly in the western and northwestern fronts, and if he gains the terrain in the North and in the West of the Capital, he is not able, so far, to occupy any objectives anticipated: Ang Snoul, Kantauk, Pochentong, Prek Phneou and Chrouy Changwer. However, the enemy succeeds in moving his heavy weapons into the areas where he can launch attack by fire on our sensitive installations with effectiveness.

> In spite of his deployment of very important forces and means of fire as well as his multiplication of obstacles on the river, the enemy fails on the Mekong.

There was no question that FANK had dealt the communists a stunning defeat in the northwest sector of Phnom Penh in January 1975. However, the Mekong situation was a disaster: the enemy controlled the riverbanks, and in January and early February the convoys lost three petroleum tankers, two cargo vessels, four tugs, and a self-propelled barge. It was difficult for us to make the Cambodians realize the criticality and to respond quickly and in force at the Lower Mekong. The lack of a sense of urgency foretold the eventual outcome. FANK's aggressiveness was about depleted. They were worn down.

By far the most important function of the tripartite deputies was the security of the Mekong. This was a most complex issue, more so since late 1973, when the resupply of Cambodia via the Mekong was greatly increased. Coordination involved three countries, many ministries, dozens of organizations, and complex contractual relationships. We gradually unsnarled the complex problems of the Mekong convoys, but not until we expanded our charter from resolving only military issues to investigating the economic and political ones.

Obviously, communications is the foundation upon which information is reciprocated. Initially, it was hard to obtain compatible equipment and then get the South Vietnamese and Cambodians to utilize it. In April 1974, the respective forces accomplished a successful test of the Cambodian MR-6/South Vietnamese MR-4 link. Thus, the two adjoining military regions could and did communicate. In January 1975, the chief of the South Vietnam study group notified his counterpart that, according to recent intelligence reports, the communists had succeeded in intercepting and deciphering FANK's radio communications. FANK did not act quickly on the information, so, unfortunately, the Khmer communists were able to relay firing data to FANK artillery units, who, as a result, fired on their own troops.

Since both militaries were most interested in order of battle data, exchange of intelligence was an ongoing affair. Both were particularly concerned with establishing Cambodian liaison detachments at South Vietnamese border outposts as well as having liaison officers with the respective J-2s. By August 1974, they had quadrupled daily radio contacts, were exchanging intelligence daily, and had senior officers visiting regional counterparts. As an example, in January 1975 the FANK disclosed intelligence information concerning the appearance of North Vietnamese tanks in the area south of Krek.[167]

The major effort of the cross-border working group was to prepare an agreement for the coordination of border operations that included concerted and unilateral operations, fire support, and the repatriation of Khmer refugees.[168] The border areas saw many serious combat incidents. In the border areas, the FANK and the RVNAF eventually took on the 1st NVA Division and decimated it to the extent that it was deactivated and the remaining troops transferred to communist units in the Tay Ninh sector.[169] By keeping communications open, exchanging military intelligence on enemy units and activities, and militarily cooperating in operations in the border areas, South Vietnamese and Cambodian forces kept both the North Vietnamese and the Khmer communists off balance and attrited them. Most important, however, the tripartite deputies smoothly effected the ground, air, and naval cooperation and coordination necessary to provide security for the Mekong convoys.

Khmer Logistics Requirements

The Cambodian military also required petroleum products, of course. In less than a year, FANK's vehicle density went from eight hundred vehicles to more than five thousand in 1974, to say nothing of the necessity for aviation gasoline and kerosene for the air force and diesel fuel for the navy.[170] The disruption and destruction of the countryside resulted in a major reduction in the production of rice, Cambodians' staple food; thus both Phnom Penh and the enclaves had become totally dependent on the United States for resupply. In addition, there was also the requirement to supply general cargo—the trucks, tools, and other necessities to operate both the military and the economy. Although the procurement of foodstuffs was USAID's responsibility, the delivery of life-saving rice to Phnom Penh and to the enclaves was mostly the responsibility of the U.S. military—either by Mekong convoy or airland/airdrop.

The provincial enclaves under siege could be resupplied only by airland and airdrop. The Khmer Air Force kept these enclaves resupplied from depots in Phnom Penh, but the U.S. Air Force and their contractors contributed all out-of-country cargo. Whenever stocks were dangerously low or there was an emergency requirement, supplies were normally airlanded at Phnom Penh. However, the most important line of communication by far was the water movement of cargo up the Mekong River from South Vietnam. Deep-water vessels could use Kompong Som, and the three maritime provinces were generally resupplied from there. But with Route 4 interdicted, these supplies could not be moved inland. Although Headquarters USSAG had no responsibility for the purchase and call forward of supplies and equipment, we had full responsibility for the coordination of all transport.

When the communists called off their attack on Phnom Penh in mid-August 1973, the stocks of ammo, rice, and petroleum at the capital had been seriously drawn down, and it was necessary to rapidly build them up in preparation for dry-weather hostilities. In fact, the stocks were at an all-time low: we not only had to meet the current MEDTC and USAID daily requirements, but we had to increase the stockage to required levels, which demanded an understanding of the commodity situations.[171]

Cambodia was an agrarian society; more than 90 percent of its people were engaged in rice production. As the population fled the countryside they left their rice paddies untended; thus, the production of rice dropped dramatically.[172] About half of the Cambodian government-controlled population became refugees. With rice production reduced by about 85 percent, from 3.81 million metric tons in 1969 to 0.56 million metric tons in 1974–1975, the free-market prices rose dramatically—increasing ten-fold between January 1973 and April 1975, far beyond the means of the huge refugee population. Malnutrition and starvation spread. To alleviate the situation, USAID attempted to maintain the Khmer's standard of living. Although that laudatory goal was not possible, since aid-financed imports could not offset reductions in production, the twenty-two AID personnel authorized in country did an outstanding job. The Cambodians became entirely dependent on the United States; without American rice they would certainly starve. Under the PL 480 assistance program, more than 470,000 metric tons of rice was delivered to Phnom Penh, 89 percent of all foodstuffs imported. Our job was to see that it was delivered to the depots. Distributing it to the people was another extremely difficult problem, which USAID handled. In October 1973, the daily PL 480 rice requirement was given as 550 metric tons, and this was certain to increase. In coordination with USAID, we set the Phnom Penh stockage objective at a ninety-day supply.

Petroleum products were essential to both the military and civilian components of the nation. The military required automotive gasoline, diesel fuel, aviation gasoline, and jet fuel. In the spring of 1974, the average daily consumption of petroleum was 690 cubic meters, of which 255 cubic meters were for the military. Use fluctuated greatly from day to day. The utility companies accounted for the major civilian uses of diesel oil and fuel oil, for water and electricity production; more than 63 percent of bulk petroleum was for civilian use.[173]

Funded by USAID, Telakhmer, the state-owned petroleum company, procured civilian supplies, although other petroleum companies (Shell, Esso, Caltex) distributed it. MEDTC requisitioned military petroleum from the DAO office in Saigon. Of the fuel for transit to Cambodia, about 75 percent was obtained at Nha Be, South Vietnam, and 25 percent at refineries in Singapore. Deliveries of petroleum were to Phnom Penh via the Mekong by small tanker vessels, to Battambang by road from Thailand, and to Kompong Som by tanker vessels.

The petroleum allocations, which varied between the wet season and dry season, averaged about 570 cubic meters per day. The storage capacity at Phnom Penh was thirty-five thousand cubic meters, so we established that as an objective. Military storage at Prek Phnom, ten miles north of Phnom Penh, was an additional seventy-five hundred cubic meters.

In December 1973, ammunition deliveries to Cambodia originated from depots in Thailand, where there generally were sufficient munitions on hand to meet requirements. MEDTC desired to maintain ammo stocks in country at a thirty-day required supply rate. The main ammo depot for both ground and air munitions was the Kantauk depot, located within the Phnom Penh perimeter. In varying amounts, stocks were also kept in some twenty enclaves throughout the country. The August 1973 enemy attack showed that the Kantauk depot could

Table 22. Storage Objectives and Replenishment Requirements (metric tons)			
	Depot stockage 1 November	Stockage objective	Monthly replenishment requirement
Rice	6,897	49,500	21,000
Ammunition	8,252	13,605	12,000
Petroleum	14,000	34,300	16,500
Cargo	—	—	7,500
Total	**29,149**	**97,405**	**57,000**

Source: Maj. Gen. Ira A. Hunt, "Increased Use and Secutiry of the Mekong LOC," November 1974, Headquarters USSAG, Nakhon Phanom, Thailand.

be vulnerable in the future. Therefore, MEDTC set the limit of storage there at fifteen thousand short tons, so as not to incur a major loss by sabotage, interdiction, or being overrun.[174]

General cargo was more difficult to get a handle on. During the last half of FY 73 (January–June), a great amount of military supplies was shipped via the Mekong. This fulfilled the accelerated delivery of military assistance equipment—code name NIMBLE THRUST. Although most general cargo was military-funded matériel, there was also civilian cargo. For planning purposes, we estimated that general cargo would be approximately 250 metric tons per day.

The depot stocks and stockage objectives on 1 November 1973 are indicated in table 22.[175]

Not only would the monthly shipments on the Mekong have to increase greatly, from the previous eight months' average of 33,700 metric tons to 57,000 metric tons (a 69 percent increase), but depot stocks of ammo, rice, and petroleum would also have to increase by 68,256 metric tons, or 134 percent, in order to meet the stockage objectives. Therefore, the United States initiated an all-out effort entitled Project PILLAR POST to resupply Cambodia via the Mekong River.[176]

Mekong Convoy Security

The immediate requirements were not only to increase the transportation of supplies and equipment via the Mekong, but to ensure the security of transit. Having determined the transportation requirements, it was necessary to address the security aspects. Since 1973 there had been eighteen severe shipping losses on the Mekong. To prevent further losses we applied operations research to optimize the situation. We had to determine the convoy makeups and schedules, what they should be, what previous damages to convoys were, where and how often they occurred, what weapons were used, whether there were seasonal factors, and finally what could be done to improve convoy security.

First, we reviewed the convoy statistics for the previous eight months (March 1973 through October 1973), as the data was readily available.[177] During the period there were 269,900 metric tons transported by thirty-four convoys totaling 230 vessels, an average of 6.8 vessels carrying 7,900 tons per convoy, with an average tonnage per vessel of 1,160 tons. The average monthly tonnage delivered was 33,700 metric tons, well below the replenishment requirements of 57,000 metric tons per month, to say nothing concerning the pressing need to rebuild stocks. If the current average number of convoys, four per month, were to continue, then the number of vessels per convoy would have to double—to fourteen. Consequently, the current contractual allocation of tugs and barges would have to be increased.

The addition of more tugs and barges to carry ammunition and rice would be no problem, since many were available from shipping contractors. However, there were only ten or eleven available petroleum tankers with the draft necessary to ply the Mekong, and their high profile made them vulnerable. (See photo 5.) At the time, only 40 percent of the petroleum stockage objectives at Phnom Penh were on hand. Consequently, petroleum resupply was critical. Therefore, it was important to determine the optimum Mekong convoy scheduling for petroleum by maximizing the tonnage transported for the given fleet while minimizing the essential troop commitments required to protect each convoy.[178] We concluded that the optimum convoy cycles were an eight-day transit and an eight-day cycle, which we recommended that the tripartite deputies adopt.

About this time Major General Murray, DAO Saigon, received a letter from Lt. Gen. Nguyen Van Manh, RVNAF JGS chief of staff, which stated that too many small special convoys to transport rice and petroleum to Phnom Penh were being requested, causing a difficult security situation for the RVNAF, which had to provide air, ground, and naval support to protect the convoys moving through South Vietnam. He cited two special convoys, one an oil tanker and a rice barge leaving Vung Tau on 17 October 1973 and the other an oil tanker and a rice barge leaving Vung Tau on 21 October. The USAID personnel in Phnom Penh obviously would have to plan to have their vessels join the tripartite scheduled convoys. Not only were these small unscheduled convoys grossly inefficient in transporting commodities, but they greatly disrupted military operations in South Vietnam's MR-4. The Cambodians had the same problem as the South Vietnamese, since air cover was essential, as was the insertion of ground troops at choke points. Each convoy, whether it was large or small, required the same security efforts.

Analysis of convoy security resulted in several major findings.[179] Summary data from January 1972 until November 1973 indicated there was slightly more than one attack by fire per convoy and that all of these attacks resulted in eighteen instances of severe loss or damage. While this was a loss rate of only 1.6 percent, from a funding aspect these were ill-afforded losses. In the first nine months of 1973 the enemy sank four ammo barges, resulting in 2,534 metric tons of ammo being lost. The ammo losses amounted to $4.7 million—an amount MEDTC certainly could not afford. To understand the security situations, we had to determine where the attacks against the convoys were occurring, when and how they occurred, and whether there were any special factors in convoy makeup or discipline that affected matters.

An analysis[180] of the 140 communist attacks against convoys traveling on the lower Mekong (that is, south of Phnom Penh to the South Vietnam border in 1972–1973) indicated that ninety-one were against northbound convoys and forty-nine against southbound convoys. Further, ninety-three were from the east banks and forty-seven from the west banks (see photo 5). All the attacks occurred in four key areas in the ninety-two kilometers from the South Vietnam border to Phnom Penh. The solution to suppressing enemy attacks by fire was, of course, to have the Cambodian military occupy the banks at these critical locations (see figure 7).

The Mekong River is more than four thousand kilometers long, and it drains an area of 795,000 square kilometers. It begins to rise

Photo 5. Convoy Passing through Mekong Narrows at Peam Reang Island with Petroleum Tanker on Fire. (Source: Headquarters USSAG, Nakhon Phanom, Thailand, produced by 432nd Reconnaissance Technical Squadron, U.S. Air Force.)

in May, following the onset of the southwest monsoon, and attains its maximum level in September or early October. At Phnom Penh, the river height is well over thirty feet in October, falling to a height of only seven to eight feet in April. During the dry season it is below its banks and the channels are narrow, giving the enemy a much easier time interdicting convoys. In 1972–1973 there were 1.6 attacks per convoy in the dry season and only 0.6 attacks in the wet season; in other words, a convoy was 2.6 times as likely to receive an attack in the dry season. Figure 8 displays this information graphically for 1973. Since the convoys usually cleared Tan Chau in early morning, the transits, which

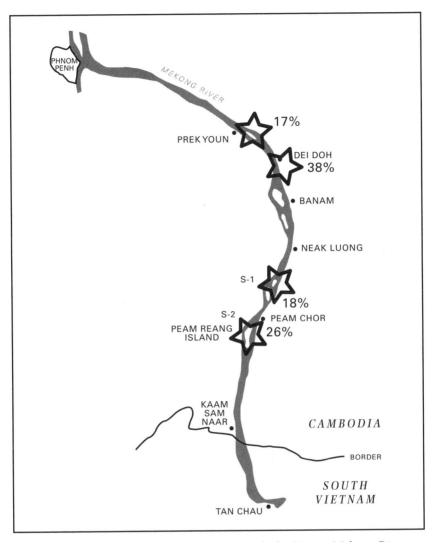

Figure 7. Locations of Khmer Communist Attacks by Fire on Mekong River Convoys. (Source: USSAG briefing, "Analysis of Mekong Convoy Security," 22 March 1974, Headquarters USSAG, Nakhon Phanom, Thailand.)

took anywhere from eight to twenty hours, were normally completed during daylight. The hours of attack, which depended on the convoy location, were generally in daytime. There were very few late afternoon attacks, and none were at night. Perhaps the key was to sail at night.

Next we asked what the nature of the attacks was. Crews could tell

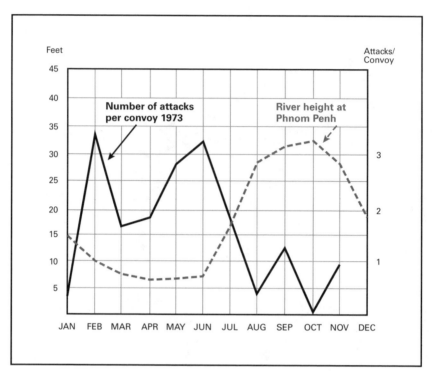

Figure 8. Height of Mekong River and Attack Rate. (Source: Headquarters US-SAG, Nakhon Phanom, Thailand.)

the weapons utilized in 102 of the 140 attacks on convoys. Normally, multiple weapons were fired, and the 75 mm recoilless rifle was the predominant attack weapon—utilized in over 53 percent of the identified attacks—with rocket-propelled grenades being a secondary means of attack.[181] The B-40 and B-41 rocket-propelled grenades' range made them effective in the dry season, when the river was narrow. However, the recoilless rifles could be effective all year around. In South Vietnam, my unit, the 9th Infantry Division, had encountered these weapons, which the enemy effectively used against defensive positions since its penetration capabilities were great. We made the weapons ineffective by erecting in front of our positions simple chain-link fences. Incoming rounds detonated on the fences and spent their lethal penetrating cores before they struck the defensive positions. Obviously, this was a solution to the communists' most destructive weapons. And sandbags could effectively protect against machine guns, small arms, and mortars.

Many advocated small convoys as the method to transit because the naval escort vessels could concentrate on protecting only a few vessels instead of being spread out along the length of a large convoy. Analysis of the data, however, indicated that except for the very small convoys of three vessels or fewer, and the very large, nineteen vessels or more (for which we had data on only one convoy), convoy size made no difference.

A debrief of the Cambodian naval escorts and the captains of the tugs and vessels indicated that the KC had built entrenched locations at choke points from which they attacked and that the attacks had a set pattern. As the convoy passed the enemy interdiction location, all of its positions would open fire simultaneously, each concentrating on a single vessel. Since not every enemy position had recoilless rifles or rocket-propelled grenades, this meant that only a few vessels were subject to lethal fire.[180]

In summary, to increase convoy security the Cambodians must position troops at known attack locations, use aircraft and artillery to suppress fire, consider travel at night, and use sandbags, sheet metal, and fencing to protect vessels and cargo. In general, each convoy required the same security efforts. Attacks by fire were a function of the number of convoys and generally not of the number of vessels in the convoy.[181] Therefore, the tonnage per convoy must be increased. Already in December, 67,006 metric tons were shipped, doubling the sizes of previous rice and ammo shipments.

To counter enemy threats, FANK implemented its Mekong Special Zone Plan, which had five main components: troop dispositions, artillery, air support, riverine protection, and overall coordination.[182] Thirty-two tubes of artillery provided coverage over the complete length of the Mekong in Cambodia. To coordinate these artillery units, the joint staff established a fire support coordination center at the Mekong Special Zone headquarters in Neak Luong. In all, FANK provided the equivalent of twenty-eight battalions on the Lower Mekong. The air force flew missions to provide continuous air cover and utilized tactical air strikes when available.

On the Lower Mekong, the navy had sixty-five vessels operating.

MNK briefed convoy security at the pre-sailing conference in Tan Chau, South Vietnam. The navy was responsible for coordinating convoy security, and it did a systematically effective job. Once the convoy was under way, to maintain communications security after the pre-sail conference, the navy passed a message to all concerned, citing frequencies and check point locations.

With my idea of standoff fencing, which could be installed relatively cheaply and expeditiously, headquarters USSAG developed a plan for protecting ammo barges, and on 8 December 1973 we forwarded the plan to the Military Sealift Command, Far East, in Yokohama, Japan.[183] It called for standoff fencing to protect against rocket-propelled grenades and recoilless rifles.

While watching the unloading of ammunition barges at Phnom Penh, I noted that the multiple layers of sandbag protection that had been placed on top of the ammo created major unloading problems, since the sandbags took a considerable amount of time to remove and often split, causing additional problems. It was important to reduce the turnaround time, since the dock area was relatively unprotected. Analysis of major attack positions along the Mekong indicated that the enemy usually fired at the ammo barges from an elevation of two meters or less and at a distance of three hundred to eight hundred meters. The slight angle of incidence to the top of the barge resulted in a flat trajectory. Therefore, I recommended using sheet steel for overhead protection, which would ensure ricochets and would be easier to both emplace and remove with cargo-handling equipment. Such covering could be easily stored and would reduce the net weight of protective material, thus increasing the ammo storage capacity.

Subsequently, to increase the chain-link standoff distance and enable more ammo cargo per barge, we recommended the use of shield barges, which would be towed alongside the ammo barges. This created much static for many reasons; most predominantly, some supposed that it would slow the tugs' advance. Regardless, we prevailed, and four deck cargo barges were outfitted for a trial run (see photo 6).

Meanwhile, on 18 February 1974, northbound convoy TP-71 was attacked and the ammunition barge *Mt. Hood* was hit by recoilless rifle and machine gun fire and sank, taking with it 1,097 metric tons of ammo. This unfortunate incident gave great impetus to the protective barge project.

Photo 6. Barge Protection on the Mekong River. (Source: Headquarters USSAG, Nakhon Phanom, Thailand, produced by 432nd Reconnaissance Technical Squadron, U.S. Air Force.)

Investigations had determined that the most suitable support system for the proposed standoff protection system was the deck cargo barges in the ARVN watercraft fleet. To facilitate the project, the South Vietnamese cooperated fully and arranged immediately for the transfer of fourteen barges.[184] The first four shield barges were completed in early March and tested on 6–7 March, with excellent results. However, several of the tug masters believed that with the shields protecting the ammo barges, the tugs themselves would become targets. They also cited their potential loss of maneuvering capability, should a barge part a line or have any other problems. The tug masters changed their tune once they actually used the shield-barge concept. Mr. Benito Cirera, the master of the motorized tug *Polaris,* wrote, "In the opinion of the undersigned the shield barges is a commendable if not magnificent improvement to our present securing arrangement."[185]

The enemy attack against TP-84 on 24 May 1974 provided the first opportunity to measure the escort barge concept's effectiveness at protecting critical ammunition cargo. One of the seven screen barges took three hits. One round created a ten-by-five-foot hole, another a basketball-sized hole, and the third ricocheted off. The ammo remained undamaged.

It took several months to put our recommended convoy procedures in place, but by March 1974 we had procured the screen barges and limited the convoys to four sailings per month, but with many more vessels per convoy. The MNK had their riverine procedures working, and marine battalions occupied several of the key choke points. However, the plan required at least three additional marine battalions. The navy generally supported each convoy with twenty to thirty vessels. Yet, on some occasions the employment of navy vessels was less than optimum, and upgrading was needed. The number of sorties flown in support of the convoys increased greatly. The air force's ability to strike threat areas and react to attacks was much improved. The fire support coordination center improved artillery effectiveness, facilitating artillery employment against targets of opportunity.

In spite of all the improvements, there were still several areas of concern. To ensure maximum utilization of assets, the Seventh Air Force flew reconnaissance flights during convoys and analyzed the results. The use of large numbers of small and sometimes underpowered rice vessels was a major problem; over the previous several months USAID had chartered such vessels to transport rice and grain to Phnom Penh. These vessels stretched out convoy lengths; photographs show one convoy in excess of twenty kilometers.[186] Discipline materially degraded when the convoys extended over great distances, severely straining both naval and air force assets. Lately, the enemy had been able to pick and choose its attack times almost free from countermeasures. Convoy vessel crews had been used to at least a one-to-one relationship between naval and commodity vessels, and they were unhappy. Therefore, to improve convoy security the tripartite deputies imposed a ceiling of twenty powered vessels per convoy, with each vessel having an over-ground speed of at least three knots. The forthcoming flood season—when the Mekong currents would increase from one knot between December and June to two knots in July–August, and to three or four knots in September–November—would only exacerbate the problem with the small, underpowered rice vessels.[187]

Notwithstanding the rice vessel problems, a review of convoy statistics indicated that there had been significant improvement when comparing the dry-season periods of the improved Mekong security—that is, March through June 1974 with the same period in 1973. In 1973 there were 208 transits, carrying 176,516 short tons, and forty-nine vessels were hit, including eight sunk and four beached. In 1974 there were 530 transits, carrying 300,732 short tons, and forty-five vessels were hit, with only one beaching.

The *Bonanza III*, part of TP-88, carrying two thousand metric tons of rice, received a grenade round in its engine room, which caused a fire, and thus on 28 June 1974 the vessel was beached at Peam Chor, losing its cargo. Although only 8 percent of the vessels in the 1974 period were hit, as compared to 24 percent in the 1973 period, the Phnom Penh run was still very dangerous. In both years four crew members were killed. Running the enemy's gauntlet of fire took great courage. However, in the 1974 period there were no SCOOT ammo tug casualties.

By early summer, the Phnom Penh stockage objectives for rice, petroleum, and ammunition had been met, and analysis indicated that either three or four convoys per month, consisting, respectively, of nineteen or fourteen vessels per convoy, could meet necessary stock replenishment requirements.

Without a doubt, the major convoy problem area was the lack of security provided by the Khmer Navy. In the early days the SCOOT program had a goal to transport two thousand metric tons per month. In those days, each tug could be protected by several river patrol boats. However, as the war increased in intensity and refugees by the hundreds of thousands fled to Phnom Penh, the requirements for ammo, rice, and petroleum increased greatly, necessitating more vessels to be protected by the same military assets. The navy and air force assets, consequently, were spread thin, and the convoy crews became disenchanted. But the navy's tactics also left much to be desired, since the navy would not aggressively counter the enemy attacks. Further, the marines were not sweeping the ground at the hot spots. Starting in June 1974, complaints from ship masters began to surface.[188] On 14 December the vice president of SEAPAC Inc. wrote: "As much as the tug officers and crew are aware that it is part of the deal to be fired upon, although this is not stipulated in the Service Agreement in so many words, they also know that they are supposed to be provided with sufficient military protection. The protections they are afforded, are inadequate and not properly executed." Others stated, "To continue in this work under the present circumstances is the height of recklessness." They wanted reassurance, or else they would withdraw their assets from the program.[189]

The level of attacks by the enemy on Mekong convoys did not abate during the 1974 wet season as it had in the past. In fact, late in the year the communists began increasing their forces on the lower Mekong. Aerial photos indicated new individual and crew-sized weapons bunkers throughout the area and that the enemy was possibly constructing barricades at two locations south of Neak Luong. The communists had an estimated forty-one battalions on the lower Mekong. Unquestionably, steps had to be taken to improve Mekong security. Obviously, the forthcoming dry season was going to be a difficult one.

Notwithstanding the problems, a review of Mekong security for calendar year 1974 indicated that it had been a successful year:

> Of all commodity inputs to Cambodia, 94 percent were via the Mekong (781,100 short tons), carried by fifty-two northbound convoys. There were seventy attacks by fire, and ninety vessels were hit, resulting in the loss of

four vessels carrying 6,006 metric tons of cargo. One ammo barge was sunk in February, but none since screen barges had been used. Cargo losses were 0.8 percent.

Of all the attacks, 96 percent were in four areas, highlighting the necessity for more troops at these locations. The real test of security was to come in the 1975 dry season. It was one thing to know the security shortcomings, but it was another to motivate the Cambodians to overcome them.

1973

June Attack on Phnom Penh

By the summer of 1973, with MEDTC's expert advice and assistance, FANK had made great progress in its reorganization. At that time the military assistance–supported force included 166 infantry battalions, about 200 aircraft, and 150 boats. Although reorganized and streamlined, FANK was still deficient in the organizational and technical skills necessary to conduct a major coordinated military campaign. However, it was receiving modern military equipment that greatly improved its firepower and mobility, which at the time provided the edge over the communists. In late June 1973, with fifty-four battalions, the enemy initiated a major attack against Phnom Penh. The situation was tough, but the newly formed infantry units, supported by the formidable U.S. air power, plus the firepower provided by ninety-one tubes of recently delivered artillery, successfully defended Phnom Penh. The enemy called off the attack on 15 August—coincidentally, the same day Congress mandated a halt to all U.S. air support of Cambodia.

At the time, many observers believed that without U.S. air support Cambodia could not possibly hold off the forthcoming communist dry-season offensive. However, recognizing the loss of firepower, the United States effected an accelerated delivery of artillery, M113s, radios, vehicles, and air and watercraft to build up Cambodia's firepower and mobility. The standardized organizations and equipment enabled the divisions and brigades to get a better handle on their situation. Additionally, a direct air support center and an artillery fire support coordination center were established in the summer of 1973 and integrated with the FANK operations center. (USSAG maintained radio contact with the operations center as well as with the MNK headquarters.) This newly improved command and control was of immediate benefit in the battle for Kompong Cham, which called for coordinated efforts by all three services.

The communists had reinforced their forces around Kompong Cham, and on 24 July 1973 they launched an attack, overrunning several villages. They followed this with a 17 August attack against Kompong Cham itself, and by 7 September they had succeeded in occupying peripheral areas of the city as well as the central marketplace, where heavy street fighting occurred. Between 18 August and 14 September, with newly arrived air force C-123s and the boats of the Khmer Navy, the Cambodians reinforced the city with four brigades of four battalions each and a navy task force. They launched offensive operations on 21 September, and they forced the communists by 2 October to begin to withdraw and by 21 November to ultimately redeploy. The combined efforts of the army, air force, and navy contributed to the success at Kompong Cham and gave morale a big boost. The stage was now set for the commencement of the 1974 dry season.

In early December 1973, Lt. Gen. Lon Nol requested a meeting with Gen. Timothy O'Keefe, the USSAG commander. O'Keefe presented him a thoughtful talking paper, covering three subjects: the spirit of the offensive, lines of communication, and joint command and control.[190] In essence, it noted that FANK generally had been oriented on the defense of population centers and had conducted few offensive operations. It listed the definite benefits to the offensive side, as it keeps opposing forces off balance, gains psychological advantages, receives favorable press releases, influences world opinions, and normally can influence events to its liking. It also stated that next to the defense of Phnom Penh and the implementation of the Mekong river plan, in the interest of lines of communication the clearance of Highway 4 was the highest priority item. Finally, it stated that we were very encouraged by the great improvement in joint command and control, particularly with the steps that had been taken to integrate air support with ground operations and the navy's contributions. A strong air force was essential, and O'Keefe suggested improved coordination between the army and the air force.

Map 8. Cambodia, Major Routes and Enclaves. (Source: FANK, Cambodian Joint Staff, Phnom Penh, Cambodia.)

Route 4 was one of the major ground lines of communication connecting the deep-water port of Kompong Som to Phnom Penh. In late 1973 and early 1974, the security of Route 4 was a major FANK objective; if the route could be secured, then the major resupply of Phnom Penh could be more easily effected over this 210-kilometer route than by using the Mekong River or by airlanding supplies (see map 8).

At least two-thirds of Route 4 runs through dense forests, mountainous areas, and high passes dotted with more than thirty major bridges and numerous culverts, making it vulnerable to enemy interdiction. The communists had three to five battalions between Kompong Som and Kompong Seila and four to six between Kompong Seila and Phnom Penh. Should extensive convoy activities commence, the enemy could be expected to reinforce the area.[191]

FANK had eleven infantry battalions deployed along Route 4 from three different brigades whose average strength was about 250 men. The Route 4 special zone commander controlled only the twenty-six territorial force companies, with an average strength of sixty men, which were positioned at outposts along the road and the ten artillery positions with 105 mm howitzers spaced along the route to provide fire support. Although FANK had substantial forces committed to Route 4 security, their success was limited because of command and control problems. A single unified command was necessary to ensure immediate response to any enemy-initiated action.[192] FANK also had to improve the positioning of artillery platoons for proper overlapping coverage and mutual support. But the real problem boiled down to its not having the manpower to form additional territorial force companies to secure the new fire support bases.

In December 1973, the joint staff directed the 1st FANK Infantry Division to clear Route 4 west of Kompong Speu. This was the first time the newly organized full division conducted an offensive operation, and some operational shortcomings were to be expected as the unit progressed up the learning curve. The assistant army attaché's field report was most enlightening; after one month the 1st Division had cleared only two kilometers of the fifteen controlled by the enemy.

The attaché reported that the division's plan lacked imagination and often violated basic elements of sound tactics. The division commander never once brought to bear the full combat power available to him; rather, he committed it piecemeal or kept it in reserve. He parceled M113s out to the brigades and did not use them effectively to take advantage of their firepower and maneuverability. However, he did use artillery and air support fairly effectively. Slowness and caution characterized the division's operations; it forfeited any possibility of achieving surprise. The 48th Brigade commander and several battalion commanders were in faraway Phnom Penh when their units were supposedly conducting a decisive engagement. Some infantry battalions had only about 150 personnel in the operational area, and the average operational strength was between 150 and 250 troops, out of 512 authorized. The almost daily enemy contact or harassment by fire, combined with relatively high casualties, high sick rates, and long separations from families lowered the morale in some units. However, the 1st Division opened Route 4 on 6 January, mainly because the communists withdrew troops to attack Phnom Penh. Later on, the division did achieve some significant successes; these resulted in a marked improvement of morale at all levels.

In 1973, the army had made substantial progress in its reorganization into military assistance–supported divisions and brigades. The major equipment infusion of artillery, M113s, and aircraft had strengthened both its firepower and maneuver capabilities. More important, FANK had successfully defended Phnom Penh, defeated the enemy at Kompong Cham, and resisted major enemy attacks at Takeo. Yet it had a difficult time keeping Route 4 open, and in October and November the communists managed to overrun several large towns. Notwithstanding these setbacks, FANK was definitely an improved force on paper, but it still lacked the leadership necessary for it to become fully operationally effective—and it had endemic manpower problems.

At year's end we noticed the redistribution of communist forces, reflecting a major buildup in the Phnom Penh area—to fifty-nine battalions, much greater than the thirty-five it had available at the initiation of the summer offensive. Countrywide, the enemy had increased its forces by about ten thousand troops and increased the number of operational battalions from 121 to 166. Many of the new units had not been battle tested, and the communists appeared to be going through a protracted period of minor skirmishes outside the Phnom Penh area to gradually test their new battalions. Once these forces had been battle tested, they would move to Phnom Penh. Additionally, we expected that once the rice harvest had been interdicted in the Battambang area four or five more battalions would be available for the main attack against Phnom Penh, which had always been the communist key objective. In 1974 the enemy would have more battalions with tighter command and control and therefore could be more effective. At the same time, however, limited junior leadership, understrength units, and possible shortages of rice and ammunition mitigated against their success.

1974

The Dry-Season Attacks

A well-planned dry-season attack on Phnom Penh proper kicked off on 6 January 1974. The enemy found a weak spot in the northwestern sector of the capital defenses and attacked with fifteen battalions. It pushed to within four kilometers of the Pochentong airbase, the most serious threat of the war. FANK reacted by ordering into the area of conflict two battalions of the 28th Brigade, reinforced with M113s. This rapid reaction, supported by effective close air support, blunted the attack and stabilized the situation. Tactical air sorties flown throughout the day also provided effective support to army units in contact elsewhere. Other enemy forces threatened the southern sector, where there were massive gaps in friendly defenses. Surprisingly, the communists displayed a lack of alertness and aggressiveness, permitting FANK to reinforce the sector in a piecemeal fashion and negating their best opportunity to enter the city. However, on 20 January, in the southwestern sector the enemy managed to move a sizeable force as far north as the Prek Thnot River, putting it within howitzer range of Phnom Penh. The communists fired more than five hundred 105 mm rounds into Phnom Penh, causing absolute panic among the population. One artillery attack on 11 February caused more than two hundred civilian casualties. By the end of February, FANK had halted the attack on Phnom Penh and seized the initiative in the outlying provinces. Its determined defense had created substantial communist casualties, which required the enemy to replace units in the Phnom Penh area with battalions elsewhere. This permitted the Cambodians to conduct highly successful population reclamation projects at Kompong Thom and Siem Reap and to expand the Takeo perimeter. For the time being, the enemy reverted to interdicting the lines of communication and conducting attacks against provincial capitals, particularly Kampot.

The war in Cambodia was unique in many ways. The following intelligence report shows the "light side" of this very real conflict:

> KC battalion 371, consisting of estimated 700 men commanded by Neang-Srey-Dos-Muoy (Translates: Miss Single Breasted Woman) were observed in March 1974 at US820765 on Route 3 en route from Kompong Speu Province to reinforce KC units attacking Kampot town. Twenty pack elephants were transporting the battalion's ammunition and crew served weapons which included two 82MM and four 60MM mortars.

It was obvious that the Cambodians enjoyed both tactical and strategic superiority in mobility, that is—trucks, armored personnel carriers, and aircraft and riverine assets versus the communists' "shank's mare" and elephants.

In April 1974, Ambassador John Gunther Dean replaced Chargé Thomas Enders. Dean was credited with bringing about a negotiated settlement to the civil conflict in Laos, and many, particularly the by now war-weary Cambodians, had high hopes that he might work some magic and broker a negotiated settlement in Cambodia. The word was that Secretary of State Kissinger had instructed Dean to maintain a strong hand in support of U.S. interests, which meant strengthening the government so it could survive and continue to fight the communists until they could be brought to the negotiating table. The pragmatic Dean realized the importance of energizing FANK so it could obtain the upper hand in the current stalemated military situation. Recognizing this, Headquarters USSAG proposed a "think piece" reviewing the current situation and proposing a concept of strategic mobility that, if implemented, would materially assist Cambodia in reacting to the upcoming enemy initiatives.[193] General O'Keefe forwarded the study in May.

It is important to note that after being repulsed at Phnom Penh, the KC overran Oudong at the end of March and Kompong Luong in April, both towns situated on the key Route 5 line of communication.

Thus, the FANK was hard-pressed to protect provisional targets or even execute the third phase of the dry-weather campaign—to open Route 5 to provide access to the agricultural area of Battambang/Pursat. At this time Kampot, Prey Veng, and Lovek were under siege.

Military Strategies

USSAG noted that the primary objective of enemy forces was the capture of Phnom Penh. The second major assault on Phnom Penh, in January 1974, greatly exceeded the May 1973 attack: the enemy used more artillery, rockets, and ground troops in multipronged but uncoordinated attacks. There was little doubt that the enemy would attack again, and in greater strength than previously. Subsequent to the major attacks on Phnom Penh, so as to maintain the initiative and keep the pressure on the government, the enemy had always mounted selective assaults against major provincial capitals. It continuously interdicted the main communication routes.

The Cambodians' military strategy was the obverse: to defend Phnom Penh, protect provincial capitals, and keep the lines of communication to Phnom Penh open. Their first priority, mirroring the communists', was to defend Phnom Penh, which also meant protecting Pochentong Airbase and the Mekong, the two absolutely vital means of resupply.

Looking to the combatants' strengths and weaknesses, the enemy had expanded its force structure, improved its combat capability, and obtained increasing levels of material support from North Vietnam. Its personnel strength had doubled to more than sixty thousand in a year, and to improve command and control it created three divisions and doubled their battlefield commands, regiments, and battalions (see table 17). On the battlefield, the enemy had exhibited a higher degree of leadership and initiative at all levels and demonstrated an aggressive offensive spirit. These improvements in material support aside, the enemy's most significant weakness was his limited ability to support forces in sustained combat. The lack of both tactical and strategic mobility also limited enemy capabilities.[194]

The Cambodians' major strengths were firepower, strategic mobility, and sustaining power. The FANK had recently greatly improved its coordination and integration of air, artillery, and naval gunfire in support of operations. The armored personnel carriers also had added shock effects. The close air support had materially improved, and the navy provided effective support for marine forces operating along riverbanks. Just as important, the air force, with its C-123s, and the navy, with its naval assets, provided the capability to deploy forces and equipment rapidly in response to enemy initiatives. The GKR's current advantage in sustaining power depended solely on continued U.S. logistics support. FANK's major weaknesses remained its progressively deteriorating personnel situation, lack of leadership and command initiative, weakness in the planning and execution of operations, and failure to capitalize on its advantages in mobility.

USSAG Concept

The USSAG staff conducted an operational analysis of the major battles in Cambodia, separating them into government successes and losses.[193] On the one hand, where FANK did not reinforce or attempt reinforcements and where there was also a paucity of artillery firepower, it lost. In every case, the losses occurred in twenty-three days or less. On the other hand, where it did reinforce and where there were adequate artillery tubes, they were successful. The successful battles lasted thirty-seven days or longer. When FANK put up a serious fight, the enemy could not logistically sustain the contact and withdrew.

Looking to the current military situation, in reacting to the enemy's attacks against outlying population centers FANK had deployed seven intervention brigades from Phnom Penh and the Mekong. This left the balance of force in these two key areas about equal. The communists had forty-eight battalions within thirty-five kilometers of Phnom Penh and they could quickly introduce reinforcements from outlying areas. The northwest and southwest sectors of Phnom Penh were both dangerously weak; neither could likely withstand a major enemy attack. So there was an urgent need to reinstate the Phnom Penh defense plan as well as to take aggressive action against the enemy at Lovek, Prey Veng, and Kompong Thom, which were under attack and did not have sufficient artillery support.

Considering these strategic strengths and weaknesses, it appeared necessary to modify the current situation to provide an effective governmental capability for countering enemy initiatives in outlying military regions while maintaining adequate security around Phnom Penh and along the Mekong. Our concept of strategic mobility capitalized on Cambodia's strengths by emphasizing the roles of intervention forces, firepower, and mobility.[195] First, the ninety-one battalions of intervention forces, whose average strength was only 295 men, had to be brought up to full strength and centralized in the Phnom Penh area. Second, the previously submitted modified Phnom Penh defense plan had to be implemented. Last, plans had to be formulated to respond decisively to enemy threats against outlying military regions by employing sufficient intervention forces, firepower, and mobility to counter the enemy. In April 1974, the military region commands had 182 separate battalions, whose average strength was about four hundred men. There was a general balance of forces between the FANK and the enemy at the provincial capitals; thus, reinforcements should be able to stabilize the combat situation and in some cases defeat the enemy. This simple and affordable plan would ensure an effective defense of the Phnom Penh capital military region and, when the security situation permitted, would provide a responsive capability for reinforcing threatened outlying population centers. The concept of strategic mobility depended greatly on the air force's and navy's abilities not only to quickly transport intervention units to the locales undergoing attack, but also to provide additional lethal firepower.

The distribution of friendly and enemy battalions within radii of twenty-five kilometers of provincial towns and thirty-five kilometers of Phnom Penh as of 30 April 1974 indicated that 80 percent of friendly battalions were located in these major population centers, whereas only 70 percent of the enemy forces were.[196] The communists required a large force just to keep the lid on the very restless natives—they used forced communization, harsh discipline, and impressed labor. They had to maintain strict control of the countryside to provide a constant influx of impressed young men and women to expand their combat forces and to make up for the severe casualties the FANK inflicted upon them.

The army did make incremental progress in increasing the strength of the intervention battalions, reaching an all-time high average of 362 soldiers in ninety-four battalions in October 1974, and it did implement the Phnom Penh defense plan. But, more important, it implemented phase 3 of the 1974 dry-season plan and attacked up Route 5 and recaptured Kompong Luong, lifted the siege of Lovek, and in July retook Oudong. These actions cleared the Tonle Sap. Some of these battles took a major toll on the enemy, particularly in its counterattack at Oudong when more than two hundred were killed. As the dry season came to a close, the government had successfully defended and repulsed major enemy efforts against Phnom Penh, Kompong Cham, Kampot, Lovek, and Prey Veng. Morale had improved, and optimism had replaced pessimism for the time being.[197]

In a June 1974 *New York Times* article, David Shipler summarized the Cambodian situation from an observer's point of view.[198] He saw the record at the ending of the dry season as slippage for the Cambodian government and disappointment for the insurgents. He pointed out that by its continuing existence, the government defied the previous August's prognostications that it would not survive without U.S. bombing and put an end to predictions of imminent communist takeover. The rebels had cut Phnom Penh highway links but had not stopped Mekong traffic, and they mismanaged some offensives. Most analysts believed that the rebels' inability to cut the Mekong lifeline was a major failure. Some credited Cambodia's survival to "new-found" military skills. Both sides benefited from U.S. military aid: the government got deliveries, and rebels captured arms. He characterized the war as having no victories or defeats, just slow, unrelenting deterioration in Cambodia's military, economic, political, and psychological facets. Politically, the country was torn by internal dissent, but the military was the real power and not politically restive under Lon Nol. Psychologically, the communist-led troops were demoralized but not panicked.

In mid-July Ambassador Dean critiqued the situation somewhat differently:

Beginning in the middle of May the situation has steadily improved for the GKR's forces. Except for a few minor setbacks, the GKR has expanded government control around Phnom Penh. . . . The vital Mekong River lifeline has been kept open. . . . The Khmer Air Force has demonstrated its ability to provide ever-increasing support to ground and riverine operations, and air-ground coordination has improved significantly. . . . By the middle of July, FANK had clearly seized the initiative from the enemy and was on the offensive throughout the country. The enemy is now reacting to FANK initiatives, rather than vice versa.[197]

There was no doubt that FANK had assumed the initiative and had recently won several major battles around Phnom Penh and several provincial capitals, severely attriting the enemy. Unquestionably, the end of the 1974 dry season was the high point of the war for FANK.

It was always amazing to me to see how much the MEDTC organization of Major General Cleland and Brigadier General Palmer accomplished with a military staff of only seventy-four. The relatively inexperienced Cambodian joint staff was not yet capable of providing effective war plans, nor did the overworked MEDTC have the time to undertake this heavy planning effort. Consequently, in November 1973, at MEDTC's request, Headquarters USSAG had prepared a draft dry-season plan for its consideration, to present to the joint staff. In late May 1974, Palmer requested that our staff prepare a wet-season plan similar to the previous dry-season one. MEDTC listed as important priorities defense of Phnom Penh, maintenance of the Mekong line of communication, opening and securing of a surface route from Battambang to Phnom Penh, and defense of provincial capitals and population centers.[199] It also listed several important points to be addressed: a preparation phase, the missions of the navy and air force, and the Phnom Penh defense.

Once the plan was developed, MEDTC reviewed it and Ambassador Dean approved it. At that time, MEDTC presented it to Lieutenant General Fernandez and the joint staff and finally to President Lon Nol.

Subsequently, USSAG assisted MEDTC in preparing a dry-season plan for the period 15 December 1974 until 30 June 1975. It considered two enemy courses of action: first, that the enemy concentrates its force for a major effort against Phnom Penh and the Mekong Special Zone; and second, it continues its strategy of attacking enclaves and provincial capitals.[200]

In the summer of 1974 Cambodia seized the offensive, and by July it had built up considerable momentum. This was the high point of the war. In June it recaptured the strategic town of Kompong Luong, and its breakout of Lovek enabled ten thousand refugees to be evacuated.

By July, FANK had breached the last enemy defensive line northwest of Phnom Penh and had retaken the historically important city of Oudong.[201] Lon Nol, enjoying the success, invited General O'Keefe and myself with our wives, who were living in Bangkok and whom we rarely saw, to visit at the presidential residence for a luncheon on 27 July. We first called upon Ambassador Dean at the embassy and then, with the ambassador and Brigadier General Palmer, went to the residence, Chamcar Mon, where we were given a briefing by the Khmer on the recently approved wet-season plan. After that, the ladies, who had been on a sightseeing tour, joined the group for lunch. All of the senior Khmer military were present, as was Prime Minister Long Boret. O'Keefe gave an excellent lead-in to a toast to the president and the Khmer Republic. There was a sincerely warm feeling, and the Khmer were deeply appreciative of the U.S. assistance in their conflict. Our wives' presence was a positive signal to all that Phnom Penh was safe and internal affairs were normal.

Although the military situation in Cambodia was at its high point and internal affairs were normal, the capital was always circulating rumors and conducting intrigues. At the end of August 1974, military initiatives around Phnom Penh came to a virtual halt because of the heavy rains, which caused extensive flooding. With military action at a standstill, the local Phnom Penh newspapers filled their space with an increase in local gossip. There was always a certain amount of unrest in Cambodia: civilian unrest resulting from increased prices, military unrest stemming from pay shortfalls, and student/teacher unrest. Several of the press reports alluded to a possible coup, but this time such rumors appeared baseless. Nevertheless, we queried the Phnom Penh Station to see whether there was any substance to it. They replied:

There is currently a flurry of press reports that Cambodia is undergoing coup d'état or something like it. However, officers in Phnom Penh had not seen or heard these reports themselves and reassured that this is not the case, at least as of 25 September 74. However, there is ferment among various significant groups, including FANK military, which creating potentially volatile and unstable situation. Within past day or so, SRF officers in Phnom Penh have produced some substantive in-depth reporting on subjects which indicate that military action against the Lon Nol regime is possible. However, there are no indications that any coup d'état is taking place in Cambodia at this time.[202]

Who Controlled What?

Putting coup rumors aside, the greatest item of interest for Cambodia in the late summer of 1974 was the political battle at the United Nations to determine which government the body would recognize—Lon Nol's or Prince Sihanouk's. Much depended upon which entity controlled the most population. Prior to the war Cambodia had been a peaceful agrarian society. Its last census, taken in 1962, indicated a population of 5,728,711. Its capital, Phnom Penh, was the only city with a population greater than a million. Battambang and Kompong Cham were two medium-sized cities, but the provincial capitals had only ten thousand to fifteen thousand inhabitants each. In 1970, at the outbreak of hostilities, great numbers of the rural population, even whole towns, abandoned their homes and farms. As the fighting became progressively more intense, thousands more were displaced. Most sought safety in and around government-controlled district and provincial capitals. The displaced initially could resume farming on unused areas at the edge of the enclaves where they sought refuge, so they were in great part self-sufficient. Those who remained in place under communist rule quickly became disenchanted, as the communists uprooted entire villages and towns and forced the inhabitants into the countryside, where it was easier to control them and exploit them economically. Many died as the result of harsh treatment. As a consequence, large numbers of the rural people attempted to flee to enclaves under Cambodian governmental control. The refugee situation became desperate; the large mass of people could no longer support themselves—they had no livelihood, no housing, no hope.

As the communists became more aggressive and cut the land lines of communication, many of these enclaves—such as Kompong Thom, Svey Rieng, Takeo, Kompong Seila, and Prey Veng—could only be resupplied by air. Whenever the Cambodian forces became aggressive and reclaimed territory from the enemy, great numbers of Khmers voluntarily fled the communist-controlled areas and sought haven in the government-controlled enclaves. Several hundred thousand liberated rural Khmers sought refuge in controlled territory in 1974. The disruption of the war dramatically reduced rice production, and the rampant inflation increased the already demand-driven prices so that many Khmer people were starving. In 1972, to alleviate this situation, the USAID personnel initiated a program to provide immediate food, shelter, and health supplies and began a resettlement program. AID was successful in distributing rice to the enclaves, and the sustenance drew ever more refugees. With this massive displacement of people, it was important to know who controlled what: far from the conflict within Cambodia, the communists were fighting for the UN's Cambodian seat. In addition to charging that Prince Sihanouk was the head of the rightful government of Cambodia, the communists claimed to control the majority of the population and territory.

It was therefore of U.S. interest to have a determination of the population situation. Headquarters USSAG was primarily interested in the enclave populations, since military resources were involved in transporting essential supplies to Cambodia. So, in mid-1974 General O'Keefe called for a study on population and territorial control in Cambodia. Since access to communist-controlled areas was not possible, USSAG had a unique resource—tactical reconnaissance. Our staff studied reconnaissance photographs in an effort to measure levels of activity in both urban and rural areas and made a special attempt to differentiate between government- and communist-controlled areas. Photography covering twenty-five Khmer communist and North Vietnamese-controlled cities and villages, nine government-controlled cities, and several rural areas under both friendly and enemy control were utilized. In July 1974 USSAG disseminated the "Khmer Population Study," which Capt. Jerry Pickar, 1st Lt. James Lord, and 1st Lt. Glenn Brazelton prepared, to all concerned.[203] This seminal study's conclusions were of inestimable value to those following the Cambodian conflict. The study summary follows:

> Earlier this year analysis of tactical reconnaissance photography of Cambodia indicated that in many cases cities under NVA control had been abandoned and that those cities controlled by the KC were sparsely occupied—in fact, there was very little market place activity and no signs of other types of economic endeavors. As a result of this rather startling

information, it was decided to undertake a study to determine the extent of population control in Cambodia utilizing the unique tactical reconnaissance assets as well as all other available intelligence data.

Urban analysis indicated that the GKR controlled population was mainly concentrated in cities and resettlement villages and that the buildings and facilities in GKR areas which had been damaged by bombing and fighting had been repaired whereas in communist areas they had not been. Analysis of rural areas indicated that most of the land was under cultivation. In GKR controlled rural areas activity was less intense as the distance from the urban areas increased while in KC-controlled areas agriculture was less intense in the vicinity of cities. In other words, the civilian population that formerly resided in enemy controlled urban areas had been dispersed into the country-side where the communists could maintain population control with minimum forces while increasing agricultural production.

The results of this study indicate that the GKR control approximately 66.9 percent of the population residing on 17.9 percent of the land area as indicated in the table below:

Population and Area Control				
Controlling Organization	Population		Area (km)	
GKR	5,348,200	(66.9)	30,560	(17.9)
KC	2,200,400	(27.5)	101,700	(59.5)
NVA	343,000	(4.2)	18,800	(11.0)
INDIFFERENT	108,100	(1.4)	19,940	(11.6)
	8,000,000	(100.0)	171,000	(100.0)

Relating population to military requirements, it was determined that the communists required a force of one soldier per 120 persons for population control. Therefore, about 18,000 KC soldiers are required, and the closer the KC area is to a GKR the more force is required to maintain this control. With a total labor force of about 980,000 men and women, the Khmer communists have enough resources to generate forces to maintain control of their area while at the same time carrying out logistic and operational missions. In the long run the control of the population appears to be the single major issue at stake in the current conflict. As the GKR seizes more military initiative, the liberation of enemy controlled areas will assume much greater importance in future strategic military planning.

The densely populated capitol region (SMR) included 3,250,000 people. The other major populated area was Battambang Province (MR-3), which, because of its rice-producing capacity and transportation connections to Thailand, was self-sufficient. It had a population of 1,650,000. A breakout of area and population control showed Phnom Penh and Battambang Province (MR-3) contained 4,420,000, or 83 percent of the population under Cambodian government control; the rest under GKR control were almost all in the provincial capital enclaves.

From a military standpoint, an item of major importance was whether the communists had a sufficient reservoir of manpower to both replace their large number of casualties and allow them to still control the countryside. According to the 1962 Khmer census, 44.6 percent of the population made up the labor force—51.1 percent of all males and 38.8 percent of all females. Applying this percentage to the 2,200,000 people under communist control would suggest 980,000 were available for military service—more than sufficient untrained manpower. To improve the effectiveness of this reservoir, the enemy established 153 training centers throughout its territory to provide rudimentary military skill training.

How the communists maintained their control is of interest. From the time of Prince Sihanouk's overthrow until mid-1974, for example, the Khmer communist insurgency went through three phases in KC MR-203 and MR-304 (northeast and southeast of Phnom Penh). The massive Vietnamese invasion that culminated in the disastrous defeat of FANK during the CHENLA II operation dominated the first phase (1970–1971), during which the NVA/VC established an administrative apparatus dominated by persons who had been trained in North Vietnam. It also set up training and indoctrination centers for the cadre who would make up the Khmer communist military leadership, some of whom had served in NVA/VC military units, and established lines of communication for delivering military equipment.

Phase 2 began in early 1972, with the withdrawal of North Vietnamese main force units. Those Cambodians who had been trained in the indoctrination centers were the cadre for KC military units. Each battalion had ten or twelve North Vietnamese advisers. The Khmer communist administrative committee then established territorial hierarchical control—regions, sections, districts, villages. As soon as the governmental apparatus was operating, it formed many associations under the banner of Prince Sihanouk to obtain popular support among the peasants. This effort was successful, and it had little trouble obtaining recruits to fill out the army. Phase 2 ended in mid-1973 when the enemy battalions had been trained and equipped and were prepared to launch large-scale main force attacks against government-controlled areas.

The third phase saw the enemy throw off the facade supporting Sihanouk, which initially was necessary to rally the peasants, and have the real Cambodian communists take control in name as well as fact. Most villagers had believed that the revolution's goal was to return Prince Sihanouk to power. Before this, there were no actively enforced social or economic programs; people conducted their lives democratically. Now everything changed, and the communists enforced highly restrictive control over the population. Villagers were forced to join communes; they could not travel outside their villages; they were forbidden to marry; and many were forced to join the military. Whenever they objected, they were forced to relocate to the countryside. Many were summarily executed by stabbing. Moral failures and improper personal conduct, particularly indiscretion with the opposite sex, were regarded as serious offenses, and those guilty were often executed.

The Khmer were predominantly Buddhist, and in the early phases of the communist revolution the communists patronized the Buddhist religion and its monks. In phase 3 the communists imposed severe restrictions on religious practices and traditional ceremonies. They destroyed temples and defrocked monks and forced them to join the military. In one major enemy attack, the communists forced monks dressed in their saffron robes to stand in the front ranks and advance—an unusual method of eliminating them.

Perhaps the most oppressive factor was the rigid communal existence. Within the communized villages, men were separated from women and then all were divided into age groups. Each group was assigned tasks to support agricultural production. They worked, ate, and slept in accordance with a strict schedule. There were only two methods of relief from this life: join the army, or escape to Cambodian government–controlled territory. Since the peasants believed either alternative would end in death, they stayed put and miserable. Obviously, this phase of the communist education outraged a majority of the population. The people's original sympathy for communist goals turned first to apathy and eventually to hatred of the KC. They had been promised democratic equality and had become victims of a harsh, godless dictatorship.

Therefore, it was no wonder that whenever FANK initiated military operations to reclaim lost territory, they received disaffected peasants by the thousands. This swelled the population under government control—but it also added to the burgeoning refugee problem. As an example, in September 1974 Capt. Kenneth Bowra, U.S. Army, reported that an enemy company in the Kompong Speu area had rallied to the government. The unit strength was ninety-two soldiers, of whom seventy were males between the ages of eighteen and forty, twelve were females, and ten were boys between the ages of eight and twelve. Their weapons included M-16s, AK-47s, M-2 carbines, Chinese weapons, 60 mm mortars, and M-26 grenades. Also included was a PRC-10 radio. All were basically uneducated, simple farmers disenchanted with the communists. The communists' harsh discipline had molded a mixed group with disparate weapons into a military unit, yet its communist ideology failed, and when enticed by a government agent they rallied.

There should have been no doubt in any observers' minds as to exactly what treatment to expect from the Khmer communists whenever they successfully occupied territory and subjugated the population. They maintained control over a large area by exercising brutal force; yet there was no question but that the Cambodian government's control over a much smaller area included two-thirds of the population.[203]

The United Nations Seat

In the fall of 1974, the military conflict in Cambodia was being conducted for an important political consideration, the UN General Assembly's recognition of the legitimacy of the Khmer government. The contest, of course, was between the government of Lon Nol, the GKR, and the government-in-exile of Prince Sihanouk, the communist government in Cambodia (GRUNK). Until the question of the seating of government in the United Nations was decided, GRUNK had categorically ruled out any negotiations or compromise with the GKR. The GKR, supported by the United States and most democratic countries, was actually attempting to improve its international credentials prior to the November 1974 UN debate. On the other side, Khieu Samphan, the KC forces' commander, trumpeted the fact that sixty-two countries (many aligned with the communists) recognized GRUNK and supported Prince Sihanouk's royal government. Samphan claimed that GRUNK held almost all the territory and was a complete state politically, economically, and militarily. In late November, the UN General Assembly voted 56–44 to support a resolution calling for talks to end the war. The resolution noted that GRUNK, presided over by Sihanouk, had authority over part of Cambodia but the GKR still controlled the preponderant number of Cambodian people. It further stated that the two parties to the conflict should solve their problems free from external influence. The resolution effectively left Cambodia with the UN seat for another year.

Besides pleasing the Cambodian government, the UN vote had special internal ramifications. The Khmer Rouge began to assert its control over GRUNK, no longer hiding behind Sihanouk, and the communists' rhetoric became much more strident. Communists no longer mentioned Sihanouk's name, and they methodically removed the pro-Sihanouk personnel.

I had many interesting experiences traveling about Southeast Asia during these times, and I must relate one of them. One morning I was to attend a meeting at Siem Reap. The city is near the ancient temple complex at Angkor Wat, which, as it was in communist territory, I had no chance to visit. So, flying over the ruins of the ancient place, I was engrossed with the scenery. As the aircraft descended to land at what appeared to be a temporary landing strip nearby, I noticed the soldiers along the runway staring at the aircraft in disbelief, their mouths wide open. The instant I saw their checkered red and white scarves, I knew they were enemy troops guarding the airstrip, and I yelled to pull up— from only ten to fifteen feet off the runway. Obviously, the pilot had chosen the wrong airstrip. We subsequently landed at the Cambodian Air Force airstrip at Siem Reap.

In the year between March 1973 and March 1974, the enemy cut Route 4 twenty-eight times. The longest period the highway was opened after 15 August 1973, when the United States terminated close air support, was the nine days between 17 and 26 October 1973. The longest period it was closed was the sixty-two days between 11 January and 13 March 1974.

So, in May 1974 USSAG noted to MEDTC that the many small friendly positions deployed along Highway 4 were highly vulnerable and could easily be isolated and overrun, resulting in unnecessary additional losses of personnel, equipment, and ammunition. The communists were particularly anxious to capture some of the 105 mm howitzers deployed and would target these locations with large forces to obtain easy victories and add to their weapons inventory. We recommended that the military situation could be strengthened and losses cut by consolidating positions along Route 4. The FANK did consolidate into several strong, defendable enclaves; one of these was Kompong Seila. Consequently, Route 4 was closed, requiring Cambodian logistical resupply to be effected solely via the Mekong and by aerial measures.

Kompong Seila was 126 kilometers southwest of Phnom Penh on Route 4. Shortly after the consolidation of FANK forces in March 1974, it came under a siege that lasted until mid-January 1975 and was one of the little-known stories of the Cambodian war.[204] The continuous siege, dating from May 1974, established a record for the Indochina wars, eclipsing the fifty-six days of Dien Bien Phu and the ninety-six of An Loc. The story of the heroism and suffering of the men, women, and children of Kompong Seila is a noble chapter of this tragic war. The enclave did not want to provide info to the enemy, so for months it sent only cryptic radio messages. Because of the necessity for a continuous airdrop of food and ammunition to the enclave, we had followed the situation as closely as possible. The U.S. Air Force delivered about four hundred short tons of ammo and a hundred short tons of rice each month. MEDTC and USSAG had considered possible relief operations to evacuate Kompong Seila since early November 1974. However, in mid-January 1975 the communists broke contact, and FANK was able to evacuate. At that point there were still some eighty-eight hundred civilians in beleaguered Kompong Seila, plus eight hundred military effectives.

During the many months this valiant garrison had been cut off, it sustained extremely heavy enemy attacks, both on the ground and by indirect fire. It often received a thousand rounds of incoming artillery, rocket, and mortar fire in a single night. Obviously, friendly casualties had been very high. There had been 390 military killed in action, 200 wounded, and another 200 hospitalized for other illnesses, malaria, and the like. No figures were received on civilians killed and wounded, though there were many.

In early 1975, when Kompong Seila was finally abandoned, the garrison troops were inserted into the northwest sector of the Phnom Penh perimeter that was under relentless attack by the enemy. The Kompong Seila forces had not been paid for several months, and when the paymaster showed up short of money (probably siphoned off to pay for ghost troops), an argument ensued and he was killed. The frustrated troops proceeded to cut out the heart of the paymaster and serve it up for lunch. This reported act shocked Phnom Penh. Obviously, the troops who had suffered so much lost their cool when put upon. It was hard to imagine these usually unimpulsive people reacting so violently.

In July 1974, when the fortunes of FANK were at their highest, the Khmer government appealed to the communists to commence peace negotiations without any prior conditions.[205] There was no response. In late November 1974 the military situation in Cambodia was still most favorable to the Cambodian government, even though the government knew that the U.S. funding situation was critical, requiring major ammunition conservation efforts and a large reduction in the procurement of other supplies and equipment.[206] This was the best of times for Cambodia to try again to initiate negotiations with GRUNK, which it did. Unfortunately, the communists reacted by becoming more intransigent. The window of opportunity had passed, though Cambodia, unlike South Vietnam, had seriously attempted to negotiate a peaceful solution.

The military situation at the end of 1974 was a stalemate. Both armies had greatly improved their capabilities during the previous year. Intelligence reports indicated that the communists intended to maintain the offensive by an all-out coordinated attack on Phnom Penh in early 1975. The country's future looked ominous: without additional

U.S. supplemental funding, the Cambodian forces would rapidly deplete their dwindling military arsenal.

1975

Communications Security

Communications security was poor on both sides—but particularly for the communists. They talked by radio about every conceivable situation and problem. Until early in 1974, a U.S. airplane sweep of the area picked up dozens of daily communist communications. The communists were a formidable force, but they did have problems—low morale; malaria; lack of ammunition and replacements; soldiers who were wet, hungry, and afraid of artillery and air strikes; and the list goes on. Nevertheless, their leaders' harsh discipline kept the units together. There was always the fear of corporal retribution to the communist soldiers or, more important, to their families.

There was one communist leader in charge of an area south of Phnom Penh, KC MR-607, who would critique his own performance after every battle, and he always lost the battles. When he came up on the air, we would laugh, knowing that the FANK had bested the enemy again. I often thought afterward that if this were in the U.S. military, with its zero tolerance for error, he would have been long gone. However, he learned and improved, and his command played a major role in closing the Mekong, the strategic move that in reality won the war. The KC military regions are shown on map 9.

We obtained several types of information by communications intelligence. For instance, a report of the Route 4 battlefield committee (southwest sector) intercepted on 6 May 1974 indicated the enemy had many wounded personnel: 1,820 were seasoned troops, 388 were women, and 761 were young men. At the same time, a message from Ran Koh Kong to Mok (southwest sector) stated: "On 6 May we captured a boat belonging to Thieu and Ky's government and seven persons including a district chief. They have been killed." Finally, in mid-November we learned that the Khmer Communist Party Central Committee had decided to launch coordinated attacks against Phnom Penh in late December. Once they were launched, the campaign would be continued vigorously. However, the initiation of attacks was delayed when the KC found that many of the troops were concerned with the lack of medicine, separation from families, unfamiliarity with the terrain, insufficient food, and the reorganization of their units under a new chief.

In November and December 1974 an interesting phenomenon occurred in KC Region 405, indicating a consolidation of Khmer Rouge leadership over the insurgency (see map 9). Ta Mok, the Region 405 commander, ordered more than thirty battalion-level political and military officers arrested and imprisoned on unannounced charges. All of the arrested officers had been trained in North Vietnam; the Khmer communist leadership was obviously attempting to purge its ranks of North Vietnamese influence.

FANK also had lapses in communications security, sometimes with serious consequences. On 9 April 1975, for the second time in three days, enemy radio operators succeeded in causing friendly artillery to fire on their own troops. The enemy called an artillery battery and directed it to fire on a communist unit in the vicinity of the 23rd FANK Brigade. Since the joint staff fire support unit sometimes called artillery units directly, without going through control headquarters, and also the command included the correct code word, FANK fired on a friendly unit. This caused the 23rd FANK Brigade to break.

In early December, the enemy-controlled radio summarized their activities against Mekong shipping, noting the importance of the waterway as the government's main line of communication for food, fuel, and munitions. The broadcast said, "If the lower Mekong is ever blocked, the clique would be choked to death." This really telegraphed one of the communists' main objectives for the dry season.

During December, enemy forces disengaged from the wet-season battlefields and made final preparations for their 1975 dry-season campaign. Communist command authorities convened several regional and inter-regional meetings to coordinate attacks. In all areas of the country, local communist leaders conducted extensive personnel recruitment programs. They stockpiled material resources such as rice and ammo in forward areas. Most important, the enemy was shifting its forces from the outlying areas to the Phnom Penh and Mekong battlefields.

Although there were excellent signs of enemy troop transfers and

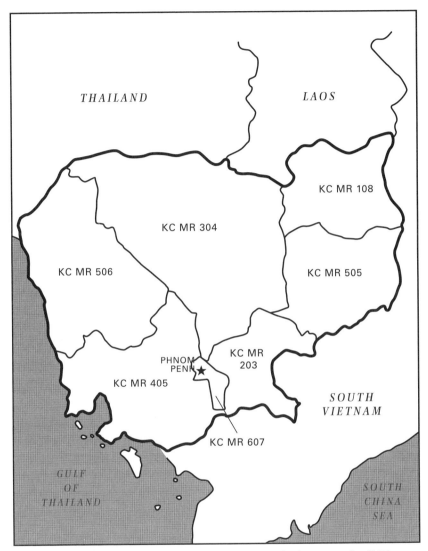

Map 9. KC Military Regions. (Source: FANK, Cambodian Joint Staff, Phnom Penh, Cambodia.)

plans in the upper Bassac and along the Mekong, there were few firm indicators of enemy plans north and west of Phnom Penh. However, intelligence reports did reveal significant relocations of high-level communist leaders. On 9 December, Ta Mok, the southwest region party secretary, moved from the vicinity of Pich Nil Pass to the Amleang area northwest of Phnom Penh. On 27 December, intelligence reports indicated that the Khmer communist central party secretary was approximately forty kilometers northwest of Phnom Penh, the same area from which he had directed the 1974 dry-season offensive. The following day, intelligence reports indicated that the northern region party secretary and the special region northern commander were in the same area. Thus, by 28 December initiation of major enemy activity appeared imminent.

On 31 December, I was in Bangkok when more meaningful intercepts by units in the Bangkok area kept occurring. All afternoon I was on the secure phone. By early evening it had become definite that the Khmer communists were going to launch an attack against Phnom Penh on 1 January. Although we already had sufficient intelligence to indicate that an attack was imminent, these latest interceptions made it absolutely certain. In order to convey this latest information to Phnom Penh I went to the American embassy, where they had a secure bubble with a connection to Phnom Penh, and passed on the latest information, which corroborated previous intelligence. MEDTC informed FANK, and before midnight Fernandez ordered his forces to general alert. Cambodian troops were ready when the enemy attack began.

The 1975 Dry-Season Attack on Phnom Penh

The enemy struck early on 1 January 1975, with simultaneous attacks against the Phnom Penh perimeter. A document the 3rd FANK Division seized from a killed battalion commander in the 2nd KC Division on 4 January provided the strategic plan for the enemy's dry-weather campaign.[207] The three prime objectives were the ammunition depot at Kantauk, the Pochentong Airfield, and the Mekong River. The troops involved in the offensive would be eleven divisions with more than a hundred battalions consisting of approximately thirty-three thousand soldiers. The offensive was divided into six sections. First, in the west section, the 1st and 3rd KC Division were to capture Pochentong in three days. Second, in the northwest the equivalent of two divisions were to sever Route 5 and neutralize the 7th FANK Division. Third, south of Route 4, the 2nd KC Division was to make a dash for the munitions depot at Kantouk. Fourth, between the Tonle Sap and the

Mekong, one division was to destroy the naval base at Chrui Chang War. Fifth, four divisions were to interdict the Mekong. And finally, in the south there were territorial or regional forces with no specific objective.

The document specified that the military operations were to be conducted simultaneously and that troops were not to dig trenches but were to launch the assault and that the capture of Pochentong Airfield would deny all governmental individuals an escape. The initial attacks played out as written. As in 1974, the main attack was from the northwest sector toward Pochentong Airfield. But this time FANK was ready. Consequently, the enemy suffered greatly. Attacks elsewhere on the perimeter—particularly from Phnom Baset in the north, from the northeast, and from the eastern banks of the Mekong—pinned down the intervention units. The communists drove a major salient in the northwest, but friendly units flown from the provincial enclaves stabilized the situation. North of Phnom Penh, excellent air support helped the 7th Division halt the enemy's advance. By 8 January, FANK had stopped cold the initial attack on the Phnom Penh perimeter and the crisis had passed. The enemy had taken very heavy casualties. This was a major victory at the Phnom Penh perimeter; nevertheless, Pochentong Airfield was constantly under sporadic 107 mm rocket fire.

On 17 December 1974, the joint staff J-2 provided its best estimates of the communist force strengths—sixty-eight thousand regulars and fifteen thousand popular forces. The popular forces and village militia were necessary for population control. The main force combatants had approximately fifty-three thousand troops available for major attacks. The popular force strength had been much higher a year previously, but it had been greatly reduced by combat losses and by many popular force battalions' being upgraded to main force combatants. Therefore, when the communist high command committed eleven divisions, encompassing thirty-three thousand combatants, to attack Phnom Penh and the Mekong in the 1975 dry-weather campaign, it was committing almost two-thirds of its available main force units, surpassing the twenty-six thousand friendly troops in the seventy-eight intervention battalions defending the capital region in late December 1974. However, FANK rapidly increased its defensive units as both sides escalated the combat in the capital region.

The communists very quickly broke off outlying units and reinforced troops at Phnom Penh and the Mekong.[208] Between December 1974 and January 1975, they withdrew fourteen battalions each from MR-6 and -9 and twenty-six battalions from MR-2 and they formed ten new battalions, thereby greatly increasing the force surrounding Phnom Penh from sixty to ninety-five battalions and the Lower Mekong from ten to forty battalions.

The enemy had overrun several marine positions of the lower Mekong. The communists had the preponderance of forces in the lower Mekong, which, because of the situation around Phnom Penh, the government had neglected. The situation was serious and required urgent attention.

The enemy pressure in the lower Mekong continued unabated and after 9 January was much more intense than around Phnom Penh. The communists planned and executed well their strategy to close the lower Mekong. Responding to this threat, FANK reinforced its troops occupying the terrain controlling three choke points on the lower Mekong River. On 4 February, utilizing water mines against shipping, the enemy forced Mekong convoy TP-114 to turn back. North of Banam, the key areas of Prek Yuon and Dei Doh subsequently fell, and the friendly positions at the lower choke points were overrun in late February. The enemy defeated two battalions on the key Peam Reang Island, with a loss of more than four hundred men. Without friendly control of the riverbanks at the narrows, the Mekong was closed—at least until the next flood stage, thereby forcing the United States to turn to a massive airlift to resupply Phnom Penh and the besieged enclaves.

At the end of February, a malaise had permeated Cambodia. A growing number of desertions were negating the government's increased efforts to implement the draft. MEDTC estimated that more than fifty-three hundred had deserted during January and February; without any effective control, the streets of Phnom Penh were full of deserters. Many of the intervention units had been severely bloodied, and there was a distinct lack of not just the offensive spirit but all combativeness. Many units were willing to abandon positions rather than stand and fight; the future performance of many units was at this time definitely unpredictable. Yet, by the end of February the enemy had not renewed its attacks on the Phnom Penh perimeter, most probably because of the heavy losses it had absorbed in the New Year's offensive. Approximately half of the enemy troops attacking Phnom Penh had been killed or injured.

This was undoubtedly a crucial period for Cambodia. In early March, to get a sense of the future, the USSAG intelligence staff prepared a special study comparing the situation at the end of February 1974 with that at the end of February 1975.[209] According to the study, in their 6 January 1974 initial attack the Khmer communists made a major penetration in the northwest sector and successfully crossed the Prek Thnot River in the southern sector, enabling them to fire 105 mm rounds into Phnom Penh. However, by the end of February, because of their piecemeal attacks and the lack of command and control, FANK had pushed the enemy back to the Phnom Penh defense perimeter except for gains in the northeastern sector.

In 1975, the communists had improved their command and control, which resulted in more coordinated attacks, and they had increased their total strength from 166 to 230 battalions. They had committed ninety-two to a hundred battalions against the capital and approximately forty battalions to the lower Mekong interdiction campaign. These forces notwithstanding, their initial attack on 1 January had been stopped cold, resulting in major casualties. Renewed attacks at the end of February resulted in inroads into the Phnom Penh defensive perimeter in the northwestern sector, letting the enemy conduct heavy attacks by fire against Pochentong Airfield. As in 1974, it also had some northeastern sector gains. The military situation around Phnom Penh was quite similar to what it had been in 1974; the major difference was that the communists had managed to successfully interdict the Mekong River.

In the beginning of January 1975 there was appreciably more ammo, rice, and petroleum stored in Phnom Penh than there had been during 1974's nearly critical shortages. The improved supply circumstances, and the enemy having not fired 105 mm artillery rounds into the city, enabled the internal situation to remain calm. Obviously, the 107 mm rocket interdiction had much less effect on the Phnom Penh citizenry: in 1975 the city received 231 rounds, as compared to only 10 in 1974. However, the KC increasingly interdicted Pochentong, trying to curtail the airland resupply. FANK's high ammo consumption rate in 1975, although it was much lower than it had been in 1974, continued to draw down stocks so that the ammo supplies for both ground and air at the end of February 1975 were lower than they had been in the same month in 1974.

While FANK was conserving ammo, the communists were expending theirs at a much faster rate than they had in 1974. As mentioned, a captured document indicated that the enemy would attack Pochentong and Phnom Penh with a great increase in its command structure from January 1974, when it had only two divisions. And it had markedly improved its organizational structure (see table 17). Equally important was that the enemy had strengthened its logistical system; its troops had many more heavy weapons. The communists had doubled their firepower and had more ammo reserves. Both were relatively small, however, when compared to FANK's.

While the enemy now utilized more forces, was better equipped, and had more firepower, FANK was encumbered by the strict ammunition conservation requirement. The average daily expenditures had been reduced from 627 short tons in January–February 1974 to 432 short tons in the same months of 1975. How much of this reduction resulted from ammo restrictions and how much from the combat situation, which cooled off somewhat around Phnom Penh after mid-January, could not be determined. I believe it was mostly the result of the situation. The expenditures at 432 short tons were 50 percent greater than the 290 short-ton conservation-authorized supply rate, which came as no surprise.

The tremendous disparity in firepower between the FANK and the communists is brought home when one recognizes that the enemy expended several thousand short tons per month of ammo and the friendly troops expended 432 short tons per day.[210] So, notwithstanding enemy improvements in command and control, weapons density, and logistics resupply, the Cambodians still had a major advantage in firepower and tactical and strategic mobility. However, they lagged in several intangibles, particularly leadership. A quick review of army, navy, and air force performance provides insights into the balance of power.

A comparison between 1975 dry-season FANK command and control techniques and those of 1974 indicates some notable improvements. For example, FANK had been much more effective during 1975 in its use of supporting artillery and air and its armored mobility in conjunction with infantry units. There were many examples of leadership initiatives at battalion and, albeit less frequently, brigade and division levels. All of these positively contributed to the fact that friendly forces had extracted a significantly higher casualty toll from the enemy than in the previous year.

However, the tactical and strategic weaknesses evident in 1974 persisted. More disappointing than FANK's failure to improve unit strengths was its lack of success in overcoming leadership and command deficiencies. Despite urgings to the contrary, the army had failed to take the initiative and continued to suffer from centralized decision-making and poor execution of plans. The indecisive and piecemeal commitment of forces in 1975 evidenced this when, for example, the general staff urgently needed to reinforce units on the lower Mekong but failed to do so.

The attrition of both sides was much greater in 1975 than it had been in 1974.[211] FANK's tactical mobility, its much improved effectiveness of the air force, its better-prepared defensive positions, and its having been forewarned of the communist attack all contributed to significant enemy losses in 1975. However, the enemy's larger, better-equipped and -coordinated force, with more weapons and ammunition, also took a toll on FANK (see table 23).

On the bright side, over the previous twelve months, under Brig. Gen. Ea Chhong the Khmer Air Force had made significant improvements. Aircrew totals had increased from ninety to 141. Sortie rates also significantly increased. For example, T-28D operational sorties increased from 2,790 in January–February 1974 to 3,848 in January–

Table 23. Countrywide Casualty Figures and Attrition							
	January–February 1974				**January–February 1975**		
	KHA	**WHA**	**MIA**	**EN KIA**	**KHA**	**WHA**	**MIA**	**EN KIA**
January	651	1,563	371	963	2,644	5,088	353	7,249
February	558	1,023	152	731	931	4,345	30	2,513
Total	1,209	2,586	523	1,694	3,575	9,433	383	9,762
Source: DAMSREP/DAO, Phnom Penh, Cambodia.							

February 1975.[212] Other improvements that lent themselves to statistics included bomb damage assessments and visual reconnaissance. Maintenance improvements were also significant.[213] The Khmer Air Force was currently conducting airlift and strike aircraft phase inspections, and a decline in aircraft losses attributed to maintenance was evident. The supply system to keep aircraft operation-ready also showed improvement. The Khmer Air Force improvements were one of the most noteworthy accomplishments of the Cambodian military.

The navy's performance was continuously rated as high during January and February 1974. Concrete examples included the successful transit of Mekong convoys with moderate damage, few casualties, and relatively little loss of cargo; the successful regular resupply of Kompong Cham and Kompong Chhnang; and the support given army operations in the Bassac and Phnom Penh areas. During January–February 1975, navy personnel performed adequately. However, the introduction of mine warfare (with the resultant equipment losses), the increased tempo of operations, and decreased maintenance of the riverine craft contributed to a greatly depleted naval force. In January, the introduction of mining tactics on the Mekong and the presence of enemy forces all along the lower Mekong sealed off this avenue of resupply to Phnom Penh. The mining tactics would not have enjoyed as much success had the marine units been able to hold their defensive positions. Cambodia lost all of its marine positions on the lower Mekong south of Koch Reah and abandoned several other positions.

In early March 1975, this comparison of forces with respect to March 1974 indicated that both combatants had advantages and disadvantages. The enemy had largely improved over 1974, with the very important exception of its severe combat losses. FANK had improved its fire support coordination, tactical mobility, and close air support. These were the key areas where the Cambodians had a great advantage over the communists. However, because of casualties and desertions, the army had not brought its units up to strength; the navy was depleted; and all were attempting to reduce ammo expenditures. More important, they did not have the offensive spirit.

In summary, at the beginning of March 1975 both sides were exhausted. FANK, with its much greater firepower, had pretty much beaten up the enemy, but it had allowed the Mekong to be closed.

Since it was superior in both firepower and mobility, if it could find the will to fight aggressively, it might deny the communists success for at least another year, thus setting the stage for a possible negotiated settlement. However, with the current military assistance funding, Cambodia would soon run out of supplies, a situation made much more tenuous by the expensive and dangerous airlift requirements. The U.S. Congress's willingness to support the war was in question, and without supplemental funding there was no hope of success. Yet, the Cambodians continued to fight.

The Lower Mekong Situation

On 1 January, as discussed, the enemy initiated its dry-weather campaign with simultaneous attacks on the Phnom Penh perimeter, working to overrun Pochentong Airfield and the Kantauk ammunition depot. While all friendly attention was focused on defending Phnom Penh, the enemy routed the 36th FANK Brigade southeast of Phnom Penh along Highway 1 and overran the marines' positions south of Neak Luong along the Mekong. The Mekong Special Zone withdrew all artillery support to Neak Luong. Preoccupied with Phnom Penh, the government hardly noticed that its vital lifeline was in serious danger of being effectively closed. The enemy dug in and consolidated its hold on both banks of the Mekong and surrounded Neak Luong. The situation was such that on 7 January 1975 the following message was sent to all concerned in advance of the tripartite meeting to be held at Phnom Penh on 10 January:

> The security situation along the lower Mekong is serious. The enemy now controls both sides of the Mekong north of Neak Luong for a stretch of 20 km. However FANK still has artillery coverage over most of this terrain. The enemy controls both sides of the Mekong at the narrows south of Neak Luong near Peam Chor and Peam Reang. This sector is without artillery coverage. Latest indications are that Neak Luong itself is an important enemy target. . . .
>
> There is always the possibility that Pochentong could be closed temporarily thus precluding any airland and making the resupply of enclaves extremely difficult. Consequently, the flexibility afforded by the Mekong

is absolutely essential to the prosecution of the war both in the short and long term. . . .

Without artillery coverage and with the enemy holding critical terrain it is entirely possible that some vessels might be severely damaged or sunk. Therefore, all concerned must be prepared to accept losses should they occur.

Mekong convoys cannot be interrupted or the storage situation at Phnom Penh will deteriorate to the critical point (15 DOS) well before the end of January. In the meantime, selected supplies of ammo and petroleum will have to be airlanded on an as-required basis. Mekong convoy TP-111 will sail in the first half of January with a limited number of vessels carrying essential cargo only. The exact date of the convoy is close hold for security purposes and will be disseminated on a need to know basis at the Tripartite conference.

Since the enemy had little, if any, communications security, friendly forces knew with precision its order of battle on the lower Mekong. Its battalions on both banks of the river were in place, including the 213th NVA/VC Battalion at gridline 21, a dangerous choke point. This was the first time North Vietnamese units had been identified.[214] We subsequently received an intelligence report that the Viet Cong Dong Thap I unit was also camped on the west bank between gridlines 20 and 36 and another NVA/VC battalion was on the east bank between gridlines 20 and 42. The intelligence source stated that their mission was to interdict the Mekong River traffic. I knew that the Dong Thap I was a battle-hardened old line Viet Cong unit; in 1969 I had fought against two of its battalions. Additionally, at Vung Tau on 17 January at 0400 hours, a mine, probably placed by a sapper, blew a hole in the tug *Ocean Star,* beaching it. This was the second such incident against ammo tugs at Vung Tau within a year. It appeared that the North Vietnamese had joined the objective of closing the Mekong.

The Khmer high command instructed the navy to formulate a plan to reopen the Mekong; Rear Adm. Vong Sarendy briefed this plan to the tripartite deputies in detail. The joint staff approved the plan, the gist of which was to use 75 percent of navy vessels and all available air force resources, to land at least five additional battalions at choke points, and to reintroduce 105 mm artillery if the situation permitted.[215]

The tripartite deputies accepted the Cambodian plan and spent additional time discussing TP-111 convoy tactics—whether to go as one entity or be broken into two sections and whether to have a night convoy, which would greatly reduce the air force's effectiveness. However, navy vessels could return fire more effectively in this situation because they could home in on the enemy weapons' flashes. The deputies decided that the navy should cross the border at daylight to gain maximum daytime operational capabilities.

We anticipated the potential use of mines but had no idea of the threat's precise nature. It could consist of sophisticated techniques, such as command-detonated mines or buoyancy mines ballasted to float below the surface of the water. Alternatively, it could be the run-of-the-mill surface-floating mines or explosive charges already encountered singularly or in conjunction with channel barricades. Mine countermeasure craft would be required for coping with the sophisticated threat, but finding and detonating floating mines would only require active reconnaissance.

Everyone understood the importance of the first 1975 convoy. Reporting to the State Department concerning the convoy, Ambassador Dean stated that the next forty-eight to seventy-two hours, between 21 and 23 January, would be crucial for Cambodia, because they would determine whether the large-scale economic and military assistance made available to Cambodia could actually be brought up the Mekong River to Phnom Penh. He believed it was imperative that TP-111 reach Phnom Penh. The Khmers—both friendly and enemy—knew it.[216] Headquarters CINCPAC stated that there was a high level of interest in Mekong convoy TP-111 and requested some type of arrangement in which CINCPAC could receive an hourly update once the convoy crossed the border.[217] To accommodate this, USSAG sent situation reports on the January convoys as information of importance developed.

The sagas of the 1975 Mekong convoys were interesting. They included owners refusing to sail, missing river pilots, crews abandoning ships, fires on-board vessels, withering attacks by fire, detonating mines, capsized ships, tugs run aground, propellers fouled by barricades, and plenty of heroics. (See appendix D.)

The January convoys managed to move 17,471 metric tons of cargo—but at what a price in both shipping and personnel casualties!

On downriver PT-112, the cargo vessel *Port Sun 1* was lost. On upriver TP-113, two petroleum tankers, the *Han Seung 2* and the *Han Seung 7* were lost, as was the rice-carrying coaster *Wah An* (see photo 7). On 3 February, the downriver convoy PT-113 lost three tugs: *Timberjack, Hawkeye,* and *Buckeye,* with their six shield barges and the petroleum tanker *Bayon Trader* as well as the self-propelled barge *Saigon 120* and three others. On upriver TP-114 the tugs *Asiatic Trust* and *Shinso Maru* were sunk and the tug *Asiatic Enterprise* went aground and was set afire—causing the convoy to turn back to South Vietnam. The Me-

Photo 7. Mekong Convoy, 29 January 1975. (Source: Headquarters USSAG, Nakhon Phanom, Thailand, produced by 432nd Reconnaissance Technical Squadron, U.S. Air Force.)

kong River below Neak Luong was a shipping graveyard.[218] Five crewmen were killed and at least thirty wounded in the month's convoy. Cambodian Navy losses also were severe.

After the "Black Monday" losses on the downriver PT-113 on 3 February, the deputies decided to have a replay of TP-111 and send the next convoy north with only two ammo barges and four tugs, all with shield barges. The convoy was scheduled to sail on 5 February.

Anticipating problems, particularly with the new mine menace, we scheduled a transportation meeting with the U.S. agencies and ship owners associated with Mekong convoys at Saigon on the same day, primarily to solicit firsthand information on how the security and operations of convoys could be improved and secondarily to head off potential withdrawals, should TP-114 encounter serious problems. At the meeting, contractors suggested that the U.S. and Khmer governments allow them to construct and operate a minesweep; provide competent river pilots when ship captains requested them; ensure that navy radio personnel provided for tugs were bilingual; arm tugs; provide a large, bunkered barge to be used as a standoff between the contractor tug and contractor sweep ensemble, with bunkered barges manned by mortar and 40 mm gun crews; have the army occupy banks at the Peam Reang choke point; have the navy aggressively sweep for mines; ensure adequate air coverage; and have the convoy commander on the lead tug be designated by the contractor.[219]

These comments were strictly informal and received from various individuals. At the meeting, the contracting office granted permission to begin the construction of a mine ensemble. All of the other matters were brought up at the tripartite deputies' meeting at Phnom Penh on Friday, 7 February. The suggestions that contractor personnel offered were agreed upon and were in the process of being implemented by the various governmental agencies with one exception: the Khmer Navy said it would not man a bunkered barge immediately behind the minesweep.

The owners, managers, and tug captains of the contracted corporations attended the transportation meeting. This was an amazing group of men. They were of many nationalities, rugged, brave—they had to be brave to willingly submit to the intense gamut of fire along the Mekong. I brought them up to date on the military situation in Cambodia and reassured them that everything possible would be done to improve convoy security. I impressed upon them the importance of the next convoy, TP-115, and asked them to agree to sail. In conclusion, I said that if we failed to keep operating the Mekong convoys, and Phnom Penh fell as a result, more than three hundred thousand Cambodians would be slaughtered. They left noncommittal.

That night, three representatives of the group asked to speak to me. They had only one question. "We know you are truthful, do you really believe that three hundred thousand Cambodians would be killed?" I told them I definitely believed they would. The delegates then agreed to sail.

I was pleased to report to the tripartite deputies that if we could ensure that the contractors' recommendations were fulfilled, the crews would sail. Several days later I received a call from the embassy in Saigon reporting that it did not concur with my statement concerning what would occur should Phnom Penh fall to the communists. Obviously, they seriously misjudged the Cambodian communists.

The Mine Threat

Now there were two major threats to shipping on the Mekong. One was the mines, which had such an impact on the SCOOT tugs, and the other was the continual intensive weapons fire from the banks at choke points, which had a devastating effect on the higher-silhouetted petroleum and cargo vessels.

Mines appeared to be the number-one threat on the Mekong. Ground fire had not stopped tugs and barges, but mines had sunk six tugs recently. However, owners and captains said they could design a minesweep that could eliminate mines as a danger. Saigon immediately grasped this suggestion, and the Military Sealift Command agreed to alter the SEAPAC contract, and the CINCPAC representative assisted by ordering foam and equipment immediately. The immediate acceptance of the contractors' requests was necessary for SEAPAC to agree on one more trip. Although at the tripartite meeting Rear Admiral Sarendy had been lukewarm to the idea of the minesweep, its use had the deputies' approval. The minesweep was to be pushed by a high-powered tug spaced from the sweep barges by an empty ammo barge. The rig would be ready in time for TP-115.

Very thorough discussions were carried on both in Saigon and Phnom Penh concerning the mine threat. To date, no mines had been recovered, and information was pieced together to determine the threat's extent. Crews had stated that whenever they ran into a mine they saw pieces of bamboo four to five inches in diameter and two to three meters long floating on the surface. Some surmised that the mines were hung from these floating platforms, two to three meters below the surface. Others believed that the bamboo marked the submersed mines on the bottom that were command detonated when the ship reached the bamboo. The personnel in the hospital in Saigon with whom the problem was discussed thought the mines were command detonated, their rationale being that the mine exploded midship. One crewman was in the hospital with severe head injuries because the mine's force hurled him upward against the bulkhead. Yet the captain of the *Timberjack,* which was sunk during darkness, claimed that it was too dark for the enemy to see to command detonate. The *Luzon* crew, though, said that before they were hit by mines the enemy fired flares. The mines' extreme impact on the shipping led experts to believe that they were 210-pound Chinese mines. The Khmer Navy had chain drags capable of sweeping to the bank to sever wiring if the mines were command detonated as well as the barricades. (See photo 8.) Sarendy firmly believed that within forty-eight hours he could successfully drag the area for the mines. We next had to discern the extent of the mine threat. Four convoys had been run between Phnom Penh and Neak Luong without encountering mines. Therefore, we believed that the minefields were located at the ends of Peam Reang Island. Since these were large mines, it would have taken a major logistical effort to provide sufficient mines to effectively close the channel here alone without considering additional locations. For the time being, all concerned surmised that the mine threat was probably at Peam Reang only. But to be certain, the tripartite deputies requested the navy sweep all of the river.

The enemy had concentrated its fire at three areas. The best way to eliminate the enemy threat, particularly the ground fire and mine threat at Peam Reang, was to land troops on the ground and take over the choke point. Until troops were made available to control the choke

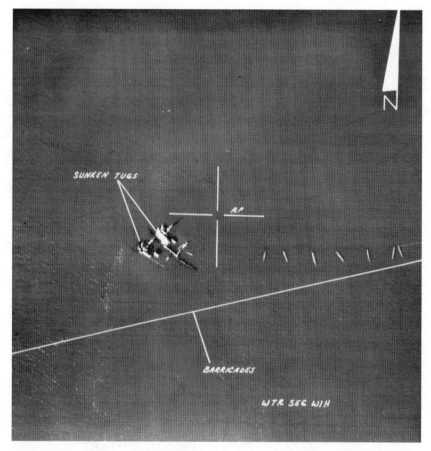

Photo 8. Barricades on the Mekong with Sunken Tugs. (Source: Headquarters USSAG, Nakhon Phanom, Thailand, produced by 432nd Reconnaissance Technical Squadron, U.S. Air Force.)

points, enemy firepower remained a major threat to ships, though not to tugs and barges. However, mines were a major threat to tugs and barges. The navy did not intend to sweep the Peam Reang area until FANK controlled the banks. The army was to send the 69th Brigade to Neak Luong to replace the 4th Brigade, which would clear the area near Peam Reang. However, landing troops would take some time.

Throughout these periods, the enemy continued to refine its interdiction tactics and in time became much more coordinated. It formed special Mekong River units. One of these operated in Kandal

Province south of Prek Doch village. This consisted of heavy weapons Battalion 260 and support Battalions 18 and 265.[220] Another battalion established ambush points further north, digging trenches 250 meters apart, each of which was for seven men and had emplacements for four 75 mm recoilless rifles and two 82 mm mortars. When the convoys traveled at night, the communists would set up a series of kerosene lamps which were shielded so that the light was visible only to their dug-in firing positions along the opposite riverbanks. As a darkened convoy approached, a downstream observer would alert the positions by firing a shot. The gunners would then aim their weapons at the kerosene lamps, and when the advancing ships blocked the light, the gunners opened fire. A sizeable percentage of enemy forces, more than eight thousand troops, had as their mission the interdiction of convoys on both the upper and lower Mekong.

On 7 February, it was important to go all-out to prepare for TP-115. Each of the Khmer services had its problem to solve. The convoy could be successful only if the Khmer, Vietnamese, and U.S. organizations worked together, and unless TP-115 was successful it did not appear possible to run subsequent convoys in the near future. Everything was riding on this convoy.

The army had established a sound plan to land troops on the banks. The navy was actively preparing for minesweeping operations, and the air force stood ready to fully support the effort. SEAPAC had made excellent progress in designing and fabricating a minesweep that would clear the river. Plans called for five tugs: one to push the minesweep and double tugs for the two ammo barges. Whether they would cross the border depended on many factors: troops on the ground, adequate river sweeps, sufficient naval escort, a deputy commander on the lead tug, machine gun crews and grenadiers aboard tugs, English- and French-speaking radio operators, and the convoy sailing on schedule. These factors would require formidable operations between then and the convoy sailing time, set as 18 February at the earliest and 20 February at the latest. It remained to be seen whether the Cambodians were up to the task.

With the 5 February failure of TP-114 to resupply Phnom Penh, the stockage situation was beginning to pinch a little.[221] There were thirty-six days' rice supply at the current consumption rate of 545 metric tons per day and about forty-five days' petroleum supply. The civilian petroleum allocation was reduced from 258 to 121 cubic meters per day—a big cut. Certain line items of ammo were below the fifteen days of supply, including 5.56 mm rifle, 60 and 81 mm mortar, and 105 and 155 mm howitzer rounds. There were only six days of napalm and cluster bomb air force munitions. To alleviate the situation the JCS directed the U.S. Air Force to augment the existing Bird Air contract to supply Phnom Penh to provide twenty sorties of airland missions per day (an increase of thirteen sorties per day), which would hopefully take care of the supply situation until the Mekong convoys were resumed.

That week, the ammo consumption for Phnom Penh alone was 640 short tons per day. The army planned to make every possible effort to reduce the rate to 400 short tons per day for the rest of February and then to 300 short tons per day thereafter. This still exceeded the 1 January 1975 strictly established authorized supply rate of 290 short tons per day, dangerously depleting the existing funding authority. Even if the Mekong convoys resumed, there would be a very severe ammo problem. The current Mekong closing and the projected ammo rationing deleteriously affected Cambodia's morale.

Reviewing Mekong security as we looked ahead, the navy's suppressive fires had not been effective, except for the monitors, which had 105 mm guns. The smaller boat platforms were, unfortunately, always below bank level, preventing an effective line of fire. The artillery fire support also was not effective, in that case because of poor leadership. Whenever the air force provided close air support, its five-hundred-pound bombs did silence the enemy trenches—but they were often unavailable during the day and obviously ineffective at night. The only really effective solution was to place troops on the ground at choke points. Recognizing this, on 6 February the joint staff made the Mekong Special Zone an army command (vice navy) and placed Brig. Gen. Noup Paramoun, the MR-6 governor and commander, in command.[222] He would have a navy deputy and an air force field-grade officer as advisers, and he would eventually have a ground force of two and a half brigades, in addition to the forces defending Neak Luong. With these troops, he was to reoccupy lost artillery positions and emplace more artillery so that mutually supporting gun positions would cover the lower Mekong from the border to Phnom Penh.

Subsequently, neither the army nor the navy could get organized with respect to Mekong security, and on 26 February 1975 we sent a very strong message to all concerned:

> Since the last update five days ago situation on the Mekong has deteriorated appreciably. . . . MNK in its Mekong convoy operations has lost 6 additional craft. . . . Now less than half of the Mekong craft are fully operational.
>
> The key to initiating convoy operations is still the bank clearing operations since it is doubtful if MNK will successfully sweep for mines (operations to sever communications for command detonated mines requires sweeps close to the banks) unless there is improved bank security. Without mine sweeps and bank security the civilian contractor tug crews probably will not sail. Bank clearing operations require additional combat battalions.
>
> The situation around the Phnom Penh perimeter has also worsened. . . . The major problem is that there are no immediately available reserves—either divisional or strategic. Any major penetrations of the perimeter could be most serious. Thus, the lower Mekong must compete with Phnom Penh, including the protection of ammo (Kantauk) and airlift (Pochentong), for desperately required reinforcements.
>
> On the plus side, in SVN the mine sweep barge array has been completed and successfully tested. The shield barge bunkers will be completed on 27 February. A decision has been made to pull the ammo barges with one tug each, thus reducing tug and crew requirements to four (considering the need for an escort tug).
>
> Considering the immediate need to bolster Phnom Penh defenses which competes with the requirement to reinforce the lower Mekong, the battered condition of the MNK, a general feeling of FANK unrest as well as the loss of additional positions on the lower Mekong it is the considered judgment of MEDTC/USSAG that the banks of the lower Mekong at critical choke points probably will not be secured in the foreseeable future. Thus, it is believed that the next convoy will be postponed indefinitely.
>
> This is a coordinated MEDTC/USSAG message.[223]

Now that the Mekong River line of communication, the lifeblood of Phnom Penh and thus Cambodia, was closed, alarm bells should have sounded at the joint staff when the battle-weary marines failed to occupy critical positions on the lower Mekong. True, they discussed a plan for the lower Mekong and they changed the command structure, but they failed to provide the one essential ingredient—more combat battalions. The chief of staff, Lieutenant General Fernandez, had stated on several occasions that he would never allow a provincial capital to be taken. However, by the end of January the preponderance of all enemy main force units had been relocated to attack Phnom Penh and the lower Mekong. It is true that in that month some troop units from outlying areas were relocated to the capital region to counter communist attacks; those troops aside, however, the bulk of the territorial battalions remained in outlying areas to protect the provincial enclaves. The cautious attitudes of the joint staff allowed the intermittent enemy local force attacks to fix those territorial units in place. The failure to substantially reinforce the lower Mekong with additional units from the outlying regions ultimately resulted in the downfall of Cambodia.[224] Coincidentally, just the opposite occurred in South Vietnam, where President Thieu's precipitous directives to withdraw forces from MR-1 and MR-2 to protect Saigon and the delta had catastrophic results, leading to the collapse of the South Vietnamese government.

Aerial Support Operations

The Khmer communists' strategic plan was to completely isolate Phnom Penh by cutting all avenues of approach. In 1975 they had driven close to Pochentong and were seriously interdicting the airfield. Notwithstanding the constant artillery and rocket attacks, the JCS had approved increased airlifts when, on 5 February, TP-114 was turned back. Now, at the end of February, when it was clear that the Mekong was definitely closed and a further increase in airlift was essential, we were concerned that additional funding would not be approved and flights into Pochentong would even be curtailed because of the increased shelling of the airfield. The airfield's interdiction was becoming more effective. The communists had obviously located artillery so they could fire directly along the narrow airfield's axis. On 23 January, when my airplane was taking off, the enemy walked six rounds smack down the center of the runway. The first four detonated behind the aircraft, each closer than the last. And when the aircraft was over a hundred feet off the ground, the last two exploded under it, rocking the plane.[292] It was really a race against time, and the enemy's timing was off by seconds.

In January and February, 745 rounds hit Pochentong Airfield and fragments severely wounded several cargo handlers. Nevertheless, higher headquarters unhesitatingly approved additional sorties to fully support Cambodia. Our military did not back off. Subsequently, our tactical analysis branch prepared a paper titled "Risk Associated with Pochentong Airlanded Operations," taking into consideration the incoming rockets' ground pattern. They concluded that there was a relatively high probability of at least one aircraft being hit or damaged if operations lasted more than thirty days. The matter was receiving the utmost attention at Headquarters USSAG; we constantly monitored firings, landings, and offloadings on an event basis.

Enemy attacks on Pochentong continued to increase, and in March 211 rounds of 105 mm artillery and 872 rounds of 107 mm rockets hit. During the dry season, more than 2,400 rounds were fired at the airfield.[225] Fortuitously, we lost no aircraft, although shrapnel damaged eight. The United States had no casualties either; however, the Cambodians supporting the operation suffered more than fifty, including eight killed. MEDTC reported on 11 April that shrapnel hit a DC-3 carrying a cargo of diesel fuel during takeoff and five crew members were killed in an attempt to land the aircraft.

Besides moving operations from one location to another and temporarily suspending operations during periods of intense attacks, the U.S. Air Force supervisors constantly strived to reduce offload times and total ground times. Obviously, the shorter the ground time, the less the risk. The average C-130 ammunition block-in to block-out offload time was 5.9 minutes, and the total ground time was 10.6 minutes. For other cargo loads the ground times averaged 29 minutes.[226]

Now that the Mekong River was indefinitely closed, the airland/airdrop delivery methods assumed the greatest importance. In mid-January, our staff had commenced planning for that possible contingency. From March to December 1974, once the Mekong convoys really started moving, airlanded cargo averaged only 230 short tons per month, less than the equivalent of one sortie per day. However, because of the enclave situation, the need for airdrops persisted all year. The average total commodity deliveries per month, exclusive of road deliveries, was 68,900 short tons. Such quantities could no longer be feasibly delivered solely by air; therefore, the American embassy, Phnom Penh, USAID, and MEDTC jointly determined an austere posture of 41,500 short tons. After they cut the requirements by 42 percent, there was still a need for ninety sorties per day. Whether that number could ever be accommodated remained to be seen; to sustain this level of airlift there would have to be a capability to load, transport, and unload about 1,350 short tons per day. Fortunately, there was an additional staging area at the southwest corner of the airfield at Pochentong, which would enable satisfactory loading and unloading. Thus, capacity would be limited only by the availability of ground equipment, U.S. personnel for surveillance, and air and ground congestion (not considering enemy interdiction). With proper equipment, we could surge to seventy-two sorties per day at Pochentong, which would require four to six U.S. ground handlers to oversee offloads and two U.S. Air Force air traffic controllers. To stay under the two hundred personnel ceiling mandated by law, U.S. personnel would have to arrive by first sortie in the morning and leave on the last sortie of the day.

Airdrops could provide the eighteen additional sorties required. However, to increase from the current ten airdrop-sorties-per-day capability, the Military Assistance Command, Thailand Support Air Group at Samae San would also require additional personnel and equipment. Since the rice resupply was critical, the most feasible solution was to support airlift requirements from Samae San and U-Tapao. This, however, would require the Thai government's permission to throughput American rice, and that permission was denied.

The major limiting factor for aerial resupply was the potential enemy interdiction of Pochentong, which could result in short- or long-term interruptions of the flow of airland sorties. In any event, planning was ongoing. Recognizing the situation, the JCS had increased the airlift capabilities on 7 February, after TP-114 failed, and again on 27 February, when it became apparent that the Mekong was closed. If the DAO in Saigon or MEDTC in Phnom Penh clearly articulated a problem, they could expect immediate CINCPAC and JCS support (within funding limits or other restrictions laid down by Congress). Higher headquarters were always very supportive in dozens of situations.

The U.S. Air Force supply airdrop had been ongoing since May 1973. At that time, the Khmer military and the civilian population had withdrawn into enclaves, after which the communists systematically cut off land routes, making airlift resupply a necessity for the enclaves' survival. In May 1974, six major enclaves required a total average daily resupply of 144 short tons, two-thirds ammo and one-third rice—which required about ten sorties per day in total. There always were end-of-month shortages of some ammo line items. To optimize the situation, our staff implemented several actions that materially improved the effectiveness of the total system. First, the staff analyzed the ammo calls forward for the major enclaves for the month of June 1974 and determined that 82 percent of the tonnage to be delivered (1,554 short tons) consisted of six major line items (plus fuses). In contrast, 18 percent (341 short tons) consisted of sixteen line items. The 341 short tons was the equivalent of sixty sorties, or two per day. Because the minor line items had low tonnage requirements, the amount of ammo on hand could fluctuate greatly. It appeared that the Khmer Air Force could respond quickly to those requirements to ensure that the enclaves maintained adequate levels. The U.S. Air Force could resupply the six major line items and thus could facilitate the programming and loading of calls forward, thereby improving response times. The requirements for Cambodian and U.S. air support to enclaves could then be balanced between the U.S. and Khmer air forces.[227]

The next step was for the U.S. Air Force to adopt both sixteen- and ten-pallet standard loads. Thus, each sortie would have much greater flexibility when several enclaves were being resupplied, if required to divert from one landing zone or drop zone to another because of weather or tactical situations. The Khmer Air Force–tailored loads could meet ammo imbalances at an enclave.[228] Again, standardized loads facilitated rigging, loading, accounting, and calls forward. None of the measures resulting from operational analysis were earthshaking, but they greatly facilitated the management of ammunition resupply to enclaves and, more importantly, we realized a cutback in sorties.

The airdrop techniques the C-130 crews used included the adverse weather aerial delivery system, a multipurpose avionics system designed to assist aircrews in performing aerial delivery missions in low visibility or darkness. With this high-velocity system, they were able to drop from altitudes above ten thousand feet and avoid the antiaircraft defenses of the enemy. At various times, airdrops using these procedures supplied twenty-five different enclaves. The overall drop accuracy was excellent. During the critical period of 1 January through 13 April 1975, out of 5,548 bundles dropped, only thirty landed off the drop zone, indicating the competence of the system and the crews. However, our streamer rate (those bundles whose parachutes did not open) always seemed to hover at about 6 percent.[229]

During these critical periods, all logistical personnel at Samae San and U-Tapao responded in an exemplary fashion to airdrop requirements in Cambodia. Positive response often involved long hours of backbreaking effort by the army and air force personnel, and they met every challenge successfully.

The enemy overran several Cambodian positions and captured equipment and supplies. In fact, it had taken forty-four 105 mm howitzers with a sizeable quantity of ammo, which it then used to shell enclaves—Kompong Cham, Das Kanchor, and Takeo to name a few. The enemy's January 1974 shelling of Phnom Penh with several hundred rounds of 105 mm had caused a near-panic situation. These attacks caused substantial casualties, mostly civilian: When the support troops at Samae San responsible for preparing bundles to be airdropped into enclaves heard of this, they thought of spiking a bundle of 105 ammo, which they proposed to have dropped outside the drop zone so the enemy would recover and hopefully use it. When the spiked ammo was fired, it would explode—destroying the gun and perhaps a few communist artillerymen. The idea seemed enterprising, but I understood that when their headquarters got wind of it they responded, "no dirty tricks." However, it was a very dirty war. For example, the communists occasionally dressed in FANK uniforms and went into towns to recruit for the army; those who volunteered or expressed interest were liquidated.

In 1974 it had been our goal to reduce airland requirements to the absolute minimum, for safety reasons, and to maximize the use of the Mekong convoys; thus, twice the tonnage had been delivered by airdrop as by airland. However, in 1975, with the Mekong interdicted, it was absolutely essential to increase airlanded deliveries. In 1974 more than 94 percent of all deliveries to Cambodia were by the Mekong, while from February to April 1975 more than 89 percent were airlanded.[232] Careful planning and great execution by all concerned made this dramatic switch possible, as the threat to aircraft landing at Pochentong from rocket and artillery attacks was much greater than ever before. With the turn back of convoy TP-114, Brigadier General Palmer told CINCPAC that Cambodia's resupply had been thrown into great jeopardy, and it was operating on a paper-thin margin.

On 7 February, there were only about seven thousand short tons of ammo in storage at Kantauk. To alleviate the situation, the Bird Air contract was adjusted to increase the daily sortie rate from seven to twenty. Additionally, the Military Airlift Command contracted for three DC-8s to airlift ammo from U-Tapao to Phnom Penh. The planes were piloted by World Airways and Airlift International crews. In February, these assets together transported 12,276 short tons of ammo, which built up stocks only somewhat, since expenditures were still high.

At the end of February, the emphasis on resupply switched to rice, and because of problems obtaining clearance from the Thai government for its import, the DC-8 operation moved to Tan Son Nhut Airfield at Saigon. Between 27 February and 17 April, 2,001 sorties were flown, bringing 56,723 short tons of essential cargo to the besieged city of Phnom Penh.[233]

Unfortunately, many members of the U.S. Congress refused to acknowledge the importance of aerial support for Cambodia's survival. The *Indochina News* reported that twenty-one Democratic congressmen filed a federal suit to halt all U.S. supply airlift and reconnaissance flights in Cambodia, alleging that such flights were in violation of a congressional ban on U.S. involvement in Cambodia.[234]

The JCS suspended all airlift support to Cambodia on 17 April 1975. The last airlift effort was a rice drop to Kompong Chhnang at 1520 hours. Headquarters USSAG summarized the Khmer airlift shortly thereafter:

The U.S. Airlift Operation in the Khmer Republic from 11 Apr 73–17 Apr 75 stands out as the largest sustained airlift operation since the Berlin Airlift. The survival of Phnom Penh and several important isolated provincial enclaves became completely dependent on U.S. airlift to provide

life-sustaining rice, ammo, petroleum, and general cargo. USAF C-130s
. . . and contracted DC-8s flew 5,413 airland missions to deliver 123,631
S/T in the two year sustained operation.

The continuous Khmer airdrop support to approximately 25 different
enclaves, such as Kampong Seila and Neak Luong, was the largest sustained airdrop effort in USAF history. . . . Approximately 98 percent of
total bundles dropped were reported recoverable even though some drop
zones had less than a 500 meter radius of security.

Obviously, the airlift was much more expensive than the Mekong
convoys. The transportation costs came out of the military assistance
funds, thereby reducing the amount available for purchasing ammo. A
day of reckoning was coming; however, it was hoped by the GKR that
Congress would provide supplemental funding to stave off a catastrophe. By 1 March 1975, the ammo stockage had been replenished and
the inaugural flights of the rice airlift from Saigon had gone smoothly,
with ten round-trip flights. Consequently, many thought that the airlift
could buy the time needed to reopen the Mekong. Ambassador Dean,
for instance, said to the press that the military situation was "grim but
not desperate." The major concern was that one of the resupply aircraft
might be shot down, which would render the situation untenable for
the U.S. airlift.

Adequate logistics are fundamental for successfully waging a war,
and the logistical supply of Cambodia was a nightmare. The lack of
funding greatly limited supplies, all land routes were cut, thirteen completely isolated population enclaves could only be supplied by airdrop,
and the Mekong main supply route was severely interdicted. It was
Headquarters USSAG's responsibility to oversee the transportation of
critical supplies to Cambodia.[235] By 1975, out-of-country transportation assets provided half of the Cambodian rice consumption, all of
its petroleum products, and all the essential logistics of war. In other
words, Cambodia was almost totally supplied by military-supervised
airland, airdrop, and Mekong convoys. Internal distributions were
the responsibilities of USAID, FANK, and Telakhmer. Except for the
Mekong and aerial resupply, Phnom Penh, the heart of Cambodia, was
totally isolated. The expensive and dangerous logistical resupply by air,
no matter how successful, could only be a short-term solution. Thus,

when the Mekong River, Cambodia's lifeline, was cut, the end of the war was inevitable.

The Final Battles

USSAG's review of the Cambodian situation indicated that on 1 March 1975 the military situation was nearly a standoff. The enemy had been seriously attrited. However, FANK had to kindle the will to fight.

Enemy units took terrible losses in their initial attack on Phnom Penh. The intensity of combat in the 1975 dry season was more than double that of any previous offensive. The enemy conducted four times as many attacks, and friendly casualties, which averaged about 71 per day in January 1974, increased to 120 per day in January 1975. Enemy kills jumped from 31 per day in January 1974 to 234 per day in January 1975. Communist prisoners of war and ralliers confirmed the heavy casualties. Personnel replacements for communist combat losses were readily available in the early part of the dry season, but by March they were hard to come by. Enemy regiments that entered combat with twelve hundred troops now had current strengths of only four hundred personnel. Whatever replacements were received were mostly poorly trained second-rate troops. For example, on 2 March the Khmer communist high command of KC Region 405 (southwest of Phnom Penh) issued an order that all men between the ages of sixteen and fifty-five must be mobilized for immediate deployment to the Phnom Penh battlefront. In February, two young prisoners captured by the 3rd FANK Division said they had been sent to the front without any training and had learned to fire their AK-47s on the road from Takeo to the Phnom Penh area. The same month, a rallier stated that many of the 152nd KC Regiment's troops were new and "did not even know how to hold a weapon." These men ended up as cannon fodder.

Nevertheless, the enemy kept reinforcing the siege of Phnom Penh with these newly formed or upgraded territorial units, so the number of battalions committed kept growing. The joint staff also realized the only way to save Phnom Penh was to pull units from the provincial capitals, but it did not reinforce with sufficient units. Although the number of FANK battalion equivalents in the capital region and lower Mekong increased, the total number of units countrywide decreased

Table 24. Force Distributions, Battalions

	FANK		KC			
Date	Total Countrywide	SMR	Total SMR	Phnom Penh	Mekong	Total Countrywide
20 December 1974	291	78	64–76	54–66	10	212–245
7 January 1975	291	100	130–137	93–100	37	231–253
7 February 1975	298	122	145–150	105–110	40	254–271
6 March 1975	289	121	156	120	36	260–271
3 April 1975	262	134	162	133	29	258–269
15 April 1975	262	134	164	152	12	258–269

Source: FANK, EMG, Phnom Penh, Cambodia.

as understrength units were inactivated to build up the ranks of viable units. The force distribution countrywide and at Phnom Penh and in the lower Mekong for both FANK and the KC is shown in table 24.

FANK's capital region and lower Mekong unit availability increased by fifty-six battalions between 20 December 1974 and 15 April 1975. Forty-one of these came from the six enclaves in MRs 2, 6, and 9, which were nearest Phnom Penh. Four outlying major enclaves in MRs 4 and 8 remained the same, but Battambang (MR 3) and Pursat (MR 9) were unbelievably reinforced by a total of sixteen battalions. (See map 10.) On 15 April, these twelve enclaves had 45 percent of all battalions and at least 50 percent of the overall combat personnel, yet by then they faced mostly understrength communist territorials, as the bulk of the enemy's main force battalions were in the capital region, engaged with the intervention battalions. Additional reinforcements for the Phnom Penh area were desperately needed but not forthcoming.

In one of his reports, Ambassador Dean described the situation as two punch-drunk fighters in the ring staggering around, each unable to knock the other out.[236] In early March, that was an apt description; both sides had taken enormous losses since 1 January. Of the intervention forces, 75 percent were understrength. The intervention brigade battalions were at only 51.5 percent of authorized strength. Estimated casualties through 3 March were 3,575 KHA and 9,433 WHA. The hospitals were full to overflowing, and the wounded kept arriving. Joint staff efforts to replace losses had fair success. They were able to

Map 10. GKR Military Regions. (Source: FANK, Cambodian Joint Staff, Phnom Penh, Cambodia.)

replace casualties. However, the great number of desertions depleted the combat ranks. The communists faced an even worse personnel situation, having lost approximately 9,700 KIA, many of whom died in their New Year's attack when the Cambodians were prewarned and ready. Enemy units also were heavily understrength, with replacements generally being young, untrained recruits. Ralliers and deserters continued to report low morale, although discipline remained firm.

That month, the Khmer communist strategy remained the complete isolation of Phnom Penh and its eventual capture. At that time, it effectively interdicted all land routes—leaving only the capture of the Mekong and the effective interdiction of Pochentong to complete their stranglehold. Although the enemy had already prevented any further convoys from resupplying Phnom Penh, it still concentrated on eliminating all friendly outposts and enclaves on the lower Mekong River. Thus, the continued preponderance of communist effort was against Phnom Penh and the lower Mekong. The forces attacking the many provincial capital enclaves in outlying regions had to keep up a reasonable pressure to fix FANK forces in place to the maximum extent possible. These enemy commanders had already sent most of their main force units to the Phnom Penh perimeter and were constantly being stripped of territorial troops to replace main force unit battle casualties. Nevertheless, they managed to initiate episodic attacks. The pressure against Kompong Cham continued throughout the month, and although FANK lost several positions, the communists were too weak to seriously threaten the city. The communists made serious inroads in MR-1 and were able to control a large portion of the rich rice-growing region and even threaten Battambang with attacks by fire. The enemy threatened Kompong Speu, but its activities at Kampot and Takeo slackened appreciably, reflecting its siphoning off of its combat troops to the Special Mekong Region. Aside from the minor pressure on outlying regions, the government's attention was definitely focused on Phnom Penh.

At mid-month, Rear Admiral Sarendy suspended all navy convoys because constant attrition had reduced operationally ready vessels to a minimum. During March the navy lost eighteen boats in riverine operations, including eight river patrol boats, two MSRs, and two monitors. Since 1 January, it had lost forty vessels—and more important,

70 percent of its riverine crew members had been casualties. At that time, the only convoys being conducted were for resupply operations to isolated garrisons, principally to Neak Luong. During the night of 6–7 March, before the stand-down, the navy successfully evacuated the embattled Mekong S-2 position. This was a major loss. Following the capture of S-2 the enemy made a three-pronged coordinated attack against Khal Salang, the ferry site opposite Neak Luong, and it fell. This was the last FANK position on the west bank of the Mekong. Using Khal Salang as a jumping-off location, the communists attacked the two remaining islands in the Mekong, thereby eliminating all FANK positions on both banks of the Mekong except the Banam–Neak Luong enclave. This enabled the enemy to consolidate its formidable forces on the lower Mekong for an all-out attack on Neak Luong. During the final week of March, it initiated the expected attack on the Banam–Neak Luong complex, which started with a major attack by fire, including rockets, artillery, mortars, and recoilless rifles. Having successfully pinned down the defenders, two regiments of the 1st KC Division made an amphibious landing on the eastern shore, shutting the highway between Banam and Neak Luong. The 1st and 2nd KC Divisions then attacked from the north and two enemy brigades attacked from the south, with incessant attacks by fire raining on the defensive position from the west bank. On 1 April, unable to withstand the assault, Neak Luong fell.

The enemy had fulfilled its objective, eliminating any government presence on the lower Mekong. More ominous, this allowed the communists to move their considerable lower Mekong forces to attack Phnom Penh. Flushed with victory, twenty-eight battalions reinforced the Phnom Penh perimeter forces. Meanwhile, the Cambodians realized they had lost the Mekong. They were also being fed a diet of negative reports regarding additional U.S. aid. Morale tumbled.

An army attaché, who attended a religious ceremony with the commanding general of the 3rd Division on 10 March, recounted an interesting story.[237] The ceremony honored the coming Khmer New Year and centered around a soldier who went into an apparent trance. When the soldier awoke, his body was believed to contain the reincarnation of an ancient warlord. The commanding general asked the soldier many questions about the enemy threat, possible successes, and tactics the

3rd Division should follow; he answered them all. After the ceremony, the attaché asked the assistant division commander, Colonel Sunthan, what he had been told, and Sunthan became extremely disturbed and vehemently told the attaché that the soldier had said it was "time for the Khmer Republic to find a country that they could count on for aid—not one that could not seem to make up its mind." Brig. Gen. Ly Kheang asked the attaché whether the United States would intervene militarily to save the Khmer Republic, and when he told him this was most unlikely, the general was visibly disturbed but said that with continued aid he believed the Republic could survive.

In early March, the U.S. State Department released a summary of the government's continued and numerous private initiatives in attempting to arrive at an early compromise settlement in Cambodia. This included several attempts, both direct and through intermediaries, to establish contact with Sihanouk and the Khmer Rouge leadership. A negotiated settlement had been the goal of U.S. policy all along. However, with the Mekong closed, the Khmer Rouge believed it had the upper hand and stepped up its in-country propaganda. Sihanouk reiterated in the harshest terms that he and the Khmer Rouge would never negotiate with the Phnom Penh "lackeys," and that no amount of U.S. aid could save Cambodia, which would fall shortly. On several occasions he also denied that a bloodbath would take place following a communist victory. He spoke of complete amnesty to all but "Seven Traitors" on the government side.

On 25 February 1975, President Ford told Congress that if his request for $222 million in military aid for Cambodia were not approved quickly, "the government forces will be forced within weeks to surrender to the insurgents."[230] He went on to declare it a "moral question" that the United States not "deliberately abandon a small country in the midst of its life and death struggle."[231] The nation's dire funding situation was known to all. In Phnom Penh, the local press was becoming bitter and very critical over the issue of supplemental aid. Among other issues, it claimed Cambodia had trusted the United States too much and criticized Congress for refusing to help an ally fighting for survival. On 4 March, a U.S. congressional delegation visited Phnom Penh to assess Cambodia's needs for supplemental military and economic assistance.

In the States, the antiwar sentiment was heating up as the Ford administration attempted to obtain supplemental aid—in his strongest statement yet, Ford asserted that Cambodia's fall would affect U.S. national security. Among the Congress members speaking loudly against the war, Senator Hubert Humphrey wanted to end all aid to Cambodia. On 27 February 1975, the *Philadelphia Inquirer* stated, "This country owes the Cambodians nothing." At the same time, other voices were raised to support the Khmer struggle; for example, on 10 February the *New York Times* asked, "Why are we so afraid to assert that what we are doing to help others defend themselves against communist sponsored aggression is the right thing to do?"

The drumbeat of U.S. antiwar sentiment was definitely heard in Cambodia, where newspapers reported the suspense resulting from the uncertainty of U.S. supplemental aid to the Khmer Republic and to South Vietnam, and the pessimistic views held by various members of the two congressional chambers in the United States. One Khmer newspaper editor said, for example, "The fate of the Khmer Republic is that of peoples betrayed."[238]

This played into the hands of the communist propagandists, whose theme of Khmer abandonment by the United States was reinforced by the Khmer communists' military successes in closing the Mekong. All of this visibly lowered FANK morale.

Battles on Phnom Penh Perimeter

During March, the intensity of combat on the lower Mekong was greater than on the Phnom Penh perimeter—but not by much. The enemy kept replenishing combat losses with young, green troops and directing its units to keep up the pressure. This resulted in a high rate of casualties, notwithstanding which, the enemy kept attacking. The main threat to Phnom Penh had always been from the northwest sector, obviously directed at capturing Pochentong. The enemy continued to build up forces on the Phnom Penh perimeter. In the southwest, it intensified the situation by using riot control gas to attack government troops; the encircled FANK troops had held their ground for over two weeks but now broke and ran from the gas. The communists managed to dig in north of the Prek Thnot River (the position from which they had fired 105 mm artillery in 1974, causing near panic in Phnom Penh). By this time, the enemy always protected its positions with plenty of land mines, the fear of which further reduced the FANK's aggressiveness to counterattack.

In the northwest sector, the joint staff directed its operations at clearing the rocket belt so as to eliminate the continual interdiction of Pochentong, the only source of airlanded resupply. Early on, the enemy took the key town of Toul Leap. However, FANK counterattacked and retook it but failed to exploit this victory, preferring instead to recoup and rest. The rocket belt was not cleared.

The communists continued to shell Pochentong almost at will. U.S. personnel on the ground at Pochentong not only kept a daily log but made impact analyses to determine patterns of incoming rounds so as to better position aircraft. Beginning on 26 March, a great number of 105 mm howitzer rounds began to impact—eighty-four in three days. Since the ground forces could make no headway against the enemy, the only deterrent was the air force. Because it was difficult for the Khmer Air Force planes to spot rocket- or artillery-firing sites, it initiated area suppression techniques in the rocket belt, often effectively cutting off the interdictions. Notwithstanding the air force's efforts, in the first few days of April the rate of interdictions more than doubled the very high rates of March, making operations at Pochentong extremely dicey.

Farther to the east in the northwest sector, the 38th FANK Brigade held off enemy attacks at Phnom Thom. The brigade started the month with more than eight hundred soldiers and finished it with about three hundred. The month ended with the 38th Brigade and 7th Division mostly surrounded, ineffective, and generally out of action. Friendly casualties were high.

Throughout March, enemy forces in the southeast sector continued to pin down friendly forces. FANK showed no initiative to retake Highway 1. Intelligence sources determined that the communists were going to move several major units into the Upper Bassac from the lower Mekong, which would provide them with a definite local superiority of forces. The southeast sector probably would become hotly contested soon.

Around Phnom Penh, it became clear that the enemy, buoyed by the halting of convoys and the lack of forthcoming U.S. supplemental aid, was fighting a war of attrition. One FANK soldier recounted that initially the communists attacked his position with artillery, mortars, and rockets. Then they started ground attacks, line after line: "We would shoot back, and the front line would crumble, only to be followed by another line and then another. They just kept coming until we were overrun." The communists' attrition objective was successful, although their casualties were high. Cambodia's personnel, equipment, and, most important, morale were all being attrited.

The combination of desertions and battle casualties severely reduced FANK unit strengths. Even if the 115 intervention battalions could have been brought up from their current near-half strength to full strength, the grossly limited funding, almost all of which had to be spent on ammunition, would have prohibited adequate reequipping. The constant depletion of the essential combat equipment, which was not replaced, continuously degraded FANK's combat capabilities.

During March, the reports of many attaché inspections were depressing; for example, it was stated that the 1st Division was in miserable condition and should be rated combat ineffective.[239] The rolling stock of the division remained in poor condition due to a shortage of repair parts. There were 250 desertions during the month (10 percent). In the 3rd Division, low foxhole strengths were also a big problem. Even greater was the loss of commanders at the platoon and company levels. Since 1 January, the 3rd Division had had over seventeen hundred casualties and received only three hundred new recruit replacements. Personal gear was old and worn out—the soldiers needed uniforms, boots, mosquito nets, and ponchos—no wonder the newspapers called FANK a ragtag army. The 7th Division had only one brigade capable of offensive operations. At some of its defensive positions, combat losses were staggering, and the remaining defenders were capable only of close-in defense, because many suffered from malaria, combat fatigue, and food-related problems. The navy had taken so many casualties that it became super-cautious. When sent to evacuate marine forces on the lower Mekong, its boats would stand off from the shore and make the evacuees swim toward them. (It is hard to maintain your weapon when forced to swim for your life.)

Notwithstanding all of their grave shortcomings, the friendly soldiers stood their ground and fought. On numerous occasions, they bloodied the enemy as the communists continued to press their attacks. It was really a shame that the infantry soldier was not better led; however, some of the Cambodian leaders were truly outstanding. Recognizing that many of the older senior officers were a definite detriment, Marshal Lon Nol attempted to shake up the senior command. On 11 March, Lieutenant General Fernandez resigned, and Lt. Gen. Sak Sutsakhan replaced him. Younger and tougher men replaced several other senior officers, but it was too late.

On Sunday afternoon, 23 March 1975, at his accommodations in Bangkok, I met with Fernandez for over an hour of frank discussions.[240] He said there were two situations in Cambodia, the military and the political, and the political situation was in disarray. He agreed with the current newspaper accounts that Marshal Lon Nol probably would not remain in the country too much longer; however, he believed there would be a major vacuum when he left and none of the four political parties had the strength to unify the country. Therefore, the military would eventually be the vehicle to unify the government and stabilize the situation. (Lon Nol left on 1 April, and Sutsakhan took over on 12 April.) Many times in our conversation, he said the politicians were not thinking of the good of their country but only their own welfare and safety. He stressed the importance of having both Brigadier General Chhong (Khmer Air Force) and Rear Admiral Sarendy (MNK) in on all military planning and considered part of the team (something initiated only since January 1975, which had greatly improved planning). He did not believe Sutsakhan could be effective at the joint staff headquarters, as Lon Nol had appointed him defense minister in addition to chief of staff, so he would probably have to spend most of his time in meetings and would not be able to follow day-to-day operations. (The next day in discussion, Brigadier General Palmer said that Sutsakhan had spent the whole day in meetings with the marshal and was not available to assist in military decisions.)

In updating Lieutenant General Fernandez on the current situation, I mentioned that the 23rd Brigade had fallen back and that this upset the schedule to retake the rocket pocket, and eliminate indirect fire on Pochentong. Fernandez said the marshal himself had appointed the commander of the 23rd Brigade, a very weak man who reported directly to the marshal. He then said he thought Gen. Lon Non and

Gen. Ith Suang were going to the joint staff operations center each day and were giving orders and directing affairs. He believed such interference could not be tolerated. (This subject had been a matter of concern to both Palmer and Ambassador Dean.)

Fernandez had put his finger on a major problem: there was no strong leader in charge of military operations. In Phnom Penh, there was a deep frustration with the poor military performance, and the government was unable to bring the Khmer Rouge to the negotiating table. This led Marshal Lon Nol to once again reshuffle his government, but to little avail, and he left Cambodia on 1 April for an extended visit to Indonesia. With the marshal out of the way and Sukham Khoy as acting president, everyone hoped that peace negotiations could be jump-started. However, by then it was obvious that Cambodia was on its last legs.

The attaché field report of the 3rd FANK Division, probably the most competent of all Cambodian army units, summarized the situation in April 1975.[239] According to the report, Lon Nol's departure at first raised hopes for the United States' increased military assistance, which would provide the soldiers with the uniforms and equipment they so drastically needed. As time wore on without U.S. assistance, however, morale dropped; and when Banam–Neak Luong was captured, it hit a new low, visibly affecting the soldiers' will to resist. On 7 April, as the division fell back along Route 4 under enemy pressure, it still managed to kill more than two hundred communists. Since 1 January 1975, the 3rd Division had undergone more than seven hundred attacks by fire and almost three hundred ground contacts. Its dry-season campaign casualty figures were high. With Chinese/NVA weapons and equipment, the enemy appeared better supported than the FANK was.

Regardless of severe shortages, the FANK fought on, severely bloodying the poorly trained and inexperienced enemy fillers. It reported that "its operations on 10 April caused heavy communist casualties. North of Route 4, the 13th Brigade reported killing 150 communists. Farther north the 45th Brigade claims 550 enemy killed, mostly by air attacks. Elsewhere on 10 April, Prey Veng reported 125 KC killed and 9 prisoners taken, while Takeo claimed 69 enemy killed and 3 prisoners."[241] If the reporting was reasonably accurate, then the heavy enemy losses—combined with a carefully planned 12 April operation utilizing three M113 squadrons, five artillery batteries, and full air support to counter the communists in the critical northwest sector—should have provided a manner of relief in the defense of Phnom Penh. Yet there was little hope.

A message from the JCS in Washington at the end of February 1975 conveyed concern that ammunition rationing and other understandably imposed restrictions had strangled Cambodian initiatives and, noting that the recently increased airlift resupply operations were temporarily building supplies at the Kantauk ammunition depot, questioned what actions could be taken in the field to encourage a higher tempo of operations.[242] The message suggested that the authorized supply rate for units actively engaged in combat be increased—that is, "shoot more." However, ammunition was not rationed, nor was it ever, and throughout the enemy's dry-weather offensive friendly units had no restrictions and greatly exceeded their funding-related authorized supply rates. Rationing would have acutely affected the army's ability to react to crisis situations.[243]

In the same time frame, a message from CINCPAC staff expressed serious concern about Cambodia's increased rate of ammunition expenditures. So as to preclude a major drawdown of ammunition, Admiral Gayler suggested a reduction in the 0.67 conservation ratio—that is, "shoot less."[244] His well-intentioned suggestion would not have solved the problem, since FANK was greatly exceeding current authorized supply rates. CINCPAC headquarters had anticipated the congressional cutback in funding and diligently monitored the need for ammunition conservation in Cambodia.

These two messages graphically highlighted the ammunition dilemma—how to successfully fight a war on a budget? Should there be all-out or constrained expenditures of ammunition? The troops combating the communists solved the dilemma. Utilizing available equipment and supplies, they were fighting all-out, and consequently, within a short period they would completely run out of ammunition without knowing it.

While all the Cambodian political and military machinations were going on, the well of U.S. funding was going dry, almost unnoticed. It was now obvious that the U.S. Congress was not willing to grant President Ford's request for supplemental funding. Cambodia was running out of supplies. It had no equipment replacement for combat losses; what equipment it had was short of repair parts; many of its troops needed uniforms; and, most important, there was little ammo left. So, on 27 March, Headquarters USSAG informed all concerned that the ammunition stocks at Phnom Penh and the enclaves were approaching critical levels.[245]

As of 26 March 1975, there were 2,309 short tons at Samae Son set aside for airdrops to the Cambodian enclaves. This ammo required palletized standard loads and special rigging. With a delivery of 105 short tons per day, the airdrop would end on 17 April. When the 2,019 short tons at Samae Son awaiting airland delivery were added to the 9,249 short tons stored at Phnom Penh, this amounted to 11,268 short tons. At the current ammunition consumption rate of 400 short tons per day, there would be zero depot stockage by 22 April. Long before then, however, there would be zero balances in many key individual line items, so in reality there would be severe ammunition shortages by mid-April. With the fiscal year only half over, the government had already exhausted its military assistance funding. No matter how valiantly Cambodia fought, defeat was inevitable.

The U.S. country team in Cambodia, led by the dynamic Ambassador Dean, was doing everything possible to shore up the flagging Cambodian situation. Dean reported:

> I do want you to know, however, the pride I feel in being part of this group of 200 dedicated Americans who are working around the clock to help our Khmer friends in meeting this supreme challenge. In this connection I should like to pay particular tribute to the professional skill and dedicated effort which BG William W. Palmer, Chief of MEDTC, has displayed during this trying period. He and his team, as well as the defense attaché and his staff, have performed efficiently and well.

We at Headquarters USSAG heartily endorsed the ambassador's tribute to Palmer, his dedicated, overworked MEDTC team, and the members of the defense attaché staff—their professional performances were truly exemplary.

The U.S. and South Vietnamese military support of the Cambodian conflict was at all times commendable. The same was definitely true of Ambassador Dean, his staff, and the USAID personnel. Unfortunately, both military and civilian in-country assistance were severely circumscribed by Congress's limit of two hundred U.S. personnel available in country.

The first of April was the turning point of the war. The overrun of Banam and Neak Luong, the last government strongholds on the Mekong River, freed up the communist forces on the lower Mekong to join in the siege of Phnom Penh. Additionally, the departure of Marshal Lon Nol indicated to all that the situation was grim. The Cambodians' morale fell drastically, although those who had assumed positions of responsibility put on optimistic faces. The malaise so evident at the end of February had taken its toll. Although it was business as usual in Phnom Penh, there was an atmosphere of great apprehension. Most of the foreign embassies had withdrawn their staffs, and it was time for Ambassador Dean to think seriously about evacuation.[246]

The Phnom Penh Evacuation

As early as April 1973, CINCPAC had tasked Headquarters USSAG to both plan and execute the emergency evacuation of Americans from Cambodia. USSAG's surface operations and plans division had completed evacuation plans for Operation EAGLE PULL, as it was called, by April 1974. The marines who were to serve as the security force had been in training for this operation at least since then. Initially, there were three evacuation options: fixed-wing civilian aircraft, fixed-wing military aircraft, and military helicopter. The continuous shelling of Pochentong by the Khmer communists generally eliminated any thought of fixed-wing aircraft evacuation. In January 1975, Lieutenant General Burns had called a planning conference at Nakhon Phanom, attended by key marine and air force personnel. The initial EAGLE PULL plan needed to be updated and closely reviewed. As was to be the case in the evacuation of Saigon, the anticipated number of evacuees kept changing. At one time, the American embassy estimated well over three thousand civilians. But that number kept decreasing, particularly since the embassy used airland resupply operations at Pochentong to backhaul both American and Cambodian personnel. On

3 April, Col. Sydney H. Batchelder and his advance group of marines arrived in Phnom Penh. His command element was extremely helpful in assisting the by now reduced embassy staff in last-minute evacuation planning as well as operational matters. Although plans initially included use of multiple landing zones, particularly the large Olympic athletic stadium, the group decided to use only one landing zone, a soccer field, LZ Hotel, about one kilometer northeast of the embassy and protected by a row of apartment buildings to the east that masked the area from probable direct fire from the communists on the east bank of the Mekong.

The choice of LZ Hotel necessitated a security force of 360 marines, to be inserted by twelve CH-53 helicopters flying in groups of three. The same CH-53s were to be used to evacuate the embassy and Cambodian personnel. Another heavy helicopter squadron would then evacuate the security force. At the last tally, about six hundred evacuees were expected, one-fourth American and the remainder foreign nationals. Actually, only 287 were evacuated, including eighty-four U.S. citizens.

Burns established L-hour as 0900 on 12 April. At 0730 hours that day, Ambassador Dean notified key Cambodian officials of the evacuation, instructing them to assemble at the embassy by 0930 hours if they desired to leave. Amazingly, only one senior official, Acting President Khoy, accepted. The others decided to stay and fight to preserve their government.

Naturally, there was formidable air cover overhead, ready to suppress enemy actions if necessary. The integration of the protective cover with the helicopter flow was effected superbly, as was the execution of the scheduling. The evacuation helicopters adhered to adjusted schedules with precision. I recall either CINCPAC or Washington asking Blue Chip where one echelon of choppers was when it was only a few minutes off schedule. Such was the senior command interest, which incidentally took time to satisfy. Another factor of great importance was the excellent maintenance of the helicopters, which worked flawlessly.

The communists got their act together about 1100 hours and attempted to interdict LZ Hotel with rocket and mortar fire—but it was too late to affect the operations. The evacuation had already been conducted, without the U.S. forces, tactical air, or marine security having to fire a single shot.

Although Washington had initially recommended against a helicopter evacuation, the operation's success was due primarily to the element of surprise. The enemy, certain that any evacuation would be from Pochentong Airfield, was caught completely unaware by the use of an in-town landing zone and was thus unable to make any disruptive efforts until too late.[247]

The recounting of Operation EAGLE PULL by the USSAG historian, Capt. Norman Felty, summarizes succinctly the successful operation (see appendix E). On 12 April American president Gerald Ford released a press statement:

> I decided with a heavy heart on the evacuation of American personnel from Cambodia because of my responsibility for the safety of the Americans who have served there so valiantly. Despite the evacuation, we will continue to do whatever possible to support an independent, peaceful, neutral and unified Cambodia. We can all take deep pride in the U.S. Armed Forces that were engaged in this evacuation operation. It was carried out with great skill, and in a manner that reflects the highest credit on all of those American servicemen who participated. I am deeply grateful to them for a job well done.

The Americans and Cambodians had both always hoped that if the military situation were to become stabilized, then the Khmer Rouge would be willing to negotiate. Many wished that Cambodian forces could hold on until the wet season in June, when the rising Mekong would flood its banks and permit convoys to run the blockades and the enemy ground forces besieging Phnom Penh would find their efforts much more difficult. This, of course, presumed that the United States would continue to provide essential funding and critical supplies. Therefore—notwithstanding the change in government, with Sukham Khoy assuming control as acting president—the Khmer fought on. The intensity of conflict in the days before the U.S. departure was the greatest of the war, exceeding the previous high point reached in the communists' initial 1975 dry-season assault, thereby accelerating the drawdown of ammunition.

By massing for its assaults, the enemy made excellent targets for the air force, which, despite the continued interdiction of Pochentong, was providing effective close air support to the beleaguered ground forces. On 10 April, for example, in the important northwest sector, the 13th Brigade reported killing 150 KC north of Route 4, and the 45th Brigade claimed 550 KC killed, mostly by air attacks. Elsewhere in the provinces, friendly forces at Prey Veng and Takeo had successful operations, killing 125 and 69 KC, respectively. These losses, even if exaggerated, were excessive, and an indication that the enemy was using poorly trained troops to press its incessant attacks. The *Christian Science Monitor*'s Dan Southerland noted, "What amazes some observers is that any (FANK) soldiers continue to fight, and some fight well."[248]

New Government

Once the United States departed, taking Acting President Sukham Khoy with it, those brave souls who remained—almost all the Khmer leaders—had to organize their third government in as many weeks. A Supreme Commission of seven, composed of four military and three civilians led by Lt. Gen. Sak Sutsakhan with Prime Minister Long Boret as deputy, took over the reins of government. Their first decision was to defend Phnom Penh and the provincial enclaves by all means possible.[249] President Ford, greatly impressed that these Khmer in positions of responsibility had stayed on, authorized the airlift to continue as long as the Cambodian government continued to resist the insurgents. FANK troops had retreated from their positions on the east bank of the Mekong River at Phnom Penh, and the Khmer communists could target Pochentong at will with artillery. The communists did not, however, shell Phnom Penh. Therefore, the airland option was no longer thinkable, not just because of the Pochentong interdiction, which the U.S. crews had continued to brave, but also because landings required U.S. controllers on the ground and U.S. cargo handler supervisors to unload the aircraft. U.S. personnel could no longer be brought into Cambodia. The Khmer were terribly disappointed that resupply had to be by airdrop; obviously the required supplies could not, in the long run, be delivered, even if they were available to call forward. Phnom Penh was running short of rice and needed about six hundred short tons per day to feed its swollen population. There was hardly any ammunition remaining for delivery, but all that remained in the pipeline would be airdropped. At the bottom of the barrel, many ammunition line-item shortages were evident. Although no airdrop sorties were scheduled on 12 and 13 April, they recommenced on 14 April, with deliveries to Takeo, Prey Veng, Lovek, and Kampot. However, nothing was delivered to Phnom Penh, because the agreed-upon drop zone was inundated. With rice critically short at Phnom Penh and ammunition quickly running out, it was obviously only a matter of time until an insurgent takeover.

Southerland reported that the Khmer had expressed a sense of U.S. betrayal, as they were left with dwindling supplies and little hope of a negotiated end to the war.[250] The feelings of the people were later given voice when President Sukham Khoy said, "The United States led Cambodia into this war, but when the war became difficult the United States pulled out."

Consequently, the Cambodian government desperately sought a cease-fire, hoping to establish negotiations. After the U.S. exodus, the communists let up in their attacks, particularly on Phnom Penh. On 8 April 1975 a communications intercept of a communist message stated:

> In the event that Phnom Penh is completely liberated, we must prepare for our objective and goals as follows: All the capital resources in the city must be protected without fail. . . . Anyone who ravages would become a traitor of the nation. . . .
>
> In addition to the matter of protecting the resources there are two other problems which we must solve immediately i.e. mobilizing the people and stopping acts of sabotage. Mobilize the civilians and, first of all, take them to a liberated sector in order to stabilize the situation. . . .
>
> As for foreign nationals such as Frenchmen and various embassy personnel who are still remaining in Phnom Penh, we must gather them and place them in areas and protect their safety.

The Surrender

On 14 April, an air force T-28 aircraft flown from Pochentong by a deserter dropped two bombs on the FANK headquarters building, killing seven.[251] A review of the Phnom Penh and Saigon endgame situations revealed how similarly the events of the final days at each location played out. This traitorous bombing act initiated a series of events that culminated during the evening of 16 April when Long Boret, Lon Non, Chhim Chun, and Thong Lim Huong capitulated. Lon Non and Chhim Chun then went to the Ministry of Information to broadcast an appeal to troops to stop fighting. Shortly afterward, Maj. Gen. Mey Sichan, speaking for the government, broadcast the decision to surrender in a recorded message our signal unit monitored in Bangkok. As Sichan, delivering Lieutenant General Sutsakhan's message, said, "I myself and the committee of the armed forces will make a decision with the delegation from our brother side about a way to bring peace to our country." The Khmer Rouge broke into the address: "We did not come here to talk." And the interrupter said, "The Lon Nol clique and some of its officers should all be hanged."[252] The Khmer Rouge then appealed to citizens and troops all over the country to lay down their arms and cooperate with the insurgents. Khmer Rouge leaders had earlier warned the government and other politicians to leave the country for their own safety.

On 15 April, our intelligence group in Bangkok informed us that in the event of the imminent collapse of Phnom Penh and the impossibility of extraction by air, the Khmer chief of naval operations, Rear Adm. Vong Sarendy, as well as other naval officers, would embark on the Mekong in navy craft in an attempt to escape the communists by exfiltrating into South Vietnam.[253] Intelligence provided us with the frequencies and call signs of the PRC-25 radios aboard the three craft. The message went on to say that the situation in Phnom Penh was deteriorating rapidly and the fall of the city was expected the next day.

Headquarters USSAG had always maintained direct radio contact with both the joint staff operations center and the navy headquarters, which enabled us, in our tripartite hat, to keep abreast of critical situations, particularly with respect to the Mekong convoys. So on the morning of 16 or 17 April I was surprised when Blue Chip informed me Rear Admiral Sarendy was on the radio and wanted to talk with me. Sarendy said, "My dear friend General Hunt, My officers and I are here at naval headquarters, and the communists are entering the city. It is only a matter of hours and they will be here. In the name of our close relationship and our good friendship I ask you to send a helicopter to extract us, or we will all be killed." I replied that I understood his situation and his request at this time but USSAG did not have the authority to dispatch a helicopter to Cambodia. I told him I would ask higher-ups for permission. Though we did not hold out much hope, we immediately called the American embassy in Bangkok to see if they could obtain permission to dispatch a chopper. It would have been a risky venture, but Cambodian Air Force helicopters had been operating in and around Phnom Penh for days without any mishaps. Within two hours we received word that U.S. assets were not to enter Cambodia. So, with a heavy heart I had to tell him we could not dispatch a helicopter. I suggested that he use naval assets to escape. He replied that they would surely die. He did not get off the net and left the radio open.

Admiral Sarendy was the most dynamic of all the Khmer military leaders. Until the last days, when both personnel and equipment had been so greatly attrited, the navy had been a formidable and valiant force. This very personal final conversation with him was extremely difficult.

Following the official declaration of surrender, the government officials took their cars to the Phnom Penh stadium, where air force helicopters were waiting for them. Long Boret and Thong Lim Huong boarded one helicopter and were preparing to depart when Long Boret's family arrived. The two men descended from the helicopter to help the others aboard, but the helicopters suddenly took off. As they ascended, passengers in the crafts could see enemy troops take Thong Lim Huong and Long Boret, along with Long Boret's family, into custody.[254] Those officials who did manage to land at Samrong said Lon Non and Chhim Chun were also captured but they were not sure of the circumstances.

Long Boret had been the glue which held together several of the Cambodian governments. He was an exceptional man who served his country well until the very end.

The Aftermath

We received debriefs from several sources as to the events of 17 April.[255] Khmer communist elements entered Phnom Penh that morning from several directions, and the situation quickly became confused, with various communist factions issuing orders and nobody apparently in overall charge. People stood on the sidewalks, waving to the insurgents. White flags and banners flew from every building in the city. We were told that the joint staff had ordered the display of white surrender flags, and friendly military vehicles could be seen flying theirs. The square in front of the American embassy was filled with hundreds of cheering people waving white flags. But the cheering did not last long.

On 18 April, the Khmer insurgents forced the entire population of Phnom Penh to leave the city. On the outskirts, the people were forced to go in different directions; however, the communists did not seem to have any organization or method in determining the directions people took. Anyone who refused to obey instructions immediately was shot on the spot. For the first several days, the enemy gave people evacuated from Phnom Penh no food or water. They had to subsist on whatever they had carried with them or could beg from villagers along the way. After the first two or three days' walk, the route was littered with dead bodies. Many of these people had been shot, while others seemed to have died of natural causes. No one was burying the dead.

I spent several hours discussing the Cambodian situation with one of the French doctors who worked at the Phnom Penh hospital. He told me that the communists had shown up at his hospital and immediately evacuated everybody. He had just finished an amputation of a soldier's leg, and they made the soldier get up and vacate. Obviously, the man died shortly thereafter.

About a thousand foreigners had sought refuge in the French embassy. The doctor said the sanitary situation there was deplorable; he and his medical associates were kept busy trying to maintain the health of this group. The communists entered the embassy to remove all Khmer. After three weeks, all foreigners there finally were loaded into vehicles and taken on a several days' journey to Thailand. Phnom Penh was completely deserted, as were Kompong Chhnang, Pursat, and Battambang, the cities they passed through along Route 5 on their evacuation. They were all ghost towns.[256]

On 22 April we intercepted a message: "Request you implement the measures you were informed about previously, that is, all the enemy leaders must be eliminated without fail. As for the provincial leaders, the senior commanders and those who owe us a blood debt, both large and small, you must implement above plan to get rid of them. Request you implement this plan secretly." And on 28 April, from Kompong Thom we received the following intercept: FANK officers between the rank of 1st lieutenant and colonel were being eliminated, wives of these officers too, "because our observations revealed that they are no different than their husbands." District chiefs and assistants plus important people were also eliminated.

There were reports after reports from all areas of Cambodia detailing incidents of communist atrocities. They would separate the military and send them for rehabilitation training at undesignated camps; they propagandized that the soldiers would not be harmed and the rehabilitation training would enable them to come back and help their country. However, upon arrival at the camps, the soldiers were accused of being traitors to the country and its people and were sentenced "by the people" to death by firing squads. Thousands of military men died.[257]

The treatment of civilians was harsh in a different way. For example, on 23 and 24 April the town of Battambang was evacuated. The people were moved approximately twenty-five kilometers out, where they were told to start farming. They were not given any food or tools to work with. To cultivate the land, they were forced to pull plows by hand, using eight men to pull each. They were divided into groups of ten and told that the remainder of each group would be held responsible if any of its members escaped. Cholera broke out in many places; without medicine, with little food, and having no hope, many died.

Later in June, those Cambodian refugees who had managed to escape to Thailand and then attempted to return home—men, women, and children—were executed on Route 5, approximately ten kilometers from the border.[258] The communists explained the executions by claiming these people were treacherous to the country; they had been brainwashed in Thailand and might be dangerous. They had to be punished as an example, to deter others from escaping, and the severe punishment was given because the country needed a strong and strict government. Well, the government was indeed strict. And so the elimination went on, targeting the intelligentsia, engineers, teachers, military, and those with glasses, among others. Close to a million were killed or died because of harsh living conditions. This was the war's legacy to this formerly peaceful and happy country.

Summing Up

With time, as the Khmer communist forces expanded and became much better supplied, the war in Cambodia grew in intensity. The October 1973 combat intensity factor was 0.73, and in October 1974 it was 4.70, but in the 1975 dry-weather campaign it was almost an order of magnitude greater than in 1974, peaking at 22.30. The enemy continually attacked the Phnom Penh perimeter and along the lower Mekong, and it had to be repulsed. A concomitant to the increased intensity of combat was, of course, a major increase in battle casualties.

The Cambodian conflict was a bloody one. On the friendly side, the troops often were poorly led, which caused unnecessary casualties. Mostly on the defensive, sometimes the troops were not made to properly dig in and to clear fields of fire. Yet they had firepower superiority, and their artillery and close air support took a heavy toll on enemy troops in the attack. Fortunately, this was an unsophisticated environment, devoid of heat-seeking missiles that would have played havoc with the slow-flying aircraft. The enemy was a determined adversary, generally on the offensive. Their commanders had no compunction about forcing their untrained troops into frontal assaults, often utilizing the cover of darkness to gain advantage. In early January we had reports that they placed refugees in the front ranks as screens during assaults. The reported casualties during the 1975 dry-weather offensive are as shown in table 25. About 60 percent of all casualties occurred in the defense of Phnom Penh.

Casualty reporting data from Cambodia was usually obtained

Table 25. Khmer Republic—Casualty Recap, 1 January–11 April 1975

			Countrywide casualties		
	Friendly KHA	**WHA**	**Enemy KIA**	**KBA**	**Total enemy**
1–31 January	2,644	5,088	5,293	1,956	**7,249**
1–28 February	931	4,345	1,948	565	**2,513**
1–31 March	1,145	5,709	3,121	1,322	**4,443**
1–11 April	259	1,376	1,016	890	**1,906**
Total	4,979	16,518	11,378	4,733	**16,111**

Source: DAMSREP/DAO, Phnom Penh, Cambodia.

from field spot reporting, and it was often difficult to reconcile—the EMG J-2 would have one set of data and the EMG J-3 another. Army reporting was, in fact, generally conservative and normally understated the situation, particularly with respect to the enemy killed in action. We worked diligently with MEDTC and the attachés to rectify any reporting discrepancies. We used the statistical information to portray trends, and for that purpose the inputs were satisfactory. In table 25, the friendly statistics are close to correct. The enemy killed in action may be overstated. However, at 3.24, the rates of enemy to friendly killed countrywide were not greatly out of line, considering that FANK was on the defensive, had firepower superiority (especially with the air force), and at the end was facing grossly untrained troops. With respect to the Phnom Penh battles, even when one discounts the enemy killed by 20 percent and takes into consideration the wounded in action, the total enemy casualties closely approximate the number of main force units that initiated the dry-weather campaign. That is why the communists were so desperate for reinforcements and replacements. The 10,667 total FANK capital area casualties during the same period amounted to over one-third of the forces in contact. By any reckoning, it was a bloody war. For the eighteen months between 11 October 1973 and 17 April 1975, the friendly casualties in the Cambodian conflict, as best as can be determined, were 11,393 KHA and 31,267 WHA, whereas the communists had 31,999 KIA.

From 17 October 1973, when Headquarters USSAG started keeping combat statistics, until the fall of Cambodia, FANK had a daily average of eighty-eight casualties, nearly one-fourth of them killed by hostile action, and the communists had an average of fifty-nine killed. The overall reported exchange ratio was 2.81 to 1, and that was probably nearly correct, considering we had no idea of the enemy wounded who died due to primitive or nonexistent medical treatment facilities. The ratio of FANK KHA/(KHA + WHA) from contacts was 0.267, somewhat higher than the 0.212 ratio in South Vietnam. But then, Cambodia's medical and evacuation facilities were not nearly as good.

When one contemplates these numbers and focuses on the carnage, it is clear what the Khmer Rouge leadership meant when it talked of "those who owe us a blood debt." Unfortunately, the Khmer Rouge knew no bounds in its debasement after the capitulation, and it set

Table 26. Combat Data, FY 75

	Weeks	ABF	Minor contacts	Major contacts	Casualties per major contact	Combat intensity factor
RVNAF 28 June 1974 to 27 March 1975	39	19,533	21,168	691	27,907	1,858,777
	avg.	500	542	17.7	715	47,661
FANK 26 June 1974 to 24 March 1975	39	18,653	9,550	375	21,006	1,216,310
	avg.	478	244	9.6	538	31,187

Sources: "Republic of Vietnam Ammunition Conservation Study," June 1975, Headquarters USSAG, Nakhon Phanom, Thailand; "Khmer Republic Ammunition Conservation Study," June 1975, Headquarters USSAG, Nakhon Phanom, Thailand.

about to systematically kill many of the Cambodian military. We had report after report of bodies seen lying along the sides of the road and in centers of towns, many of them men in military uniforms who had been shot or had their throats cut. We had verifiable information concerning the Khmer Rouge penchant for harsh discipline (read as "atrocities"), and although I anticipated a retribution of three hundred thousand deaths, I never dreamed of the extent of the Khmer Rouge's killing fields.

I developed the combat intensity formula for the RVNAF above all to determine the levels of combat. It related to artillery ammunition expenditures, since our premise was "Ammunition demands vary in direct ratio to the intensity of combat."[296] By the summer of 1974, FANK had a data reporting system that enabled us to calculate the combat intensity factor for Cambodia on the same basis as for South Vietnam. Table 26 gives a summary of the FY 75 combat data for both countries.

A review of these combat statistics for both countries in FY 75 is most revealing. It shows, surprisingly, that Cambodia had almost as many attacks by fire per week as South Vietnam, 478 versus South Vietnam's 500. This was because the communists, faced with fixed defensive positions at the enclaves, resorted to attacks by fire to keep FANK under pressure. In FY 75, 26 percent of all attacks by fire (124 per week) were against the major forces defending the Phnom Penh Special Military Zone, and the rest were generally against the enclaves into which the military and the general population had withdrawn.

Conversely, the multitude of RVNAF dispersed military positions resulted in many more minor contacts, with a cumulative large number of casualties. Both conflicts were wars of attrition. Of all ground conflicts, the major contacts were 3.2 percent in South Vietnam and 3.8 percent in Cambodia. However, the average casualties per major contact were 39 percent higher in Cambodia, 56.0 versus 40.4, probably reflecting both the tactics and training of the troops. Overall, as was to be expected, the combat intensity in South Vietnam was 53 percent greater than in Cambodia.

As President Lon Nol was willing to give up control of land to protect the majority of the Khmer population, fourteen major enclaves existed; the largest, of course, was Phnom Penh. This strategy allowed FANK to have defined defensive positions with interior lines; however, it created a severe logistical resupply problem. This issue was solved primarily by the USAF airland/airdrop operations supported by the Cambodian Air Force. Thus, the army was not spread out attempting to protect thousands of villages and outposts, as was the military in South Vietnam.

The success of the enclave strategy created an ultimately fatal mind-set at EMG Headquarters. Lieutenant General Fernandez had stated that the joint staff would never allow a major enclave to be captured, leaving too many battalions to protect the enclaves even though in 1975 the enemy had concentrated its forces on two objectives—Phnom Penh and the lower Mekong. It had pulled its regular battalions away from the enclaves, leaving territorial units to create harassing pressures, hoping to tie down friendly units. Many battalions were unnecessarily kept at the enclaves when they could and should have been utilized at the Phnom Penh Special Military Zone.

The enclave strategy also created a defensive orientation. When FANK attacked out of the enclaves, it was often successful, but it did not sally forth to any great extent. In South Vietnam, however, to keep the enemy off balance, the RVNAF, directed to protect all of its territory, took to the offensive, initiating more attacks than the communists did in FY 75.

As late as 15 April 1975, FANK had seventy-five battalions in defensive positions located at the six enclaves in MR-2, -3, -4, and -9, where the combat intensity was lowest, versus thirty-eight enemy battalions, mostly understrength territorials. Many of these units were desperately needed at Phnom Penh and the lower Mekong. The only area, notably, where FANK troops did not have a perimeter-type defense with interior lines was in the lower Mekong, and it was there where, because of a lack of combat strength, they could not successfully defend their positions, losing them one by one.

The Cambodians' enclave strategy worked. They took the heavy poundings of the enemy's attacks by fire—Kompong Seila was a good example. When available, the artillery and close air support mauled the enemy, and the ground contacts attrited it. But they could not muster the troop strength to control the Mekong. As their supplies dwindled because of the drastic cut in funding, their morale and fighting spirit degraded.

Why Did Cambodia Fall?

It is difficult to precisely analyze why the Cambodian efforts failed to hold off the Khmer communist insurgency. Some reasons are obvious. The failure of the Cambodian military leadership certainly was a major cause. The Khmer culture did not lend itself to the hands-on, take-care-of-your-men leadership prevalent in the West. There was a definite innate lack of a sense of urgency at all levels; the joint staff's inability to react to the enemy's interdiction of the Mekong in 1975 is a prime example. High-level corruption was a cancer, particularly with respect to the practice of padding the rosters with ghost soldiers. The army's inability to maintain combat effective strengths in its intervention units was certainly also a prime cause; the government would not even crack down on the great number of desertions until late in the game. Yet, all of these factors were prevalent throughout the entire course of the war.

Only in February and March 1975 did the Cambodian defenses start to unravel, and a serious malaise accompanied by a precipitous drop in morale ensued. The U.S. Congress's failure to provide the funding necessary to adequately support the war effort caused much of this defeatism. Had the Cambodians not capitulated, they would have completely run out of ammunition within days. All funds had been utilized to provide critical ammunition, so they were not available for replacement equipment, repair parts, or even uniforms. FANK was derided as a "ragtag" army. This visible lack of support unquestionably had a severely deleterious effect on morale, to say nothing of combat effectiveness.

The Khmer communists, in contrast, seemed to become better equipped and supplied as the war wore on. They certainly did not lack either sufficient ammo or replacements. Whereas the government was reluctant to enforce conscription or crack down on deserters, the communists had no qualms about enforced conscription and rigid discipline. That these units all had a cadre of North Vietnamese or North Vietnamese–trained Khmers enhanced their combat capabilities, whereas, unfortunately, U.S. advisers were not authorized to support Cambodian units and were limited to two hundred in-country personnel.

Another key factor was that, as in South Vietnam, the United States withdrew its supporting combat forces; on 15 August 1973, Congress forbade the U.S. Air Force from contributing its formidable firepower support. As in South Vietnam, we attempted to augment that loss by providing the fledgling Cambodian forces with additional armor, artillery, and tactical air equipment. However, funding constraints seriously undercut the effectiveness of the increased firepower and mobility.

The fall of Cambodia was due to a clash of ideologies: the cautious democratic approach of the Cambodian government versus the communists' harsh disciplinary methods; the failure of the U.S. Congress to support the war versus the People's Republic of China's and North Vietnam's continual support of the Khmer communists.

In these wars by budgets, the U.S. budgets were woefully insufficient. Vietnamese and Cambodian combatants bravely fought the communist aggression and gave their lives in futile efforts. Both countries were doomed. They could not have prevailed militarily because they lacked the sinews of war—ammunition, petroleum, and equipment. They were doomed by the budget—the United States' lack of financial support and resolve. We had a commitment to the peoples of South Vietnam and Cambodia, and we let them down. The killing fields of Cambodia need not have happened. The loss of Southeast Asia is not in the United States' national conscience; its citizens generally are unaware of how Congress abandoned our allies in South Vietnam and Cambodia.

4

The *Mayaguez* Incident

USSAG/7AF had just completed its responsibilities for the emergency evacuations of American citizens from Cambodia and South Vietnam, and with the loss of those two countries to the communists our headquarters was due to stand down on 30 June. Personnel were enjoying the calm after the hectic days of April 1975. Shortly after noon on 13 May we received an important message from the JCS that the Cambodians had commandeered a U.S. merchant ship in the Gulf of Thailand and we were to immediately launch aircraft to locate the ship. We quickly went to the command center and directed two standby F-111 aircraft, which were on an alert status, to locate the vessel. They found it at anchor about one kilometer off Koh Tang Island. Subsequently, the JCS directed us to maintain constant surveillance and take any actions necessary to ensure that the vessel did not enter a Cambodian port. Koh Tang Island was only thirty miles from the major port of Kompong Som.

The Seventh Air Force battle staff took over the operation, with the aircraft assets available from the airbases in Thailand, which included F-4s, F-111s, A-7s, OV-10s, C-130s, KC-135s, and helicopters, as well as an airborne command and control aircraft, which was deployed from Clark Air Force Base in the Philippines.

The U.S. merchant vessel was a container ship called the SS *Mayaguez*. Washington obviously was very displeased with this affront by the Cambodians, and strong actions might have to be taken to secure the release of the *Mayaguez* and its crew. CINCPAC directed Lieutenant General Burns to plan for a helicopter assault operation to land on top of the *Mayaguez*'s containers and take the vessel by force. The only troops in country at that time trained for such an operation were those in the air force security police unit stationed at NKP. When the unit was asked for volunteers, every member stood tall. So USSAG made plans for a helicopter assault at first light on 14 May. That evening, about a hundred air force security police went by helicopter to U-Tapao, the closest U.S. base in Thailand to Koh Tang, which was to be used as the staging area. During the transfer, a CH-53 crashed, killing eighteen security police and five crew members on board. It was downed in the same area in which a previous helicopter crash had occurred several months earlier. This caused some serious initial concerns: at the time, there were many unidentified aircraft reportings from southern Laos. However, the cause of the accident was definitely established as a mechanical failure.

At U-Tapao, at 0400 hours on 14 May, the security police and helicopter crews were ready to seize the *Mayaguez*. However, the order to execute was not given. Subsequently, two platoons of marines from Cubic Point in the Philippines and a marine combat battalion from Okinawa were deployed to U-Tapao. As the marines arrived, they replaced the security police, who were still on alert status.

Late in the day on 13 May, USSAG/7AF received instructions to sanitize the island—that is, to isolate the area so no boats could leave the island for the mainland, and, in particular, no shipping could reinforce Koh Tang. Only movement between the *Mayaguez* and the island was to be allowed. During the evening, AC-130 and F-111 aircraft monitored watercraft in the area. In the morning, tactical aircraft were on station. The Seventh Air Force had established rules of engagement and ordinance requirements as well as the aircraft tasking necessary to ensure constant surveillance.

On the morning of 14 May, I was at the command center observing activities and Lieutenant General Burns and the Seventh Air Force staff were in a planning session. A little after 0800, the aircraft on station reported that three vessels had departed Koh Tang, heading in different directions toward the mainland. In following instructions, the fighter aircraft engaged the leading vessel. It first fired rockets and .20-caliber machine guns forward of the craft. When the craft did not alter its course, A-7s dropped CBU-30 canisters filled with the riot-control agent CS on the speeding patrol boat. When this had no effect, the pilot asked for instructions and I responded, "Sink it"—which he proceeded to do. When our aircraft initiated the same procedures on the second boat, it turned back toward Koh Tang. Attention now turned to the third boat, still holding a course for Kompong Som. On the first pass the aircraft fired rockets. Then it made a second pass, firing its machine guns. One of the pilots reported, "I think I saw a 'round-eye' on board but I can't be sure." We requested the aircraft make several additional passes to see whether it could verify that potential sighting. It could not. The A-7s then dropped riot control agents on the vessel. The boat did not veer from its course, and no additional personnel verifications could be made. The lead pilot then stated that the boat was nearing land and asked for his instructions. I instructed the command center officer in charge to tell him to "Let it go." I then said I would take the responsibility for the decision if there was any fallout from letting the vessel reach land. It turned out later that by the grace of God all the *Mayaguez* crew was on board that boat. If not for the sharp-eyed pilot, it could have been a disaster.

At midday there was a conference call among the National Military Command Center, CINCPAC, CINCPACFLT, CINCPACAF, and COMUSSAG to discuss the concept of operations for the recapture of the *Mayaguez* and its crew. The concept was to board and secure the ship, conduct selected air strikes on the Cambodian mainland, and carry out a helicopter assault on Koh Tang to recover the crew.

By this time the USS *Harold E. Holt,* a destroyer escort, was in the vicinity of Koh Tang Island, so it was decided to have three CH-53 helicopters lift a boarding party onto the *Holt.* The boarding party was made up of forty-eight marines of D Company, 1st Battalion, of the 4th Marines, who were to secure the *Mayaguez,* six military sealift personnel and six naval crew who were to place the vessel under steam, two ordinance experts to defuse any booby traps or explosives found on board, and an army linguist. The helicopters deposited their troops about 0600 hours, and the *Holt* maneuvered expertly up against the container ship. Fortunately, its main deck matched the elevation of the main deck of the *Mayaguez,* facilitating an old-fashioned assault boarding. There were no Cambodians on board. By 0800 hours, the *Mayaguez* had been secured (see photo 9).

The aircraft carrier *Coral Sea,* previously bound for Australia, was ordered to make all speed to the vicinity of Koh Tang Island. This proved very fortunate for two reasons. First, the aircraft from the *Coral*

Photo 9. The Recovery of the *Mayaguez*. (Source: Headquarters USSAG, Nakhon Phanom, Thailand, produced by 432nd Reconnaissance Technical Squadron, U.S. Air Force.)

Sea would carry out the directed air strikes against the Cambodian mainland, and second, the flight deck of the carrier was indispensable to the helicopters extracting the marines from Koh Tang on the evening of 15 May. Some have criticized the National Security Council decision to bomb selected targets on the mainland to prevent potential Koh Tang reinforcements. However, I believe the decision was a wise one. It showed the United States' determination. A-6 and A-7 aircraft from the *Coral Sea* bombed the Ream navy base, the Ream airfield, and warehouses at the port of Kompong Som. Bomb damage assessment

Photo 10. Bomb Damage Assessment, Kompong Som, 15 April 1975. (Source: Headquarters USSAG, Nakhon Phanom, Thailand, produced by 432nd Reconnaissance Technical Squadron, U.S. Air Force.)

indicated that the effort was successful. The assessment at Kompong Som showed major damage to two warehouses (see photo 10).

The military actions taken by the air force, navy, and marines to secure the *Mayaguez* and conduct an assault on Koh Tang Island were primarily for the purpose of recovering the crew. The air strikes against the mainland were also conducted to leverage the crew's recovery. Yet, the crew's status was still unknown on the morning of 15 May. No word or sightings had been received.

Consequently, all concerned were absolutely amazed when an

aircraft identified a Thai fishing boat flying white flags and heading toward the guided missile destroyer USS *Henry B. Wilson,* which had just arrived in the area—as having some of the *Mayaguez* crew on board. It was 1000 hours when the Thai boat came alongside the *Wilson,* which determined that all forty crew members of the *Mayaguez* were on board. What a fantastic change of events!

According to an official translation of a Thai Army report based on the debriefing of five Thai fishermen after they had been released by the Khmer communists along with the crew of the *Mayaguez* and had returned to Thailand, on 12 May, KC gunboat 126 had taken the Thai boat *Sin War I* while it was sailing in international waters in the vicinity of Koh Tang Island, where it was forced to land. There were also two captured Vietnamese vessels at Koh Tang. Khmer communists had executed seven Vietnamese abducted in late 1974 while sailing in adjacent waters; the pirating of the *Mayaguez* was definitely not an isolated incident.

Once the *Wilson* confirmed that the *Mayaguez* and its crew had been recovered unharmed, at about noon the order went out from the National Military Command Center to immediately cease all offensive operations against the Khmer Republic related to the seizure of the *Mayaguez.*

The Assault on Koh Tang Island

Koh Tang was about 3.5 kilometers long and 1.7 kilometers wide at its base, and it was covered with dense vegetation. The only clearing on the island was at the base of a small spur on its northwestern tip. The *Mayaguez* was anchored about a kilometer offshore from the eastern edge of the spur. If the crew were on the island, they would likely be here (see map 11).

Under the command of Lt. Col. Randall W. Austin, the 2nd Battalion, 9th Marines was deployed from its base in Okinawa to the U-Tapao Air Base by C-141s, arriving on 14 May.[259] Austin made an aerial reconnaissance of the island late that afternoon. He determined that there were two suitable landing zones for a helicopter assault, one a small cove on the western edge that could handle two helicopters, and the other an open beach on the eastern side, with more than sufficient

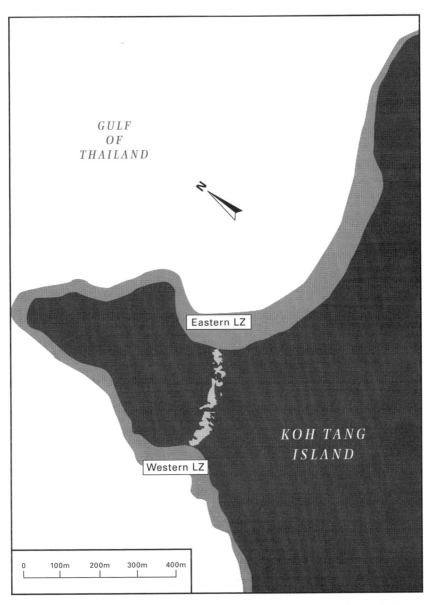

Map 11. Northern Koh Tang Island, Indicating Landing Zones. (Source: From photographs produced by the 432nd Reconnaissance Technical Squadron, U.S. Air Force.)

space for multiple helicopter insertions. The two landing zones were about four hundred meters apart.

The air force helicopter assets available for the assault were nine HH-53s and eight CH-53s. Two of the nine HH-53s of the 40th Aerospace Rescue and Recovery Squadron remained on ground alert at Korat in case emergency requirements arose elsewhere.[260] The HH-53s (call sign "Jolly Green") were air-refuelable, which was very important considering the great distances involved. Just as important, the helicopters had 450-gallon foam-filled tip tanks. The CH-53s of the 21st Special Operations Squadron (call sign "Knife") were not air-refuelable, and they had 650-gallon non-foam-filled tip tanks, which made the helicopters much more vulnerable to ground fire. The distance from U-Tapao to Koh Tang was about 210 miles. The fact that the Jolly Greens could be refueled from the HC-130s provided much greater flexibility.

The initial assault force consisted of a 180-man battalion landing team from the 2/9 Marines, which were to be inserted by three HH-53s and five CH-53s. The helicopters launched about 0415 hours in four successive sections of two helicopters each for the approximately two-hour flight to Koh Tang. Knife-21 and Knife-22 were to insert on the western landing zone, while the other six were to insert on the eastern landing zone, Knife-23 and Knife-31 first, then Knife-32 and Jolly Green-41, and finally Jolly Green-42 and Jolly Green-43. Knife-21 unloaded twenty-one marines into the western landing zone but was shot up in the process, and the pilot ditched the aircraft about one mile offshore. One airman was lost at sea. Attempting to cover Knife-21, Knife-22 lost an engine and had a ruptured fuel tank and was forced to withdraw and make an emergency landing on the Thai coast. At the eastern landing zone, Knife-23 received intense fire and crashed at the water's edge, but the twenty marines and five air force crew members made it to shore (see photo 11). Knife-31 was hit by ground fire and its fuel tank exploded; it crashed about fifty meters offshore. Ten marines, two navy medics, and one air force crewman were killed, and the other thirteen on board were swept out to sea, where, fortunately, the *Wilson* picked them up. Austin then decided that the remaining four helicopters should insert at the western landing zone. Knife-32 rescued the crew from the downed Knife-21 and then inserted its troops into the western landing zone. Jolly Green-41 made several attempts to insert

Photo 11. Destroyed CH-53 Helicopters on Koh Tang Island. (Source: Head-quarters USSAG, Nakhon Phanom, Thailand, produced by 432nd Reconnaissance Technical Squadron, U.S. Air Force.)

its troops and finally about 0930 hours was successful. Jolly Green-42 inserted its troops, but Jolly Green-43 was driven off by heavy fire and inserted its team about one kilometer to the south of the western landing zone. Austin was on Jolly Green-43. After successfully offloading its marines onto the *Holt*, Jolly Green-13 attempted to rescue Knife-23's group of twenty-five on the eastern shore but was badly damaged and had to withdraw.

So, by mid-morning the battalion landing team was dispersed in three areas: twenty men at the eastern landing zone, eighty-two at the western landing zone, and twenty-nine one kilometer south of the western landing zone. The exact count of the troops on the ground was difficult to determine with precision because of all the battle damage and the fog of combat—but 131 of the 180 marines in the first assault group were now on Koh Tang. The air force had only one helicopter operational out of the eight that initially inserted the marines.

In the first moments of contact, ten marines, two navy medics, and two airmen had been killed. These, except for three marines missing in action and presumed dead and one other marine, were to be the total losses in the engagement. There were about fifty men wounded in action. However, we at NKP always considered the eighteen volunteer security police and five crewmen of the crashed CH-53 part of the *Mayaguez* casualties.

At noon we received a JCS directive to cease all offensive operations. However, for the embattled marines on Koh Tang to effectively disengage and withdraw, Lieutenant General Burns deemed it necessary to reinforce them with additional troops. Subsequently, Knife-51, Jolly Green-11, Jolly Green-12, and Jolly Green-43 successfully inserted a hundred marines into the western landing zone. Knife-52 was badly damaged attempting to insert into the eastern landing zone and had to make a forced landing near Royong, Thailand.

Intelligence concerning the Cambodian forces on Koh Tang was sparse. One estimate, based on a Cambodian refugee debrief, indicated eighteen to twenty troops and their families were on this island. An intelligence estimate stated there could be a battalion of from one hundred to three hundred troops with small arms, light machine guns, 82 mm mortars, and B-40 rockets. The captain of the Thai fishing boat said in his debrief that the Khmer force at Koh Tang numbered about sixty. Lieutenant Colonel Austin estimated about 150. Whatever the number, the enemy was well armed and highly disciplined.

Two relatively serious problems surfaced almost immediately upon contact. Both related to the ground troops' ability to coordinate supporting air strikes. The battle area was so compressed that absolute identification of the marines' positions was necessary before close air support could be provided. Unfortunately, the marine forward air controller and his radios were lost when Knife-31 crashed. The troops on the eastern landing zone used an emergency survival UHF radio to coordinate with the tactical air, whereas those in the western landing zone had only their FM radios. The marines on the east could not talk with those in the western landing zones; consequently, the limited communications with the ground forces as well as the dispersed positions of the marines made close air support difficult. The time compression in the planning process meant insufficient time to deploy OV-10s and still provide adequate crew rest and mission preparation for early morning insertions. Consequently, A-7 aircraft were committed to the forward air controller mission.[261]

The A-7s were very familiar with helicopter operations and had a greater ordnance capability. However, whenever the A-7 acting as the tactical air controller had to refuel, it handed its responsibility off to another A-7, and it took valuable time to reorient the new controller with the ground situation. About 1630 hours, OV-10s relieved the A-7s of the control responsibilities and along with the C-130 gunship handled the evening evacuation of the several hundred marines. Incidentally, none of the navy tactical aircraft from the *Coral Sea* were equipped with FM radio capability, which precluded their use in close air support.

With nightfall approaching, Burns decided that the position of the twenty-five men in the eastern landing zone was too tenuous and they definitely would have to be evacuated. About 1730 hours, with supporting fires from the USS *Wilson* and its gig as well as Jolly Green-12 and Knife-51, Jolly Green-11 successfully evacuated the twenty-five marines and airmen. Both Jolly Green-11 and Jolly Green-12 were severely damaged in that operation, which left only three helicopters available for the extraction of the marines in the western landing zones. Notwithstanding the limited resources, Burns decided to evacuate the remainder of the ground forces, even though it meant this must be done at night. At 1830 hours, Knife-51 extracted forty-one marines and deposited them on the deck of the *Coral Sea,* now, fortunately, within sixty miles of Koh Tang. Next, Jolly Green-43 extracted fifty-four marines, who it also deposited on the *Coral Sea.* Jolly Green-44, newly arrived from NKP, extracted thirty-four troops and quickly deposited them on the nearby USS *Holt* and returned to extract another load of forty marines. Knife-51 extracted the last of Austin's marines, a group of twenty-nine troops, which proceeded again to the *Coral Sea.* All operations in support in the recovery of the SS *Mayaguez* and crew were terminated at 2245 hours on 15 May.[262]

President Ford reacted forcefully to this serious affront by the Cambodians, only two weeks after the U.S. withdrawal from South Vietnam. The U.S. government had to respond vigorously to this seizure of a U.S. ship sailing in international waters, since the lives of its citizens had to be protected. The compressed time schedule set by the National Military Command Center has often been criticized. Yet, acting quickly most likely accelerated the recovery of both the crew and the ship. The *Mayaguez* recovery operations displayed the will and determination of the United States and were important in restoring the confidence of our allies, particularly in Asia.[263]

However, the Thai government expressed great displeasure over the United States' use of its territory to attack neighboring Cambodia. In fact, there was an interesting sequel to the *Mayaguez* incident. A few days after the capture, Cambodian gunboat E-311 entered the Thai port of Sattahip, and its crew confessed to Thai officials that it had captured the *Mayaguez*; they asked for refugee status. There were two accounts of gunboat E-311's activities. One, related in the 20 May 1975 issue of the *Washington Post*,[264] was that the crew mutinied, threw their communist officer overboard, and sailed to Thailand seeking asylum. The crew's members said they were members of the Cambodian Navy pressed into service by the Khmer communists and that their boat had been used to intercept a number of ships sailing near Cambodia over the past several weeks. The other (perhaps more plausible) account was that the gunboat was at sea when Cambodia fell and that the crew decided to impress the new government with its loyalty, so they captured the *Mayaguez*.[265] This backfired when the new government was told of their act. At that point, in fear for their lives, the crew members decided not to return to Cambodia—and sailed for Thailand. Whatever the story, the arrival of the Cambodian boat at Sattahip, Thailand, was causing the Thai government embarrassment and nervousness, and it tried to keep the matter quiet.

5

Thailand

Thus far, I have discussed affairs in South Vietnam and Cambodia, with only tangential references to Thailand and Laos, both of which had important roles in the wars in Southeast Asia, which were definitely regional conflicts. The common enemy operated extensively in Laos, Cambodia, and South Vietnam and continuously exerted pressure on northeast Thailand. The communication routes inextricably wove the four countries into a single region. For example, the Mekong River convoys, Cambodia's lifeblood, providing more than 92 percent of its supplies, originated in Thailand, were assembled in Vietnam, and transversed the interdicted part of the river in Cambodia to arrive at Phnom Penh. The major infiltration of men and matériel by the North Vietnamese, which turned the tide of combat in South Vietnam, came through Laos and Cambodia. I will touch on several of the events occurring in Thailand and Laos between 1973 and 1975.

The day before I arrived in Bangkok, a student-led movement had suddenly and startlingly toppled the military government on "Bloody Sunday," 14 October 1973. Seventy persons were killed, and more than eight hundred were wounded. The ruling clique, as the Thais addressed the military leadership, consisted of Premier Thanon Kittikachorn, his powerful son, Colonel Narong (who was the liaison officer from the Queen's Cobra Infantry Regiment in Vietnam to my division for a year), and Deputy Premier Praphat Charusathien—the trio they called "The Father, the Son, and the Wholly Gross." Field Marshal Thanon was prime minister, minister of defense, and foreign minister, and Field Marshal Praphat was commander in chief of the army, deputy supreme commander, deputy prime minister, minister of the interior, and acting director general of the Thai National Police Department. The idealist students wanted to turn the country away from this dictatorship and toward democracy. When I arrived, Bangkok was relatively calm, but not a policeman or military person could be seen; they had all taken cover. Uniformed Boy Scouts were directing the horrendous traffic for which Bangkok is famous.

An interim regime headed by Prime Minister Sanya Thammasak, took office; and a January 1974 national election resulted in the 269 seats in parliament being held by twenty-two different political parties, which made meaningful legislation impossible. Nevertheless, the Thais were working to lay the foundation for a parliamentary democracy. The Sanya government's major political contribution was the creation of a new constitution, the ninth in this century.[266]

In July 1974, youths rioted in the Chinese sector of Bangkok, and the civilian government forcefully suppressed the riot; this did much to improve the morale of the security services that had been sorely treated in the October 1973 uprising.[267] In demonstrating its ability to maintain law and order, the Sanya government also improved its image and as a result could act with much greater confidence in relations with its critics. And there were many critics, for the new democracy encouraged the public to speak out strongly on a multitude of issues, foremost among which was the U.S. military presence in Thailand.

The U.S. military's relationship with our host country was extremely important. Our ambassador held periodic political-military conferences, at which we discussed such topics as the Indochina Assessment Update, trends in U.S.-Thai relations, special reports of activities, and U.S. base closure problems.[268] U.S.-Thai relations were never smooth. In Bangkok, the well-organized Thai students repeatedly staged massive demonstrations against the presence of American forces in their country. In August 1974, the Democrat Party leader, Seni Pramot, said publically that it was not proper for Thailand to help the U.S. transport weapons to Cambodia and urged the abolition of any agreement that Thailand might have with the U.S. government on this matter. He further stated that Thai assistance in transporting weapons undermined Thailand's claim to neutrality in the Khmer conflict and that it might cause the communist side in Cambodia to seek revenge. Later, in January 1975, the government would not permit the United States to import its rice to Thailand for transshipment to Cambodia, so the airlift support had to be transferred to South Vietnam.

The Thai government was always very concerned about communist aggression in neighboring countries and its effect on Thailand. In July 1974, Thai foreign ministry officials made public their uncertainty about the future stability and security of Asia and showed a deep-seated resentment toward the United States.[269] The U.S. military was conscious of these sentiments and always did all it could to ameliorate the situation. For example, in January 1975 Thailand had to contend with a major flood, described as the country's worst natural disaster in a hundred years, which caused great economic damage in southern Thailand, killing 239 persons and leaving fifteen thousand homeless. His Majesty, the King of Thailand, requested that the U.S. Air Force provide airlifts in support of flood relief operations. We immediately did so.

Insurgency and Counterinsurgency

There was a serious communist insurgency problem in northeastern Thailand.[270] In the last quarter of 1974, the Second Thai Army conducted sustained operations in the Thai communist heartland of the southern Na Kae District of Nakhon Phanom Province. It had fifteen rifle companies conducting its counterinsurgency operations, the largest contingent in six years. The fighting escalated to 1975, and in early April, in an unusually bloody battle, guerrillas killed thirty-three Thai soldiers about seven miles from the Laotian border. The Thai defense minister, Pramarn Adireksarn, said the North Vietnamese had backed the guerrillas who launched the attack.

Northeast Thailand had always been a hotbed of communist activities, and the Thais were sincerely concerned that the communists would try to annex the area to gain control of the Mekong River. So, they were particularly disturbed in late February and March 1975, when there was a large increase in unidentified air activities in northeastern Thailand.[271] Many of these activities were in the vicinity of Nakhon Phanom. HUMINT reported six helicopter landings in Nam Dong. The wreckage of a small, black-painted aircraft with no identification markings was found 155 miles southwest of NKP. Between 24 February and 4 March, villages reported helicopters flying very low and slowly between 1900 and 2100 hours, just twenty miles northwest. In the same period, other HUMINT sources reported fifteen separate instances of unidentified air activities. With all of these reported incidents, the situation was heating up, particularly as the communists were having successes in Cambodia and South Vietnam at the same time.

Most of these HUMINT sightings reported the unidentified aircraft as flying at treetop level.[272] Because of an occurrence earlier that year when I had several visitors, I was concerned whether the NKP radar could pick up the tracks. I had provided my guests with an escort so they could visit the town of Nakhon Phanom. When they returned, they asked why the black-painted aircraft were landing at Thakhek, just across the Mekong River. I responded that they must be mistaken, since our command section had received no reports of air activities at Thakhek. They insisted it was so. I checked with our radar station, which had seen no air activities. Consequently, I had an inquiry made, and sure enough, Laotian planes did land at Thakhek with troops, to quell a student demonstration. These planes had flown low along the Mekong, below the NKP radar screens.

However, in the case of the unidentified air activity without lights being reported by ground observers, the NKP radar did pick up the tracks. In fact, three different radars registered the activity (INVERT, radar approach control, and the weather radar scopes), increasing the validity of the reports.[273] We asked our radar technicians to take photographs of the observed activities on their scopes, which they accomplished several nights later. The situation was puzzling.

On 27 April, the INVERT radar carried three good tracks and confirmed eight to ten RAPIAN radar close-in tracks. With such good verification, an AC-130 and a Jolly Green chopper were launched to monitor the situation. No results. On 30 April an aircrew reported a hundred-yard square with fire around its perimeter and a round, beaten-down area in the grass, about twenty-five yards in diameter, at its center. Was it a man-made fire marker for helicopter landings? On another occasion, a Jolly Green was consistently in the middle of three or four tracks. On two occasions its pilot observed the lights of a flight of two helicopters, each of which went into a dive and turned out its lights when they saw his running lights.[274]

I kept a makeshift log of all these occurrences, and in three and a half months our radar picked up hundreds of unidentified tracks near NKP. We could make no determination of identity or mission. The tracks peaked during a seven- to eight-day period commencing two days before the full moon (for visibility?) and proceeded at 60 to 120 knots at elevations from treetop to twelve hundred feet.

These occurrences had not been seen previously. Given the HUMINT reports, there could have been some validity to the occurrences. The situation kept the Thais in the northeast edgy, and it provided the airbase a diversion after the all-encompassing activities accompanying the evacuations from Phnom Penh and Saigon.

On 9 May, a bomb exploded at a NKP bus station, killing three Thais.[275] This was one of the first terrorist activities of this type. Given this sort of terrorist act, along with the increased insurgency and unidentified flights, the Thai government was very concerned about the northeast provinces. With the fall of Cambodia and South Vietnam, the balance of power in Southeast Asia had been dramatically altered in favor of the communists and their powerful backer, China. The continued presence of U.S. troops in Thailand therefore was a very touchy subject.

The Mayaguez Incident

The subject was brought to a head with the *Mayaguez* incident. Prime Minister Khukrit Pramot presented a Royal Thai government aide-mémoire on the U.S. military use of Thailand to our embassy at 1600 hours on 14 May, and the Thai ministry of public affairs released it to the public two hours later:

> It is recalled that on May 13, B. E. 2518 the Prime Minister in his capacity as Acting Minister of Foreign Affairs had informed the Charge d'Affaires of the American Embassy that Thailand does not wish to become involved in the dispute between the United States and Cambodia over the seizure of the vessel Mayaguez, and that Thailand will not permit its territory to be used in connection with any action which might be taken by the United States against Cambodia.
>
> On May 14, B. E. 2518, the Thai Government learnt that the United States Government has sent some elements of its Marine Forces into Thailand as part of its reaction against Cambodia.
>
> The Thai Government considers that this action by the United States Government is not consistent with the goodwill existing between Thailand

and the United States. And unless these forces which have entered against the wishes of the Thai Government are withdrawn immediately, the good relations and co-operation existing between Thailand and the United States would be exposed to serious and damaging consequences.[276]

When Ambassador Charles Whitehouse arrived at Don Muong Airport about 1800 hours the same day, he was met with fifty to sixty demonstrators, most from Thammasat University. Many of the demonstrators displayed crudely drawn posters: "Bastered [*sic*] Ford, Get Your Troops Out," "U.S. Get Back," "Go Home."[277]

On the next day, the English editorial in the *Bangkok World* also protested the situation:

So America is back fighting again in Indochina. It is a relatively small military engagement but the consequences will be colossal.

And we in Thailand are right in the middle of it. The Americans get back their crew and depart. Thailand cannot, if the Cambodians decide to retaliate, what can they do? They cannot attack America, so the natural target must be Thailand, right next door, and especially since the troops and planes involved in the Mayaguez incident have come from Thai soil.
. . .

The handling of this episode is a downright insult to the Thai Government and people, but when you look at the United States track record on Indochina, perhaps it is in keeping with what has gone before. The wounds to Thai-American friendship will not be easily healed.[278]

Thailand was attempting a very difficult balancing act, trying to avoid a rift with the United States while acknowledging a dramatic expansion of communist influence in Southeast Asia and at the same time facing serious labor strikes, insurgency, and a declining economy.[279] The United States did withdraw its forces from Thailand. By the end of June, the F-111 fighter-bombers and F-4 phantom jets were leaving Thailand as the major air force units were rapidly being transferred and U.S. logistics support bases were downsizing. Headquarters USSAG was to be deactivated on 30 June 1975. The U.S. military's major presence in Southeast Asia was a thing of the past.

6

Laos

On 21 February 1973, not a month after the 28 January signing of the Vietnamese cease-fire agreement, the Royal Laotian government (RLG) and the communist-inspired Lao Patriotic Front (LPF) signed an agreement on the restoration of peace and reconciliation in Laos. The agreement ushered in a period of major political and military changes in Laos.

The most dramatic consequence was the rapid diminution of both the frequency and intensity of military hostilities.[280] Conflicts, which had totaled 225 in the first week following the agreement, were reduced to only five per week by August. Casualties of the RLG armed forces were reduced from sixty killed in the first week to two per week by April. T-26 aircraft sorties lowered from 610 in March to only 6 in December. However, in the LPF zone the North Vietnamese maintained an estimated fifty thousand troops, who had full control over the upgrade and maintenance of the Ho Chi Minh Trail. North Vietnam was the major supporter of the LPF troops.

Politically, the agreement prescribed a framework for settlement. It stipulated that a new provisional government of national unity (PGNU) and a joint national political council would be formed. Working deliberately and steadily the RLG and LPF improved prospects for the general acceptance of a new coalition government.

Ultimately, Prime Minister Souvanna Phouma, a neutralist, moved to form a coalition government; he formed a PGNU cabinet on 5 April 1974, and there appeared to be an even balance of forces. The Vientiane side (RLG) blocked several communist initiatives, such as the recognition of Sihanouk's GRUNK and the Viet Cong Provisional Revolutionary Government. One aspect of the agreement was to authorize the LPF to station twenty-five hundred Pathet Lao troops in both Vientiane and Luang Probang, to neutralize the situation there. The LPF took advantage of its lawful presence in the capital to cultivate students and labor organizations and to foster and exploit dissatisfaction.

In early 1975, the coalition government appeared to be operating satisfactorily, with cooperation between the Vientiane side and the LPF in carrying out the various governmental projects.[281] However, the LPF managed to covertly spread student dissension in Ban Houei Sai and Thakhek (just across the Mekong River from Nakhon Phanom), where the LPF used its forces to quell student demonstrations although they were within the Vientiane side's zone. But generally, the situation was quieter and both sides were making progress in the effective functioning of the PGNU.

In Laos, the developments in Cambodia and South Vietnam, although they had no immediate military consequences for the nation, did embolden the LPF with the possibility of adopting much tougher positions and produced a serious despondency on the Vientiane side.[282] The subsequent falls of Phnom Penh and Saigon very negatively affected the morale of the Force Armée Royales officers.[283] Since the agreement, U.S. military assistance had fallen from $274.7 million in FY 73 to about $80.0 million in FY 74. Junior RLG officers were more concerned with the lack of strong leadership in the army than the reduction of U.S. aid and presence. Just as in Cambodia, here they also contrasted what appeared to be a disciplined communist force supported by the North Vietnamese with their own less disciplined organization.

As anticipated, LPF militant actions did increase. On the morning of 9 May, several organizations had assembled in Vientiane at the Monument for War Dead, when a group of 150 students began marching around it with signs and banners chanting slogans, among them, "Americans Go Home, Down with the CIA." They marched to the American embassy, where, under cover of rocks and bricks, several scaled the embassy gates and tore down the American flag.[284] That started a series of events that culminated on 13 May with an attack on the USAID compound in Luang Probang, where the protesters broke windows and destroyed whatever they could get their hands on.[285] All Americans employed by our government left that city. On the same day, demonstrations spilled over to Savannakhet, where USAID employees and dependents were held hostage.

At a 14 May PGNU cabinet meeting, Prime Minister Phouma accepted the resignations of most of the key Vientiane cabinet members: the foreign minister, defense minister, deputy public works minister, and deputy foreign affairs minister. Additionally, Gen. Vang Pao (the MR-2 commander and the director general of the defense ministry) also resigned.[286] The Vientiane side of the coalition government collapsed overnight, largely because it had little political foundation. When faced with the ominous combination of events—the collapse of Cambodia and Vietnam, the LPF militant pressure, and demonstrations in which cabinet members were attacked by name—they had had enough.[287]

The LPF moved additional troops into Vientiane, bringing the estimated number of Pathet Lao troops in the capital to ten thousand. By 23 May, the LPF wielded almost total military and political control of the Vientiane side's zone.[288]

That day, the United States prudently began an emergency airlift evacuation of all dependents and nonessential personnel.[289] A week later there were 147 government-associated Americans in Vientiane, and by 28 June the number was to be reduced to fifty-six. All thirty-three USAID personnel and fourteen of the twenty-one DAO personnel were to be evacuated. By mid-June, the LPF had completely reduced the Vientiane leadership and had commenced the integration of its personnel into all levels of governmental offices. It had also established control of the Forces Armées Royales and installed its own troops in all provincial capitals. The reeducation of military and civilians alike had commenced.[287]

On 26 June, the embassy informed the PGNU that the United States had decided to terminate USAID.[290] The PGNU promptly responded by asking for all materials held by USAID and the DAO and the departure of all civilian and military personnel attached to these organs of assistance. The U.S. presence in Laos was being greatly reduced.

Now that the Pathet Lao and their North Vietnamese allies had triumphed in Laos, it was difficult to forecast what type of society would emerge. The LPF said it would continue a coalition government. Since the fighting was over, it could turn its attention to healing the wounds of war and improving the economy, which was in tatters.[291] The withdrawal of the United States and the cut in aid would have serious economic consequences.

"Red Prince" Souphannouvong, a leader of the communist element and half-brother of Prime Minister Souvanna Phouma, said the LPF would survive on its own. Now that the communist revolution in Laos was completed, one thing was obvious: the United States no longer had influence in Indochina.

Epilogue

I left Southeast Asia to return to the States on 4 July 1975, with very mixed feelings. On the day we Americans were celebrating the birth of our nation and our freedoms, the heavy yoke of communism had brutally suppressed the freedoms of the people in Southeast Asia. Already there were mass killings going on in Cambodia, and indoctrination camps were established in Vietnam. It appeared the American sacrifice of lives and treasure had been in vain. Had the United States continued to adequately support its allies, though, it would not have needed to end this way.

Today's Afghanistan situation is similar in many respects to the one in Southeast Asia in the 1970s. By 1970, the American people had tired of the Vietnam War and were clamoring for a withdrawal of our forces. So our government decided to build up South Vietnam's military capabilities so that it could protect itself from communist aggression—the "Vietnamization Program." It took several years of huge military equipment and supply transfers to enable the Vietnamese forces to become self-sufficient. By early 1973, the cease-fire with the communists had been signed and the United States withdrew all its forces, leaving in place the enemy troops in South Vietnam. However, in reality there was no cease-fire and the communist aggression continued unabated. With strong political leadership, the U.S. funding support for South Vietnam initially was adequate, and the country fared very well. However, the U.S. leadership changed, and the communists became more aggressive. Concurrently, the U.S. Congress drastically reduced its funding to the extent that South Vietnam could no longer adequately protect itself, and both South Vietnam and Cambodia fell to the communists. This was indeed a sad ending for all the blood and treasure we had expended.

Today, many Americans clamor for a troop withdrawal from Afghanistan. To facilitate a possible withdrawal, our government has initiated what I term an "Afghanization Program." As we did in Vietnam, we are expeditiously supplying and training the newly formed Afghan army and police. Ultimately, the government of Afghanistan will determine that its forces will be able to control the internal conflicts by themselves and, as in Vietnam, the United States will gradually withdraw its forces, leaving the insurgents in place to continue their disruptive efforts. With strong political leadership, the United States has thus far adequately supported the Afghan forces. How long will Congress continue to provide our support? Will Congress reduce funding and our military support to a grossly inadequate level, as it did in Vietnam? If this is the case, an unstable regime will surely take over, and again, as in Vietnam, our expenditure of blood and treasure will have been for naught. If, however, Congress continues to support Afghanistan adequately, then possibly there could be a stable, friendly country, and democracy might flourish.

The lesson to be learned concerning the defeats of South Vietnam and Cambodia is that U.S. military aid to embattled nations must be matched by our country's political strength and popular support to ensure a positive outcome. Lacking this resolve, military assistance will inevitably be withdrawn, thus abandoning the embattled nations to their fates.

Glossary

ABF	Attack by Fire
ARVN	South Vietnamese Army
ASR	Authorized Supply Rate
CIF	Combat Intensity Factor
CINCPAC	Commander-in-Chief, Pacific
COMUSSAG	Commander U.S. Support Activity Group
CONPLAN	Contingency Plan
COSVN	Central Office South Vietnam (Communist-controlling headquarters)
DAO	Chief, Defense Resource Support, and Termination Office, Saigon, commonly known as the Defense Attaché Office
DOS	Day of Supply
EMG	Cambodian Joint Staff
FANK	Cambodian Army
FREQUENT WIND	Operation to evacuate personnel from South Vietnam
GKR	Government of the Khmer Republic
GRUNK	Communist government in Cambodia
GVN	Government of Vietnam
HES	Hamlet Evaluation Survey
HUMINT	Intelligence obtained by personnel
J-2	Intelligence Section of the Joint General Staff
J-3	Operations Section of the Joint General Staff

JGS	South Vietnamese Joint General Staff
JOC	Joint Operations Center
KBA	Killed by Air
KC	Khmer communists
KHA	Friendly troops killed by hostile action
KIA	Enemy troops killed in action
LPF	Lao Patriotic Front
LZ	Landing zone
MACV	Military Assistance Command Vietnam
MAP-CB	Military Assistance Program, Cambodia
MEDTC	Military Equipment Delivery Team Cambodia
MNK	Khmer Navy
MR	Military Region
NKP	Nakhon Phanom, Thailand
NVA	North Vietnamese Army
PF	Popular Forces
PGNU	Laotian Provisional Government of National Unity
POL	Petroleum products
PROJECT ENHANCE	Effort to provide military equipment to the RVNAF
PSDF	People's Self Defense Forces
RF	Regional Forces
RLG	Royal Laotian government
RSR	Required Supply Rate
RVN	Republic of Vietnam
RVNAF	Republic of Vietnam Armed Forces
SCOOT	Effort to supply ammunition to Cambodia out of Thailand
7AF	Seventh Air Force
SMR	Capital Military Region
SVN	South Vietnam
USAF	U.S. Air Force

USSAG	U.S. Support Activity Group
USSAG/7AF	U.S. Support Activity Group and Seventh Air Force headquarters at NKP
USARPAC	U.S. Army Pacific
VNAF	South Vietnamese Air Force
VC	Viet Cong
VCI	Viet Cong Infrastructure
WHA	Friendly troops wounded by hostile action

General Definitions and Processing Ground Rules for Combat Analyses

1. General Definitions and Processing Ground Rules

The generic types of incidents considered are ground contacts, attacks by fire, mine and booby trap incidents, terrorism, sabotage, and political incidents. Each of these can be further decomposed into either enemy- or friendly-initiated.

The definitions used for the purpose of data processing, and interpretation of the data are given as follows:

(1) A ground contact is any troop combat engagement between friendly and enemy forces, initiated by either side. The size of forces involved may vary from platoon size to divisional size. A ground contact may result in enemy, friendly, and/or civilian casualties. Ground contacts may be decomposed into four distinct categories, defined as follows:

   (a) A contact is normally any open engagement between opposing forces, initiated by either side.

   (b) An ambush is an action initiated by the enemy as an element of surprise.

   (c) Harassment is an action initiated by the enemy against friendly forces which may result in very few or no casualties. The purpose of harassing action is not to engage friendly forces in combat, but is more geared to a type of psychological warfare.

   (d) A penetration incident is a probing action designed to test the strength of the opposing force. This type of action may be friendly or enemy initiated.

(2) An attack by fire (ABF) is an enemy or suspected enemy delivery of standoff fire from artillery, mortar, rocket, or recoilless rifles against a friendly position not accompanied or followed (within time constraints to be discussed later) by a ground attack. An ABF can result in any type of friendly (including civilian) casualties.

(3) Mine and booby trap incidents are those in which friendly military forces physically detonate an enemy placed mine, or fall prey to an enemy placed booby trap.

(4) Terrorism is any action initiated by the enemy against a civilian element. For example, enemy rockets or mortars directed against civilians will be treated as an incident of terrorism, and not an attack by fire. Kidnapping and assassinations of civilian officials are classed as incidents of terrorism.

(5) Sabotage is any action initiated by the enemy against lines of communication (LOC). Lines of communication are defined as physical structures such as bridges, dams, ammo dumps, military equipment, etc. For the purpose of definition, sabotage will never result in any casualties of any type. (Casualties associated with this type of incident will cause the incident report to be changed to that of either harassment or terrorism, depending on the target of the attack.)

(6) Political incidents are actions initiated by the enemy which may result in a show of force, but never any casualties of any type. This type of action is used to gain the attention of any person(s) to the enemy's political goals and ambitions in South Vietnam.

The critical facets of the incident definitions given are the purpose of the action and who the action was directed against. There is certainly some subjective judgment involved in categorizing the data into the different types of incidents.

It must be noted at this point that only reports subsequent to 2 December 1973 identify the generic type of friendly unit involved in an action. Prior to that date, the data is aggregated, and can be treated only in reference to the total armed forces (RVNAF).

The unit definitions used in the report are given below:

(1) Main force units are those units consisting primarily of the Army of the Republic of Vietnam (ARVN), but also includes the Vietnamese Navy (VNN) and the Vietnamese Marine Corps (VNMC).

(2) Regional Forces (RF) consist of units assigned to protect areas falling within the Government of South Vietnam (GVN) provincial boundaries.

(3) Popular Forces (PF) consist of units assigned to protect areas falling within GVN district boundaries in any province.

(4) The People's Self Defense Forces (PSDF) are elements which act as a local militia to guard their hamlet of residence.

(5) The National Police Field Forces (NPFF) is an agency which acts as a civilian police force with normal responsibilities of a policeman. It is also used as a tactical force to combat against enemy activities.

(6) Civilians are personnel not paid by the GVN to bear arms.

(7) The Rural Development (RD) cadre consists of personnel paid by the GVN to assist the population in the development of farms, land areas, etc. RD cadre personnel bear arms, but only for self-protection. (RD cadre personnel are treated as civilians in incident reporting.)

(8) Territorial Forces (TF) consist of any combination of Regional Forces (RF), Popular Forces (PF), People's Self Defense Forces (PSDF), and/or National Police Field Forces (NPFF).

Having discussed the incident and force unit definitions used in the report compilation process, it is now necessary to discuss the various ground rules associated with incident classification.

Perhaps the most critical ground rule or assumption used is that incidents occurring within specified time and space constraints are treated as a single incident. The guidelines specified are that incidents occurring within 300 meters of one another, and within a twelve hour period, are combined and treated as a single incident. The primary rationale for doing this is to make some attempt to account for events which may be reported as separate, but are in reality part of a single encounter. A few examples may help illuminate the incident combining procedure and the rationale for doing it.

(1) Suppose the enemy rockets or mortars a friendly position with four rounds at a specified time, and sends in ten more rounds two hours later. For the purpose of this report, we would only show one ABF incident of fourteen rounds.

(2) Suppose the enemy initiates an ABF on a friendly position, and then within the twelve hour time constraint, either attacks the position, or the friendlies initiate a ground attack (within the space constraints), then one incident of an enemy-initiated contact (with rounds) would be reported. In the case of an ABF followed by an enemy attack, the rationale for combining incidents is that the initial ABF was probably designed to soften up the friendly defenses in preparation for a ground attack. The rationale for combining an initial ABF followed by a friendly-initiated attack on enemy positions (again within the temporal and spatial constraints) into one incident of an enemy-initiated contact is that the ABF was the first event (enemy-initiated) and may have a direct causal relationship to the initiation of the friendly security operation. In either case, the number of incoming enemy rounds associated with the incident is in the data file.

It must be noted that although the temporal and spatial constraints for incident combinations are somewhat arbitrary, military combat experience appears to support such incident aggregation in a vast majority of cases.

Some other general ground rules include:

(1) The time and location reported for each incident are the time and location of incident initiation. Although some contacts could last several hours, and the engagement location could move substantially, the report considers only the time and location at the beginning of the incident.

(2) In situations where incidents are combined, the time and location of the incident is taken to be that of the initiator event. For example, in the case where the enemy initiates an ABF followed by a ground attack (which when combined would report one incident of enemy-initiated contact), the time and location of the combined reported incident would be that of the initial ABF attack.

(3) Summarizing the incident types in terms of who can initiate an incident we have the following rules:

> contact—enemy- or friendly-initiated
> ambush—enemy-initiated only
> harassment—enemy-initiated only
> penetration—enemy-initiated
> terrorism—enemy-initiated against civilians only
> attack by fire—enemy-initiated only (against military units)
> mines & booby traps—friendly-[triggered] (by definition)
> sabotage—enemy-initiated only (against LOC)
> political—enemy-initiated only

(4) Enemy casualties resulting from VNAF airstrikes in a close air support role (i.e., in conjunction with a ground operation or contact) are counted as part of the casualties associated with the contact incident. However, VNAF air strikes not in conjunction with ground operations are not counted as incidents, and consequently, enemy casualties which result in such an action are not utilized in the data base or report.

Further ground rules will be discussed in the next section on data collection procedures and manual and machine editing processes.

2. Data Collection Procedures; Manual and Machine Editing Processes

A. Data Collection Procedures

As incidents occur in the field, the friendly element involved files a report of the incident with its operations center. This initial report is relayed from there through command channels to the military headquarters of the region in which the incident occurred. [As a matter of note, South Vietnam is divided into four military regions: MRs -1, -2, -3, and -4. A special zone, the Capital Military District (CMD), encompasses Saigon City and portions of the city's immediate surrounding areas (the CMD can be compared to the Military District of Washington in the US). However, for the purpose of reporting cease-fire incidents, the CMD is included as part of MR-3.] From the MR headquarters the cease-fire incident reports are encoded and transmitted telephonically to the Joint Operations Center (JOC) located in the JGS compound in Saigon. The reports are transmitted hourly, or sooner if required. Updated information is reported as it is received by the MR headquarters. The JOC decodes the messages and includes the information in one of two reports: "The Morning Situation Summary (1800–0600)" and "The Evening Situation Summary (0600–1800)." Each report is published daily for the time period specified and each is checked and authenticated by the team chief on duty in the JOC.

Up to this point, the cease-fire incident reports have remained strictly in Vietnamese reporting channels. Copies of the reports or situation summaries now enter into US hands. They are furnished to the DAO Liaison Office by the JOC and translated into English by Vietnamese military translators using AOSOP Form 13, "Daily Report." The AOSOP Form 13 and the Vietnamese spot reports are divided into two sections: Section I contains enemy-initiated incidents by MR, and Section II contains friendly-initiated activities, referred to by the Vietnamese as "security operations." The AOSOP Form 13 is the source document used to record raw data which is later verified and added weekly to the data master tape. From the AOSOP Form 13, the information is formatted onto AOSOP Form 15EV, "Daily Results of Ceasefire Violations," from which DAO key punch operators prepare the data cards for input to the master file.

The cards when completed by the DAO keypunch section are either transmitted to USSAG via autodin or in some cases, part of them are hand carried back from Saigon. At this point, as the cards arrive, and again at the end of the reporting week, the manual and machine editing of the input data is accomplished.

B. Manual and Machine Editing Processes

As cards are received at USSAG, certain field validation processes must occur prior to update of the master data file. The first process involves a computerized sort (called a UTM sort) of certain information on each card. A printout is obtained displaying all data on the card which is utilized to ensure that errors in the cards (both keypunch errors and consistency errors in relation to our established ground rules previously discussed) are minimized prior to entry into the computer editing routine. Applied conscientiously, these manual checks (which includes combining incidents) will ensure that the data is as consistent with respect to our ground rules as possible, and save a large amount of computer editing time.

Regardless of the care taken in the manual editing process, the amount of information contained on each card, and the sheer number of incidents reported on a weekly basis, make it imperative to have a second editing process performed by the computer. The computer editing routine not only performs consistency checks of the data, as does the manual procedure, but also performs certain reasonableness checks of the data, in order to ensure that potential biasedness in reporting is minimized. As a result of the computer editing process, records (incidents) which do not pass all the formatting and reasonableness checks are printed out, and each record is then compared with the translation (AOSOP Form 13) to ensure the validity of the data on the card. As soon as all necessary corrections have been made, the cards are reinput to the computer, and the master data file is updated on a weekly basis.

3. RVN Cease-Fire Violations Criteria

Because of the large numbers of incidents, most of which result in very few casualties, if any, it was deemed necessary to differentiate cease-fire violations into two categories, major or minor violations, in order to enable responsible military personnel to focus on the more important conflicts taking place. The JGS, of course, had a major input in determining the criteria, which as always was subjective. The criteria for cease-fire violations follows:

    I. MAJOR VIOLATIONS constitute one or more of the
       following situations:
       A. An ABF during a short period of time in which 20 or
          more rounds of mortar, artillery or rocket fire are received.
       B. An ABF as described in "A" above consisting of less than
          20 rounds but in which 5 or more friendly casualties are
          taken.
       C. One or more acts of terrorism involving extensive use of

mines, grenades or demolitions whether or not casualties were suffered.

D. An act of terrorism involving grenades or command detonated mines in which 5 or more friendly casualties are suffered.

E. A multiple company ground attack with or without supporting fires.

F. A ground attack of less than multiple company size in which a total of 20 casualties of friendly or enemy are suffered (to include enemy detained or friendly MIA).

G. A ground to air attack which results in the destruction of a friendly aircraft.

H. Any incident such as an assassination attempt, assassination or abduction of a prominent personage such as a province, village or hamlet chief or other VIP.

I. An interdiction of any line of communication to include highways, navigable rivers or rail lines.

J. An attack against the Mekong Convoys to Cambodia which results in the loss of a ship or barge.

K. Any incident involving U.S., Four Party Joint Military Team or ICCS Personnel, aircraft, or facilities.

II. MINOR VIOLATIONS constitute one or more of the following:

A. An ABF during which less than 20 rounds of mortar, artillery, rocket or small arms fire are received and in which less than 5 friendly casualties occur.

B. A small ground attack that is unsupported by significant mortar, artillery or rocket fire in which less than 20 casualties are taken by both sides.

C. Small acts of terrorism involving the use of grenades, mines or demolitions in which less than 5 friendly casualties are suffered.

D. Ground to air attacks which result in only minor injuries and do not result in destruction of an aircraft.

JGS Assessments on Friendly/ Enemy Activities of the Ceasefire

REPUBLIC OF VIETNAM
MINISTRY OF DEFENSE
JOINT GENERAL STAFF/RVNAF
J-3
TEL: 32.325
MEMORANDUM
No 3823 /TTM/P343

APO 4002, 11 Oct 74

SUBJECT: Assessment on Friendly/Enemy Activities after the Cease-fire.

1. General:

This memo is designed to present considerations regarding enemy/friendly activities after the Ceasefire on 28 Jan 73 and particularly after 2 Dec 73, on which date started strong enemy strategic changes.

The data and facts used in this assessment are provided by Corps + MRs' reports through recordings and statistics of computers, and are compiled through the following 3 parts:
  a. Activity level
  b. Combat effectiveness
  c. Activity time during the day

2. Activity level:

    a. Enemy activity (Inclosure 1)

        (1) Although they had signed the Ceasefire Agreement the Communists have not abandoned their intention of taking over South Vietnam by arms so they have pursued their aggressive attacks against RVNAF units. Since early Dec 73, they have launched again large scale attacks at regiment level, typically through violations at Quang-Duc Front (MR2) the level of enemy attacks in 1974 seems to decrease, (in average 55 incidents per week) but on the contrary, a striking fact reveals that since March 74 the Communists have launched repeatedly large scale campaigns at division level with tremendous intensity not inferior to that of their offensive in 1972. The difference between the war situation in 1974 and 1972 is about rate. In 1974, big battles have occurred in separate locations and times while in 1972 the battles happened simultaneously and were equally distributed according to time and space.

        (2) Enemy attacks by fire are also noticeable as to intensity and degree. ABF level was recorded as 69 incidents in average per regular force units, increased to 124 incidents/week during the 2nd quarter CY.74 and kept rising to 169 incidents/week during the 2 months of July and August 1974.

        Another noteworthy fact is that since Aug 74 the enemy has employed 130mm guns in the Quang Nam area (while in 1972 these guns were only used in Tri Thien area) and 100mm, 105mm guns and howitzers in Binh Dinh area, etc. . . .

    b. Friendly activity (Incl 2)

        Since early Dec 73 the RVNAF has not been able to remain passive in face of more and more serious violations so it has had to react with energetic retaliations. RVNAF initiated fire contacts from 4 incidents/week in the 1st quarter CY.74 rose to 60 incidents/week during the period up June 74 and kept ascending to 109 incidents/week in the months of July and August 74. This fact shows that the RVNAF in general, and the regular force, in particular, have been determined to safeguard the integrity of the territory and to pulverize the Communists land and population grab attempt.

3. Combat effectiveness:

The data furnished by Corps & MRs during the period since Dec 73 on which date strong activities of both sides started until 7 Sep 74, are recorded and analyzed to evaluate the combat effectiveness of regular force units and enemy forces.

a. RVNAF Regular Force combat effectiveness: (Incl 3)

   (1) Fire contact rate:

Among the total figure of 5,087 clashes between the regular force and the enemy, 2,518 incidents were initiated by the regular force, or 49%.

Analysis by separate MRs:

- MR1   :   47%
- MR2   :   39%
- MR3   :   59%
- MR4   :   59%

The above results indicate fire contacts during security operations initiated by the regular force in MRs 3 and 4 claim the highest rates (59%).

   (2) Fire contact results:

Through 5,087 clashes, the RVNAF regular force killed 23,410 enemy troops. In average in every clash 4.6 enemy troops were killed.

Analysis of enemy killed in each clash in different MRs:

	RVNAF initiated fire contacts	Eny initiated and reacted by regular force	MR Regular Force Rate
- MR1	3.9	2.9	3.4
- MR2	4.8	5.3	5.1
- MR3	4.7	1.8	3.5
- MR4	9.8	0.8	6.2
Nationwide	5.8	3.4	4.6

In general the results of friendly initiated fire contacts are more successful.

In MR3, as compared with fire contact rate, friendly forces score a very high rate, but the results are equal to MR1 and fewer than MR2.

In MR4, the results obtained in friendly initiated fire contacts are 10 times higher as compared with those scored from reactions to enemy initiated attacks.

b. Enemy combat effectiveness versus RVNAF Regular Force (Incl 4)

(1) Enemy fire contact results:

Also among 5,087 clashes recorded since 2 Dec 73 through 7 Sep 74, the enemy caused to the RVNAF Regular Force 3,487 KIA's. In average in each clash the enemy inflicted 0.68 friendly killed.

Analysis by separate MRs:

	Eny initated	Regular Force initiated	MR rate
- MR1	0.55	0.61	0.58
- MR2	0.78	0.47	0.65
- MR3	0.92	0.96	0.94
- MR4	0.31	0.88	0.64
Nationwide	0.71	0.65	0.68

The above results reveal that the friendly killed rate caused by the enemy in MR3 is the highest.

(2) Results of enemy attacks by fire:

Since 2 Dec 73 through 7 Sep 74 the enemy realized 4,707 ABF's targeted against RVNAF regular force units, distributed as follows:

-MR1	:	1,666	(35.4%)
-MR2	:	856	(18.2%)
-MR3	:	1,314	(27.9%)
-MR4	:	871	(18.5%)

Causing to friendly forces:

	KIA	MIA	Total	Compared with MR Regular force common losses
- MR1	312	1,576	1,888	20%
- MR2	258	1,123	1,381	23%
- MR3	293	1,961	2,254	32%
- MR4	101	786	887	22%
Total	964	5,446	6,410	27%

Notably, in MR3 among the total figure of regular force personnel losses 32% was caused by enemy ABF's.

MR2 level is equivalent to MR4 (856/871 incidents) on the contrary the figure of KIA's in MR2 is over 150% (258/101).

c. Weapons losses: (Incl 5)

In comparing regular force personnel losses with weapons losses, enemy personnel killed with weapons captured by the regular force, the following results are recorded:

(1) Regular force:

Common rate: $\underline{2,545}$ (wpns lost)   =   0.55
                    4,573 (killed)

In average, 2 friendly troops were killed for every weapon lost.

-MR1   :   0.80
-MR2   :   0.60
-MR3   :   0.30
-MR4   :   0.51

Regular Force/MR3 weapons losses rate is relatively lower than other MR's.

(2) Enemy:

Common rate: $\underline{5,234}$ (captured wpns)   =   0.21
                    24,651 (Killed)

In average the regular force had to kill 4 to 5 enemy troops to recuperate 1 weapon.

Enemy weapons losses caused by the regular force in all MR's:

-MR1   :   0.24
-MR2   :   0.18   (5 had to be killed to recover 1 wpn)
-MR3   :   0.21
-MR4   :   0.24

4. Activity time during the day:

The following statistic results record the facts which occurred within 3 months (from 16 May 74 through 14 Aug 74) during which time the enemy started the 74 summer campaign.

a. Regular force frequent fire contact time:

According to the recorded results, the time of regular force frequent fire occurred more often in the daytime than at night. The level starts increasing every day from 0600H and reaches the highest point at 1100H. From 1600H on regular force fire contacts decrease gradually until 0500H of the following day (Incl 6).

This fact demonstrates that regular force night security activities, if any, only bring in very few results (Incl 7 exposes time of regular force frequent fire contacts in 4 MR's).

b. Time of enemy frequent attacks against regular force:

Unlike the previous years, most enemy attacks took place in the daytime—about 0600H, 1700H, mainly at 1100H, time at which the enemy usually attacks friendly forces (Incl 8).

The above facts show that the enemy has chosen the moments when friendly units are most subject to fatigue and when our troops are busy with individual toilet cares or recreation to attack.

Inclosure 9 analyzes time of enemy frequent attacks against the regular force in 4 MR's. It is worth mentioning that in MR1 enemy night and day attacks are equal in level, highest at 0900H, relatively increase again at 2000H. In MR3 most enemy attacks take place during the interval between 0100H until 1200H; on the contrary, fewer attacks occur at 0900H.

c. Time of enemy frequent attacks by fire:

In general enemy ABF's happen more often in the daytime than during the night, most frequently at 0700H and decrease gradually since 1800H (Incl 10).

Inclosures 11 and 12 record time of enemy frequent ABF's in MR1 and MRs 2 & 3 & 4.

5. Corps & MRs and Divisions are requested to base on the above considerations to:

a. Study enemy habits in different areas to pre-empt his attacks. Pay particular attention to the time he usually takes advantage to launch ground and fire attacks on us.

b. Have our troops get rid of habits such as lack of vigilance, neglect on guard duties during dangerous time such as at dawn, at noon during bivouacs for lunch and rest, at sunset when troops are tired and observation means are limited.

c. Apply effective measures to counter enemy attacks by fire, a tactic the enemy employs easily to cause significant losses to friendly forces regarding personnel and equipment losses caused by ABF's claim 27% of total personnel losses, which demonstrate that:

Our troops still are not vigilant in the defense against ABF's.

Combat positions, storage dumps are not adequately protected to resist against enemy shelling destruction.

Detection and counterfire measure are not appropriately applied.

d. Properly conceive and implement the conservation of weapons and equipment to minimize losses, concurrently intensify the campaign 'Competition in capturing enemy weapons and preserving our own'.

e. Increase small unit activities at night. According to statistics, these activities are usually less effective. In view of regressing this deficiency units should pay more attention to quality than to quantity, use initiative and positive execution as guidance for action, avoid perfunctory and outward show performances.

General CAO VAN VIEN
Chief of JGS/RVNAF
S/S

DISTRIBUTION:
-Corps & MRs 1, 2, 3, 4
-ABN Div-Marine Div
-Inf Div's 1, 2, 3, 5, 7, 9, 18, 21, 22, 23, and 25
For action

COPIES TO:
-Office of Chief JGS/RVNAF
--Dep Chief JGS for Opns
--Dep Chief JGS for Community Sec. and Dev.
--Chief of Staff/JGS
--Dep CofS Opns/JGS
'For info'
- Files — Archives.

Appendix C

JGS Letter to DAO on FY 75 Funding

REPUBLIC OF VIETNAM
DEFENSE MINISTRY
JOINT GENERAL STAFF, RVNAF
OFFICE OF THE COMMANDING GENERAL

Ref 4201/ TTM/ VP/ TMT

General CAO VAN VIEN
Chief, Joint General Staff
Republic of Viet Nam Armed Forces

Major General IRA A. HUNT
Acting Defense Attache
Embassy of the United States of America
SAIGON

Subject: FY.75 fund.

1-The Joint General Staff has been informed by the Defense Attache Office that the Military Assistance Fund for the Republic of VietNam may stay at the 700 million US dollars level.

2-DAO also informed that within the 700 million the following expenditures will be included:

-F.5E purchase... 77.4 million
-Ammunition pipeline.....................................55.0   "

```
-Transportation................................................ 47.0    "
-DAO............................................................. 35.0    "
-Training in FY74........................................... 9.9    "
-    "        in FY75................................... 2.5    "
-F5A............................................................... 3.3    "
```

                                                    _____

                                        230.0 million

Therefore, it will remain 470 million reserved for OM, and it will be allocated to 3 branches of services as followed:

Army	:	329 million
Air Force	:	130 million
Navy	:	11 million

3- With such really small OM fund (470 million over 1.219 million required) the combat efficiency and the moral of the RVNAF troops will be severely hurt.

- In the past year, the RVNAF has endeavored in the field of protection and saving of ammunition of fuel, and of other military equipment by using them at the right place on the right time, and by avoiding waste and pilferage.

- Even with a tremendous effort, the RVNAF feels it is impossible to operate with *such a small military aid fund* mostly during the period of communist readiness for a *possible* general offensive in Winter or Spring.

The communism is exploiting the fact that the United States have cut down the Military Aid Fund to South Vietnam. They propagandize among their territorial troops that the RVNAF will not be supported effectively due to the shortage of ammunition, of fuel, of artillery etc. . . . when the communism besiege, shell, or launch an attack on the RVNAF. The communism also increased regularly their sabotage actions over the RVNAF logistics depots in order to destroy the RVNAF potential that they know the replenishment of which is quite difficult at the present time.

The communism acquired more freedom in building up their resupply routes, in the transportation of supplies and men to replenish their logistic depots and their units, and specially they can *cut short* the time needed to reinforce the front in the South Vietnam with reserved divisions stationed in the North.

4-To assist the RVNAF in the duty of protecting South Vietnam, in which the United States Armed Forces had invested hundreds of billions of dollars and thousands of American lives, the Joint General Staff requested that the Defense Attache Office recommend to Washington the followings:

    a - Review the purchase of F.5E aircrafts this year, if it is possible to carry this program over next year.

    b - Review the ammunition resupply system in order to reduce the pipe line costs; allow the RVNAF to be resupplied with ammunition from depots situated in the South East Asia mostly during critical periods.

    c - Review other expenditures included in the 230 million, to reserve to the maximum this amount of money for the OM mostly for the purchase of ammunition, fuel and pharmaceutical products.

    d - Strongly recommend for an early increase of military aid fund to the minimum of one billion dollars for FY75.

5-In short with 700 million, in which 230 million will be set aside for the above mentioned obligated expenditure, the RVNAF will be short of ammunition, of fuel and of pharmaceutical products while carrying out the duty of defense South Vietnam against the communism aggression.

The military aid fund of 1 billion in FY75 is highly necessary for the RVNAF.

Excerpted Entries from a Mekong Convoy SITREP

In January 1975 the KC positioned forty battalions to interdict the Lower Mekong. They were assisted by several NVA/VC battalions. The communists successfully occupied both banks of the Mekong at several of the narrows. Thus, for the first time Mekong convoys were required to run a gauntlet of fire from many KC positions throughout most of the length of the river in Cambodian territory. The following excerpts of a SITREP provide pertinent details concerning the transit of convoy TP-113 (TP was the nomenclature for northbound convoys, Tan Chau to Phnom Penh, and PT was for the southbound convoys). On 28 January 1975 the first large convoy (consisting of eleven vessels—two ammo barges, three rice coasters, and four POL ships) attempted to transit the interdicted Mekong. The rice and POL vessels with their bulky profiles were very vulnerable.

MEKONG CONVOY TP 113

SITREP **1.** The vessels making up TP-113 have arrived at An Long/
No. 1 Tan Chau from Vung Tau and Phnom Penh.
281130Z As matters now stand the convoy makeup will be as
follows:
    A. AMMO:
       Barge 192-1 1400 S/T
       Barge L-44 1231 S/T
Four tugs will be used for ammo and will probably be Saigon 240, Timberjack, Asiatic Trust and Asiatic Stamina.

B. RICE:

Port Sun II 1650 M/T
Port Sun III 1800 M/T
Barge 201-67 1661 M/T
Barge 201-68 1642 M/T
Wah An 1652 M/T
Tung Lee 1800 M/T

Four tugs will pull the rice barges. They will be Geronimo, Hawkeye, Buckeye, and Wolverine.

C. POL:

Boo Heung 7 1200 C/M
Han Seung 2 1600 C/M
Han Seung 7 1582 C/M
Vira IV 1600 C/M

D. SALT:

Adriana 1800 M/T

2. The Vira IV is still steaming and should arrive 290500G. If so it will join the convoy. The Adrian is aground in the Mekong. It should arrive prior to convoy departure. It will not sail if the Wah An and Tung Lee are at Tan Chau. They have refused to sail twice previously. USAID rep is talking with them now.

3. Weather is now a problem. Convoy is scheduled to cross the border at 290600G. At that time ceiling will be 2500 feet, visibility 2-1/2 miles and there will be ground fog. By 0900 when convoy reaches Peam Reang Island ceiling will have risen to 3500 feet allowing Khmer Air Force coverage. If the convoy is delayed in crossing they will reach Neak Luong in the dark. The area 3 km south of Neak Luong has seen the most intense fire to date from both sides of the river. FANK wants to transit this area in daylight so that Khmer Air Force and artillery can suppress fire.

4. The maximum convoy size is 12 vessels/barges. It will be protected by 19 MNK vessels. This is larger than the game plan originally called for because of recent intelligence concerning tactical situation around Phnom Penh. It is probable that several vessels will not sail.

5. Current tactics are to sail the ammo vessels, which are well protected by shield barges, first and to follow with the rice and POL vessels. If enemy fires on ammo barges then Khmer Air Force and artillery will strike positions in preparation for the less protected and possibly more vulnerable cargo vessels. Lack of fire on PT-112 this morning indicates perhaps KC ammo is running low.

No. 2
290055Z

1. Reference first SITREP. The Wah An sailed with the convoy. The Tung Lee refused to sail. The Adriana is still aground in Southern Mekong. The Vira 4 arrived at An Long 0500G and is clearing customs. It is scheduled to join the convoy. Therefore, there are two ammo barges; two rice barges; three rice coasters; three POL ships definite and possibly four.

2. The convoy was made up and proceeding well with a scheduled border crossing at 290800G. At the last moment the crew of the Asiatic Trust, SEAPAC contract, pulling an ammo barge refused to sail. The tug turned around and steamed independently back to An Long where another crew has been put aboard and the Asiatic Trust is now steaming north to the border. Convoy remains at border awaiting Asiatic Trust. This has postponed border crossing until approximately 1030G.

No. 3
290345Z

1. The Port Sun I received an ABF between parallels 24 and 25. The bridge was hit and caught fire. One crew member on board the ship was killed and another crew member who jumped into the water was killed. Three additional crew members were wounded out of a total crew of 32. The Port Sun I was beached at parallel 22 on the northeast side of the island. The crew is no longer aboard. Discussions are underway with MNK in an attempt to tow the ship to the border.

2. In the meantime, TP-113 is rearranging itself and should be across the border at 1030G. The Port Sun II, probably because of information on the Port Sun I refused to go. However, the VNN Commander ostensibly has talked it into going. Until the ships cross the border, we will not have a final on the exact convoy makeup.

No. 4   **1.** The head of the convoy crossed the border at 1020G. At
290515Z 1150G the convoy was moving well and four vessels had still not crossed. However, Vietnamese Commander indicates that all are willing.

2. Ref SITREP 1, all vessels with the exception of Tung Lee and Adriana are in the convoy.

3. In summary, we have two ammo, five rice and four POL or a total of 11 barge/vessels.

No. 5   **1.** At 1345G Convoy head at Peam Chor. Until they ar-
290740Z rived at Peam Chor received small arms only. When head of convoy arrived at Peam Chor Island came under intense fire. Asiatic Trust received one hit on the main deck, barge L44 two hits port side on shield barges, Asiatic Stamina two hits port side, Timberjack four hits on shield barges. Boo Heung 7 also hit, large fire, situation unknown.

No. 6   **1.** Boo Heung 7 beached at parallel 27, west bank.
290800Z **2.** Han Seung 2 capsized and sunk at parallel 26.

No. 7   **1.** The Han Seung 2 received two hits just above the water
290110Z line. The ship capsized almost immediately. The crew was picked up by MNK.

2. The Boo Heung 7 had two hits in the bridge. Fire broke out and crew abandoned ship. Fire appears not serious. MNK is trying to get the crew to reboard the vessel. Will advise.

No. 8   **1.** Head of convoy at Neak Luong at 1615G. Rest of convoy
291000Z together (except Boo Heung 7) and proceeding well.

2. Although one ship has been capsized and another beached the general intensity of fire is much less than noted against previous convoys.

3. MNK reported that the Boo Heung 7 did not need to be

beached. This is a skittish crew who almost aborted earlier today and MNK is trying to talk them back on the ship.

No. 10   **1.** Status of TP-113 as of 291745G, based on reports from
291400Z ALUSNA Phnom Penh and MSCOV Saigon: is:

A. Han Seung 2 capsized and sunk parallel 26.

B. Han Seung 7 has Khmer personnel on board and fire out. Aground near parallel 27. Hopeful of salvaging overnight. Note that Han Seung 7 and Boo Heung 7 were confused in SITREP 6. Boo Heung 7 reported now at Neak Luong.

C. Wah An is reported aground and possibly afire 2 km south Neak Luong. Tug Asiatic Stamina assisting.

D. Port Sun II and Port Sun III both at Neak Luong. Both with unidentified engine problems.

E. All other ships/barges at Neak Luong with no reports of damage.

2. Convoy will remain at Neak Luong overnight as it would stretch limited Khmer Air Force night capable air assets if required to operate in support of convoy operations both north and south of Neak Luong. This will also allow reassembly of convoy ships, repair of damages and salvage, if possible of Han Seung 7 and Wah An.

No. 11   **2.** MNK escorts providing security for Han Seung 7 and
291630Z Wah An. Reportedly no civilian crews on board either. MNK plan salvage operations night of 30 Jan on these two ships as well as Port Sun I. With exception those casualties previously reported aboard Port Sun I, no civilian wounded or killed have been reported thus far on TP-113.

No. 13   **1.** Convoy at parallel 71. The Vira IV went aground at paral-
292230Z lel 62 but came under its own power and is moving on to
Phnom Penh. The tug Shinano, harbor tug from Phnom
Penh refused to sail to assist the Vira IV.

No. 14   **1.** The first element of the convoy arrived Phnom Penh
300135Z 0530G. There are two ammo barges, two rice barges and
one POL ship at Phnom Penh. The Vira IV, which earlier went aground, freed herself and is now three km from
Phnom Penh.

2. Remaining ships of convoy will be policed up this evening and will make the move to Phnom Penh once they
have been assembled at Neak Luong.
4. Of the 11 ships in the convoy that started out, four were
barges and all made the trip with little or no problems. Of
the four POL vessels which sailed, one was sunk and one
was beached with a fire. Of the three rice vessels, two have
damage related engine trouble and are at Neak Luong and
the other had a fire and is grounded three km south of Neak
Luong. We hope to close Phnom Penh ultimately with 10
vessels. It is obvious that the previously agreed upon all
barge Mekong convoy concept is the most viable one. Steps
are being taken to implement this as soon as possible.

No. 18   **2.** Owner of Wah An will not sign release for any tugs to at-
301535Z tempt to pull that ship from its grounded location. MNK is
now contemplating operations to off-load rice cargo. Date/
Time of off loading is unknown at this time.

No 19   **1.** USAID downriver convoy did not depart Phnom Penh
310115Z due to difficulties locating crews and pilots.
2. Port Sun II and Port Sun III departed Neak Luong at
310300G and arrived at Phnom Penh at 310600G.

No. 20   **2.** The three convoys in January transported the following
310520Z commodities:

Ammo 6494 S/T

POL 5321 S/T

Rice 7444 S/T

19,259 S/T

Appendix E

" . . . Execute EAGLE PULL"

Author's Note: U.S. Air Force evacuation and tactical aircraft in Thailand were on alert 11 April anticipating the command to execute EAGLE PULL, Noncombatant Emergency and Evacuation Plan for the Khmer Republic. Amphibious Ready Group Alpha (ARG ALPHA), with her flagship, the USS *Okinawa*, was on station just off the coast of Cambodia. ARG ALPHA, with Marine forces and helicopters of the 31st Marine Amphibious Unit, had been in position since 27 February when the alert status was increased for the possible evacuation operation.

It was reported that about 780 evacuees might be expected. The USS *Hancock*, with Marines helicopters placed upon her deck in Hawaii steamed at maximum sustained speed to take her position with ARG ALPHA. She arrived at 1800 hours on the 11th.

Conditions had eroded in the Khmer to such a point that options in the EAGLE PULL plan to utilize fixed wing aircraft and Phnom Penh's Pochentong Airport were impractical. The Khmer Rouge had moved to within three miles of the airfield and were pounding it daily with about 40 rounds of 107 mm rockets and 105 mm artillery shells. Several Khmer nationals working at Pochentong with the American Airlift of supplies had been killed or injured by exploding rockets and artillery, and a few fires had been started. While resupplying Phnom Penh, no U.S. casualties or major damage to U.S. aircraft had occurred.

The Communist insurgents had strengthened their position around the capital city and appeared to be preparing for an all-out drive. A commercial C-47 had been hit by enemy fire during takeoff this day (11 April). It crashed while attempting to return for an emergency landing at Pochentong, killing the crew of five.

When the situation seemed to have become irreversible, U.S.

Ambassador John Gunther Dean requested through the Department of State that the Department of Defense evacuate the remaining U.S. citizens and designated aliens from Phnom Penh.

USSAG at Nakon Phanom Royal Thai Air Force Base received the "execute message" on 11 April.

The USSAG/7AF Tactical Air Control Center, "Blue Chip," was a bee-hive of activity by 0400 hours on 12 April. Noncommissioned officers busily plotted the vast number of sorties that had been fragged for the day on 15 display boards. Weather personnel, after making last minute checks of Phnom Penh wind direction and speed, reported 2/8s cloud cover and an anticipated high temperature of 95 degrees—a perfect day, weatherwise.

Operations specialists carried out communication checks and veri-fied sorties schedules with all involved organizations. All organizations were ready and all systems were operational.

USSAG Assistant Chief of Staff/Operations, Major General Earl J. Archer, Jr., evacuation force director, conducted a brief staff meeting about 0430 hours. "Okay, this is it!," he told the fifty-man battle staff. "We've done our homework and the plan is in being, but we know that we can anticipate questions as the situation develops. I want you to be ready to provide the answers and keep us informed in the cab (Direc-tor's Room). There will be worldwide interest in what transpires today and rightly so."

USSAG/7AF Commander, Lt. Gen. John J. Burns and USSAG Deputy Commander, Major General Ira A. Hunt, Jr., (USA) arrived at the nerve center of the operation to exercise command and control.

The Airborne Command and Control Center, an Air Force C-130—"Cricket" launched from U-Tapao Royal Thai Navy Base at 0500 hours. EAGLE PULL was in progress!

An RF-4 took off from Udorn Royal Thai Air Force Base at 0514 to make yet one more check of the weather conditions. Another C-130—"King" was airborne at 0609 hours from Korat Royal Thai Air Force Base. "King" would provide helicopter control, as well as search and rescue coordination should anyone have trouble during the events of the day. A variety of tactical aircraft was aloft.

At 0654, a four-man Combat Control Team left Ubon Royal Thai

Air Force Base aboard HH-53s belonging to the 40th Air Rescue and Recovery Squadron. The team was inserted at Landing Zone Hotel (LZ "H") at 0850 hours and joined the U.S. Marine Ground Security Force Command Group which was already in position. Colonel Sydney H. Batchelder led the command group. LZ "H" was a soccer field near the American Embassy. The field could hold three helicopters at one time. It was open on three sides and a four-story building bordered the fourth side.

Three minutes later, three CH-53s from the *Okinawa* landed carrying the first elements of the 360-man Marine ground support force. There was no way to anticipate what resistance the ground support force would face as it moved in to secure and control the LZ. But any temptations that anyone among the thousands who gathered to watch the evacuation might have had gave way when they observed the heavily armed Marines tactically deployed around the LZ.

The Marines helicopters lifted off 13 minutes later carrying the first 123 of the 287 persons to be evacuated. The smaller than expected number of evacuees was accounted for, in that many persons had left the besieged city in recent days aboard contract C-130s returning to Thailand after delivering supplies to Phnom Penh.

A second wave of choppers quickly extracted 68 persons. No passengers were ready to board when the third wave landed and, not wanting to remain on the ground needlessly, they returned to the *Okinawa* empty.

At 1000 hours, the fourth wave of choppers lowered into LZ "H." Among the passengers boarding these three aircraft was Ambassador Dean. They were off the ground by 1015.

The ambassador reported that all U.S. personnel who wanted to leave the city had been evacuated and the Marines immediately started extracting the ground support force. The first two waves of choppers removed Marines swiftly and without incident. Then at 1050 hours—exactly two hours after the evacuation had begun—LZ "H" reported incoming rockets.

The 14-member ground support force command group and the embassy evacuation coordinator still remained on the ground, but the last wave of Jolly Greens, HH-53s, had to wait for a pause in the incoming fire to extract them.

Then came an unnerving silence in Blue Chip. At 1101, the HF radio frequency—the communications lifeline—went out. Five seconds later it came back on, but those were a long five seconds.

Shortly, "Cricket" reported that the choppers had gotten in and that all Americans had been cleared from the landing zone at 1115 hours.

EAGLE PULL operations on the ground in Cambodia had lasted two hours and 25 minutes. Sighs of relief were audible throughout Blue Chip. Smiles began to spread across the faces of seasoned combat veterans.

No shots had been fired by the Marines, who had encountered only minimum indirect fire, and no tactical airpower, though visibly present, had been required. At 1243 hours, upon learning that all EAGLE PULL aircraft were over friendly territory, General Archer directed all aircraft still airborne to return to their home base. EAGLE PULL had been executed!

—Captain Paul Felty,
USAF USSAG Historian

Sources

1. Col. Vo Dong Giang (NVA), Weekly News Conference, 21 August 1974, Compound, Tan Son Nhut Air Base, Saigon, South Vietnam.

2. "Protocol, Agreement on Ending the War and Restoring Peace in Vietnam," 27 January 1973, Secretary of State, Washington, D.C.

3. Terms of Reference, USSAG/7AF, 1973, Headquarters CINCPAC, Hawaii.

4. Col. John P. Vollmer, "End of Tour Report," 12 May 1976, Joint Casualty Resolution Center, Nakhon Phanom, Thailand.

5. Joint Resolution of the Congress, 30 June 1973, Washington, D.C.

6. DAO Position Paper, "US Military Assistance Objectives in the Republic of Vietnam," 15 November 1974, DAO, Saigon, South Vietnam.

7. "Quarterly Review and Analysis," DAO, Saigon, South Vietnam.

8. "Communists' Assessment of the RVNAF," November 1973, JGS J-2, Saigon, South Vietnam.

9. "Enemy Capabilities versus RVNAF Potential," December 1973, DAO, Saigon, South Vietnam.

10. Gen. Phillip R. Davidson, *Vietnam at War* (Novato, Calif.: Presidio Press, 1988).

11. "Enemy Activity, Friendly Activity, Logistics," August 1974, J-4, JGS, Saigon, South Vietnam.

12. Agent Report, "COSVN Briefings of Key Cadre of Subordinate VC Military Regions," Field No. FVS-32, 855, 6 September 1973.

13. COSVN Resolution 12, Lao Dong Party Resolution 21 disseminated in South Vietnam, North Vietnam.

14. "COSVN Resolution for 1975," interim resolution closely tied to COSVN Resolution 12 of 1974, Issued by Lao Dong Party, North Vietnam.

15. Agent Report, "COSVN Estimate of US Intentions in South Vietnam," Field No. FVS-12, 855, 6 September 1973.

16. Working papers, Headquarters USSAG, Nakhon Phanom, Thailand.

17. Chronology, "NVA/VC 1975 General Offences," 1975, Headquarters USSAG, Nakhon Phanom, Thailand.

18. Message, "RVNAF Order of Battle," 161723Z January 1975, DIA, Washington, D.C.

19. Briefing, "Briefing on the Military Situation in South Vietnam," 2 October 1974, JGS, Saigon, South Vietnam.

20. "South Vietnam Threat Assessment (January–June 1975)," November 1974, Headquarters USSAG, Nakhon Phanom, Thailand.

21. Report, debrief from ralliers, "NVA Problems," August 1974, 500th Military Intelligence Detachment, Saigon, South Vietnam.

22. "Khmer Population Study," July 1974, Headquarters USSAG, Nakhon Phanom, Thailand.

23. President Nguyen Van Thieu, briefing to Vietnamese officers, 11 May 1974, Saigon, South Vietnam.

24. Maj. Gen. Ira Hunt, memorandum for General O'Keefe, orientation visit to DAO Saigon and RVN JGS, 23–24 October 1973, Headquarters USSAG, Nakhon Phanom, Thailand.

25. Lt. Gen. Dong Van Khuyen, *The RVNAF* (Washington, D.C.: Indochina Monographs, U.S. Army Center of Military History, 1978).

26. "Quarterly Review and Analysis," 2nd Qtr FY74, DAO, Saigon, South Vietnam.

27. "Logistics," August 1974, J-4, JGS, Saigon, South Vietnam.

28. "RVNAF Modernization Requirements," 1973, OP-523-73, J-3, JGS, Saigon, South Vietnam.

29. Position paper on South Vietnamese force levels, 19 November 1974, DAO, Saigon, South Vietnam.

30. Message, "Command and Control of VNAF Air Assets," 29 April 1975, 7602 AINTELG, Fort Belvoir, Virginia/INP.

31. "Destruction and Damage of Enemy Tanks in SEA," 29 October 1973, Headquarters USSAG, Nakhon Phanom, Thailand.

32. Memorandum, "Improvement of Capability for Countering Enemy Tanks," 7 December 1973, JGS, Saigon, South Vietnam.

33. Col. W. F. Ullmer, Team Chief, "Trip Report, Technical Assistance Team—Visit of 12–16 November 1973," 16 November 1973, DAO, Saigon, South Vietnam.

34. Fact sheet, "Background, ARVN Armored Units," December 1973, DAO, Saigon, South Vietnam.

35. "Combat Vehicle Status (26 Nov 73)," 26 November 1973, DAO, Saigon, South Vietnam.

36. Presentation, "GVN Defense Efforts in 1974," Minister of Defense, Saigon, South Vietnam.

37. Message, "DAO Quarterly Economic Report, Oct–Dec 1974," 080051Z February 1975, DAO, Saigon.

38. "Economic Stress," July 1974, DAO Economic Section, DAO, Saigon, South Vietnam.

39. Lt. Gen. Ngo Quang Truong, briefing, "Organization and Assessment of Enemy Forces in MR-1," 10 April 1974, CG MR-1, Da Nang, South Vietnam.

40. Maj. Gen. Ira A. Hunt, *The 9th Infantry Division in Vietnam: Unparalleled and Unequaled* (Lexington: Univ. Press of Kentucky, 2010).

41. Capt. Richard L. Hutchings, memorandum: "General Definitions and Processing Ground Rules for Combat Analyses," 2 December 1974, Headquarters USSAG, Nakhon Phanom, Thailand.

42. Analysis, "Summary of Ceasefire Statistics," June 1975, Headquarters USSAG, Nakhon Phanom, Thailand.

43. File, "Report on Terrorism in the GVN," November 1973, Saigon, South Vietnam.

44. Message, "Summary of RVN Activity" (daily, 30 June 1974–21 April 1975), Chief of Operations and Plans Division, DAO, Saigon, South Vietnam.

45. "Daily Summary of Major and Minor RVNAF Incidents," JGS via DAO, Saigon, South Vietnam.

46. Gen. Cao Van Vien, report to the president, "Implementation Results of Improvement and Upgrade of Territorial Forces in MR-4," 13 October 1974, Chief of JGS/RVNAF, Saigon, South Vietnam.

47. Document, "Hamlet Evaluation System (HES)," MACV Doc DAR R70-79, 1 September 1971, MACV, Saigon, South Vietnam.

48. Hamlet Evaluation System (HES), Report 1973–1975, Office of the Prime Minister, 28 March 1975, Saigon, South Vietnam.

49. Brig. Gen. Tran Dinh Tho, *Pacification* (Washington, D.C.: Indochina Monographs, U.S. Army Center of Military History, 1977).

50. Message, "Intelligence Information Report" (COSVN Directive 4, New Strategy), 100236Z September 1974, DAO, Saigon, South Vietnam.

51. USARPAC Regulation No. 710-15, "Ammunition Supply Rates, Southeast Asia," 24 May 1974, USARPAC, APO 96558, Honolulu, Hawaii.

52. "Republic of Vietnam Ammunition Conservation Study," June 1975, Headquarters USSAG, Nakhon Phanom, Thailand.

53. Memorandum, "Ammo Conservation," No. 2562, Central Logistics Command, JGS, Saigon, South Vietnam.

54. Message, "SEA Ammunition Perspective," nine sections to multiple addressees, 131930Z December 1974, Headquarters USSAG, Nakhon Phanom, Thailand.

55. "Khmer Republic Ammunition Conservation Study," June 1975, Headquarters USSAG, Nakhon Phanom, Thailand.

56. Message, "Ammunition Consumption," 102245Z December 1974, ODCSLOG, DA, Washington, D.C.

57. Message, "Ammunition Consumption," 122204Z December 1974, ODCSLOG, DA, Washington, D.C.

58. "ARVN Ammo Issues," ARVN Records via DAO, March 1975, Saigon, South Vietnam.

59. Message, "RVNAF Ammunition," 111045Z March 1975, Headquarters USSAG, Nakhon Phanom, Thailand.

60. Message, "RVNAF Ammunition," 080341Z April 1975, Headquarters USSAG, Nakhon Phanom, Thailand.

61. Message, "Departing Visit with LTG Toan," 050808Z August 1974, DAO, Saigon, South Vietnam.

62. Message, "Departing Visit to CG IV Corps, LTG Nghi and CG 7th Div, MG Nam," 061054Z August 1974, DAO, Saigon, South Vietnam.

63. Message, "MR-4 Ammunition," 190900Z September 1974, Headquarters USSAG, Nakhon Phanom, Thailand.

64. Message, "Talk with General Vien," 171100Z June 1974, DAO, Saigon, South Vietnam.

65. National Intelligence Bulletin, "South Vietnam," 1 October 1974, conveyed by Col. LeGro, DAO, Saigon, South Vietnam.

66. Maj. Gen. Ira A. Hunt, personal notes concerning NVA/VC intentions, December 1973, Headquarters USSAG, Nakhon Phanom, Thailand.

67. Message, "President Thieu's Instructions on the Present War Policy," 015620Z August 1974, DAO, Saigon, South Vietnam.

68. Message, "Visit with Senior Military Officers of JGS RVNAF," 190245Z August 1974, Nakhon Phanom, Thailand.

69. Message, Lieutenant General Kornet, DCSLOG, Washington, D.C., to Major General Smith, DAO, Saigon, South Vietnam, 191435Z September 1974.

70. Message, Lieutenant General Kornet to Major General Antonelli, DCSLOG, DA, Washington, D.C., 170619Z February 1974.

71. Message, "FY75 DAV Funding," 030442Z September 1974, DAO, Saigon, South Vietnam.

72. Message, "Army Furnished Munitions Support to MAP—Cambodia and DAV," 022115Z October 1974, DALO, DA, Washington, D.C.

73. "FY1976 VNN Defense Assistance to Vietnam Program," November 1974, DAO, Saigon, South Vietnam.

74. Message, "September 27 Press Summary," 272344Z September 1974, Secretary of State, Washington, D.C.

75. Message, "VNAF, FY75," 200536Z September 1974, DAO, Saigon, South Vietnam.

76. Message, "DAV Funding," 030442Z September 1974, DAO, Saigon, South Vietnam.

77. Message, "Meeting of 29 and 30 Aug at JGS," 1 September 1974, J-3, JGS, Saigon, South Vietnam.

78. Message, "Crisis Management," 240610Z August 1974, CINCPAC, Honolulu, Hawaii.

79. Gen. Cao Van Vien, "Briefing on the Military Situation in South Vietnam," 2 October 1974, JGS, Saigon, South Vietnam.

80. Message, "Communist Military and Economic Aid to North Vietnam," 1970–1974, 070105Z March 1975, Defense Intelligence Agency, Washington, D.C.

81. Letter, Headquarters USSAG to CINCPAC, "RVNAF Study FY75," 21 August 1974, Headquarters USSAG, Nakhon Phanom, Thailand.

82. Special bulletin, "Ambassador Graham Martin's Testimony at US Foreign Relations Committee on U.S. Economic Aid for South Vietnam," 25 July 1974, Department of State, Washington, D.C.

83. Message, "September 6, EA Press Summary," 062153Z September 1974, Secretary of State, Washington, D.C.

84. Mr. P. Sabol, fact sheet, "RVNAF Casualty Reporting," 26 December 1974, AOSOP-OL, DAO, Saigon, South Vietnam.

85. Message, "Casualty Reporting," 211045Z February 1975, DAO, Saigon, South Vietnam.

86. Message, "RVNAF Casualties," 061914Z January 1975, Erich F. Van Marbod, Principal Deputy Assistant Secretary (Comptroller), The Pentagon, Washington, D.C.

87. Message, Major General Murray, DAO Saigon, to Major General Guthrie, CINCPAC, concerning Senate Armed Services Committee report dealing with MASF, 111004Z July 1974, DAO, Saigon, South Vietnam.

88. Message, "Casualty Reporting," 190200Z October 1974, DEPCOM USSAG, Nakhon Phanom, Thailand.

89. "Report Vast Viet Military Corruption," *Pacific Stars and Stripes* (2 September 1974).

90. COSVN Resolution for 1975, unnumbered resolution issued mid-November 1974.

91. "South Vietnam Threat Assessment (January–June 1975)," 25 November 1974, Headquarters USSAG, Nakhon Phanom, Thailand.

92. W. R. Dobbing and J. J. Koelhl, intelligence report, "Shell Fuel Storage Area, Saigon," 15 December 1973, Saigon, South Vietnam.

93. Gen. Cao Van Vien, discussion, "Communist Intentions and Capabilities for 1975," 18 December 1974, JGS, Saigon, South Vietnam.

94. Message, "Executive Summary," 280200Z December 1974, USSAG, Nakhon Phanom, Thailand.

95. Message, "Communist 1975 Plans and Information Collected in Communist-Controlled Areas," 040100Z February 1975, DAO, Saigon, South Vietnam.

96. Message, "Intelligence Information Report," 100056Z January 1975, USDAO, Saigon, South Vietnam.

97. "Summary of All Aircraft and Air Crew Losses for the Ceasefire Period 28 January 73–27 January 75," 3 February 1975, TOCC, AOC, JGS, Saigon, South Vietnam.

98. Message, "Executive Summary SVN Combat Activities, 104th Week," 300520Z January 1975, USSAG, Nakhon Phanom, Thailand.

99. "NVA/VC 1975 General Offensive, A Chronology," May 1975, Headquarters USSAG, Nakhon Phanom, Thailand.

100. Executive Summary, "116th Week, Percentiles of Activity," Headquarters USSAG, Nakhon Phanom, Thailand.

101. Message, "MR-2 Plans for Defense of Hue/Danang," 310739Z March 1975, DAO, Saigon, South Vietnam.

102. IPAC Special Report No. 28, "RVN: All Fini," 080449Z May 1975, COMIPAC, Honolulu, Hawaii.

103. Message, "Spot Report" (Nha Trang), 070120Z April 1975, DAO, Saigon, South Vietnam.

104. Message, "Evacuation from VNAF Airbases," 212030 May 1975, 7602 A Intel Gp., Fort Belvoir, Virginia.

105. Message, "March 27 Press Summary, Indochina," 272358Z March 1975, Secretary of State, Washington, D.C.

106. "Spot Report," 7 April 1975, taken from a collection of reports in possession of Major General Hunt concerning the North Vietnamese final offensive.

107. Message, "The Battle of Long Khanh," 160351Z April 1975, DAO, Saigon, South Vietnam.

108. Notes from teleconference on 20 April 1975 with Gen. Tran Dinh Tho, J-3, JGS, Saigon, South Vietnam.

109. Message, "Developments on the Long Khanh Battlefield," 140600Z April 1975, DAO, Saigon, South Vietnam.

110. Message, "Spot Report," 080630Z April 1975, DAO, Saigon, South Vietnam.

111. Press release, news summary, 7 March 1975, Saigon, South Vietnam.

112. Message, "Spot Report," 240145Z April 1975, CHSPECACTS, Bangkok, Thailand.

113. Maj. Gen. Ira Hunt, notes taken from discussion with JGS, 23 March 1975, Saigon, South Vietnam.

114. Gen. Frederick C. Weyand, "Report to the President of the United States

on the Situation in South Vietnam and Options Open to the United States," 2 April 1975, Washington, D.C.

115. Conversations, Maj. Gen. Ira Hunt with Gen. Cao Van Vien, April 1975, Saigon, South Vietnam.

116. Message, "Spot Report," 020900Z April 1975, DAO, Saigon, South Vietnam.

117. Message, "Non-Combatant Emergency and Evacuation (NEMVAC) Plan, Vietnam," 111050Z June 1974, DAO, Saigon, South Vietnam.

118. Message, "After-Action Report—Frequent Wind," 030500Z June 1975, USSAG/7AF, Nakhon Phanom, Thailand.

119. Telegram, "Emergency and Evacuation: Estimated Number of Potential Evacuees," 14 April 1975, U.S. Embassy, Saigon, South Vietnam.

120. Maj. Gen. Ira Hunt, memorandum for the record, visit with Gen. Cao Van Vien, JGS, 19 April 1975, Saigon, South Vietnam.

121. Message, "Chronology/Discussion of Events that Occurred at Tan Son Nhut AB, Saigon, RVN between 1800H 28 Apr. and 2000H 29 Apr," 150723Z May 1975, DAO Saigon, Fort Shafter, Hawaii.

122. Maj. Gen. H. D. Smith, "End of Tour/End of Mission Report," 30 May 1975, Residual DAO, Saigon, Hawaii.

123. Message, "Vietnam Evacuation Operation SITREP," 301158Z April 1975, CINCPAC, Honolulu, Hawaii.

124. Radio transmission, CINCPAC to Blue Chip, 291521Z April 1975.

125. Message, "Final Frequent Wind SITREP," 301000Z April 1975, USSAG/7AF, Nakhon Phanom, Thailand.

126. Message, "After Action Report Frequent Wind," 021510Z May 1975, CTG Seven Nine PT One.

127. Message, "Evacuation Operation SITREP," 301158Z April 1975, CINCPAC, Honolulu, Hawaii.

128. Internal memorandum, "Frequent Wind Firing Incidents," April 1975, Headquarters USSAG, Nakhon Phanom, Thailand.

129. Capt. Aannio and Maj. Brake, transcript, "Events/Discussions that Took Place on the Secure Voice Conference Net during the Execution of Frequent Wind, 7 May 1975," Headquarters USSAG, Nakhon Phanom, Thailand.

130. Message, "Vietnam: Communist Victory, Plus 60 days," 260239Z June 1975, COMIPAC, Honolulu, Hawaii.

131. Message, "Cambodian Representation Issue," 031353Z September 1974, Secretary of State, Washington, D.C.

132. "Cambodia's Prince Sihanouk," Special report of USSAG daily news summary, 24 March 1975, USSAG, Nakhon Phanom, Thailand.

133. "Cooper-Church Amendment," Special Foreign Assistance Act of 1971—Section VII(a), Amended by Section 408, Washington, D.C.

134. "Limitations on United States Personnel and Personnel Assisted by United States in Cambodia," Section 756, PL 92-226, "Foreign Assistance Act (FY)72," Washington, D.C.

135. Maj. Gen. John Cleland, "End of Tour Report, MEDTC 1973–1974," 20 February 1974, MEDTC, Cambodia.

136. Message, "Debriefing Information," 500th Military Intelligence Detachment, 010330 October 1974, Headquarters USSAG, Nakhon Phanom, Thailand.

137. "Khmer Communist Order of Battle Document," DAO, Phnom Penh, Cambodia.

138. "FANK Forces Effective Strength," April 1975, MEDTC, Cambodia.

139. Table, "Analysis of FANK Intervention Force Strength," 20 July 1974 Issue of the Khmer Order of Battle, 25 July 1974, DOSO, Headquarters USSAG, Nakhon Phanom, Thailand.

140. "KAF Air Operations," February 1975, MEDTC, Phnom Penh, Cambodia.

141. Message, "KAF Aircraft Self-Sufficiency," no date, USMACTHAI, Bangkok, Thailand.

142. Message, "FY75 Cambodia MAP," 030858Z February 1975, CHMEDTC, Phnom Penh, Cambodia.

143. Staff summary, "Khmer Air Force Aircraft Status" (trends from February 1974), 16 May 1975, MEDTC, Phnom Penh, Cambodia.

144. Message, "Khmer Air Force (KAF) Activity 13–18 April 1975," 221705 April 1975, CHMEDTC, Phnom Penh, Cambodia.

145. Commander Herig, Khmer Navy, report on number of Khmer Navy Vessels, 12 June 1974, KNN, Phnom Penh, Cambodia.

146. Message, "Khmer Naval Order of Battle," 150345Z February 1974, DAO, Phnom Penh, Cambodia.

147. Table, "Working Class/Consumer Price Index—All Items (1949-100)," GKR National Institute of Statistics, 3 March 1975, Phnom Penh, Cambodia.

148. Maj. F. R. Pocock, memorandum for the record, "Ammo Funds Recouped from FY-74 MAP—CB Overcharge," 30 May 1975, Headquarters USSAG, Nakhon Phanom, Thailand.

149. Brig. Gen. W. W. Palmer, letter to Lt. Gen. Sosthene Fernandez, 28 August 1974, MEDTC, Phnom Penh, Cambodia.

150. Message, Maj. Gen. Ira A. Hunt, "Reply to CINCPAC ASG 190324Z Jun 74," 020819Z July 1974, Headquarters USSAG, Nakhon Phanom, Thailand.

151. Message, "Mekong Water Levels," July 1974, Headquarters USSAG, NIP, Thailand.

152. USSAG file, "Quarterly Major Equipment Items/Weapons Destroyed in Cambodia Oct 73–Mar 75," Headquarters USSAG, Nakhon Phanom, Thailand.

153. Message, "Logistic Considerations/Planning for Cambodian Wet Season," 190324Z June 1974, CINCPAC, Honolulu, Hawaii.

154. Table, "Daily Consumption Rates on a Weekly Basis," 18 August 1973–12 April 1975, MEDTC, Phnom Penh, Cambodia.

155. Message, "CB MAP Ammo Short Ton Experiences," 042213Z January 1975, CINCPAC, Honolulu, Hawaii.

156. Message, "FY 75 CB MAP CRA Priorities," 190325Z January 1974, CINCPAC, Honolulu, Hawaii.

157. "Ammo Price Changes," DACOM MASL Part1, Change 10, August 1974, Washington, D.C.

158. Memorandum, "Review of Pricing of Ammunition for the Cambodian Security Assistance Program in 1974," 16 December 1974, Assistant Secretary of Defense, Washington, D.C.

159. Message, "CB Funding Situation," 190421Z December 1974, CINCPAC, Honolulu, Hawaii.

160. Message, "FY75 CB MAP CRA Funding," 191048Z June 1974, CHMEDTC, Phnom Penh, Cambodia.

161. Message, "Surface Support of Cambodia," 100541Z December 1974, Headquarters USSAG, Nakhon Phanom, Thailand.

162. Message, "SCOOT and SCOOT-T Operations," 310829Z July 1974, USSAG, Nakhon Phanom, Thailand.

163. Staff summary sheet, "Trip Report" (discussion of cost advantages and faster response time of SCOOT-T over SCOOT), 22 May 1974, Headquarters USSAG, Nakhon Phanom, Thailand.

164. News release, 5-75 (detailed discussion of Improved SCOOT-T), 24 February 1975, Military Sealift Command Far East, FPO Seattle 98760.

165. File, "Brief History of the Tripartite Concept," 15 October 1973, Headquarters USSAG, Nakhon Phanom, Thailand.

166. Maj. Gen. Thong Van Fanmoung, "Presentation at Tripartite Deputies Meeting," 7 February 1975, Phnom Penh, Cambodia.

167. Report of RVNAF Study Group, Tripartite Deputies, "Report of the Khmer—VN Study Group," 28 January 1975, Phnom Penh, Cambodia.

168. "Repatriation Plan for the Refugees Khmer," 21 September 1974, CG MR-4, Can Tho, South Vietnam.

169. Message, "Dissension Between Khmer and UN Communists," 100939Z July 1974, DAO, Saigon, South Vietnam.

170. Message, "MAP-CB Logistics Movements," 160430Z January 1975, USSAG/7AF, Nakhon Phanom, Thailand.

171. Message, "Logistic Considerations/Planning for Cambodia," 040725 June 1974, Headquarters USSAG, Nakhon Phanom, Thailand.

172. Briefing paper, "Rice Situation in Cambodia," June 1974, USAID, Phnom Penh, Cambodia.

173. "Analysis of Cambodian POL Consumption," September 1974, MEDTC, Phnom Penh, Cambodia.

174. "J-4 Logistics Data, Cambodia," 6 May 1975, Headquarters USSAG, Nakhon Phanom, Thailand.

175. Message, "Mekong Requirements," 110830Z November 1973, COMUSSAG, Nakhon Phanom, Thailand.

176. Maj. Gen. Ira A. Hunt, "Increased Use and Security of the Mekong LOC," November 1974, Headquarters USSAG, Nakhon Phanom, Thailand.

177. Fact sheet, "Commodity Movement, Mekong River 1973–1975," April 1975, Headquarters USSAG, Nakhon Phanom, Thailand.

178. "Optimal Mekong Convoy Scheduling," April 1974, Headquarters USSAG, Nakhon Phanom, Thailand.

179. Maj. Gen. Ira Hunt, "Mekong Convoy Security," December 1973, Headquarters USSAG, Nakhon Phanom, Thailand.

180. Maj. Gen. Ira Hunt, briefing to Tripartite Deputies, "Analysis of Mekong Convoy Security," 22 March 1974, Headquarters USSAG, Nakhon Phanom, Thailand.

181. File, "Mekong Convoy Operational Data," J-3, CINCPAC, Honolulu, Hawaii.

182. Message, "Mekong Security," 201350Z December 1973, MEDTC, Phnom Penh, Cambodia.

183. Maj. Gen. Ira Hunt, letter to commander, Military Sealift Command, "Security of Convoys," 8 December 1973, Headquarters USSAG, Nakhon Phanom, Thailand.

184. Brig. Gen. Ralph J. Maglione, letter to Lt. Gen. Dong Van Khuyen, 4 February 1974, Deputy Defense Attaché, Saigon, South Vietnam.

185. Benito Cirera, Representative of TOP SERVICE, Inc., to MSC Saigon, "Report on Experience with Shield Barges," 7 April 1974, Vung Tau, South Vietnam.

186. Message, "Security of Mekong Convoys," 181012Z June 1974, SSO, Nakhon Phanom, Thailand.

187. "J-3 Mekong Convoy Operational Data," September 1974, Headquarters USSAG, Nakhon Phanom, Thailand.

188. Message, "Reply to MSCO Msg No4280 Refusal of SCOOT Tug Masters to Transit Mekong River to Phnom Penh," 260724Z June 1974, Headquarters USSAG, Nakhon Phanom, Thailand.

189. R. H. Plank, letter to commander, Military Sealift Command Office, "Security-SCOOT Program," 20 June 1974, SEAPAC, Saigon, South Vietnam.

190. Talking paper, "Gen. O'Keefe's Presentation to Marshal Lon Nol," December 1973, Headquarters USSAG, Nakhon Phanom, Thailand.

191. "Khmer Route 4 Security Status," 1974, Headquarters USSAG, Nakhon Phanom, Thailand.

192. Message, "Route 4," May 1974, Headquarters USSAG, Nakhon Phanom, Thailand.

193. "Assessment of the Military Situation in the Khmer Republic," April 1974, Headquarters USSAG, Nakhon Phanom, Thailand.

194. "Update, Assessment of the Military Situation in the Khmer Republic," November 1974, Headquarters USSAG, Nakhon Phanom, Thailand.

195. Gen. T. E. O'Keefe, letter to Honorable J. G. Dean, "Assessment of the Military Situation in the Khmer Republic," 3 May 1974, Headquarters USSAG, Nakhon Phanom, Thailand.

196. Order of Battle, "Khmer Communist Command and Control Organizations," April 1974, Headquarters USSAG, Nakhon Phanom, Thailand.

197. Message, "Recent FANK Successes," 171045Z July 1974, Ambassador John G. Dean, U.S. Embassy, Phnom Penh, Cambodia.

198. Press summary, 19 June 1974, David Shipler, article in *New York Times*, "Cambodia Situation."

199. Message, "Wet Season Plan," 230945Z May 1974, CHMEDTC, Phnom Penh, Cambodia.

200. Message, "FANK Dry Season Campaign Plan," 141155Z October 1974, CHMEDTC, Phnom Penh, Cambodia.

201. Message, "Recent FANK Successes," 171243Z July 1974, U.S. Embassy, Phnom Penh, Cambodia.

202. "Recent Flurry of Coup Rumors in Cambodia," 25 September 1974, CIA, Phnom Penh, Cambodia.

203. "Khmer Populations Study," July 1974, Headquarters USSAG, Nakhon Phanom, Thailand.

204. Message, "Kompong Seila—Gallant Footnote to the War in Cambodia," 270945Z January 1975, U.S. Embassy, Phnom Penh, Cambodia.

205. Message, July 9 EA press release, 092144Z July 1974, Secretary of State, Washington, D.C.

206. Message, "Assessment of 1974 Wet Season Campaign in Cambodia," 121115Z November 1974, U.S. Embassy, Phnom Penh, Cambodia.

207. Brig. Gen. Kim Eng Kouroodeh, letter to CINC/FANK, "Transmittal of Intelligence Documents," 5 January 1975, Chief, J-2, FANK, Phnom Penh, Cambodia.

208. Chronology, "1975 Khmer Communist Dry Season Offensive," April 1975, Headquarters USSAG, Nakhon Phanom, Thailand.

209. "Review of Cambodian Situation," 20 March 1975, Headquarters US-SAG, Nakhon Phanom, Thailand.

210. Staff summary, "KC Ammunition Expenditures," 12 March 1975, Headquarters USSAG, Nakhon Phanom, Thailand.

211. Message, "March Casualties Soar," 030458Z April 1975, U.S. Embassy, Phnom Penh, Cambodia.

212. "KAF Air Operations," 21 January 1975, MEDTC, Phnom Penh, Cambodia.

213. Col. Delbert E. Smith, staff summary sheet, "Khmer Air Force Aircraft Status," 16 May 1975, Headquarters USSAG, Nakhon Phanom, Thailand.

214. Message, "Cambodia," 081049Z February 1975, 7602 AIG OLB Det5, Saigon, South Vietnam.

215. Adm. Vong Sarendy, Khmer Navy, briefing to Tripartite Deputies Conference, 7 February 1975, Phnom Penh, Cambodia.

216. Message, "Cambodian Situation," 251450Z January 1975, Headquarters USSAG, Nakhon Phanom, Thailand.

217. Daily journal, 14 January 1975, secure call from CINCPAC, 0310hours, Headquarters USSAG, Nakhon Phanom, Thailand.

218. Message, "The Mekong Ship Graveyard—What's Next?," 040920Z February 1975, U.S. Embassy, Phnom Penh, Cambodia.

219. Message, "Preparations for TP-115," 140100Z February 1975, Headquarters USSAG, Nakhon Phanom, Thailand.

220. Intercept, "Special Mekong Unit," October 1974, 7602 AINTEL, Bangkok, Thailand.

221. Message, "Cambodian Status Report—February 7," 071153Z February 1975, U.S. Embassy, Phnom Penh, Cambodia.

222. Message, "Reorganization of Mekong Special Zone (MSZ)," 041040 February 1974, CHMEDTC, Phnom Penh, Cambodia.

223. Message, "Mekong Convoy Update," 261330Z February 1975, Headquarters USSAG, Nakhon Phanom, Thailand.

224. Message, "Lower Mekong Convoy," 131502Z January 1975, CHMEDTC, Phnom Penh, Cambodia.

225. Maj. John D. Murphy, USAF, memorandum for the record, "Pochentong Interdiction Campaign," 12 May 1975, Headquarters USSAG, Nakhon Phanom, Thailand.

226. Message, "Ground Times at Pochentong," 271140Z March 1975, SEAAC 7AF SOA, U-Tapao Airfield, Thailand.

227. Message, "Standard Airdrop Load Configurations," 040320Z June 1974, CHMEDTC, Phnom Penh, Cambodia.

228. Message, "Airdrop Scheduling," 100817Z July 1974, Headquarters US-SAG, Nakhon Phanom, Thailand.

229. Message, "Khmer Airdrop Activity," 150805Z April 1975, USSAG/7AF, Nakhon Phanom, Thailand.

230. President Ford statement to Congress, 25 February 1975, *Stars and Stripes* 31, no. 57 (27 February 1975).

231. News summary, editorials, *Philadelphia Inquirer,* 27 February 1975.

232. "C-130 Sorties Flown in Support of Khmer," August 1973–March 1975, Headquarters USSAG, Nakhon Phanom, Thailand.

233. Message, "Daily Aircraft Report—TH/RVN to Cambodia No. 50," 180725Z April 1975, USSAG/7AF, Nakhon Phanom, Thailand.

234. Message, "Network News Summary for February 2, 1975," 031824Z February 1975, Secretary of Defense, Washington, D.C.

235. Message, "News Release on Cambodian Airdrop," 060130Z May 1975, USSAG/7AF, Nakhon Phanom, Thailand.

236. Message, "KC Situation in West/Northwest Sector of Phnom Penh," 241116Z March 1975, U.S. Embassy, Phnom Penh, Cambodia.

237. AARMA comment, 10 April 1975, DAO, Phnom Penh, Cambodia.

238. Message, "March 30 Khmer Language Editorial," 310500Z March 1975, U.S. Embassy, Phnom Penh, Cambodia.

239. Message, "Monthly Assessment of Military Situation in Cambodia— March 1975," 190406Z April 1975, DAO, Bangkok, Thailand.

240. Maj. Gen. Ira A. Hunt, memorandum for the record, "Meeting with General Sosthene Fernandez," 24 March 1975, Headquarters USSAG, Nakhon Phanom, Thailand.

241. Message, "Reporting Military Operations in Cambodia," 11 April 1975, DAO, Phnom Penh, Cambodia.

242. Message, "Cambodian Ammunition Resupply," 262237Z February 1975, JCS, Washington, D.C.

243. Message, "Ammunition Rationing," 041125Z October 1974, CHMEDTC, Phnom Penh, Cambodia.

244. Message from AFSSO NKP for Rear Admiral Hugh G. Benton, J-4, CINCPAC, 240851Z July 1974, Headquarters USSAG, Nakhon Phanom, Thailand.

245. Message, "CB Ammo Status Report," 270650Z March 1975, Headquarters USSAG, Nakhon Phanom, Thailand.

246. Message, "Evacuation of Phnom Penh: Military Situation," 061200Z April 1975 ZFF-4, U.S. Embassy, Phnom Penh, Cambodia.

247. Message, "Observations on Eagle Pull," 161313Z April 1975, CHMEDTC/JLO CP, Samae San, Thailand.

248. Press release, Dan Southerland writing for the *Christian Science Monitor,* April 1975.

249. Message, "Request from GKR Finance Minister for Continuing US Assistance," 150628Z April 1975, U.S. Embassy, Bangkok, Thailand.

250. USSAG Public Affairs news summary, 14 April 1975, Headquarters USSAG, Nakhon Phanom, Thailand.

251. API News Special, 14 April 1975, Saigon, South Vietnam.

252. USSAG Public Affairs—Special News Summary #2, 17 April 1975, Headquarters USSAG, Nakhon Phanom, Thailand.

253. Message, "Spot Report—Situation in Phnom Penh and MNK Intentions," 150753Z April 1975, CHSPECATS, Bangkok, Thailand, MACT J252.

254. USSAG Public Affairs news summary, 17 April 1975, Headquarters USSAG, Nakhon Phanom, Thailand.

255. USSAG Public Affairs news summary, 18 April 1975, Headquarters USSAG, Nakhon Phanom, Thailand.

256. Message, "Spot Report—Situation in CB," 050715Z May 1975, CHSPECATS, Bangkok, Thailand, //MACT J25G//.

257. Message, "Khmer Communist (KC) Executions of FANK Officers," 160513Z June 1975, Det 5 7602, AINTELG, Bangkok, Thailand.

258. Message, "Executions of Cambodian Refugees upon Return to Cambodia," 230210Z June 1975, Det 5, 7602 AINTELG, Bangkok, Thailand.

259. News briefing by key marine participants, 191902Z May 1975, CINCPAC Rep Philippines, Subic Bay, Republic of the Philippines.

260. News briefing by five key AF Officers, "Recap of the SS Mayaguez Operation, 12–15 May," Headquarters USSAG/7AF, Nakhon Phanom, Thailand.

261. Message, "Effectiveness/Availability of FAC Control during Mayaguez Operations," 231402Z May 1975, USSAG/7AF, Nakhon Phanom, Thailand.

262. Message, "Casualty Reporting," 190202Z May 1975, USS *Coral Sea*.

263. Message, "Recovery of the SS Mayaguez," 162229Z May 1975, JCS, Washington, D.C.

264. Message, "May 20 EA Press Summary," 202202Z May 1975, Secretary of State, Washington, D.C.

265. Message, no subject, 191020Z May 1975, U-Tapao Command Post, U-Tapao, Thailand.

266. Message, "Thailand Has Changed since October 1973," 231234Z July 1974, U.S. Embassy, Bangkok, Thailand.

267. Message, "Comments on Bangkok Chinatown Riots," 081246Z July 1974, U.S. Embassy, Bangkok, Thailand.

268. Memorandum for the ambassador, "POLMIL Meeting," 20 June 1974, U.S. Embassy, Bangkok, Thailand.

269. Message, "Foreign Ministry Officials Express Resentment about THAI/US Relationship," 180627 July 1974, U.S. Embassy, Bangkok, Thailand.

270. Message, "Quarterly Report on the Insurgency and Counter-Insurgency in Northeast Thailand," 140700Z June 1975, U.S. Consulate, Udorn, Thailand.

271. Message, "Unidentified Helicopter Sightings," 040110Z June 1975, Det 5, 7602 AINTELG, Bangkok, Thailand.

272. Message, "Unidentified Helicopter Activity in Northeast Thailand and Laos," 210830Z April 1975, Det 5 7602 AINTELG, Bangkok, Thailand.

273. Spot Report, "Unidentified Air Traffic in NE Thailand," 301530Z April 1975, Headquarters USSAG (Blue Chip), Nakhon Phanom, Thailand.

274. Spot Report, "Unidentified Air Traffic in NKP Area 27Apr75," 281930Z April 1975, Headquarters USSAG (Blue Chip), Nakhon Phanom, Thailand.

275. Intelligence report, "Bomb in NKP City," 091045Z May 1975, INOE, Headquarters USSAG, Nakhon Phanom, Thailand.

276. Message, "RTG Aide Memoire on the US Military Use of Thailand," 141230Z May 1975, U.S. Embassy, Bangkok, Thailand.

277. Message, "Airport Demonstration at Ambassador's Arrival," 141401Z May 1975, U.S. Embassy, Bangkok, Thailand.

278. Message, "Bangkok Paper: US Handling of Mayaguez Saga 'Insult to Thailand,'" 151041Z May 1975, FBIS Bangkok, Thailand.

279. Message, "Is RTG on the Brink?" 040357Z May 1975, DAO/U.S. Embassy, Bangkok, Thailand.

280. Message, "One Year after the LAO Ceasefire Agreement," 160130Z February 1974, U.S. Embassy, Vientiane, Laos.

281. Message, "The LAO Settlement Two Years Later," 040510Z March 1975, U.S. Embassy, Vientiane, Laos.

282. Message, "LAO Reactions to Developments in Vietnam and Cambodia," 260633Z March 1975, U.S. Embassy, Vientiane, Laos.

283. Message, "Current FAR Morale," 050600Z March 1975, DAO, Vientiane, Laos.

284. Press release, "Rally at Monument to the War Dead," 9 May 1974, U.S. Embassy, Vientiane, Laos.

285. Message, "Demonstration in Luang Prabang, US Officials Forced to Leave," 141210Z May 1975, U.S. Embassy, Vientiane, Laos.

286. Message, "Cabinet Meeting Deals with Vientiane Side Resignations, Demonstrations in Savannakhet," 151026Z May 1975, U.S. Embassy, Vientiane, Laos.

287. Message, "Laos: Calm before Another Storm," 151040Z June 1975, U.S. Embassy, Vientiane, Laos.

288. Message, "PL Official's Comments on Current LAO Situation," 020441 May 1975, DAO, Vientiane, Laos.

289. Message, "Proposed Timetable for Reduction of Mission Staff," 050450Z June 1975, U.S. Embassy, Vientiane, Laos.

290. Message, "PGNU Note Asks for Immediate Turnover of All Economic and Military Assistance Property and Termination of USAID," 261057Z June 1975, U.S. Embassy, Vientiane, Laos.

291. Message, "Habib Call on Foreign Minister Phoumi Vongvichit," 031038Z June 1975, CINCPAC, Honolulu, Hawaii.

292. Message, "SPIREP (Ground Fire)," 231700Z January 1975, 56 SOW RTAFB THAI/DOI.

293. Gen. Vo Nguyen Giap, *The General Headquarters in the Spring of Brilliant Victory* (Ha Noi: The Gioi Publishers, 2005).

294. Spot Report, prisoner of war debrief, "Withdrawal from Tong Le Chan," April 1974, Saigon, South Vietnam.

295. Cen. Cao Van Vien, memorandum, "Restricted Employment of Artillery and Tactical Air," No. 1185, 12 March 1973, JGS/RVNAF, Saigon, South Vietnam.

296. *U.S. Army Field Manual, FM 101-10-1/2, Staff Officers' Field Manual, Organizational, Tactical, and Logistical Data Planning Factors,* vol. 2 (Washington, D.C.: Headquarters, Department of the Army, October 1987).

297. Major General Ira A. Hunt, "South Vietnam Assessment," December 1974, Headquarters USSAG, Nakhon Phanom, Thailand.

Index